Work and Control in a Peasant Economy

WORK AND CONTROL IN A PEASANT ECONOMY

A History of the Lower Tchiri Valley in Malawi, 1859–1960

Elias C. Mandala

The University of Wisconsin Press

The University of Wisconsin Press
114 North Murray Street
Madison, Wisconsin 53715

3 Henrietta Street
London WC2E 8LU, England

5 4 3 2 1

Printed in the United States of America

Library of Congress Cataloging-in-Publication Data

Mandala, Elias Coutinho.
Work and control in a peasant economy: a history of the lower Tchiri Valley in Malawi, 1859–1960 / Elias Mandala.
424 pp. cm.
Includes bibliographical references (p.) and index.
1. Peasantry—Malawi. 2. Agriculture—Economic aspects—Malawi. 3. Shire River Valley (Malawi and Mozambique)—Economic conditions.
I. Title.
HD1538.M26M36 1990
305.5′633′096897—dc20
ISBN 0-299-12490-8 90-50093
ISBN 0-299-12494-0 (pbk.) CIP

Why Tchiri and Not Shire?

"Shire" I would state is absolutely unknown as a native name. . . .

—Harry Johnston, 1894

Contents

Part 3: The Limits and Contradictions of Rural Struggle

Illustrations

Figures and Tables

Figures

Tables

Acknowledgments

I wish to thank the Social Sciences Research Council and the American Council of Learned Societies for funding the research leading to the dissertation on which this book is based; the National Endowment for the Humanities and the Mellon Foundation, whose fellowships enabled me to devote full attention to revising the dissertation for three semesters; the Fulbright Student Exchange Program for financing my graduate studies in the United States; and the University of Rochester for providing money to visit Michigan State University Library. I am also indebted to the archivists and librarians at the Malawi National Archives in Zomba, the Africa Evangelical Fellowship center in Wimbledon (London), the National Library of Scotland (Edinburgh), Rhodes House at Oxford University, and the libraries of Michigan State University and the University of Edinburgh.

During the year I spent in Malawi researching this study, I enjoyed the hospitality of Joseph Mizedya and his wife, the late Mrs. Lucy Mizedya, Lucy and Steven Mutuwawira, Gertrude and Enoch Mvula, Rose and Edward Pereira, Kings Phiri, Steven Valeta, and Joe Verbelen. In addition to opening their doors to me, Edward Pereira, Enoch Mvula, and Kings Phiri assisted in the collection of some of the data used in this study. I could not have expected more than what these good friends gave.

A special note of thanks goes to my friends and teachers at the University of Minnesota. I owe an intellectual and moral debt to Allen Isaacman, my adviser and friend. His support has proved indispensable to my development as a graduate student and teacher over the past ten years. Susan Geiger and Lansine Kaba were always ready to give a helping hand when I needed it. Cecinha and João Reis and their son, Damien, provided the off-campus social environment that makes me look to Minneapolis with a sense of nostalgia. Doug Dorland extended his previous experience as a Peace Corps volunteer in Malawi by editing the original dissertation.

As a traveling scholar at the University of Wisconsin–Madison, I had the opportunity to discuss the original proposal with Steven Feierman. Jan Vansina painstakingly read and commented on the proposal. Some of the questions embodied in the proposal were inspired by his *Tio Kingdom*.

At the University of Rochester, many friends and colleagues assisted me in revising the dissertation. Stanley Engerman, Eugene Genovese,

William B. Hauser, and Joseph Inikori read the entire manuscript and offered incisive criticisms and positive comments. Karen Fields and Jesse Moore commented on different aspects of the work and provided the friendship that will outlive my life at Rochester. Jean DeGroat and Joyce Ostberg were always generous with their administrative and secretarial expertise whenever I needed it.

I also feel indebted to Jane Guyer, Marcia Wright, and the late Joel Gregory for their intellectual input at different stages in the development of this project. A special note of thanks goes to Rachel Davila, my copy editor, and Barbara Hanrahan, acquisitions editor at the University of Wisconsin Press. Barbara Hanrahan spared me the trauma that many unknown writers like myself have had to go through in seeing their first works through publication.

I thank my wife, Flora, for the patience that allowed me to take so much time away from my domestic obligations, particularly the caring for our two sons, Nyatwa and Wangani. The two boys make me appreciate better what my own parents must have gone through in raising me.

To all my informants in the Lower Tchiri Valley I extend my thanks for sharing with me their own experiences and those of their ancestors. I owe them not only the information but also their ideas about history. The year I spent with them was the most important time in my life as an academic. They made me realize the simple fact, often ignored by scholars, that peasants are workers. I often had to follow them to the fields in order to interview them. The conditions in which they worked during the drought of 1980 drew my attention to the significance of the natural environment in the labor process.

I dedicate this book to three men whose work among the peasants of the Valley has shaped my own life in many different and important ways. As young missionaries who died in the service of the people of the Valley, the late Jan Dirkx and Gerald Hochstenbach taught me how individuals can make this world a happier place for others. Matthew Schoffeleers's researches opened my eyes to the spiritual, cultural, and historical richness of the peasant world in the Valley; this book would not have been what it is without his pioneering studies.

Preface

The following study, which is a contribution to the debate on peasants in Africa, utilizes a wide range of oral and documentary sources. For the reconstruction of Mang'anja society in the early 1860s (Chapters 1–2), I have relied heavily on the published and unpublished journals and letters of two British expeditions to the area. The first was the Zambesi Expedition led by Dr. David Livingstone. After abandoning his original plan to explore the Zembezi River, Livingstone and his companions visited the Tchiri Valley and Lake Malawi area six times between January 1859 and January 1864. Among the published reports resulting from the six visits are *The Narrative of an Expedition to the Zambesi,* coauthored by David Livingstone and his brother Charles, and the two-volume journals of David Livingstone and of Dr. John Kirk. The unpublished reports include David Livingstone's "Shire Journal," edited by G. W. Clendennen,[1] and a corpus of unedited letters to friends and government officials in the United Kingdom and the United States. Most of these letters are now housed in the National Library of Scotland in Edinburgh.[2]

The second expedition was that of the Universities Mission to Central Africa, led by Bishop Charles Mackenzie. The missionaries entered the country through the Tchiri Valley in May 1860. Their first settlement was at Magomero on the Highlands. After encountering many setbacks, including the death of Bishop Mackenzie, the missionaries moved to Chikwawa in the Valley where they lived from May 1862 to September 1863.[3] Like the staff of the Zambesi Expedition, the members of the Universities Mission were prolific diarists. Their works include Henry Rowley's *Story of the Universities Mission to Central Africa;* Lovell Procter's journal, published in 1971;[4] and the unpublished letters and diaries of Horace Waller, which are now kept in Rhodes House at Oxford University. Another published journal which belongs to this generation is that of James Stewart, who visited the area in 1862–63.[5] Stewart had been sent from Scotland to explore the possibilities of founding a Scottish mission.

I have found the records of the two expeditions both valuable and challenging. They are the first detailed eyewitness accounts of the people of the region in the English language. The choice of the late 1850s as the baseline of this study was partly determined by the availability of these sources, particularly the diaries of the Universities Mission party, who lived with the Mang'anja for two full years. Even a cursory reading of these documents would lend no credibility whatsoever to the charge that the missionaries were too involved in doctrinal issues to see what was going on in Mang'anja society at the time.[6] Unlike their successors who came to the country under the protection of the British colonial state, the Universities Mission party did not enjoy the luxury of indulging in academic issues. They depended on Mang'anja hospitality, and their writings are primarily an account of their daily struggles for physical and moral survival in what was apparently an uncertain sociopolitical environment.

The fact that I was not able to complement the British records with those of the Portuguese has not, I hope, seriously prejudiced my interpretation of the history of the area in the 1859–64 period. I am particularly concerned about the possibility that as committed abolitionists, the British might have exaggerated the disruptive effect of the slave trade, and that a reliance on their testimonies could lead to what Kjekshus has termed the "maximum population disruption" theory.[7]

I have tried to minimize this danger by applying the comparative method. I have subjected the observations of any one traveler against those of another on the premise that although they were all abolitionists, each reporter remained his own person. At one extreme was David Livingstone, who, as an employee of the British government and industrialists, tended to see things against the official objectives of his mission. At the other end were "marginal" men like Richard Thornton[8] and Horace Waller, whose memoirs cannot be said to have been tailored for an official audience. The two groups have left different impressions about the slave trade and other issues, such as the region's potential for cotton production.

Another important area of comparison is provided by the existence of two types of documentary evidence dealing with the same period. These are the books and journals. The Livingstone of the highly structured *Narrative* is a slightly different reporter from the Livingstone of the journals edited by others many years after his death. As a rule, I have tried to follow the journals more closely than the books. The fact that there are many more journals than books for the period has, I believe, raised the degree of objectivity of the modified version of the maximum population disruption viewpoint that I propose in Chapter 2. This view is consistent with the nature of the events of the period, including the failure of the Universities Mission expedition and the rise of the Kololo as power brokers in the Valley. There is a broad consensus among Kololo and Mang'anja oral historians regarding the connection between the chaos brought about by the slave traders and the emergence of the Kololo as a dominant group in the area.

Whatever their limitations, the written accounts of 1859–64 are a far more valuable source for the history of the Valley than the dispatches of British consuls from the east coast or the diaries of European visitors to the Tchiri region after the mid-1870s.[9] Like consular letters, the published and unpublished travelogues of the post-1870 era throw hardly any light on what was going on within the local communities at the time.[10] They are helpful only as a source of diplomatic history, especially the Anglo-Portuguese conflict for control over the Valley and the role of the Kololo ruling families in that international dispute. The same may be said about the early colonial reports, with the notable exception of Harry Johnston's summary written in 1894 of his activities during the first three years of British rule in Nyasaland.[11]

The single most important resource for the colonial history of Nyasaland is the Malawi National Archives, located in Zomba. The critical documents are the Department of Agriculture files and the annual and quarterly district reports and district books. The district books cover the same administrative issues as the annual and quarterly district reports. Like the latter, district books are the official diaries in which heads of districts (known variously as collectors, residents, or district commissioners) were supposed to record their activities and observations since 1907.[12] Since not many district commissioners actually entered their observations on a regular basis, the district books are sketchy. They are indispensable, however, for anyone interested in the period before 1918, because the parallel annual and quarterly district reports for the period were destroyed by fire. Thereafter, one may safely ignore the district books in favor of the annual and quarterly district reports, which are a mine of information on the social, political, economic, and religious life of the village community in the Valley. It is to be regretted therefore that my analysis of the 1950s in Chapters 6 and 7 did not benefit from these reports, which were still closed to researchers in 1980.

Of still greater relevance than both the annual and quarterly district reports and district books are the Department of Agriculture records. These are monthly and annual reports compiled by local agricultural officers after 1909. Because of the general trajectory of Malawian historical research, these files have not begun to be fully exploited by historians. They are, however, extremely valuable in determining colonial agricultural policies, peasant reactions to the policies, and their effect.

They are second only to oral data as a source for the region's agricultural history.

The oral data base is over one hundred interviews that I recorded between 1973 and 1980. The interviews conducted in 1973 covered Matthew Schoffeleers's project on spirit mediumship and my study of the Tengani chieftaincy.[13] The data from a second trip in 1976 were collected in connection with my master's thesis on the Kololo interlude. Another field trip in 1980 was designed to complement earlier oral testimonies and to answer questions specific to the present study.[14]

Because the focus of my research in all four projects was on events after 1850, there is very little information that can be categorized as traditions of origin. I recorded only those stories about Mang'anja origins that had a direct bearing on post-1850 developments. I discuss the general features of these traditions, including the problem of chronology, in a separate essay.[15] The traditions utilized in this study refer to events for which there is a considerable body of written data. And, with the exception of songs and folktales, of which I have made little use in this study,[16] the information was obtained through the answer-to-question method.

The data collected in the four field trips demonstrate the almost limitless potential of oral tradition as a source for the reconstruction of the region's history after 1850. Respondents were forthcoming with information on such topics as political, economic, social, and religious change.[17] The quality of the material obtained this way depended on the nature of the questions, the patience with which I pursued an issue, and my sensitivity to the methodological problems raised by this kind of evidence. I have found traditions about the recent past to be highly personalized and more susceptible than traditions of origins to three sources of distortion. These sources are the informant's social position, his or her geographical location, and the particular history of the institution or activities under discussion. Testimonies on the recent past are highly particularistic, although some are more so than others. Some traditions are subject to only one of these sources of distortion, others to two, and still others to all three sources of distortion.

The stories about the Kololo rise to power are the least personalized or particularistic. They are widely distributed in the Valley. They are also considerably formal. The most formal are the official histories obtained from the descendants of Kololo immigrants and from the Mang'anja, whose ancestors were displaced as rulers by the Kololo. The narratives given by the two parties also exhibit a high degree of ethnic bias. The differences are sharpest with respect to the events surrounding the Kololo takeover between 1861 and 1870. Official Kololo versions portray the immigrants as protectors of the Mang'anja population harassed and molested by slave dealers and as providers of meat and food to a famished population. The Mang'anja version highlights the image of Mang'anja ancestors as a peaceful people whose generosity was violently abused by an ungrateful group of immigrants.

The two sets of traditions also differ on the target of Kololo violence. Kololo accounts, like contemporary British reports, present the politically competent Mang'anja chief Mankhokwe as the main adversary of the Kololo. In Mang'anja traditions the protagonist is one Tsagonja, a lineal descendant of the *lundu* paramounts who had ruled the Valley as a united polity from the sixteenth to the eighteenth century. It is the Kololo murder of this inoffensive and small headman rather than the surrender of Mankhokwe that constitutes the watershed in Mang'anja historical perspective. The British takeover, which is a landmark in Kololo traditions, is barely an event in Mang'anja history. These are, however, the only stylized accounts in which ethnicity is a determinant factor.

Traditions on domestic slavery require an understanding of the institution's history, particularly the fact that the British abolished it against the wishes of the Kololo rulers. Elders today either deny the institution's historical existence or are unwilling to talk about it. When they admit its existence, they almost invariably present it as a benign institution.[18] Quite interestingly, this is also the standard picture given by the descendants of former slaves. It was only under cross-examination that elders admitted the violence of the institution. The cross-examination took the form of questions about the role of slaves in religion and in nonagricultural production and exchange.

I have found oral testimonies about economic change the most particularistic. Unlike the narratives on the Kololo episode or the more politically sensitive issue of slavery, "free" accounts about the economy are subject to all three sources of distortion mentioned above. These are history, the social position of the informant (which in this sphere often takes the form of gender differences), and geography. The fact that iron smelting and smithery were essentially male activities is reflected in the greater knowledge which men have about this branch of production. Similarly, it was female elders who provided the best accounts about salt making, an activity that was dominated by female labor. Information given this way proved extremely valuable in determining the social relations and ideology characteristic of nonagricultural production at different historical periods after 1850. There are no written sources that can rival oral history in this respect.

The only major problem I encountered here is that such knowledge is not evenly distributed in the Valley. Elders living outside the former iron or salt centers had almost nothing to say about these activities. More important, many of them were quick to deny the existence of these branches not only for their areas but for the entire Valley. The assertion that the Mang'anja never made their own iron implements or cloth before the coming of the British is becoming a very well-established tradition in the area. It reflects not only regional differences but also the fact that iron smelting and cloth manufacturing barely survived the nineteenth century.

This discovery, which, quite fortunately, was made early in the 1980 research trip, necessitated some changes in my itinerary and interviewing procedures. Instead of administering the questionnaire randomly throughout the Valley, I decided to concentrate on ecologically defined areas. My knowledge of the area as a native and through earlier field trips proved helpful in identifying zones. I adapted the questionnaire in such a manner as to obtain the most of what is best known in each of the six ecological zones.[19] The results were quite startling. Women living on the western fringes of the Dabanyi, from which captives were taken to the Lower Zembezi until the end of the nineteenth century, gave the most lively accounts of the slave trade. Similarly, the most elaborate accounts of the short-lived plantation agriculture came from men in areas most affected by the system during the first three decades of colonial rule.

The "universal" colonial peasant economy emerges in these memoirs as many local economies insofar as the systems of production were concerned. It is also revealing to note in this connection that, probably because colonial intervention in the production process was so superficial, information on this aspect of the cotton economy had to be squeezed from interviewees with a great deal of patience. This was in contrast to information about the market, which was given spontaneously by male and female respondents, particularly the latter.

Unlike men's memoirs, which are rather flat, women's accounts of the cotton-marketing system have a well-defined perspective or message. Women's views of the market during the prosperous cotton era (1907–40) confound the crudities of underdevelopment theory. Women remember the market during this period as a fair system which helped them improve their economic status vis-à-vis their husbands. It is only in connection with the Depression and the events leading to the collapse of the cotton economy after 1940 that one can discern a sense of bitterness and resentment in women's recollections about the operations of the colonial economy. Women place the blame for the reduction in cotton prices on the greed of specific European buyers, and for the failure of cotton agriculture on the ruthlessness with which African agricultural instructors introduced new cultivation techniques, techniques that disregarded the requirements of the food economy. It is also from female elders that I have heard the most critical comments on contemporary rural society.[20] Theirs is a distinctively moral view of the economy, a view that I hope I will be able to transmit faithfully in the following pages.

Work and Control in a Peasant Economy

Introduction

The Labor Process in African Agrarian History

1

Obviously we cannot fabricate new use-values out of nothing, and since we must always work upon pre-existing substances we have to acknowledge the fact that so-called "environmental" constraints do have a significant effect upon societies.[1]

Like the peasant world itself, the Lower Tchiri Valley is a partially isolated geographical unit. Mount Thyolo, which rises to four thousand feet, is a formidable physical barrier separating the Mang'anja—the original inhabitants of the Valley before the Sena immigrations of the late nineteenth century—from their neighbors in the Tchiri Highlands. Similarly, the southern extension of the Kirk Range has separated the people of the Valley from their neighbors to the west. Finally, the convergence of the two mountain systems has broken the Tchiri River, which has its source in Lake Malawi, into a series of rapids that have rendered the river unnavigable between Matope and Mathiti (Murchison) Falls.[2]

These barriers notwithstanding, the Lower Tchiri Valley has been, like the peasant world, also partially accessible to outsiders. In addition to the many passes that truncate Mount Thyolo and the Kirk Range, the Valley forms part of a larger physical world. It represents the southern extension of the Great Rift Valley that runs from Jordan in Palestine to a little south of the Zembezi River. As such, the Valley forms the northern extension of the Mozambican coastal plain. It has been accessible to the peoples of the east coast by land and by the Tchiri River.

That section of the Tchiri River that lies between Mathiti or Mamvera Falls and the Zembezi River—a distance of some one hundred miles—is

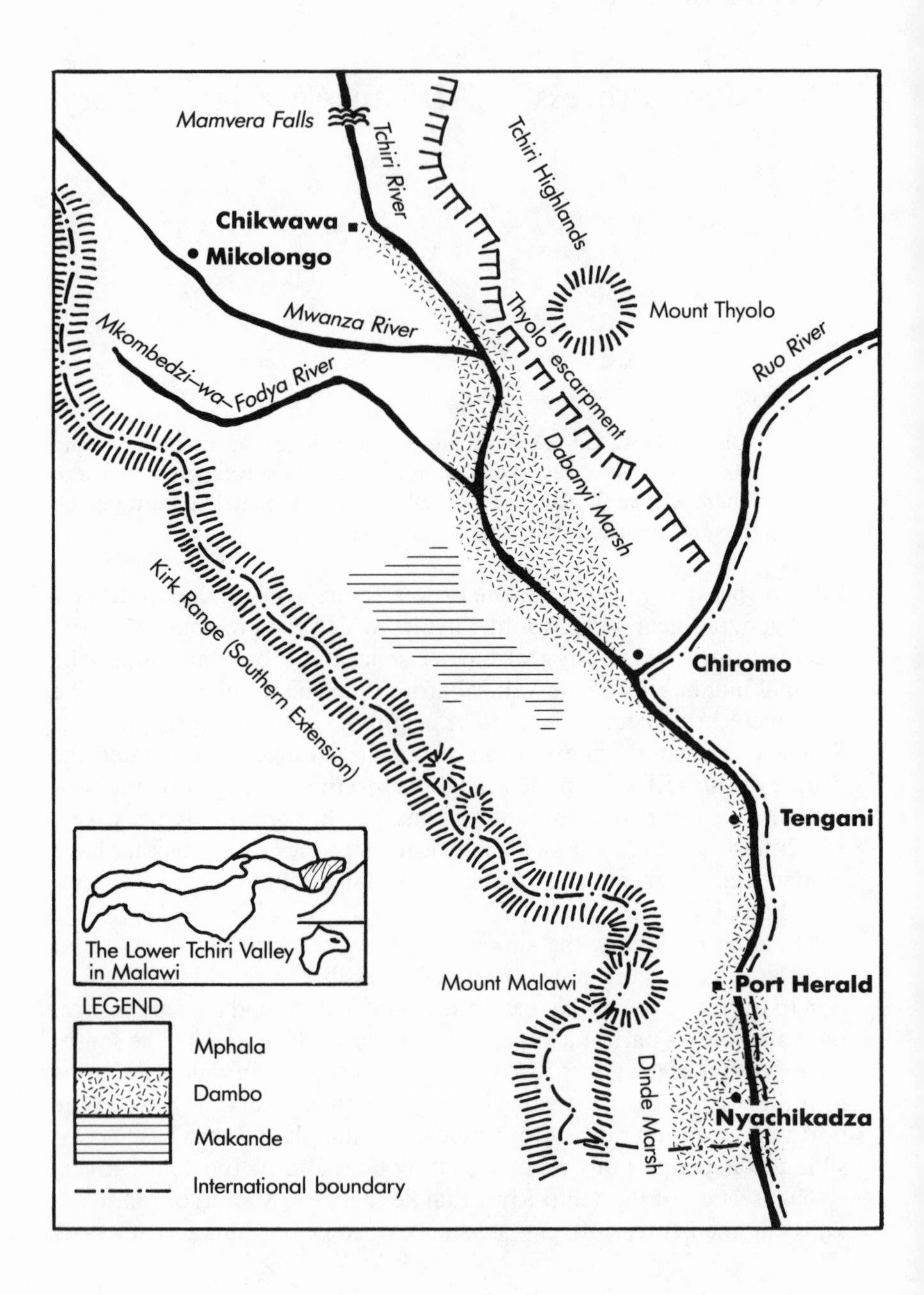

Figure I.1. Map of Topography of the Lower Tchiri Valley

completely navigable by dugout canoe.[3] The river has provided the people of the Valley with an outlet to the east coast as well as to the northern banks of the Zembezi. The southern frontier of the Valley has been open to all sorts of foreign influences.

The extent to which the Tchiri River has shaped the external relations of the people of the Valley is directly related to its influence on the local economy. In particular, the fluctuations in the river's water levels had a significant effect on the relationship between the *mphala* (dryland) and *dambo* (floodland) ecological zones (see Figure I.1).

The dambo occupies a comparatively small area, often limited to the banks of the Tchiri River. In many places it does not extend more than three miles from the riverbanks. The exceptions are the Dabanyi Marsh, also known as the Elephant Marsh, and the Dinde Marsh. The Dinde starts at Nsanje township in the north and joins the Dziwedziwe lagoon in Mozambique. The Malawi section measures fifteen miles in length. The Dabanyi is much longer. It stretches some forty miles between the confluence of the Tchiri with the Ruo River in the south and with the Mwanza River in the north. Both marshes reached a width of over ten miles during the early 1940s, when the Tchiri River carried a high volume of water.

Bordering the dambo is a belt of poorly drained alluvial and calcimorphic soils. They are of little agricultural value, but were valued for their high salt (*mchere*) content. The best salt deposits are trapped in the triangle formed by the Tchiri-Mwanza confluence. A large forest of *mvumo* or *midikhwa* palm trees (*Borassus aethiopum*) used to flourish in this same area until the 1930s.

Inside this ring of salty soils lies the dambo proper, which is made up of very fertile soils of stratified alluvium with considerable sand content.[4] The soils are covered with nothing but grasses like *bango* reeds (*Phragmites mauritianus*), the *bande* (*Echinochloa haploclada*), and elephant grass. When cultivated under the *dimba* system of wetland agriculture, the dambo supports a wider range of crops than the competing *munda* (rain-fed) agricultural regime, based upon the cultivation of the mphala drylands.

The mphala consists of two mini-ecosystems. The first coincides with the mountain slopes, which are steep, rocky, and covered with mopane (*tsanya*) and ebony (*mphingo*) trees. The second is the more extensive flat mphala from the foothills down to the marshes. In much of the Ngabu chiefdom of the Chikwawa administrative district on the west bank of the Tchiri River, the flat mphala is made up of *makande* soils: basalt deposits from the Kirk Range. Elsewhere, the mphala features brown and gray soils, which support such vegetation as the *mbvunguti* sausage tree (*Kigelia aethiopica*), the *mtondo* (*Codyla africana*), *mnjale* (*Sterculia appendiculata*), and *mlambe* baobab tree (*Adansonia digitata*). When cultivated under the munda regime, the mphala carries a narrower range of heat-resistant crops than the dimba system.

The significance of the munda system in the region's economy depended on the availability of the dambo for agricultural production. The availability of the dambo depended in its turn on fluctuations in the level of the Tchiri River, which were partly regulated by alterations in the level of Lake Malawi (see Figures I.2 and I.3). The Tchiri River overflowed its channel and flooded the dambo in some seasons but not in others. Floods receded faster in some years and slower, or not at all, in others. The result was an ecological history that has been relatively independent of human activity.

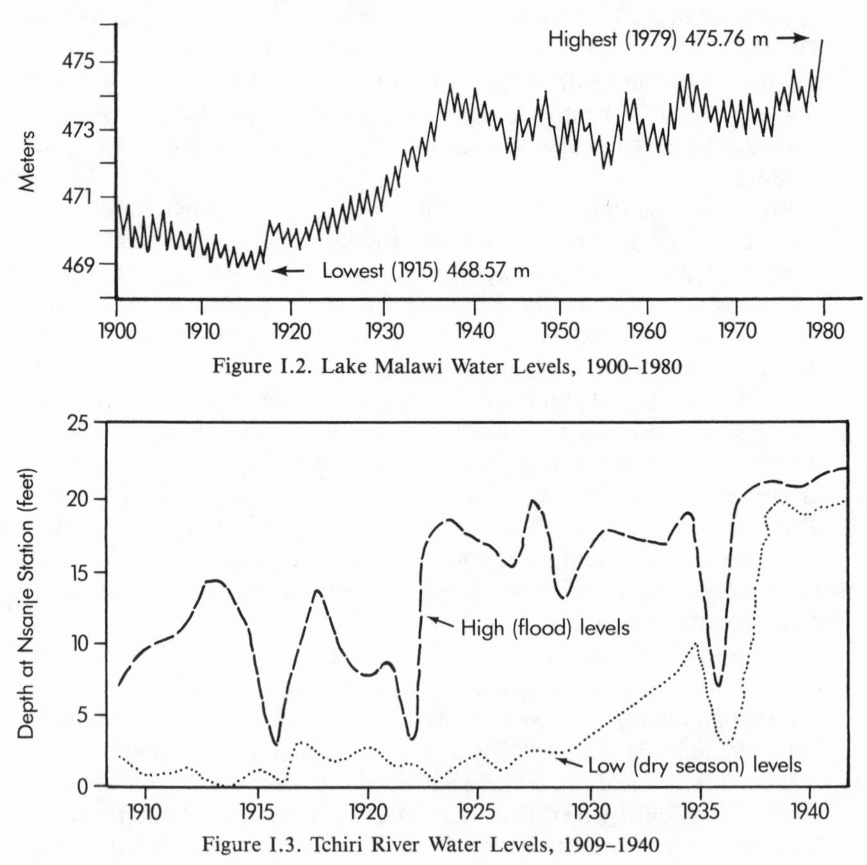

Figure I.2. Lake Malawi Water Levels, 1900–1980

Figure I.3. Tchiri River Water Levels, 1909–1940

The river has flowed in three broad long-term patterns or cycles since the mid-nineteenth century. The cycles will be referred to by the dominant agricultural systems facilitated by the fluctuations in water level: the dimba, the munda, and the dimba-munda cycles. The munda cycle has dominated since the early 1940s. It is characterized by the persistence of high flood levels which have largely confined agricultural activity to the mphala. Much of the dambo has been under permanent inundation.

The situation was different during the dimba cycle that prevailed from the 1880s to the end of the 1930s. The flood seasons were brief, lasting no more than three months, from late December to March. The dambo was under cultivation for nearly nine months, allowing people to raise several food crops consecutively in addition to the slow-maturing cotton, which had been grown only as a mphala crop during the dimba-munda cycle of the nineteenth century.

We do not know the origins of the dimba-munda cycle which formed the background to the events of the mid-nineteenth century and lasted until the 1880s. The dambo was then under water for a period of about six months, which permitted the local population to distribute their agricultural labor time more or less evenly between dimba and munda farming.

The sharp ecological shifts have sometimes mitigated and at other times exacerbated the effect of climatic factors on the region's history. Lying between one hundred and three hundred feet above sea level, the mosquito-infested and troughlike valley floor is one of the hottest places in Malawi. Mean minimum temperatures are 56°F during the coolest season (June–July) and 81°F during the hottest months (October–November) of the year. Daily maxima of up to 105°F have been recorded for the period preceding the first rains in November.[5]

Rainfalls are both erratic and low. The area receives only thirty-two inches of rain in a normal year, of which 85 percent falls between December and March. Drought or semidrought conditions occurred every five to seven years during the first three decades of this century.[6] However, the availability of the dambo for cultivation during this period minimized the effects of drought. Droughts came to play a more critical role in creating the natural conditions of famine only after the 1940s, when agricultural production became restricted to the rain-dependent mphala drylands.

The story of ecological fluctuations paralleled the rapidly changing forms of capitalist penetration. The inhabitants of the Valley were subjected to all major forms of capitalist domination during the brief century covered by this study. The international slave trade, which in other regions of Africa was protracted for over three centuries, lasted for only three decades in the Valley, from the 1840s to the 1860s. Equally brief was the era of legitimate trade. Starting in the late 1860s, informal empire waned and finally came to an end in 1891, when the British took political control of the Valley and incorporated it in the Nyasaland Protectorate. And, as they did in other parts of the colony, the British initially tried to establish settler agriculture in the area. A state-sponsored plantation economy struggled for survival from the turn of the century until the mid-1920s, when it collapsed in competition with a vigorous smallholder cotton agriculture. Started largely on peasant initiative about 1907, cotton production dominated the regional economy until the early 1940s, when it gave way to male labor migration, cattle raising, and commercial fishing.

2

> Labour is, first of all, a process between man and nature, a process by which man, through his own actions, mediates, regulates and controls the metabolism between himself and nature.[7]

The rapid succession of events marking the different phases of capitalist penetration and the extreme ecological discontinuities draw the student of the Valley into two potentially conflicting historical interpretations. There are, on the one hand, all the ingredients of a crude underdevelopment perspective in the story of the various capitalist colonial attempts to control the local economy.[8] In this view, the history of the region would be nothing but a mere derivative of the logic of capitalist expansion. It is equally tempting, on the other hand, to read the history of the region—including the local effect of capitalism and colonialism—as a simple reflection of ecological change, particularly the fluctuations in the water level of the Tchiri River that established the material conditions of different systems of land use.

The fundamental problem with these two interpretations is that they leave no room for postulating the effects of human agency at the local level. The first would make the local population the hapless victims of unequal exchange and of ruling class agendas generated outside the Valley. The second would reduce the population to mere captives of the blind forces of nature. Neither allows us to theorize the ways in which the Mang'anja and Sena inhabitants domesticated and humanized the imperialist and ecological pressures for change.

Modes of production analysts have gone a long way toward answering the first part of the problem, namely, how local agency can be conceptualized in the history of capitalist expansion. Implicit in the idea that the social formations of the Third World are an articulated combination of capitalist and precapitalist modes of production[9] is the possibility of turning the history of European expansionism into the story of how non-Western peoples struggled to retain their autonomy within the limits imposed by their own class structures. The intervention of preexisting class, gender, and other forms of conflict explain, in part, the differential effect of capitalism and colonialism on non-Western societies. As in other parts of the Third World, capitalism in the Valley did not eliminate but has coexisted with and in many significant ways reinforced the content of precapitalist structures of control. The ambiguities are reflected in the continued existence of the peasantry as a social class.

Modes of production analysts have not, however, adequately addressed the second part of the problem: how patterns of human appropriation of nature intersect with precapitalist and capitalist structures of domination. Africanists have not paid sufficient attention to productive forces in their reconstructions of precapitalist modes of production and their articulation with capitalism. As John Tosh rightly pointed out almost a decade ago, the entire debate about the emergence or decline of the peasantry in Africa has been conducted in an ecological vacuum.[10] There is an arbitrary antithesis between Nature and Society in much of the literature on rural Africa. The result has been a kind of social relations determinism that has turned a large part of "what passes for 'agricultural history' " into nothing more than "agrarian history with most of the agriculture left out."[11]

The bias against productive forces in African studies has four principal sources. The first stems from the Althusserian definition of a mode of production, which assigns causal primacy to the relations of production.[12] Under this conception, which represents only one possible interpretation of Marx's views on the subject,[13] African scholars have seen no theoretically compelling reason to explore the Man-Nature relationship in history.[14] On the contrary, they have greeted the new perspective as a healthy antidote to the many varieties of environmental and technological determinism that have plagued African studies from their inception.[15]

Revolt against environmental and technological determinism has acted as the second major force that has heightened the antithesis between Nature and Society in recent African studies. Eager to distance themselves from the Malthusian paradigm that posits population pressure and environment as long-term determinants of African agriculture, many students have turned to other models that emphasize social over natural constraints in the development of African economies. Some of the most interesting analyses of famine in Africa, for example, have been informed by Sen's theory of entitlements, which is more about distribution than production.[16]

The third major force militating against a proper analysis of productive forces in African studies has its source in the evolutionary thesis that since rural Africa did not experience a technological revolution comparable to the one that accompanied the rise of capitalism in the West, rural productive forces must be uniformly undeveloped:

> By their rapid development of the forces of production, the capitalists actively subjected nature to human control and thus forced the institutional framework of society into passive adaptation. In previous modes of production the trend had been the reverse: the institutional framework was the active force, the forces of production the passively adaptable.[17]

Productive forces in precapitalist societies do not, in other words, have explanatory power; they lie outside history. Only social relations, as an active force, articulated with capitalism.

The fourth and, for the purposes of this study, the most significant source of bias against productive forces is to be found in what Andrew Sayer aptly calls the "ideology of 'no labour.'" Generally rooted in the structure of capitalist society in which "the social character of labour [is not] immediately obvious," the ideology has proved to be particularly effective in peasant studies.[18] The various trends listed above have not only conspired against asking meaningful questions about the labor process in the development of rural productive forces. They have also limited the ability of Africanists to challenge many myths about the peasant world, a world that is infinitely more remote to most of them than the world of the proletarian. Chief among these myths is the idea of a peasant world that is perpetually underemployed and from which capital can draw unlimited supplies of labor.[19] Thus, in spite of the general axiom that labor rather than land has been the constraining factor in the development of many rural economies, Africanists have tended to present peasants as if they were anything but workers. A good deal has been written about rural differentiation, peasant struggles, peasant rationality, and peasant consciousness, but outside the confined circles of feminist discourse precious little about peasant labor. Scholars have treated peasant work, like female domestic labor, as a historical backdrop to be invoked periodically only when there is a need to explain the assumed political passivity of the peasant community. Even the sophisticated literature coming out of Southern Africa does not yet show an appreciation of the simple fact that, unlike most of their interpreters who do not have to engage in manual labor, peasants spend the greater part of their brief life spans working with their hands in order to meet basic human needs; that on this count alone peasants cannot be removed from their natural environment.

This study explores the process of the formation of a peasantry and the related problem of articulation of modes of production from the perspective of the labor process. As an analytical concept, the labor process offers a strategic entry into the problem of human interactions with nature, including the ecosystem. It has compelled this study to confront a wide range of issues that have usually escaped the attention of other scholars. These include soil structures, techniques of production, and division of labor by age, sex, or class within and between households. The concept highlights the possibility of change in productive forces despite and sometimes because of the very absence of a technological revolution. The failure of capitalism to radically transform the technology of production in the Valley became a principal factor in the development and underdevelopment of rural productive forces. Capitalist colonial demands made in the context of the existing technology heightened the significance of one critical element of productive forces—human labor power—with serious implications for the development of other aspects of productive forces and their relationship to the preexisting and colonial structures of control.

Study of the labor process raises critical questions about the social conditions in which work is carried on. It draws attention to the political, legal, and ideological dimensions of material production. It necessarily follows out the consequences of struggle for control over human and natural resources at the domestic, village, and national levels. It illuminates the ways in which the capitalist colonial state sought to organize peasant labor and the ways in which peasants sought to organize themselves and control their own destinies. It turns this work into a study of both the potential and the limits of social struggle.

Finally, the concept of labor process brings to the surface the wider problem of how the social conditions of production interact with physical processes. But answers to this question are necessarily ambiguous.

Like other workers, peasants unite in a contradictory relationship the physical and social processes that, for analytical purposes, scholars isolate as the forces and relations of production. Social life determines consciousness, but the human architect, unlike the bee, builds "the cell in his mind before he constructs it in wax."[20] Only concrete analysis of particular situations can decide the issue of causal primacy between the forces and relations of peasant production.

Part 1
Transformations in Productive Forces

One further crucial problem that has received relatively little attention from French Marxist "economic anthropology" is that of the determination of the level of productive forces.

—Jean Copans and David Seddon, "Marxism and Anthropology: A Preliminary Survey"

Labour, though traditionally overlooked in geography, is the most active and transformative process in changing Nature and society.

—Andrew Sayer, "Epistemology and Conceptions of People and Nature in Geography"

The tendency toward greater African dependence on exchange with the capitalist sector was matched by an upward tendency in the effort-price of African participation in the produce market.

—Giovanni Arrighi, "Labour Supplies in Historical Perspective: A Study of the Proletarianization of the African Peasantry in Rhodesia"

1

Major Tensions in the Political Economy of the Lower Tchiri Valley, 1859–1863

> The fact is, therefore, that definite individuals who are productively active in a definite way enter into these definite social and political relations. Empirical observation must in each separate instance bring out empirically, and without any mystification and speculation, the connection of the social and political structure with production.[1]

The political economy of the Mang'anja of the Lower Tchiri Valley during the mid-nineteenth century displayed anything but an evenly developed or harmoniously articulated set of institutions. This chapter focuses on five major inconsistencies in the sociopolitical system that are important for an understanding of the nature and effect of the region's incorporation in the capitalist world economy. These five are the pronounced economic equality characterizing the relations between free adult women and adult males against the religiously sanctioned subordination of the youth and slaves (*akapolo*) to their social elders and masters; the coexistence of a highly developed agricultural sector with undeveloped branches within nonagricultural production and exchange; the primacy of the village community in matters relative to land and labor organization within the nonagricultural sector and its invisibility in the process of food cultivation; the incoherence of the *banja* household as a social unit and its indispensability as a unit of agricultural labor; and, finally, the pressures that both supported and undermined the unity of the Mang'anja as a nation. These were among the principal inconsistencies constituting the dynamics of Mang'anja social formation.

1.1. The Mang'anja Nation: Myth and Reality

There were powerful political, economic, and ideological forces during the mid-nineteenth century that tended to contradict the autonomy of the Mang'anja village community (*mudzi*). Slave raiding and the Yao invasion of the Highlands forced independent rulers like Bobo and Kankhomba to recognize Mankhokwe's claims as lundu, the paramount or king of the Highlands and the Valley. In June 1862 they came down to Mbewe-ya-Kumadzi in the Valley, paid Mankhokwe tribute in slaves and hoes, and asked for his military assistance against the Yao invaders.[2] Two months later, in August, Mankhokwe received another delegation of Mang'anja chiefs from Khulubvi, near the modern township of Nsanje in the south. This delegation begged Mankhokwe to provide a "spirit" wife to the region's guardian spirit, Mbona. The hope was that upon receiving the "wife," Mbona would end the drought that had devastated the area since January 1862.[3] The combination of drought and the slave raids with the Yao invasion had provoked a vision of a united Mang'anja nation under the lundu paramounts. The lundus had ruled over the Valley and parts of the Highlands and had played a major role in the history of the Mbona cult from the late sixteenth to the mid-eighteenth century.[4]

Based on the notion that only royal spirits can defend the population against natural disasters like floods, locust invasions, and drought, the Mbona cult had developed as an integral part of the lundu state.[5] As in the Christian tradition, the central figure in the Mbona cult is a human being, Mbona, who, like Jesus, was born of a virgin and royal mother—the sister of the first lundu. Jealous of his nephew's success at rain-calling, the lundu ordered the murder of Mbona, which was carried out at Khulubvi. But vanquished in the flesh, Mbona triumphed in spirit. The miracles and wonders that accompanied the death he willingly accepted converted his enemies, including the lundu, into his worshipers. Whenever drought threatened the land, the Mang'anja turned to Mbona under the leadership of the lundu, who had two main responsibilities. These were to organize the rebuilding of the shrine over the place where Mbona's head was buried at Khulubvi and to install a new spirit wife, known as *salima* ("she who does not hoe")—a woman past childbearing age who lived in seclusion at the shrine and who during the mid-nineteenth century acted as Mbona's principal medium.[6] By giving in to the demand of the delegation from Khulubvi, Mankhokwe gave substance to his claim as the successor to the old lundu paramounts vis-à-vis his rivals Chibisa, Chingwandu, Kaphwiti, Nkanga, Tengani, and Tera.[7] The crises of the mid-nineteenth century provided a popular base for Mang'anja unity in the image of the defunct lundu state.

There were, in addition to the crises, more permanent structures at the disposal of the various contenders to the title of lundu. A common language, traditions of origin, the Mbona myths, and the mere survival of the old lundu family at Mbewe-ya-Mitengo all served to distinguish the Mang'anja from other peoples of the region. A network of economic exchanges in such items as cotton cloth, iron implements, salt, dried fish, and human beings reinforced the interdependence of the Mang'anja of the Highlands and those of the Valley. Finally, a set of socioreligious institutions below the Mbona cult created a series of loose political units that tended to breach the principle of village autonomy.

Most significant among the latter category of institutions were the annual rites of passage—the *chinamwali* initiation for girls and the all-male *nyau* secret societies—and the *mgwetsa* rain-calling rituals that were often performed as an alternative to the regional Mbona ceremonies. Unlike the periodic Mbona ceremonies, the execution of mgwetsa and the rites of passage presupposed the existence of an intermediate layer of political authority—below the lundu and above the village headman (*abambo* or *nyakwawa*). This is the sphere of the *mafumu* (singular *mfumu*), the senior headmen or chiefs who headed a group of mudzi villages.[8] The existence of this layer of sociopolitical organization constitutes an argument against conceptualizing the Mang'anja political system in static terms as an unrelated aggregate of autonomous village communities. No village community could reproduce all of its internal relationships in isolation from other communities.

However, neither the permanent structures nor the more contingent crises were powerful enough to destroy the reality of village autonomy at this point in Mang'anja history. The three-tier structure composed of the lundu claimants, mfumu chiefs, and nyakwawa headmen did not form a tightly integrated system. Neither the claimants to the lundu paramountcy nor the mafumu were able to translate their ritual authority into real control over their subordinates:

> Each little community had its head man, or chief, and too often its separate inerests; and though the subordinate chiefs were nominally under a superior . . . and those superior individuals under a Rundo . . . yet this arrangement produced but little good. Central authority existed but in name, unity of action was not the result of it, and patriotism did not exist.[9]

Regardless of his claim or position within the three-tier complex, every ruler was an ordinary nyakwawa (plural *anyakwawa*) insofar as real power was concerned. He exercised effective control only over his immediate dependents within the village community. Mankhokwe rarely received tribute from his supposed subordinates. Like his competitors, he "derived but little profit from" the position.[10] He could not give military assistance to the chiefs of the Highlands in 1862. Controlling no more than the labor of their immediate dependents, most Mang'anja rulers "worked in the field as much as others."[11] They were not in a position either to accumulate surplus foodstuffs for redistribution during a famine or to organize labor-intensive activities like elephant hunting and ivory trading. There was a clear discrepancy between claims to territorial authority and real economic position.

It is important to underline the discrepancy. Although it did not compromise the rulers' religious authority among the ordinary Mang'anja, the discrepancy did affect the region's position within the emerging system of international trade. Although they had developed one of the strongest and most self-sufficient regional economies in East and Central Africa,[12] Mang'anja rulers failed to compete with the *prazo* holders[13] of the Lower Zembezi (and their Chikunda retainers) and the Yao and other middlemen in the ivory and slave trades (see Chapter 2). They acted mainly as local suppliers in the slave trade, and responded to the demand for ivory by reasserting the prerogatives the lundu paramounts were supposed to have once enjoyed as owners of the land.

As owners of the land, Mang'anja rulers of all grades demanded from Portuguese and Chikunda hunters from the Lower Zembezi tribute in the form of "ground tusk"—any tusk that touched the ground.[14] The rulers used the tusks to purchase merchandise brought by foreign traders, who were required to pay for the right of passage (*chipata*)[15] as well as the privilege of speaking to the chief (*mlomo*).[16] Other Mang'anja rulers tried to procure foreign goods by imposing heavy fines on traders who were found guilty of breaking real and fictitious laws of the land. This was the famous *mlandu* system of court proceedings and fines that victimized many defenseless visitors to the region.[17] Through this system a powerful chief could rob a trader of his merchandise and prevent him from visiting other communities. A merchant was a prize to be won by one chief at the expense of others.[18]

With well-armed travelers who, like Livingstone, could not easily be intimidated, Mang'anja rulers resorted to gift (*mphatso*) exchange in order to acquire foreign merchandise.[19] They would give a visitor whatever they could offer, including "disposal" dependents, in anticipation of a present of the same or higher value.[20] There would be no bargaining in such exchanges, although dissatisfied Mang'anja givers did not conceal their displeasure.[21] Gift exchange was the principal mode of economic interaction between the Mang'anja and those foreigners who like Livingstone and the members of the Universities Mission to Central Africa did not take slaves. "It is not customary," observed Waller, "for chiefs to sell in this country. Presents, with equally beneficial understanding, are the order of the day."[22]

The combination of gift exchange and the extortions exacted through claims to territorial authority, with defensive measures adopted by warlords such as Tengani against slave raiders from the Lower Zembezi,[23] had the overall effect of discouraging traders from the Tchiri River region. Portuguese traders like Ferrão at Sena had stopped sending their Chikunda caravans to the area after many of them had been robbed, especially through the mlandu system.[24] The historical commercial relations between the Valley and the Lower Zembezi were at their lowest in the period immediately before the escalation of the international slave trade from 1861. The pressures for Mang'anja unity did not succeed in breaking the autonomy of the mudzi.

1.2. The Mudzi Village Community: Locus of Social Struggle

Pulled in the direction of national politics by the exigencies of social reproduction and fractionalized by the organization of the household-based agricultural sector, the mudzi community constituted the primary arena of social struggle in the Mang'anja political economy. Unlike the lundu or mfumu rulers, nyakwawa headmen exercised real, though geographically and demographically limited, power. As custodians of the ancestral lands, they could determine, in cooperation with the heads of the matrilineage segments, what type of land to make accessible to different categories of cultivators. Moreover, as owners of the more scarce resources for nonagricultural production, the anyakwawa stood to their subjects as nonproducers to workers, as exploiters to the exploited. The ways in which producers actually experienced this contradiction varied greatly. The variations depended on how the quasi-class relation intersected with developments in the economy.

1.2.1. Settlement Patterns

In his provocative study of social differentiation at the height of lundu power from the late sixteenth to the early seventeenth century, Matthew

Schoffeleers hypothesized that the agricultural systems of the area could have supported a maximum population of fifteen thousand persons.[25] Actual population figures gleaned from the incomplete tax records of the British administration toward the end of the nineteenth century (see Chapter 2) appear to support the hypothesis, although no attempt has yet been made to compute the region's population during the late 1850s and early 1860s—the notional baseline of this study. The only conclusion one can draw from British records for the period is that the contemporary Malawi section of the Lower Tchiri Valley was more densely populated than the Lower Zembezi.[26]

Mainly because of the importance of dimba agriculture in the food economy, the Mang'anja population was concentrated along the line separating the mphala drylands from the dambo floodlands. There were few if any permanent settlements in the extensive Dabanyi and Dinde marshes.[27] The workers who cultivated the marshes during the dry season lived several miles away from the Tchiri River on the borderline between the dambo and the mphala. The people who took the elephant killed on the banks of the river by Livingstone and his companions are said to have come from several miles away from the river.[28] Only those sections of the riverbanks that did not have extensive marshes were inhabited. Some of the largest settlements in the region, like Khulubvi (or Mbona) and Tengani (or Mpatsa), were located on the riverbanks between the Dinde and Dabanyi marshes in the south and north, respectively. Similarly, the villages of Mankhokwe (Mbewe-ya-Kumadzi) and Chibisa occupied the area between the northern end of the Dabanyi in the south and Mathiti Falls in the north. It was after they had left the Dabanyi that Livingstone and his companions were greeted by large crowds in January 1859.[29] Mikolongo was the only famous village outside the Tchiri River; it was located on the banks of the Mwanza River. According to estimates taken during 1859–63, there were up to forty, eighty, and fifty houses making up Khulubvi, Mankhokwe, and Chibisa, respectively.[30]

Whether large or small, most Mang'anja villages were physically discrete entities, as if to emphasize their political autonomy. The houses, the small gardens, and the *bwalo* meeting place of each community were enclosed by a forest of euphorbia plants that acted as a hedge or *linga*. Each village was surrounded, according to David Livingstone,

> by a stockade of growing Euphorbias. The branches are small and round, like rushes, easily broken and exude a milky juice instantly. It runs down to the ground, it is in so much abundance. The dark shade the stockade gives prevents one outside from easily seeing within, but those inside have

1. Village scene, Lower Tchiri Valley, 1960s

> a good view of those on the exterior. If arrows are employed the milky juice, dropping from the broken branches, would endanger the eyes of the invaders.[31]

Two considerations caution against viewing the linga formation as a mere response to the violence of the international slave trade. First, the hedges appear from British accounts to have dated from long before the beginning of the slave trade, which started in the region only during the 1840s. Second, the linga also characterized the spatial organization of the Chewa visited by Gamitto in contemporary central Malawi in 1831–32.[32] The international slave trade may have reinforced the linga, but it did not create it. At any rate, it provided little or no defense against firepower. It only protected the population against arrows in intervillage conflicts organized by Mang'anja elders.

1.2.2. Gender: A Case Against the Universal Subordination of Women?

> And there was nothing the men could do about this since the women were the rightful owners of the village.[33]

The nucleus of each mudzi was made up of married sisters, their daughters, and unmarried sons belonging to one or several matrilineage segments (*mbumba*). Except for the headman, who would have at least one wife in his natal village, all married men in the community were as a rule foreigners from other villages. Polygynous husbands, including village headmen, moved from one mudzi to another in order to see their wives in their natal communities.[34] Male mobility was an integral feature of the Mang'anja matrilineal system.

Like their Chewa cousins, the Mang'anja did not pay bride-wealth in their marriage exchanges. Only labor service to a prospective mother-in-law sealed the marriage contract.[35] The bride-service (*chikamwini*) conferred on the man only limited rights over his wife. It did not give him control over her reproductive capacities. Like the land the husband worked or the house he built, the children ensuing from a man and a free woman always belonged to her and her matri-kin.[36] Finally, husbands were never held responsible for the actions of their free wives: as Rowley elaborated, "If she offends, and is adjudged to pay a fine, her brother, not her husband, is liable, supposing she has no means herself of paying."[37] The "brother" Rowley referred to was known as the *nkhoswe*—the marriage surety or guardian of social anthropology.

The position of the nkhoswe (plural *ankhoswe*) in Mang'anja society has changed considerably since the mid-nineteenth century. The nkhoswe of the time did not by any means represent the embodiment of male dominance, as most twentieth-century interpreters of similarly organized communities have assumed.[38] Although in everyday language the term *nkhoswe* referred to any male sibling, it was not every brother who did in fact act as a guardian to his sisters and their children. As a social category, the term denoted either a woman's elder brother or her mother's brother. Social age rather than gender determined the distribution of power within the mbumba. Mang'anja historical traditions prioritize the struggles based on social age by portraying the conflicts between the mother's brother and his sister's sons as one of the central forces that gave rise to the major political and religious institutions of the Mang'anja, such as the lundu state and the cult of Mbona.[39] The nkhoswe was the incarnation, at the level of the matrilineage segment, of the male elder in the same way as the *mwini-mbumba* ("owner" of the matrilineage segment and source of the nkhoswe's authority) epitomized the female elder. That the age factor in the definition of the nkhoswe did in many situations erode in favor of gender is a historical development whose beginnings in the Valley can be traced to the slave raids.[40] As Chapters 4 and 7 will demonstrate, this transformation proved to be a complicated process that was neither linear nor complete by the end of the colonial era.

Just as one would not take as evidence for matriarchy the presence of female nyakwawa headpersons (such as Alindiana, Kavuma, or Mafale) or female mfumu chiefs (Nyachikadza) and lundu paramounts (Nyangu), the preponderance of men—drawn mostly from the ranks of senior ankhoswe—in positions of political leadership in the mid-nineteenth century did not imply generalized male dominance.[41] To understand gender, one has to go beyond these formal positions into the workings of the larger society. An examination of the economic, ideological, and political organization of the Mang'anja at the time shows that women's relationships to men varied greatly from one context to another.

Mang'anja women formed an integral part of the political process during the mid-nineteenth century. Mankhokwe's sister, for example, did more than just influence her brother from behind the scenes. She was one of the high-ranking members of the village council and attended all the council meetings. Her brother could not make an important decision without first consulting with her, as is evident from Procter's description of the meeting between Mankhokwe and Livingstone's party in July 1861:

> Of those near us . . . one was a sister of the Chief . . . , apparently having considerable influence with him, if anything was to be inferred from the manner in which she joined in the conversation & the attention he seemed to pay to what she said.[42]

At the end of the meeting, she made "a somewhat long speech to him."[43]

The real significance of the official integration of this select group of privileged women in the decision-making process is that it drew ordinary women into politics. Mankhokwe's sister was followed to the bwalo conference place by "a number of women [who] stationed themselves on the right hand of the chief [and who] took a lively interest" in the discussions that would eventually affect their lives. The European visitors, who were not accustomed to seeing women take part in political deliberations, "thought [the women] were the chief's wives at first, but it turned out otherwise."[44] Women's political clout vis-à-vis that of men was even more pronounced in Nyangu's region.[45]

Although women made up only a small percentage of the country's formal political officeholders, they did more or less monopolize the important positions in the religious sphere. The mwini-mbumba or her representative acted as the senior instructress (*nankungwi*) in the communally organized chinamwali female initiation rites that brought together girls from several villages forming a school (*mzinda*) under a mfumu.[46] The end of chinamwali, which took place in the bush for several days, also marked the beginning of the *chikwati* wedding feast for some of the initiates. Their fiancés had gone through their own initiation rituals organized by male elders belonging to the all-male nyau secret societies. Wearing masks, the men joined the female elders in celebrating the end of puberty rites and the commencement of chikwati festivities. It is instructive to note that the top leadership of the otherwise exclusively male nyau cult included the mwini-mbumba (or headman's sister) in her capacity as nankungwi.[47]

In local rain-calling ceremonies, or mgwetsa, the mwini-mbumba was the chief priestess (*mbudzi*). A description of a mgwetsa ceremony at Magomero in early 1862 highlights the central role played by women, and therefore deserves quoting in full:

> Chigunda assembled his people in the bush outside the village, then marched with them in procession to the appointed place for prayer, a plot of ground cleared and fenced in, and in the middle of which was a hut, called the prayer hut. The women attended as well as the men, and in the procession the women preceded the men. All entered the enclosure, the women sitting on one side of the hut, the men on the other; Chigunda sat some distance apart by himself. Then a woman named Mbudzi, the sister of Chigunda it was said, stood forth, and she acted as priestess. . . . The supplications ceased, Mbudzi came out of the hut, fastened up the door, sat on the ground, threw herself on her back; all the people followed her example, and while in this position they clapped their hands and repeated their supplication for several minutes. . . . When the dance ceased, a large jar of water was brought and placed before the chief; first Mbudzi washed her hands, arms, and face; then water was poured over her by another woman; then all the women rushed forward with calabashes in their hands, and dipping them into the jar threw the water into the air with loud cries and wild gesticulations. And so the ceremony ended.[48]

Female leadership in the religious sphere took a national character in the Mbona cult during the mid-nineteenth century. Like the cult itself, the salima wives of Mbona had emerged from their centuries-old subservience to the original lundu paramounts as the only living symbol of Mang'anja unity. Their installation and survival in office depended more on grass-roots support than on the goodwill of a small political elite. It was Mang'anja villagers who, threatened by the prospects of famine resulting from drought, initiated the campaign for the installation of a new salima and the rebuilding of the Mbona shrine at Khulubvi in 1862.

The response of the leading Mang'anja politicians to the popular demand reflected the importance of the position of the salima at this time. Tengani correctly perceived the salima as a potential rival and acted accordingly. He resisted the popular pressure,[49] hoping it would die on its own. For Mankhokwe the salima was a prize to be won, and to be turned into a lever in his bid for preeminence in the region. The plan fell to pieces against the hard realities in the Valley at the time (see Chapter 2), leaving the salima he had elected and helped put in office the undisputed authority in the land. She was "a woman all powerful" whose word as Mbona's medium was the law of the land and, as in the political sphere, whose influence extended to "her sisters" in the vicinity of Khulubvi where, according to Waller, "the fair sex have their own way a great deal."[50]

Even the androcentric testimonies of European observers of Mang'anja religious and social life during the mid-nineteenth century cannot be construed to establish a case for a deformed version of patriarchy. The most one can infer from the evidence is that the outcome of the battle between the sexes had not yet been decided—although for observers like Rowley who had a special interest in religion, women appeared to have won the struggle:

> The position of the woman with the Manganja . . . was in no way inferior to that of the man . . . men and women worked together in the fields, and the special occupations of the women were thought to be no more degrading that [*sic*] the specialities of our women are to our own women at home. The men seemed to have much kindly affection for the women; such a thing as ill-usage on the part of a husband towards his wife I did not once hear of. Frequently, as I shall have to illustrate, the position of the woman seemed superior to that of the man.[51]

Any model based on the static matriarchy-patriarchy dichotomy would impede rather than facilitate an understanding of what was a very dynamic relationship. The conflicts were not, as will become apparent in the discussion of economic relations, yet settled in favor of one or the other gender. Age was then a more reliable marker of social position.

1.2.3. Social Age and the Hegemonic Function of Religious Ideology

> In[to] the misty realm of religion . . . the products of the human brain appear as autonomous figures endowed with a life of their own, which enter into relations both with each other and with the human race.[52]

Emmanuel Terray, Claude Meillassoux, and Georges Dupré and Pierre Rey have raised a fundamental question about the social organization of precapitalist African societies by confronting the problem of social age in their analyses.[53] But their answers are not entirely convincing. Terray, for example, has defined the elder as someone who appropriates and hoards prestige goods:

> In the last analysis, there is a perfect correlation between the holding of prestige goods and the position of elder. All those, regardless of their [physical] age, who actually or potentially dispose of these goods (heads of compounds or their successors) are thought of as elders. Equally, all those who are excluded from the possession of these goods are considered youths.[54]

A class relation, which is what social age is in Terray's model, is built around the holding of certain material goods.

For Meillassoux the important issue is not the holding but the circulation of material goods in the form of bride-wealth. Elders as a group maintain their authority as a result of their control over the circulation of matrimonial goods against nubile women. They make sure that these articles do not fall into the hands of their juniors for fear that the latter may get access to women on their own terms and subvert the entire social system:

> The maintenance of the authority of the seniors over the juniors is thus the outcome of a permanent contradiction between establishing social relationships designed to strengthen the existing kinship system and the ability of these relationships to form autonomously outside the framework of kinship as established at a given moment, and challenging it.[55]

Dupré and Rey have offered a more sophisticated explanation. They have refined Meillassoux's model by subordinating the circulation of matrimonial and elite goods to that of women and slaves. Elders maintain their power by keeping youths under the threat of being denied a wife or of being sold into slavery. The two threats constitute the elders' control over the demographic reproduction of the relations of production and over exchange. Control over demographic reproduction is an economic fact whereas control over exchange is a political fact.[56]

None of the above models would explain the nature of social age among the Mang'anja. Built into the three models is a sexist definition of social age that equates seniority with the male section of the population, whereas among the Mang'anja differentiation based on age cut across sex boundaries. Moreover, it was boys rather than girls who were circulated between village communities in the Valley, and their circulation did not involve the exchange of matrimonial goods. The labor of the boy under chikamwini bride-service sealed each marriage contract. Elders' control over demographic reproduction could not have rested on their monopoly of matrimonial goods—a category that did not exist in the Mang'anja political economy. Finally, control over the circulation of elite goods against slaves—Dupré and Rey's "political" fact—became a significant component of the authority of the elders only during the brief period of the international slave trade. A different conceptual framework is required in order to understand the dynamics of social age among the Mang'anja.

A different approach is needed not only because of the dissimilarities between the social structures of the Valley and those that informed the analyses of Meillassoux and the others.[57] The ethnographic differences are only a small part of a larger theoretical problem. Dupré and Rey's explanation, and to some extent Meillassoux's, assumes the primacy of exchange over production. Questions about social relations of production are raised only to the extent that they illuminate the issue of exchange.[58] The other distinguishing feature of the three models is that none of the authors—including Meillassoux, who raises the issue when he speaks of "artificial fields"[59]—gives enough attention to the role of ideology.

The model I propose relies on different premises. Not only does it eliminate matrimonial goods as a category, it also shifts the emphasis from exchange to production relations, and argues that in order to understand the nature of control in precapitalist societies, one has to pay as much attention to economics as to ideology, particularly religious ideology—"the dominant form of primitive people's spontaneous ideology."[60] Although not determinant, religious ideas constituted the dominant sphere in the Mang'anja social formation, just as politics dominated feudal society. Religion provided the mechanisms and terrain in which conflicts based on social age—as well as the relations of slavery and tribute—were actually played out. Religious ideology was to the Mang'anja system of control what the law was to the slave society of the American South: an instrument by which the dominant groups compelled social conformity without having to resort to open violence on a daily basis.[61]

Thanks to the work done by Schoffeleers over the past two decades, it is now possible to delineate the broad outlines of Mang'anja religious ideology.[62] Rigorous and consistently historical in perspective,

Schoffeleers's studies allow for the kind of Marxian analysis of "primitive" ideology suggested by Maurice Godelier.[63] Mang'anja religious ideas have a dual origin in subjective and objective consciousness. As part of the latter, they are a by-product of what Marx characterized as the "low stage of development of the productive powers of labour and correspondingly limited relations between men [and] limited relations between man and nature."[64] Limited in their ability to control nature, the Mang'anja have, like many other precapitalist peoples, conceptualized the natural world analogously: as a world peopled with beings who are endowed with consciousness, willpower, and the ability to communicate among themselves and with the human race, and as a nonhuman world of superior beings capable of influencing the course of human history.[65] The Mbona cult is a perfect instance of such analogous representation rooted in the objective conditions of social existence. Its origins and history are a living expression of the limited ability of Mang'anja workers to control nature through the labor process. It is, according to one definition, an ecological religion "concerned with man's role as a transformer of and recipient from his natural environment."[66]

Schoffeleers also makes it clear in his other studies that the ecological definition represents only one way of looking at the cult. As part of a larger religious complex, the cult cannot be reduced to a mere "effect in the consciousness of a particular type of social relations" as determined by the structure of productive forces. It is also what Godelier has called an "effect of the consciousness on itself."[67] It has a subjective component whose boundaries did not always coincide with changes in the objective world. No structural changes in the physical conditions of production accompanied the rise of the lundu state and the subsequent radicalization of Mang'anja religious thought: the representation of the other world as a realm inhabited by the impotent spirits of commoners and the all-powerful ancestors of the ruling class. Mbona sits at the top of the latter category of spirits and can be reached only through the intercession of the living representatives of his class. The persistence of the new belief long after the demise of the lundu state testifies to the autonomy of religious ideology. It has a life of its own, independent of the very political struggles that had stimulated its birth.

Equally relevant for this study is Schoffeleers's insistence that the elitist version of Mang'anja religious ideas conflicted with an equally well-established system of representation, according to which the other world is made up of undifferentiated spirits. These are the ancestors of each village community, who are as effective in influencing the history of their respective communities as are the aristocratic spirits in relation to the affairs of the state or Mang'anja nation.[68] The coexistence of the two worldviews provided one central dynamic in Mang'anja political life during the mid-nineteenth century. It was impossible for anyone to determine in advance the political outcome of an event like a drought. It could complicate or enhance the position of either a lundu aspirant (as a custodian of the Mbona cult) or a mfumu in his role as the organizer of the locally oriented mgwetsa rain rituals.

The conflict between the two versions of Mang'anja ideology was more about the scale or spheres of influence than about the nature and effect of religious representation itself. The elitist version pointed to a larger form of social and political organization than the competing "commoner" perspective. Functionally, the two were similar. Both tried to answer the question of social control. In the Valley—as in many other societies in precolonial Africa[69]—no segment of the population could compel others to social conformity on the basis of its monopoly over the material means of production, including land. Ownership of land or any other material resource became a mechanism of control only in the context of "deified" social relations. The dominant group had to believe, act, and be accepted by others as living representatives of the spirit world, capable of bending the will of sublime beings to the benefit of every social group. The lundu state had fed on the paramounts' claims to exclusive control of the Mbona cult.[70] Similarly, the primary division within a Mang'anja village community followed the contradiction between those who could—the elders—and those who could not—the youth—deal directly with the dead ancestors of the community. The belief that some members of the community could bend the will of the otherworld formed an essential element in the definition of social age. Like the law in the antebellum South, religious ideology among the Mang'anja functioned as "an instrument by which the advanced section of the ruling class impose[d] its viewpoint upon the class as a whole and the wider society."[71]

In the Mang'anja system of representation a social junior was neither a human being nor a member of the community. He had no role to play in the communally organized magico-religious activities that, among other things, periodically reenacted the primeval harmony between man, animals, and spirits.[72] Born in the bush like animals,[73] the youth did not take part in such ceremonies as mgwetsa rain-calling prayers. In death, they were denied the important second funeral rites that normally took place nine months after the death of an elder and that were solemnized by the nyau masked dance.[74] Like an animal, a youth could not become a spirit capable of influencing the fate of human history.[75]

Defined as nonhuman beings by religion, the youth occupied a distinct position in the system of production. They were either alienated workers or nonlaborers. Mang'anja youth were not allowed to take part in some of the communally organized sectors of the economy, such as salt manufacturing and iron making. These were the primary sources of elite goods, the production of which required the intervention of magic, religious rituals, and the observance of certain taboos (see section 1.2.5). The equivalence of the youth with elite goods at the level of exchange can thus be seen as an expression of their position as nonlaborers in those branches whose forces of production combined technical skills with artificial fields.

The religiously sanctioned exclusions served many purposes, many of which converge on the problem of control at the banja household level. Like the lundu, mfumu, and nyakwawa rulers, no head of a household could establish authority on the basis of exclusive control of the means of production (land) or technical skills. In particular, the head of each household was within the more secular agricultural economy a labor equivalent of the junior. The two were technically interchangeable in most productive activities. Nothing within agriculture itself could justify the subordination of youth labor. It was only in reference to their dominance outside of agriculture that the labor power of social elders within agriculture earned higher social value despite its technical equivalence with youth labor. The artificial inflation of the labor power of social seniors formed the basis of the differential application within agriculture of the notion that actual work conferred on the agent the right to control his product. This notion, which regulated the relations of production and distribution in many precapitalist African societies,[76] was not applicable to the socially inferior labor contributions of Mang'anja juniors. They were alienated laborers, without control over what they produced together with their parents in the family field or the products of their separate *chigunda* or *chilere* gardens. Their exploitation reached a culminating point in the chikamwini bride-service, which exploited male rather than female juniors.

Coming toward the end of his life as a junior, chikamwini tested a boy's socialization as an agricultural worker. Under the control of his prospective mother-in-law (*apongozi*), the boy had to open and maintain a new field for at least one growing season before he was allowed to start his own household in the girl's village. He was the first to go to the fields in the morning and the last to return home in the evening.

When others took a break at midday, he would go on working in the dead heat of the sun.[77] Back in the village, he ate alone in a dormitory, which exposed him to the inequities of the Mang'anja system of food distribution and consumption, especially during times of scarcity. Should he displease his mother-in-law or show any sign of laziness, he would be returned to his natal village with nothing but a blanket, regardless of the amount of work he had done. A prospective son-in-law (*mkamwini;* plural *akamwini*) was, in the words of one Mang'anja informant, "a D-7 [tractor]. He was there to fell the largest trees" for the mother-in-law. The persistence of this type of exploitation into the twentieth century led some missionaries, who were otherwise quite favorably disposed to the chikamwini arrangement as it did not involve the "sale of women," to condemn the system for allowing parents-in-law to work their akamwini "without any remuneration."[78]

There are several strands of tradition that suggest the possibility that this kind of exploitation might break into open conflict. Mang'anja myths of origin portray the struggle between the mother's brother and his sisters' sons—the prototype of the antagonistic relations of social age—as the leading force causing village segmentation and the formation of such key institutions as the Mbona cult and the lundu state.[79] Then there is the classic Orwellian story recorded among the Chewa cousins of the Mang'anja. The story tells of a bloody revolution in which the male segment of the youth wiped out the entire older generation and took control of the village community because, as the narrative goes, "it was the young ones who did all the work while the elders merely ate and slept."[80] One could surmise from other traditions that the leaders of the revolution came from the military wing of the village youth. These were the chief's bodyguards, who defended the local community against outsiders and were feared for their aggressiveness. There is not one but two conflicting images of the male youth in Mang'anja culture: "an aggressive minority around the chief's compound, and a meek majority that was kept in check, inter alia, by their aggressive peers."[81] One can, in other words, theorize a direct relationship between the oppression of the youth and their capacity for revolt.

It is clear, however, that as in many other human situations, the conflict could come into the open only during periods of serious social crisis. Otherwise, social conformity prevailed. For one thing, there were limits to the exploitation of youth labor, resulting, quite paradoxically, from the very weakness of the young men. In particular, the confinement of young laborers within the agricultural and the more peripheral branches of the nonagricultural sector meant that the products of their labor had a very limited market value in comparison to the artificially overvalued labor of the seniors. The production of use-values set a "natural" limit to their exploitation. The development of petty commodity production from the late nineteenth century on would raise the ceiling and, as a consequence, intensify the conflict.

For another thing, social juniors, unlike most slaves, could always look to the day of their eventual emancipation as adults. The various magico-religious rituals that punctuated the agricultural cycle reiterated this message of salvation both positively and negatively. Exclusion from rituals like the mgwetsa declared social conformity as the high road to membership in the community of adults. Through rituals like chinamwali and the chikwati wedding celebrations the youth could see how some members of their group were in fact advancing toward the status of seniority. The intensification of the exploitation of youth labor under the influence of petty commodity production was accompanied, as we shall see in Chapter 4, by an increase in and elaboration of the magico-religious practices that validated the authority of the seniors in the eyes of both the oppressed and their oppressors. The fear of being sold into slavery, which looms as one of the two main pillars of the authority of the elders in Dupré and Rey's model, became a major factor in the relation of social age for only a brief period in the history of the Valley—the era of the international slave trade, which had a contradictory effect on the development of slavery among the Mang'anja.

1.2.4. Conflicting Trends in Ukapolo Servitude

Chapter 2 will examine the political and economic consequences of the international slave trade in the Valley. This section seeks to contribute to the debate on the relation between the export trade and internal slavery and other forms of social inequality. No consistent picture has emerged from the evidence. Some evidence supports the late Walter Rodney's thesis on the subject.[82] The export trade created a floating population that could be turned into dependents of various types. Foreigners like the Kololo exploited the chaos that accompanied the slave trade to subjugate the Mang'anja and develop a restricted version of state slavery. But the same conditions of instability failed to transform and tended to weaken the system of servitude, or *ukapolo,* among the Mang'anja indigenes.

Although I will, for lack of a better term, often refer to akapolo (singular *kapolo*) as slaves, slavery as an institution with its own laws of reproduction had not yet taken root in Mang'anja society by the time of the international slave trade.[83] Mang'anja external economic relations and internal politics had ruled out the development of slavery as a social institution. No ruler in the area, including Mankhokwe, maintained a military force that could be used to reproduce slaves as a distinct class of oppressed people. Even under the volatile conditions of the early 1860s, intervillage warfare and kidnapping (*uchifwamba*) could generate only a limited number of captives for internal use.[84] It was also difficult to keep the victims of either form of organized violence in perpetual bondage. They could be redeemed by their relatives, or they could buy their freedom themselves by running away. Sporadic intervillage warfare and kidnapping supported the external market better than internal servility. Finally, Mang'anja trade relations with the non-Mang'anja in the region were such that they did not bring to the area foreigners who could augment the kapolo system.[85] The majority of the akapolo owned by chiefs, and whom the British referred to as slaves, were victims of the legal system.

Chiefs and headmen acquired akapolo by manipulating the laws of the land. The Mang'anja compensated for a crime like murder by giving the grieved party either the convicted criminal himself or other forms of property like goats. The criminal's relatives were responsible for paying the fine, but if they failed the chief could assume the responsibility and retain the convict as his kapolo.[86] That the system was open to abuse is clear from the records of the early 1860s. Some rulers did not give the matri-kin a chance to exercise their legal rights before taking a criminal—including even those who had not been tried—as their kapolo.[87] Finally, some plaintiffs, like husbands of women convicted of adultery, preferred taking criminals as their akapolo to any other form of compensation.[88] Although some of these practices represented a response to the external demand for captives, the perversion had its roots in the Mang'anja legal system. The system had been one major source of ukapolo servitude.

Like many other productive resources, a kapolo was not a privately owned piece of property. He was the property of the mbumba community.[89] The mbumba was collectively responsible for the kapolo's continued existence as a permanently dispossessed person—as a nonhuman being. As such, he was a nonparticipant in those activities that united the community of free adults. Akapolo did not take an active part in publicly organized religion, but lived under the constant threat of being either buried alive with their dead masters or mutilated for magical purposes.[90] As a group, akapolo were also nonlaborers within the critical branches of the nonagricultural sector, particularly salt and iron production. The "labour of enslaved men" was not, as some observers of slavery in Central Africa have correctly surmised, "devoted to the production of mercantile goods for exchange."[91] Akapolo were not even allowed to carry arrows with iron heads, which was the badge of every free adult Mang'anja male.[92] As nonhuman beings, akapolo were equivalent to but not creators of those articles whose circulation formed part of the Mang'anja exchange network.

As in slave societies, the denial of the kapolo's humanity among the Mang'anja constituted only one dimension of the system of control. The other aspect required the recognition of the kapolo as a human being: at least as an agricultural laborer who could resist oppression and, in the process, create what Eugene Genovese calls "customary rights."[93] Masters were in particular expected to provide their male akapolo with wives. As one informant, whose maternal grandfather had owned akapolo, put it:

> Isn't that what our ancestors used to say? That to take care of a male slave is to give him a wife. Give him a wife and he will not run away when he grows up. . . . That is the only way to settle down a male dog. . . .[94]

Marriage represented the highest form of manumission in the Mang'anja system of servitude. Masters kept their akapolo in place by dangling the possibility that they too could one day also reproduce themselves biologically.

Whereas the marriage of a female kapolo to a free man—usually the master—implied a structural breach of the matrilineal system, the need to provide a male kapolo with a wife had the opposite effect. Few masters had disposable female akapolo to give away to their male
Few masters had disposable female akapolo to give away to their male
akapolo. They turned to the mbumba matrilineage for nubile women: their younger sisters' daughters (*adzukulu*), over whom they exercised complete control.[95] The notion that a kapolo belonged to the mbumba or kinship group was therefore no idle talk, as some of the critics of Susan Miers and Igor Kopytoff have implied.[96] What Miers and Kopytoff failed to see is the discrepancy between control and usage. Kin relations were essential to the system of control; but it was individuals as members of the banja household who used akapolo.

The Mang'anja valued their akapolo both as producers and as biological reproducers. Marriage to a female kapolo gave a free man the opportunity of controlling a woman's children, which he could not do if he was married to a free woman.[97] But free Mang'anja men and women also valued the productive labor of their akapolo. The members of the Universities Mission to Central Africa, which established a camp of fugitives at Magomero in the Highlands and at Chikwawa in the Valley during 1861–1863, found themselves in an undeclared war against free married women who prowled the mission station for young girls.[98] The women needed extra hands as much as some men did. A man at Magomero risked starvation in 1862 by disposing of his corn in order to purchase a kapolo because, as he told the European missionaries, he "had no wife, he had no child, he wanted a girl to grow up in his hut to grind corn for him, and fetch his water."[99] The use of akapolo as biological reproducers did not preclude their gainful employment as workers in the home and in the fields where they labored side by side with their owners.

The idea that because akapolo worked side by side with their masters in the fields their status was not very different from that of free women and men[100] confounds technical with social equality. Although technically interchangeable with their masters as units of agricultural labor, akapolo were, like the youth, members of a socially deprived category. They had no control over the products of their labor.[101] Moreover, like the mkamwini prospective son-in-law, a kapolo often worked harder than a free person:

> Everyone knew who a kapolo was . . . he or she was an outsider (*wapambali*). Whenever there was a hard job to be done, they always gave it to a kapolo. He or she would work the whole day without rest; and no one really cared because a kapolo was not a real human being.[102]

The members of the Livingstone expedition found, in June 1859, male akapolo hard at work opening dimba fields on the banks of the Tchiri River. The unpaid workers were, quite significantly, non-Mang'anja fugitives who had fled the Lower Zembezi "on account of the war and slave trade."[103]

The export trade had created a new source for the indigenous ukapolo system. The fugitives from the Lower Zembezi were subsequently joined by displaced people from the Tchiri Valley itself. The availability of this floating population presented unprecedented conditions for the intensification and transformation of the old relations of servitude.

The Mang'anja did not realize this potential, as the next chapter will demonstrate. The era of the international slave trade was too brief for a complete readjustment of the ancient ukapolo regime. More significantly, the Tchiri Valley was incorporated into the export trade not as a society of merchants or middlemen but primarily as an original source of captives. Every Mang'anja, regardless of his social position, became a potential victim of the violence organized from outside the Valley, with disastrous consequences. The slave raids and the famine they helped bring about nearly exterminated the local population, destroyed the economy, and expedited the political conquest of the area by the well-armed Kololo immigrants. Political conquest reduced the Mang'anja to a generalized state of servitude and denied them the chance of working out the contradictions of the old ukapolo system. The latter emerged from the catastrophes of the early 1860s barely distinguishable from other forms of social oppression like those based on social age. In the Tchiri Valley the export trade both invigorated and stifled the indigenous system of servitude with serious long-term implications for the development of the agricultural and nonagricultural sectors of the economy.

1.2.5. Nonagricultural Production and Exchange

The nonagricultural sector of the nineteenth-century Mang'anja economy comprised a wide range of activities, although the evidence permits a reasonable discussion of six branches only: food collecting, fishing, hunting, cloth making, salt distilling, and iron producing. This was obviously not a homogeneous sector. Some branches, like food collecting, fishing, and hunting, were closer to agriculture than the classification implies. As in agriculture, production within the three branches was geared toward the creation of foodstuffs. The distinction between agriculture and nonagriculture can be misleading on another and even more fundamental ground. Unlike in other parts of Africa, in the Valley it was the labor of the same free men and women that underwrote the two sectors. The two did not definitely lay the foundations of two distinct modes of production, as Terray once theorized.[104]

I will treat the six branches as a unit distinct from agriculture for two main reasons. The first is to highlight the complexity of the precolonial economy: the different uses of social labor and the variations in technical and social arrangements of production over time. The other is to seek principles of economic organization that, although not common to all the six branches, are better represented in the nonagricultural sector as a whole than in agriculture. It will be seen, for example, that with the possible exception of food collecting, production in the other branches formed a more secure basis of exchange relations than did agriculture at this point in Mang'anja history. It was principally as cloth makers, salt distillers, and ironworkers that the women and men of the Valley related their activities to the economies of the Highlands and other regions beyond the Mang'anja region. Those branches that, like food collecting, did not play this role can be distinguished from agriculture on other grounds.

The banja household featured less prominently as a labor unit in the six branches than it did in agriculture. Production within the nonagricultural sector was for the most part organized around the community. Work teams were formed on the basis of one's belonging to a neighborhood, matrilineage segment, village, or even chiefdom.[105] Group cooperation was a matter of convenience designed to speed up work in some activities; in some it was a technical necessity; in others, it represented nothing but a social necessity.

Another distinguishing feature of the production process within most if not all branches of the nonagricultural sector was the noted intervention of religious rituals as an essential component of productive forces. The intervention was most pronounced in salt and iron production, which, together with cloth making, were the premier branches in terms of their role in trade and social reproduction.

Because of its centrality to reproduction, the nonagricultural sector constituted the focus of social struggle. It was the contested arena of the economy, opposing akapolo and the youth against the elders at the same time that it cemented the alliances between members of the latter group. A husband and his wife were allies at the level of exchange because they both controlled the products of the sector either jointly or separately. Finally, whereas ownership of land did not give rise to a social relation, ownership of the more scarce resources of the nonagricultural sector provided the material content of political authority. As owners of these resources, anyakwawa, mafumu, and lundu paramounts were opposed as a class of nonproducers to the rest of the population regardless of their social age or gender. Producers in all the branches, with the exception of food collecting, had to hand over part of their product to those with exclusive claims to the ownership of fishing pools, game reserves, and salt and iron deposits. Karla Poewe's characterization of the Luapula political economy as one that rested on the contradiction between private (household) use and public ownership of the means of production[106] illuminates the dynamics of Mang'anja agriculture only. A totally different contradiction underlay the Mang'anja nonagricultural sector: publicly organized labor worked the means of production claimed by individual members of the dominant group. Forcing some coherence on the variegated nonagricultural sector reveals a more complex precolonial economy than is possible by either concentrating on the discreteness of each branch[107] or, still worse, ignoring the existence of the sector.

The apparent "invisibility" of the community as a unit of material production in many contemporary African societies is a by-product of history, resulting mainly from the demise of the nonagricultural sector.[108] A technical necessity in some branches of production, teamwork was socially determined in others, such as the collection of *nyika* (water lily) bulbs, which best exemplified the principles of food gathering during the mid-nineteenth century. Groups of women descended on the Dabanyi and Dinde marshes to collect nyika every year from about September to December. When the local lagoons could not meet the demand, parties of men would travel in canoes to the larger Dziwedziwe Marsh in what is today Mozambican territory. They would return to the Valley with their canoes filled with nyika bulbs.[109] But as cooperation had remained external to the "production" process itself, each man would take to his family what he had collected. It does not appear that the chiefs in whose land the lagoons were found demanded tribute in nyika.[110] They did, however, receive tribute from certain categories of fishermen.

The Tchiri River and its tributaries, such as the Ruo and Mwanza, abounded with fish in the middle of the nineteenth century.[111] *Chambo* (a fish of the genus *Tilapia*) and *mlamba* (mudfish) were the most common species in the area.[112] The Mang'anja employed many techniques to catch the fish, although some of the popular contemporary methods were introduced by the Sena during the late nineteenth century.[113] Some Mang'anja techniques required group cooperation whereas others did not. *Mono* fishing was one example of the latter. Every married Mang'anja male living near a major river owned a mono trap made of *nchesi* stalks or split bamboo (the largest seen by Livingstone measured six feet long, four feet in diameter at the opening, and was fitted with two traps inside).[114] The traps were moored with a rope to bushes along the riverbank, facing downstream. Every morning or evening the owner would return to the river to collect (*kuonja*) any fish trapped inside the mono. Angling (*kuwedza*) was another form of fishing that did not require group cooperation.[115]

Fishing with a rounded iron spear attached to a long bamboo pole from a canoe required the cooperation of at least two men, one steering the canoe and the other doing the spearing (*kusompha*). This mode of fishing was most common and productive during the flood season, when fish moved close to the surface of the water. "Natives in canoes," wrote Livingstone at the height of the rainy season in January 1862, "were busy spearing fish in the meadows and creeks, and appeared to be taking them in great numbers."[116] No headman or chief laid claim to the catch resulting from this or the other techniques listed above. They did, however, extract tribute from the men and women who killed mlamba and *dowe* (lung fish) and other fish left in *thamanda* pools by the receding floodwaters.

Catching fish in such pools (*kugwa thamanda*) at the height of the dry season represented the highest form of communal fishing. Men and women from many villages participated in this kind of fishing regardless of their social age.[117] They converged on the pool on a day announced in advance by the headman in whose area the pool was located. Women scooped fish with baskets, whereas men employed spears and small mono traps. Before returning to their villages, the participants were required to hand over a part of their catch to the headman or his representative at the pool. This was in recognition of one main service. Headmen were supposed to apply magic that protected the villagers from attacks by crocodiles and water snakes as well as from accidents involving the men's spears.[118] The danger of bodily injury also loomed large in the all-male hunting activities.

Mang'anja hunting activities fell into two broad categories. There was, in the first place, the more popular kind of hunting in which every male villager, including boys, took part during the dry season.[119] Dogs, arrows, and bows were the main weapons used in killing such game as gazelle, kudu, waterbuck, and the like. Group coordination was technically necessary in this undertaking. There were leaders who set fire to the bush, expecting their followers on the other side to kill any animal issuing from the fire. The hierarchical ordering of technical activities resulted in an unequal distribution of the product. Leaders reserved for themselves the best part of the meat after setting aside a portion—usually the hind leg—for the headman or chief of the area.[120] The Mang'anja were apparently more proficient at this than at the second type of hunting, involving large game such as elephants (*njobvu*) and hippopotami (*mvuu*).

The Tchiri River teemed with hippopotami in the mid-nineteenth century. Their teeth were very white though narrower and lighter in proportion to their length.[121] Equally numerous were elephants. Large herds of elephants were found in the Upper Mwanza Valley and in the area to the west of the Dabanyi. The beasts in the latter location invaded the Dabanyi Marsh for water and pasture and for midikhwa palm nuts during the dry season. Livingstone reported having once sighted a herd of about eight hundred animals in the Dabanyi, which he subsequently called the Elephant Marsh.[122] The teeth of the elephants were described as fine, weighing on the average between eight and nine pounds.[123] The Valley had every potential for a thriving trade in ivory.

The Mang'anja did not take full advantage of this natural resource. Not only did their rulers lack the manpower necessary for large-scale hunting, as the lundu paramounts had probably done before or as the Kololo would definitely do later, but what little hunting there was was done in small teams and was largely determined by requirements of the food economy. Mang'anja men killed elephants and hippopotami partly as a source of meat but mainly as a defensive measure designed to protect their dimba floodland fields during the growing season from June to December.

The two specifically Mang'anja hunting devices were the *tchera* and *mbuna*. The mbuna was a pitfall dug in the ground about eight feet in depth and two and a half feet in diameter. The bottom was planted with pointed stakes facing upward, and the top was covered with grass.[124] The idea was to trap an unsuspecting animal that would fall to the bottom and be impaled on the stakes. The tchera, according to Dr. John Kirk, consisted of a beam of up to six feet long "with an iron spike which carries poison. This is suspended from the top of a pole overhanging the path by which the beast comes out to feed. It is let go by a string which pulls a sort of trigger."[125] The hippo was the principal target of the tchera, which lined the riverbanks during the dry season. There were so many of them that Livingstone and his companions were able to observe one in action:

> One [hippo] got frightened by the ship, as she was steaming close to the bank. In its eager hurry to escape it rushed on shore, and ran directly under a trap, when down came the heavy beam on its back, driving the poisoned spear-head a foot deep into its flesh. In its agony it plunged back into the river, to die in a few hours, and afterwards furnished a feast for the natives.[126]

The poison affected only the wounded part, which was removed before the animal was eaten.

Effective only during the dry season when hippos emerged from the river and elephants trekked to the marshes, the two techniques did not provide the Mang'anja with ivory for long-distance trade. Hunting was not professionalized among the Mang'anja as it was among the Chikunda, Phodzo hippo hunters, or Zimba hunters who, together with the Kololo, would dominate the ivory economy during the era of legitimate trade (see Chapter 2). Mang'anja rulers could not translate their claims to territorial control into ivory. They had no ivory to offer for sale to Livingstone and his companions.[127] All they had were agricultural products and the locally made cotton cloth.

Because of their interest in Central Africa as a potential source of raw cotton (which would reduce the dependence of the British textile industry on the American South), Livingstone and his companions paid more attention to the indigenous cotton economy than any other branch of Mang'anja production.[128] A "cotton controversy" centers on the extent to which the Mang'anja cultivated cotton and made and wore cotton cloth. Although this debate must remain unsettled, there is, as I will show, no doubt about the position of the Valley as the leading cotton-growing area in the Tchiri River and Lake Malawi region. The fame of the Lower Tchiri Valley as a cotton-producing area goes as far back as the sixteenth century, when the region supplied the Lower Zembezi with the famous *machila* cloth.[129]

Mid-nineteenth-century British accounts present cloth manufacturing as a complex and extremely slow process. Two different methods were employed to remove wool from the cotton seeds. The first method used nothing but human fingers.[130] This was a very tedious procedure that resulted in group cooperation to speed up production. Every potential worker—children as well as men and women—took part in the process.[131] In the second technique, fingers were replaced "by an iron roller, on a little block of wood, and rove [the cotton] out into long soft bands without twist."[132] Male labor appears to have dominated in this method of production as it did in the spinning and weaving that followed.[133] In spinning and weaving, group cooperation appears to have been essential. The smallest group of weavers seen in the area consisted of two men. The men made thread with a spindle and distaff and later wove on looms (*gondo*) consisting "of a reed and treadles" supported by "sticks driven into the ground."[134]

> The alternate threads are held apart by rods placed at intervals. Two men (not women) work it, one passing the woof through on one side, & the other receiving it on the other side. The threads are attached to a long piece of wood, & are so passed across. . . . The cloth when finished has the appearance of a large towel with blue borders.[135]

According to some calculations, it took two men four days, working four hours a day, to complete a piece measuring one by two yards.[136] Gondo cloth, which was at this time also known as *maria,* was of much better quality than the imported American calico.[137]

2. Cotton weaver smoking a tobacco pipe, early 1860s

Relatively rich on technical details, British accounts cannot answer questions about the social significance of the cotton economy. The sources are especially silent on how the product was distributed among the workers or between the latter and nonproducers—the rulers. Partly as a result of this silence, it is impossible to settle the debate, which was first raised by James Stewart, about the extensiveness of cotton weaving and the use of cotton cloth at the time. Stewart accused Livingstone of having exaggerated the depth of the cotton economy in the region.[138]

There are three points about this controversy that must be clarified at the outset. First, Stewart's accusation was part of a general critique of Livingstone's overly optimistic presentation of the Tchiri River and Lake Malawi region as a potential British colony.[139] Second, Stewart's view of the region was as unrepresentative on the negative side as Livingstone's was on the positive. Stewart visited the region at the height of the disastrous famine of 1862–63 which, together with the slave raids, completely paralyzed the Mang'anja economy.[140] Third, the diaries of the other British travelers who visited the area prior to the famine and who later contributed to the debate make it clear that, in his eagerness to attract British settlers, Livingstone did indeed make unwarranted generalizations about the cotton economy in the region.[141]

There can be no doubt, for example, that Livingstone misled his readers when he asserted that "everywhere we met with it [the cotton industry], and scarcely ever entered a village, without finding a number of men cleaning, spinning, and weaving."[142] As I will show in the next section, cotton growing and weaving were not as universal even in the Lower Tchiri Valley as the statement intends to portray. Moreover, the statement obscures the fact that what weaving went on in the Tchiri Highlands was dependent on raw cotton imported from either the Upper or the Lower Tchiri Valley. As the members of the Universities Mission to Central Africa found in 1861–62, and as the Nyasaland colonial regime would discover at the turn of the century, the Mang'anja of the Highlands did not grow cotton. The area was too cold for cotton cultivation.[143] In presenting the Highlands as another rich cotton-producing area, Livingstone clearly ignored what people like Chibisa of Chikwawa had told him in March 1859: that, unlike the Mang'anja of the Valley, those of the Highlands had "no cotton and clothe themselves with the bark of trees beaten into a kind of cloth."[144]

How widely the Mang'anja of the Valley made and wore cotton cloth is a question that cannot be settled by the existing evidence. The data allow nothing more than a few hypotheses that may guide future researchers interested in the issue as part of the wider problem of social control. The wearing of cotton cloth expressed one's position in society. It favored those who could mobilize labor for the making of the cloth or those who had the means of purchasing it. The ruling elite enjoyed an advantage on both counts. Livingstone's generalization can thus be read as a reflection of his more regular and intimate interactions with the ruling elite. One can also read his assertion that women were more likely than men to wear the locally made cloth as evidence of the privileged status of Mang'anja women.[145] The statement supports the general thesis that in this, as in other sectors of the Mang'anja economy, the problem of control cannot always be reduced to that of technical organization. Mang'anja males dominated the labor process without at the same time exercising monopoly on the use of the product of their labor.

The second hypothesis is about the effect of contact with foreign merchants. The greater popularity of cotton growing and cotton cloth in a settlement like Mikolongo (some fifty miles to the west of Chikwawa)[146] may be taken as an indication of the relative isolation of that community in the emerging network of international trade. Conversely, the indigenous cotton economy was weaker in those areas that, like the banks of the Tchiri River, were visited more regularly by foreign traders.[147] Villagers in these more open areas could acquire foreign calico in exchange for a wide variety of local goods, including captives.[148]

The third area for investigation concerns the effects of the slave raids during the first part of the 1860s. The chaos, instability, and famine produced by the slave raids must have paralyzed the cotton economy as it did other branches of production. Stewart was wrong in his broad attacks on Livingstone on the basis of what he saw at the height of the famine in September 1862.[149] The conditions were not conducive to any form of organized production, including salt making.

Salt production was a predominantly female enterprise. Mang'anja women extracted salt from two main sources. Grasses were the less important source, and the processing of this type of salt was an individual affair carried on within the village.[150] The mining of ground salt, which was found all along the marshes, particularly in the triangle formed by the Mwanza-Tchiri confluence, was a communal activity although there was nothing in the labor process itself that necessitated interhousehold cooperation.

Women from one or several villages, together with their husbands, went to mine salt in the Tchiri-Mwanza confluence at the height of the dry season. The husband collected firewood for boiling the salt-laden earth, built a temporary hut (*msasa*) in which he lived with his wife, and constructed a roofless compound in which the distilling (*kutcheza*) took place. The wife alone was responsible for the actual distilling—a complex process that attracted the attention of the missionary Lovell Procter in May 1862:

> Two large pots rested on a wooden frame about two feet in height, underneath each of which, & side by side, were ranged two wooden troughs of a hollow log shaped like a canoe, & about a yard long. The bottoms of the pots are pierced, &, a quantity of the salt impregnated mud being put in, water is poured upon it, soaking through the mud & carrying off the salt which it contains through the holes. I tasted some of the salt water thus obtained, & brackish enough I found it. The canoe shaped troughs having received this liquor, it is poured into another large pot, &, the water being suffered to boil away, the salt remains as a deposit behind. If any dirt is found with it, & in any case that is wondrously little, the salt is washed well, & the water again boiled after draining. They are never able, however, to get the salt above the color of fine moist sugar.[151]

Some of the manufacturers hailed from villages twenty and more miles away.

As with other European observers, Procter was so fascinated by technical details that he did not pay enough attention to the social and religious aspects of production. One wishes he had asked the salt maker why she greeted him with indignation and suspected "some nefarious design on our part."[152] The woman might have confessed her fear of coming into contact with "hot" persons—individuals who had had sexual intercourse the previous night. Everyone who lived in the compounds, including the buyers, had to abstain from sexual intercourse. Breach of the taboo would not only jeopardize the enterprise but would also endanger the salt makers themselves.[153] The taboo partly explains the predominance of women past childbearing age in, and the exclusion of social juniors from, salt production. The Mang'anja could not trust their juniors on the question of sexual abstinence—a powerful ideology that guaranteed elders, including tribute receivers, control over a product that was second only to iron as an item of trade between the Valley and the Highlands.

Just as the people of the Highlands were dependent on salt and cotton imports from the Valley, the inhabitants of the Valley looked to the Highlands for iron implements as well as unprocessed iron ore. The Valley was less well endowed with iron deposits than the Highlands, especially the area around Mpemba, which Kirk once described as "an iron working country" where every village had its forge and smelting furnaces in the forest.[154] Rowley underlined the complementarity of the Valley-Highlands relationship when he wrote:

> The people in the highlands were rich in iron, those in the Valley were poor; so when a highlandman wanted cotton to make himself a cloth, he sent down hoes, and such like things, to the Valley, and obtained cotton in exchange.[155]

Rowley should have added that the Valley also received raw iron that was processed by local blacksmiths.[156]

A major consequence of the relative poverty of the Valley in iron deposits is that oral traditions in the area have little to say about the smelting phase (*ng'anjo*) of iron production. They are rich, however, on the labor organization involved in the importation of iron ingots from the Highlands. A village headman or blacksmith would go to the Highlands with his own men.[157] The men were needed to mine the ore and to collect *masuku* wood, which was used in making charcoal. The earth-laden ore and the charcoal were later turned over to the smelter, who was invariably described as headman or chief.[158] He supervised the smelting process, which was always conducted in the bush amid

3. Blacksmith's forge, early 1860s

great secrecy and religious ritual.[159] As in salt production, everyone who took part in smelting had to abstain from sexual intercourse. The smelter received, for his technical and ritual expertise, some of the ingots, or goats, fowls, or cotton cloth.

Back in the Valley, the blacksmith worked under a "thatched roof supported on wooden poles." His instruments included bellows made of goatskin, tongs of split bamboo, a stone anvil, and a stone hammer. The tongs were continually dipped in water to retard burning. The *chipala* furnace was cylindrical in form and about three feet in depth.

> It was filled with charcoal and iron ore, the latter previously roasted on an open hearth by the side of the furnace. From the back, a clay pipe moulded on a stick communicated the blast to the furnace, the bellows were of goat skin, of the usual rude construction, the valve being opened and shut by the hand. On the opposite side, the opening by which the ore seemed to be taken out, was closed with earth but occasionally a rod was introduced to stir it up. As the materials sunk down, fresh ore and charcoal were put on the top.[160]

The end result was an array of articles: anklets, arrows, axes, bracelets, hoes, knives, needles, and spearheads that Rowley described as "of such excellent workmanship that they might have come from the hands of some of our workmen." Rowley qualified his statement by noting that the Mang'anja of the Highlands made better iron tools than their cousins in the Valley, who "otherwise excelled in wood-curving."[161]

The reference to wood curving is apposite. It appears that Mang'anja cultivators in the Valley depended as much on wooden as on iron hoes; the Mang'anja writer William Chafulumira is very emphatic on this point. Although his informants did not flatly deny iron manufacturing in the precolonial era—as some of the traditions I recorded do[162]—they insisted that hoes of large iron blades were not widely used in the past. Only well-to-do families were able to purchase iron hoes. The only iron hoes that poor cultivators could get were those discarded by the rich (*misikiri*).[163] There may not have been a direct correlation between the progress made in agriculture and the increased use of iron hoes during the nineteenth century, as some analysts have suggested.[164]

British sources do implicitly support the claims of oral history. Only a few eyewitness accounts list the hoe as a by-product of the Mang'anja iron industry. Many, including Procter's description of Chibisa's blacksmith, do not mention the hoe. The lists are heavily biased toward ornaments and objects of religious function.[165] More significant, when the hoe appears in the texts, it does so not so much as an instrument of agricultural production but as an item of exchange. Iron hoes feature as one of the articles that headmen in the Valley frequently presented to Livingstone for sale—a regular hoe weighing about two pounds fetched calico "of about the value of fourpence."[166] Read against the claims of oral sources, British accounts suggest one possible scenario. The ruling elite of the Valley may not have produced or acquired iron hoes for local use in the first place. They may have hoarded the product primarily with a view to selling it at a higher price to foreigners, especially the inhabitants of the Lower Zembezi.

On the eve of its fateful encounter with the forces of the capitalist world economy, the Mang'anja economy was more inward-looking than it had been during the sixteenth and seventeenth centuries.[167] There was little organized trade besides that in slaves going on between the Lower Tchiri Valley and the Lower Zembezi in the late 1850s and early 1860s. Section 1.1 identified one set of factors leading to this outcome: the discrepancy between the claims to territorial authority and real economic power that tended to discourage organized foreign traders from the region.

But it was the rise of the international slave traffic that was mainly responsible for weakening normal trade relations between the Zembezi and Tchiri river regions. European and American cloth brought by the foreign slave traders must have reduced the dependence of the Lower Zembezi on cloth from the Tchiri Valley. Cloth was not one of the articles that Livingstone's Zembezi workers were eager to buy from the Mang'anja in 1859–63. The Mang'anja had lost their traditional role as suppliers of cotton cloth to the Lower Zembezi.

The slave trade dealt a blow to the organization of long-distance trade between the two regions in another way. Slave raiding contributed to the development of defensive warlordism among both the Mang'anja and non-Mang'anja rulers living along the traditional trade routes linking the two regions. The confrontations between the rulers of the Makhanga state and the Mang'anja chiefs of Mikolongo virtually paralyzed the trade route between Chikwawa and Thete.[169] In the south, Tengani responded to the attacks and raids by Matekenya and other raiders by organizing an army that for all practical purposes closed the Tchiri River to normal traffic from the Lower Zembezi:

> The way to Tette is pretty well closed by Tshisaka while Tingane in the marshy lands of the Shire kills any who would go to Senna. So they are pretty well shut out of the world.[170]

Livingstone penetrated Tengani's defenses only because of the terror that his steamship created and because of his readiness to use firearms.[171] Instead of exporting cotton cloth and other nonhuman products, the Mang'anja of the Valley were being taken away as captives and receiving as their guests the thousands of uprooted fugitives from the Zembezi region. The chiefs who hoarded items like hoes had no regular outlet for their goods, which was probably one reason these items were sold so cheaply to occasional visitors, including the British.[172]

It is important, however, not to exaggerate the significance of the developments outlined above. Long-distance exchange between the Valley and other non-Mang'anja regions, including the Lower Zembezi, was essentially a trade in luxuries that was largely restricted to the domain of the ruling elite. Its rise or decline affected the relations of ordinary Mang'anja only indirectly. It could not have disabled the reproductive cycle of the village community, which was more dependent on relations with the Mang'anja of the Highlands. Exchanges between the Highlands and the Valley cemented the ecological, political, and cultural interdependence between the two sections of the Mang'anja population. It was more durable and provided the Mang'anja with a model that informed their interactions with foreign traders.

The products of the nonagricultural sector formed the staple of barter between the Valley and the Highlands.[173] Exchanges in foodstuffs were important only in times of serious food shortages at either end of the relationship.[174] Raw cotton, cotton cloth, salt, dried fish, goats, and fowls were the main exports from the Valley.[175] These fetched a wide range of articles in the Highlands, including animal skins, raw iron, finished iron implements, and in some cases human beings. Livingstone referred to this kind of barter when he wrote, "A great deal of trade is carried on between villages."[176]

The absence of middlemen in this trade network removed the screen long-distance exchange creates between production and circulation. In intervillage barter the seller was the producer and the buyer the actual consumer. Female producers of salt often carried their product to the Highlands in *mbaza* bags just as ironmongers came down to the Valley with the products of their labor. Wives were as actively engaged in this type of trade as their husbands.[177] No husband could conclude a bargain without consulting his wife, so that each exchange became a protracted affair in which sellers and buyers haggled over the price and husbands and wives had to reach a consensus. "It [is] amusing," wrote Rowley, "to see the deference [the men] paid the woman, going to her and asking her opinion before they concluded a bargain."[178] Gender equality or complementarity in the production process found an expression at the level of distribution.

Open to all free adult producers, intervillage trade tended to discourage individual accumulation. The presence of an itinerant trader in a Mang'anja village drew every adult member of the community, including those who had nothing to sell. They came out to see who, if anyone, was trying to acquire more than what was socially needed for subsistence. Those who appeared to be amassing goods beyond what they needed became liable to accusations of witchcraft (*ufiti*):

> Kasimba was prevailed upon to sell us a goat, of which there were several about, but the sale was not effected without a prolonged . . . consultation with his brother. . . . I now discover that these consultations, which are so constantly annoying, are to avoid jealousies, & consequent machinations with mfiti [i.e., *afiti,* witches]. Such would probably be the case if one brother, though a superior chief, were supposed to be amassing property in secret, or even acting too much on his own responsibility with probable designs against his family. A general & open palaver avoids any evil suspicions.[179]

New settlers were particularly vulnerable in this respect. Khwama immigrant rice cultivators at Khulubvi had to sell their rice to British travelers at night for fear of being ostracized by the Mang'anja.[180] The Mang'anja must also have resisted the fact that the immigrants were turning agriculture into the new high road to individual accumulation, a role that that branch of production had rarely played in the local economy.

1.3. The Banja Household and Food Production and Consumption

> When telling the people in England what were my objects in going out to Africa, I stated that, among other things, I meant to teach these people agriculture; but I now see that they know far more about it than I do.[181]

> But here the men seemed evidently a domesticated race; some were nursing their children, and fondling them with much apparent affection.[182]

Mang'anja agriculture, in contrast to many branches and forms of nonagricultural production, presupposed the existence of the otherwise socially incoherent and impermanent banja household as a labor unit. Headed by the wife and her husband, the banja included the wife's dependent children, her elderly relatives such as her mother, and in some instances the communally owned akapolo. As at meals, at night the banja dispersed to merge with members of other households within the mbumba matrilineage or village community. Some children slept with their mother's mother, whether or not she had a husband and an independent household. Others slept in the sexually segregated communal dormitory (*gowelo*). Only the youngest shared the same house with their mother, who did not always spend the night with her husband. The wives of polygynous husbands (*amitala*) were scattered in different village communities.[183] Divorce was as easily accessible to women as to men.[184]

The apparent looseness and fragility of the Mang'anja banja expressed at least one fundamental reality of social organization: the fact that unlike the standard Western nuclear family, the banja did not constitute a unit of (productive) property relations. Not only akapolo but land itself belonged, as in many other precapitalist societies, to the community:

> The land is the property of the tribe; no individual can possess a freehold. The separate possession of individuals is secured to them only so long as they occupy: no one can transfer land to another. The chief has the power of allowing the alienation of land, but the common rights of the

community restrain him: without the common consent he could not dispose of any part of his territory.[185]

Wives and husbands looked to their respective communities insofar as their rights to productive property were concerned. Parents did not leave productive property to be inherited by their children.

The goods that a wife and her husband controlled as members of the banja were, as a rule, either unproductive or perishable. These included *nyumba* houses, *nkhokwe* granaries, foodstuffs, fowls, cats, and such instruments of domestic production as arrows, bows, grinding mills, mortars, and hoes. Some of these items, like the nyumba, nkhokwe, foodstuffs, and domesticated animals, were held jointly by the wife and husband.[186] Little is known about the struggles arising from the principle of joint ownership at this level except for the contests that filter through British accounts of trade relations with the Mang'anja, as discussed in the foregoing section. Other goods, especially the instruments of domestic production, were held separately. They were discarded at the death of their respective users:

> The graves of the sexes were distinguished by the various implements which the buried dead had used in their different employments during life; but they were all broken as if to be employed no more. A piece of a fishing-net and a broken paddle told that a fisherman slept beneath that sod. The graves of the women had the wooden mortar, and the heavy pestle used in pounding the corn, and the basket in which the meal is sifted, while all had numerous broken calabashes and pots arranged around them.[187]

The practice of burying a married woman or man with what the person had used in life eliminated the possibility of conflict arising from competition over the property of the banja household. Intrahousehold relations were inherently fragile and unstable, as many commentators have correctly argued.[188]

The banja does emerge, however, as a cohesive unit from the viewpoint of the labor requirements of the food economy. Notwithstanding its importance in the system of land distribution, the formation of consumption units as well as the organization of rituals like the mgwetsa that guaranteed the fertility of the land, the Mang'anja mbumba remained at the periphery of agricultural production. Kinsmen did occasionally help a stranded grower, but kinship never formed a regular channel for mobilizing agricultural labor. Agricultural work instead united the otherwise socially impermanent banja household. Competence in agriculture, rather than competence in communally organized nonagricultural production or warfare, marked off those men who could and those who could not obtain a wife among the Mang'anja—"the real owners and chief cultivators of the soil."[189]

Most Mang'anja households during the nineteenth century maintained two main fields, dimba and munda (plural *minda*). The dimba was located on the dambo plains surrounding the Tchiri and other rivers; the munda was on the mphala drylands.[190] The labor schedules for the two fields did not then conflict as sharply as they would during the second half of the twentieth century. Regulated by the flow of the Tchiri River, much of the work on the dimba started and ended at the close and beginning of the munda cycle.[191]

The amount of labor time that growers spent in preparing munda fields from August to October varied according to the age of the munda, which in its turn was a factor of the social position of the banja within the community. Well-established households did not as a rule open new munda fields. The labor demands and productivity of dimba farming reduced the possibility and necessity of shifting cultivation of the mphala. The majority of fresh minda opened during any season belonged to migrants or newly married couples before they were given the highly prized dimba gardens.

The opening of a new munda (*kuswa mphanje*) was a strenuous exercise that fell on men. With the help of an ax made of "soft iron," a man would cut down the bush and trees about a foot from the ground, leaving the stumps standing to rot.[192] Once the branches had dried up, he would gather them into heaps over the stumps, set them on fire, and spread the ashes on the ground before the planting rains in November and December.

The preparation of old minda, which approximated what Livingstone termed grassland cultivation, was less labor intensive:

> If grass land is to be brought under cultivation, as much tall grass as the labourer can conveniently lay hold of is collected together and tied into a knot. He then strikes his hoe round the tufts to sever the roots, and leaving all standing, proceeds until the whole ground assumes the appearance of a field covered with little shocks of corn in harvest. A short time before the rains begin, these grass shocks are collected in small heaps, covered with earth, and burnt, the ashes and burnt soil being used to fertilize the ground.[193]

The tall grass referred to in the passage included the stalks of crops from the previous season. Women also took part in this form of munda preparation.

Just before or immediately after the first rains, Mang'anja women and men sprayed the seeds of the staple food crops: *mapira* or *gonkho* (*Sorghum vulgare*), millet of the slow-maturing variety, and *mchewere* or *machewere* millet (*Pennisetum typhoides*). These were planted on the flat ground and were usually intercropped with groundnuts, pumpkins, *nandolo* peas, cucumbers, and other minor crops.[194] In the northeastern part of the Valley cultivators also grew on the minda a small-grained but heat-resistant variety of maize known locally as *kanjere-mkwera.* Unlike other munda crops, kanjere-mkwera was raised on *mathutu,* mounds constructed by "collecting all the weeds and grass into heaps, covering them with soil and then setting fire to them. They burn slowly, and all the ashes and much of the smoke is retained in the overlying soil."[195]

Mchewere, mapira, and maize required constant weeding from mid-December to the end of February, for although rainfall was low in the area, the high temperatures and humidity promoted rapid plant growth. The demand for agricultural labor reached a peak during this season. The struggle against weeds demanded the collaboration of every able-bodied member of the banja, including the youth, who were normally introduced to agriculture at this time of the year. Only the very weak and small were excused from hoeing:

> All the people of a village turn out to labour in the fields. It is no uncommon thing to see men, women, and children hard at work, with the baby lying close by beneath a shady bush.[196]

Theirs was a long day. It started about sunrise and ended, for the male cultivators, at sunset. It was broken briefly at midday with a snack prepared in the field itself or in the village, depending on the distance between the two. Women left the field earlier in order to attend to domestic chores.[197]

As we shall see in Part II, weeding turned out to be one of the major factors shaping Mang'anja responses to the labor demands of the capitalist colonial economy. The race against weeds complicated the problem of food security during the "months of hunger" from December to March.[198] The average Mang'anja household struggled to keep its field properly weeded while searching for food to maintain the labor force. Only large households with many able-bodied dependents were comfortably able to combine weeding with other activities, including the guarding of crops against birds and other predatory animals—a series of activities known collectively as *dindiro.*[199]

4. Women hoeing, early 1860s

Dindiro was the second major task during the months of hunger. Its intensity and duration varied between crops and locations. Maize, mapira, and mchewere fields located at the edge of a thriving animal habitat such as a mountain range had to be protected throughout much of the growing season.[200] In most cases, however, dindiro proper started only after the crops had begun shooting flower (*kumasula*) and was largely a day operation. March through April was the typical dindiro period for maize and mchewere, May for mapira.

Boys did much of the bird scaring from an observatory tower (*tsanja*) built in the center or corner of the field. From the tower radiated strings connecting reeds or trees planted at short intervals throughout the garden. To chase birds from any part of the garden, children would pull the strings while singing or shouting at the predators.[201] Dindiro was a more pleasurable activity than weeding for many boys, especially during a year following a good harvest when they would be well provided for. Bird scaring was an ordeal only when there was not enough to eat.

Parents joined their children after the crops had fully formed ears and had become the target of birds as well as larger animals like baboons along the river valleys and hills. To guard the crops against such animals, the Mang'anja built temporary dwellings (*makumbi*) in the fields.[202] The villages would be more or less empty during the season because wives and husbands lived in the fields, doing all their cooking in the tents. Poor families would not wait long before they started eating the new crops, which heralded a period of merriness in the community. The village would be moving toward the major festivities of the year, the chinamwali initiation rites for girls and the nyau rituals for boys, which coincided with the harvesting season: mchewere and maize in April and mapira in May and June.[203] Cotton (*thonje*) was the only major munda crop that did not require dindiro.

Of the three varieties of cotton that European travelers identified in what is now Malawi, only two were found in the Valley.[204] These were *thonje-kaja* and *thonje-manga,* the one being indigenous and the other of foreign origin. Thonje-manga was a semiperennial. It was planted once every three years under conditions that are not entirely clear from the literature. When fully grown it reached six feet in height, started to yield only three months after planting, and produced a longer staple than the indigenous thonje-kaja.[205]

As indicated in the preceding section, the Tchiri Highlands were climatically unsuitable for cotton growing. The weavers seen in the area imported the raw material from the Upper or Lower Tchiri Valley. It is also evident from Rowley's candid responses to Stewart's criticism of Livingstone that cotton growing in the Lower Valley was not as universal as Livingstone's enthusiastic statements tend to suggest.[206] Cotton growing demanded extra labor, and many villagers were unable to combine food production with cotton cultivation.

Thonje-kaja was planted in April,[207] either in its own field or in the gardens from which growers had harvested mchewere (and, in a few instances, kanjere-mkwera maize) but which did not carry the slow-maturing gonkho sorghum. Growing to over six feet in height, gonkho could not be mixed with the dwarfish thonje-kaja, which was between one and a half and two feet tall, without stifling the latter.[208] Raised alone after the harvesting of maize and mchewere in April, cotton could be identified easily by British travelers, who estimated that an average field did not measure more than a quarter of an acre.[209] Like other crops, thonje-kaja required constant weeding during the first phase of its growth.[210] Equally labor-demanding was the harvesting process that took place from September to the time of the first rains in November. Workers had to pay special attention to thonje-kaja because the wool adhered tightly to the seeds.[211] That the harvesting coincided with one of the peak seasons of the dimba cycle must have made it extremely difficult for labor-deficient households to engage in cotton agriculture. "In the Shire Valley," Rowley pointed out, "when drought does not prevent, some two or three persons of every village of any note cultivate a little cotton, generally sufficient to make the grower a large wrapper of native cloth."[212] If inhabitants of the region had ever grown more cotton before, the situation in the mid-nineteenth century represented a new development. The area was moving in the same direction as other parts of modern-day Malawi such as Kasungu, where few cotton plants were seen "not from soil or climate being unsuitable for them . . . but from the fact that the people can supply their wants by exchanging grain for foreign calico, as the slave-traders pass."[213] Only those Mang'anja without easy access to foreign calico combined, as did the people of Mikolongo, cotton and food cultivation on the mphala with dimba agriculture.

In contemporary Chimang'anja (the language of the Mang'anja) the term *dimba* denotes a supplementary field, which is precisely what the few plots on the edges of the Tchiri River and the now permanently inundated Dabanyi and Dinde marshes have become since the early 1940s. Dimba farming has become so insignificant that the researchers attached to the Shire Valley Development Project in the early 1970s did not incorporate it in their initial surveys.[214] During the nineteenth and early twentieth centuries, however, dimba farming contributed as much to the food economy as, if not more than, the alternate munda system. As Mang'anja elders once told Chafulumira:

> Famine visited frequently only those lands in which the people did not practice *dimba* agriculture. Where they did, as was the case among the Mang'anja, famine was a rare event. Indeed, people from many lands used to come here in search for food. Many of them never returned to their famine-ridden homelands and decided to settle here permanently.[215]

In the absence of a well-developed system of food distribution and exchange, the decision to settle permanently in the Valley implied a readiness to adapt to a new pattern of work schedules. The struggle for food security in the area was not merely a moral struggle, as much of the literature on the peasantry suggests. It required above everything else close and extensive communication with nature through the labor process.

Situated on the banks of the Tchiri River, dimba farming in the nineteenth century attracted greater attention from travelers than the munda regime. Livingstone and his companions could not, for example, fail to notice in August 1859 the ways in which the dambo had altered since their first visit at the height of the rainy season the previous January:

> A great change has taken place over the face of the district. In many places the grass has become dry enough to be burned off, while by the water edge and by the margin of the many secondary streams, the people have come down and cultivate. . . . We had observed no people but a few hunters on our former trip. . . . Whether this emigration be some universal thing, we do not know.[216]

The diarist, John Kirk, must have later confirmed for himself that what he saw was indeed an annual event: the beginning of the dimba agricultural season.

Areas of high elevation in the Dabanyi and Dinde marshes would have been under cultivation for about a month or two by August. Only the very low-lying portions of the marshes would have just been opened for cultivation at this time. As in woodland munda cultivation, the preparation of dimba fields was done exclusively by men, which led Livingstone to generalize, "The Manganja cultivate the soil very extensively and more men than women were sometimes seen at this occupation."[217] The absence of women, who were at this time busy storing munda crops, was especially conspicuous among farmers from the hills.

Dimba agriculture brought together two features of Mang'anja social inequality. First, some of the men from the hills seen at work were not independent producers. They were akapolo, clients, and other dependents sent down by their masters.[218] Second, the plots worked by such migrants did not belong to them. They were leased under the *nchoche* arrangement, according to which the producers had to give a portion of their harvest to the owner of the fields—usually a headman.[219] Ownership of the scarce but fertile dambo, like that of salt or iron deposits, signified a social relation. New settlers in the village, including sons-in-law, had to prove themselves before being granted access to dimba fields. The principles of communal ownership applied automatically only in connection with the extensive mphala drylands.

Independent and dependent workers on the dambo did not have to deal with trees. Except for the northern section of the Dabanyi, which was rarely cultivated because of the high salinity of its soil, and which until the 1930s carried an extensive forest of midikhwa palm trees, the marshes were devoid of trees.[220] Common vegetation found in the marshes included elephant grass (*tsenjere*), bango reeds, and bande grass. Whereas elephant grass and bango were for the most part confined to areas not previously cultivated, the bande was ubiquitous. The two-meter-long stems that formed a dense and tangled mass were loosely attached to the ground by very short and thin roots.[221] A strong current during the flood season could uproot large sections of the bande mass, which would then move like floating islands along the river and into the adjacent marshes.[222] As the floods receded, the bande would settle on the dambo to constitute a major natural constraint on dimba farming.

The easiest method of opening a dimba garden was to wait for the ground to become thoroughly dry and then to set fire to the bande.[223] This was the common practice in areas of high elevation that became dry as early as February or March. Owners of the more low-lying portions of the marshes that became dry only in June had to begin work immediately in order to give their crops enough time to mature. They cut the bande in vertical sections and turned the sections upside down in order to expose the undergrowth to the sun before burning everything in a couple of days. Stems and twigs that did not burn completely were gathered in small heaps and planting started on the cleared areas. Most dimba crops were planted in holes about six inches deep and two feet apart.[224]

Although much smaller than an average munda, the dimba sustained a greater variety of crops. Large-grained maize (*chimanga*) was the principal dimba crop in the mid-nineteenth century. It was intercropped with beans (*nyemba*), pumpkins (*maungu*), tobacco (*fodya*), sugarcane (*mzimbe*), and many kinds of vegetables and legumes.[225] In addition to these crops, which grew during the dry season, villagers in the Dinde Marsh also raised wetland rice (*mpunga*). Sown at the beginning of the rainy season, the rice grew in the floodwaters and was harvested about April or May.[226]

The crops were so interlaced that, in addition to providing the soil with a thick cover protecting it from the sun, they also prevented the uncontrolled growth of weeds. Weeding was especially easy where bande, with its thin and short roots, had been the dominant natural vegetation. However, where elephant grass, *nansongole* (a tall perennial grass with stiff, sharply pointed leaf blades), and especially *dawe* nut grass had predominated, weeding the dimba was a constant struggle. It demanded the cooperation of all banja members, including women.[227] The only major dimba activity besides the initial clearing in which women did not take part was guarding the crops against birds and predatory beasts.

Boys scared birds from rice fields in the same manner as they guarded mchewere and mapira on the minda. The exercise lasted about three weeks. Full dindiro arrangements were made to protect maize from elephants and hippopotami. Husbands and dependents of farmers from the hills sometimes spent the entire period from planting to harvesting guarding the plots.[228] They combined dindiro with many other activities. They watered the plants in the event of unusually dry weather.[229] But the most common undertaking was fishing and hunting. Mbuna and tchera snares were constructed during this time in order to trap elephants and hippopotami both for meat and as a means of warning the beasts to keep away from the fields. Much of the hunting that was done along the Tchiri River was not, in other words, independent of the requirements of agriculture, although some of the tchera traps remained standing along the banks after the dimba growing season had come to an end in December.[230]

Dimba farming was the primary insurance against food shortages resulting from drought. Annually replenished by floods that brought all sorts of vegetable and mineral matter, the dambo was exceptionally fertile.[231] In addition to carrying many crops at a time, the dimba system permitted the cultivation of several consecutive crops within the same growing season. In 1862 Waller identified maize in five different stages of growth because, as he put it, "so rich is the soil [that] one crop is taken up and another [is] put in the same day the moisture filtering through to the roots of the corn."[232] Three years earlier, in 1859, Kirk had contrasted the impoverishment of the Lower Zembezi (largely because of the slave raids) with the abundance of the Valley: "There is no lack of food in these regions and a fine crop for the next year [is] in the fields."[233]

Mang'anja physical appearance seemed to have attested to this abundance. Again, contrasting what he had seen in the south, Kirk commented: "The men are strong fellows, the women good natured and not the scraggy things of the Zambesi."[234] At Mikolongo, Rowley remarked, everyone "looked well fed, all were well clothed, all were profusely ornamented with beads, ivory, and brass rings."[235] This was in mid-1862, when the Mang'anja of the Highlands were coming down to the Valley to cultivate the dambo in order to avert famine occasioned by drought.

Reliance on dimba farming for food security helps make sense of at least two features of Mang'anja socioeconomic organization. The first concerns the Mang'anja's utilization of the mphala drylands. Although not yet as high as they would become toward the end of the century, the labor requirements of dimba cultivation are to be considered a key factor preventing the widespread application of labor-intensive techniques to munda agriculture. The restricted use of such methods as raising mathutu had as much to do with the problem of labor distribution as with purely ecological factors. The problem of labor distribution combined also with the high productivity of the dambo to reduce the need for shifting cultivation of the mphala. Thus, although the population densities of the Valley and the Highlands were not markedly different, the Mang'anja of the Valley did not practice shifting cultivation as much as did their cousins on the Highlands.[236]

The second ramification relates to settlement patterns. As noted in section 1.2.1, the population of the Valley was concentrated on the edges of the dambo floodlands and the riverbanks. Some of these places were liable to flooding during years of high floods, but people took the risk in order to avoid the inconvenience of having to migrate to the marshes every year at the beginning of the dimba agricultural season. Heads of important families who lived far away from the dambo could maintain dimba fields only through the labor of their dependents. Ordinary villagers had to keep close to the life-giving floodlands. This proximity also made it easier for women to combine agricultural with domestic production.

The technical equivalence of female and male labor within agriculture did not extend to all forms of household production. Some forms, like the construction of nyumba houses and nkhokwe granaries and the making of mats, were specifically male. The specifically female activities included beer brewing, pot making, and, more significantly, food processing.[237] As in many other societies, food processing among the Mang'anja occupied the largest part of female labor outside agriculture. Unlike in the capitalist West, however, the Mang'anja accorded as much value to this kind of labor as they did to specifically male activities. Mang'anja women usually released themselves from hoeing in order to do domestic chores like pounding grain and storing foodstuffs in the nkhokwe.[238]

Attached to each banja was a nkhokwe: a small round grass-plaited building on a raised platform with a conical thatched roof. Built by the husband, the nkhokwe was the wife's domain.[239] In it she stored all grain as it came from the field. At a later stage she would, with the assistance of her children and sometimes her husband, remove the grain from the granary and prepare it for permanent storage. The preparation

5. Nkhokwe granary, 1960s

involved the removal of ears from the cobs, after which the former would be put in baked clay pots and returned to the granary. Some pots would be reserved for seed, and the rest of the grain was used to feed the family.[240]

There were two stages in the preparation of maize, mchewere, or mapira before it reached the cooking pot. The grain was moistened, placed in a *mtondo* mortar—a "log of wood about 3½ feet long and 1 foot in diameter hollowed out in one end."[241] Next the grain was crushed with a heavy wooden pestle. One or several women, each with her own pestle, did the crushing (*kusinja*) simultaneously. The crushed grain was "then shaken on a flat tray of bamboo [*lichelo*] [and] by a dexterous movement [of the lichelo] the bran is cast out and the crushed grain remains behind."[242] The procedure was repeated until the grain was free of any bran.

In the second stage the women turned the crushed grain into flour (*ufa*). Sometimes the two stages were separated by several days during which the grain, especially maize, remained soaked in earthen pots. Otherwise the second stage immediately followed the first. Flour was made either by pounding the soaked grain in a mortar or by grinding it on a *mphero* mill: a "block of granite, syenite, or even mica schist,

6. Women pounding grain, 1914

fifteen or eighteen inches square and five or six thick, with a piece of quartz or other hard rock about the size of a half brick, one side of which has a convex surface, and fits into a concave hollow in the larger and stationary stone."[243] The workwoman,

> kneeling, grasps this upper millstone with both hands, and works it backwards and forwards in the hollow of the lower millstone, in the same way that a baker works his dough, when pressing it and pushing from him. The weight of the person is brought to bear on the moveable stone, and while it is pressed and pushed forwards and backwards, one hand supplies every now and then a little grain to be thus at first bruised and then ground on the lower stone, which is placed on the slope, so that the meal, when ground, falls on to a skin or mat spread for the purpose.[244]

The flour was then dried in the sun and stored in a pot to be used for preparing porridge (*nsima*).

The nsima was cooked inside the house in a clay pot "supported over the fire by others reversed" or by stones.[245] Flour was continually added to the gruel until it reached the desired consistency. The resulting nsima was served in wooden or earthen plates, one for women and the other for men. Another set of plates contained relish (*ndiwo*) in the form of cooked vegetables, fish, or meat. A full meal for the Mang'anja, as for many other peoples of contemporary Malawi, consisted of both nsima and ndiwo.

7. Woman at work on a mphero grinding mill, early 1860s

8. A girl cooking, 1960s

The meal, which was eaten outside the nyumba, reproduced some of the major contradictions of Mang'anja society. On the one hand, it emphasized the equality of and divisions between the sexes. Men of different households making up a mbumba segment ate together but separately from the women of the same group.[246] On the other hand, the meal enacted some of the basic inequalities between agricultural workers. Although the literature is not clear on how the children of the mbumba were treated in this regard, there is sufficient evidence pointing to the unenviable position of the prospective or recently married mkamwini son-in-law. Like the kapolo, he did not take part in the communal meal. He ate separately in the dormitory.[247] The amount and quality of food given to him did not reflect his actual contributions to the food economy; rather, it reflected how the community perceived him. A disenchanted mother-in-law could punish a son-in-law from the kitchen. She would tell her daughter:

> Take the maize husks,
> Give them to your husband
> Come back
> To eat the cornmeal.
> Take the bones,
> Give them to your husband.
> Come back
> To eat the steak.[248]

A famine, like the one that hit the land in 1862–1863, could exacerbate the inequities.

2

From the Slave Trade to the Rise of a Peasantry, 1859–1925

> The discovery of gold and silver in America, the extirpation, enslavement and entombment in mines of the indigenous population of that continent, the beginnings of the conquest and plunder of India, and the conversion of Africa into a preserve for the commercial hunting of blackskins, are all things which characterize the dawn of the era of capitalist production.[1]

As in many other regions of Africa, the end of the slave trade opened the Valley to the era of legitimate commerce. The long-term effect of legitimate trade on the processes associated with agricultural and nonagricultural production was uneven in at least two respects. The revival of certain branches of nonagricultural production resulting from the initial opening of the region to legitimate trade during the 1870s proved to be a short-lived phenomenon. The earlier trend toward the marginalization of the sector reasserted itself irreversibly from the early 1880s. The region entered the colonial era with very distorted patterns of work within the nonagricultural sector. In contrast, there was a complete restructuring and diversification of agricultural labor processes as cultivators intensified the production of old crops and adopted new ones, including sesame. This study locates in these contradictory economic developments the emergence of a peasantry as a partially subordinated class against a backdrop of new population movements into the Valley.[2]

For a variety of reasons, including the inadequacy of the data base, this chapter does not address some of the issues that have preoccupied specialist attention on the slave trade: its organization, demographics, profitability, and so forth. The special contribution of the chapter to the debate lies in the demonstration that, insofar as the Mang'anja were concerned, the slave trade was an unmitigated disaster. The Mang'anja did not, either as a group or as individuals, reap any political, economic, or social benefit from the trade.

2.1. The Era of the Slave Trade, from the 1840s to 1865

The era of the slave trade, which initiated the systematic integration of the Valley into the capitalist world economy, was by definition a period of extreme violence. The victims and direct perpetrators of the violence changed considerably over time. Internal violence generated some of the captives who left the Valley during the initial phase of the trade, which lasted from the mid-1840s to about 1860. Foreign slave dealers at this time relied also on the cooperation of Mang'anja elders who supplied the international traffic with what were on the whole the underprivileged members of the local community. From the perspective of the village elders, the traffic in its first phase constituted "peaceful" exchange over which they exercised some control. But selective violence directed against the underprivileged became an indiscriminate war against all the Mang'anja during the second phase, which reached its first climax in 1861–64. Mang'anja elders had lost their limited control over the traffic, with the result that women who had until then enjoyed protection against the slave dealers became victims of externally organized violence as well.

2.1.1. From Slave Trading to Slave Raiding

A careful reading of the edited diaries of Livingstone and those of his companions during the first three expeditions to the Lake Malawi–Tchiri River region in 1859[3] shows that men like James Stewart, who criticized Livingstone for portraying the Tchiri River region as a paradise unaffected by the slave trade, were correct up to a point.[4] The disruptions resulting from the opening of East Africa to slave dealers from Latin America, the Caribbean, the Mascarene Islands, and Zanzibar were not confined to the Lower Zembezi. The Valley, like the Tchiri Highlands and the region around Lake Malawi, had also been drawn into the expanding network of the international slave trade.

Mang'anja oral historians, whose ancestors participated in the trade mainly as local suppliers or as victims but never as direct agents of the foreign buyers based on the Indian Ocean, associate the origins of the slave trade with three principal names: Chisaka (Pedro Caetano Pereira), Matekenya (Paul Marianno II), and Nyaude (Joachim José da Cruz). These were the rulers of, respectively, the Makhanga, Matchinjiri, and Massangano prazo estates or kingdoms.[5] The name Chisaka dominates the traditions recorded between Chikwawa and

Thete,[6] and that of Nyaude in the memoirs collected on the western fringes of the Dabanyi Marsh.[7] Matekenya nearly monopolized the lower reaches of the Tchiri River from its confluence with the Zembezi in the south and with the Ruo in the north. To these areas the three prazo barons and other residents of the Lower Zembezi sent their Chikunda retainers to procure slaves.

Livingstone and his companions became aware of the activities of the slave dealers as soon as they entered the Zembezi River region in 1858. They were informed, for example, that Cruz Coimbra, who was stationed on the coast, was the chief agent of the engagé scheme, which allowed the French and their African suppliers to ship thousands of captives to Réunion as "free laborers."[8] It was also common knowledge that Coimbra was dependent on several suppliers operating in the interior. Prominent among the latter were one Francisco as well as Matekenya, who lived near the confluence of the Zembezi with the Tchiri River.[9] The name Matekenya was on the lips of every Mang'anja Livingstone met with in the lower part of the Tchiri River in January 1859.[10] At Chikwawa the expedition heard testimonies about Chisaka's activities in the region between Thete and the Tchiri River.[11] Finally, the journeys to Lakes Chilwa and Malawi in, respectively, April and September 1859 exposed Livingstone to the thriving traffic in human beings in the two areas.[12] The Lake Malawi–Tchiri River region of 1859 was not the paradise that Livingstone's highly structured *Narrative* tends to portray for the purpose, among other things, of attracting British settlers to the area.

Yet it is possible to defend the overall impression created by the *Narrative* in regard to the Valley during 1859. The region was not suffering from the slave raids as much as was the Lower Zembezi. Slave-raiding activities appear to have declined considerably, probably as a result of the arrest of the chief slave dealer, Matekenya, and the disbanding of his Chikunda army in mid-1858.[13] Other slave dealers operating in the area appear to have cooperated with village elders more than Matekenya had done. The typical victims of such exchanges were those members of the local community—"unfriendly orphans, slaves and witches"—who would otherwise have filled the regional exchange network which, according to Livingstone, explained the "ugliness" of the captives that foreign dealers obtained in exchange for calico, beads, mirrors, and other trifles.[14] Such transactions were highly secretive and not easily detectable by travelers like Livingstone.

The few references to the prices set during this period suggest that the slave dealers who supplied the east coast market did, as was the case in the transatlantic system, prefer male to female slaves.[15] If this was so, one reason Mang'anja male and female elders did not strongly resist the trade can be hypothesized. They themselves placed more value on female than on male labor. There was, in other words, a convergence between what the traders demanded and what the suppliers were ready to give.

The temporary predominance of "peaceful" exchanges in 1859 could not, however, conceal the effects of the preceding slave-raiding activities. People were everywhere still suspicious of traveling parties from the south. The sight of such parties revived memories of the dreaded Matekenya and placed every community in the Valley on the alert. The residents of Khulubvi village were frightened when they saw Livingstone and his entourage: "When they saw white men, they were afraid as the people of 'Matakenia' (Mariano) had done so much mischief and killed so many in the lower country. . . ."[16] The activities of Matekenya and other freebooters must also have led to the reinforcement of the linga, the defensive hedges that enclosed most Mang'anja villages,[17] and to the emergence of local warlords like Tengani. Finally, the wars "in the lower country" had sent thousands of refugees to the Valley. Mikolongo teemed with fugitives displaced by Chisaka and Nyaude, whereas Matekenya's depredations in the south and east had brought to the Valley immigrants like the Khwama who settled at Khulubvi and the chieftainess Nyachikadza and her following who established themselves at Thuka in the Dinde Marsh.[18]

In 1859 the forced migrations had not yet, however, adversely affected the food economy. On the contrary, as Chapter 1 showed, the migrations tended to stimulate agricultural production. The villages that absorbed the largest share of the refugees were also among the most agriculturally advanced communities in the region. The Mang'anja were still able to contain the effects of the international traffic. Livingstone did indeed idealize the situation in the Valley in 1859. But in the larger picture of things, the *Narrative* simply overstated the contrast between the Tchiri and Zembezi regions. The account is not as unrealistic as Livingstone's detractors have often made out. The Tchiri Valley became as chaotic as the Lower Zembezi only after 1860, when raiding replaced trading as the dominant mode of acquiring captives.

The escalation of the slave trade during the first half of the 1860s was the result of many contradictory developments of both local and international origin. The severe drought of 1862–63 weakened the position of Mang'anja elders as local suppliers vis-à-vis the middlemen in the trade at a time of generally rising prices for both sugar and cloves produced by slave labor in the French Mascarenes and in Arab-dominated Zanzibar.[19] The fact that the increasing demand for slave labor coincided with British attempts to outlaw the traffic on the Indian Ocean produced two major developments. On the one hand, middlemen who managed to bring captives clandestinely to the east coast became more aggressive because of the higher prices such captives fetched on the coast. On the other hand, the more cautious traders, especially Portuguese officials who felt constrained by the Anglo-Portuguese treaties banning the traffic, turned to the ivory trade. But like the more skillful dealers who surreptitiously continued to supply Arab and French slave users, ivory traders also turned to the Valley and the Highlands for captives.

In the Highlands Portuguese officials, the prazo barons, and their Chikunda retainers collided and sometimes cooperated with Yao traders who for the most part supplied Arab and Swahili middlemen and slave users on the east coast. The combined operations of the Portuguese and Yao slave dealers turned the Highlands and the adjacent Valley into one slave-hunting territory. Within a fortnight in July 1861, Livingstone's party and the recently arrived members of the Universities Mission to Central Africa met with more than a dozen Chikunda raiding bands. At Mbami the British were greeted by eighty-four captives chained by their necks and legs and bound for Thete.[20] After freeing the captives, the British came across more slave parties as the former headed for Magomero, where the Universities Mission was to establish a station largely on the basis of what Livingstone had said about the region in 1859.[21] The captain of one of the gangs was a servant of the governor of Thete.[22] From him the British learned about other bands operating in the neighborhood of Chikwawa in the Valley.

When John Kirk, a member of the Livingstone expedition, returned to Chikwawa, he found the armed marauders gone. They had crossed the Tchiri River at Chibisa, Mankhokwe, and Mathiti. He found only the raiders of another prazo baron, Bonga, in Chibisa's village with their guns and trade goods.[23] The Chikunda of Belshior, Mello, Sequasha, and other lesser-known figures concentrated their operations on the western fringes of the Dabanyi Marsh. "The whole country," wrote Kirk, "is deeply engaged in the slave trade."[24]

Livingstone later wrote to the governor of Thete, criticizing him for his role in the slave trade. The governor's reply was that the treaties Lisbon had entered with London banning the traffic were applicable only to the Indian Ocean system. They did not cover the inland traffic, so in his opinion the prazo barons and their Chikunda retainers had every right to resist the British with force.[25] The slaves-for-ivory network lasted until the dawn of the twentieth century—long after the decline of the Indian Ocean system, whose most important point-man in the Valley was Matekenya.

Matekenya's career from 1858 on deserves close scrutiny for more reasons than its catastrophic effect on the lives of the people of the Valley. It illustrates the fragility of Portugal's claim to sovereignty over the Zembezi region and the nature of the alliances that local Portuguese authorities forged with the rulers of the prazos. Taken to prison for a wide range of crimes early in 1858, Matekenya was released from prison in August of the same year before completing the three-year sentence imposed on him; his brother-in-law Cruz Coimbra had bribed the governor-general of Mozambique island.[26] When Matekenya was apprehended again in December of the same year on murder charges, he managed to "escape" from the guards within a few weeks.[27] Two years later, in 1861, he defeated an army set to apprehend him, killing twenty Portuguese and ten African soldiers. He expropriated from the defeated army nearly eight thousand rounds of ammunition.[28] With these and other arms he had obtained earlier from Quelimane, Matekenya headed his reconstituted army of about two thousand Chikunda up the Tchiri River. He settled at Mount Morumbala before moving to Chironje or Mthumbi in the heartland of the Mang'anja country.[29] Chironje and/or Mthumbi became the center of his slave-raiding operations and the Matchinjiri state that evolved from these activities.

From 1861 on, Matekenya's operations throw a great deal of light on the methods employed by slave raiders during the early 1860s. Slaving ceased to be an exchange for the local Mang'anja as naked force replaced cloth, beads, and other trinkets that had been given to the elders before. The armed Chikunda would come to a village, burn it, kill the elderly, and take away every able-bodied person they could lay their hands on. The Mang'anja system of village fortification crumbled against the firearms.

Matekenya's settlement in the Valley placed every Mang'anja community on the alert.[30] The men sent by the Universities Mission to procure food from Livingstone on the Lower Zembezi in 1862 had to return to Chikwawa from the Tchiri-Ruo confluence after being briefed on Matekenya's plundering down the river.[31] When the missionary Procter tried the journey himself later that year, he was greeted with burned-out villages all the way from Malo Island on the Tchiri-Ruo confluence.[32] Tengani's army had been broken, and the chief was "sleeping in the bush." Matekenya captured and murdered the chief in early 1863, when he also destroyed the Mbona shrine at Khulubvi.[33] When the murderer and destroyer also died in late 1863, it was left to his well-trained Chikunda to spread the trail of desolation. They looted Chikanzi village at Malo Island before heading northeast toward Chipoka on the foot of Mount Mulanje.[34] The depredations began to subside during the second half of the decade, partly as a result of the abolition of the engagé system in 1864.

The change in the methods of recruitment and the development of the slaves-for-ivory traffic combined to bring about significant changes in the social composition of the captives. Grown-up males began to drop out of the market. The traders who sold ivory in the Lower Zembezi region were not interested in male slaves. Moreover, whenever the marauders set upon a village, able-bodied men who were foreigners to these communities almost invariably took to their heels, leaving behind them—as did headman Bawi—their wives and children.[35] Women and children would straggle behind "the main body of fugitives" to become booty for the hunters. Only a small number of the eighty-four captives rescued by the British at Mbami had been bought. The majority had been caught after their villages had been set on fire.[36] They were, as a result, "all young, from 1 year to about 20." Some were "mothers with children at their backs."[37] Women and children also dominated the cargo destined for the Indian Ocean markets.[38] Mang'anja traditions in the Valley have preserved the names of female captives only. Raiding effectively removed elders from their role as local suppliers; it also undercut whatever relationship the international system had with the internal patterns of exchange involving children and other underprivileged members of the community. Women who had previously enjoyed greater security among the Mang'anja became the primary target of the traffic and its violence.

From the Valley the predominantly female captives were shipped off in large canoes to the east coast or driven to Sena or Thete on foot. They were tied by the neck either with ropes or the *goli,* a forked beam of wood about the thickness of a man's thigh and six feet long. The neck was secured to the fork with an iron pin.[39] Captives carried their own provisions and those of their drivers on their heads. In addition, nursing mothers would have their babies on their backs. Mothers who failed to keep pace with the rest of the team were killed or became the sad witness to the murder of their children:

> One poor woman, the mother of a babe not more than one month old, was given a heavy bundle of hoes to carry. She was a weakly woman;

she could scarcely stagger along that rough mountain-path with the babe at her back; her friends said it seemed as though she would fall down by the way. She could not carry the hoes and her babe; and the babe . . . was in the estimation of the slavers of less value than the hoes . . . so they took the babe from its mother's arms, and dashed its head against the rocks, throwing the little body on one side, as though it had been that of a dog.[40]

A portion of those women who survived the one hundred fifty to two-hundred-mile forced march to Sena or Thete were sold to local merchants for £1 to £3. The majority were taken to ivory markets such as Zumbo, where a woman of about twenty years fetched sixty pounds of ivory, which was the equivalent of £10 to £12 in 1862. In two separate trips two Thete merchants sold four hundred fifty Mang'anja women for ivory.[41] The few male captives who accompanied the women returned to Thete carrying ivory. Such men normally ended up in the hands of itinerant slave dealers from the coast.[42] Not many Thete or Sena slavers managed to ship their captives to the Indian Ocean as easily as Matekenya did.

Matekenya had no difficulty disposing of his cargo at the coast. His agent, Cruz Coimbra, was a sophisticated dealer who knew how to evade British gunboats patrolling the coast. Coimbra sold the captives to the French at one of the many mouths of the Zembezi.[43] Between 1863 and 1864 Matekenya and his successor, Paul Marianno III, sent as many as twenty large canoes each day laden with chained Mang'anja captives.[44] The figure might have been even higher in 1861. It appears that Matekenya and his competitors in the trade supplied the French so abundantly that prices for captives at the coast were eight times lower in 1862 than they had been in the late 1850s.[45] Each canoe sent down the river returned to the Valley filled with the arms and alcohol that fueled the system. Portuguese government officials at Sena encouraged Matekenya when they started buying his captives with food.[46] It was then impossible to procure provisions from the Mang'anja in the Valley. Famine had descended on the region.

2.1.2. The Great Famine of 1862–63

Famine benumbs all the faculties. We tried to induce some to exert themselves to procure food—but failed. They had lost all their former

> spirit, and with lacklustre eyes, scarcely meeting ours, and in whining tones, replied to every proposition for their benefit—"No, no!" (Ai! Ai!)
>
> . . . .
>
> But the slave-trade must be deemed the chief agent in the ruin, because, as we were informed, in former droughts all the people flocked from the hills down to the marshes, which are capable of yielding crops of maize in less than three months, at any time of the year, and now they were afraid to do so.[47]

By subordinating climatic to sociopolitical forces, Livingstone's explanation of the *chaola,* or famine, of 1862–63 rises above the simplicities of the Malthusian paradigm and comes close to the position taken by some recent studies on famine in Africa. The new anti-Malthusian model, which highlights the social dynamics of famine, is not as novel as its proponents would make it; Livingstone anticipated it by more than a century. But more significant for the argument of this study is the fact, ignored by most parties to the debate, that most preliterate peoples have not viewed famine as the inevitable consequence of an inclement climate. The Mang'anja have no place for "natural" causes in their ideas about famine or, for that matter, about drought itself. Droughts and other ecological disorders, like locust invasions, are preeminently "social" events. It is only because they have rarely attempted to integrate their theories with African conceptions about human interactions with nature that the anti-Malthusians can claim to have "discovered" a social theory of famine.

The Mang'anja have two broad theories about drought. The first holds that certain categories of afiti, or witches, and magicians can withhold rain. Chiefs would typically lead the masses in the search for withholders of rain when drought coincided with a general social crisis, as was the case in the late nineteenth century, when the combined forces of British and Portuguese imperialism threatened the position of the Kololo rulers. The resulting witchcraft cleansing allowed the Kololo rulers to eliminate their internal political rivals.[48]

The other and more common explanation opposes the general population to their rulers. According to this theory, drought follows from the failure of chiefs to perform their ritual functions in relation to the Mbona cult, namely the rebuilding of the shrine at Khulubvi and the installation of a new salima. Drought is a natural expression of distorted social relations. The rulers had milked their subjects without attending to their public responsibilities. A standard response to drought has, therefore, taken the form of a popular demand for the chiefs to fulfill their duties to the Mbona cult.[49]

Thus, according to the Mang'anja a prolonged drought that kills munda crops is possible only when chiefs either cannot take effective measures against individual rain-holders (to curb the process of individual accumulation) or are unwilling to perform their ritual duties on behalf of the population (that is, to follow out the consequences of their privileged status). But both oral and documentary evidence also make clear that the mere failure of munda crops could not by itself lead to chaola (as distinct from localized food shortages, or *njala*). A prolonged drought could lead to chaola only when combined with the failure of dimba cultivation. And, as was pointed out in Chapter 1, dimba agriculture rarely broke down completely from purely natural causes prior to the 1940s.

Mang'anja traditions are therefore correct in presenting chaola as a unique event in the precolonial era. Behind every famine was a three-tier chain of causation that could not be repeated frequently: the mere existence of social evil or conflict (drought); the inability of those in power to resolve the conflict (end a drought that killed munda crops); and, finally, a generalized social crisis that precluded dimba cultivation. Famine was chaola: a social upheaval that marked the end of one and the beginning of another social order. According to the main thrust of Mang'anja structured traditions, there were only two chaola in the precolonial period. The first formed part of the events leading to the establishment of the Mbona cult and the lundu state. The second coincided with the collapse of the lundu state and the conquest of the Valley by the Kololo immigrants in the 1860s.[50]

Read against their actual responses to the chaola of 1862–63 and 1922–23, Mang'anja theory about famine becomes more sophisticated than much of the academic thinking on the subject. Unambiguously anti-Malthusian, the Mang'anja also understood the limitations of their system of food exchange. They did not ignore production in the spurious search for the goddess of distribution. Whenever drought threatened the land, they confronted their rulers while at the same time they intensified their efforts at dimba cultivation. They did not limit the struggle for survival to the political arena, but combined politics with work in the fields. Any model that sacrifices production at the altar of distribution would not explain famine in the precolonial Tchiri Valley. The famine that descended on the Valley in 1862–63 can be understood only in terms of the three levels of causation.

The chaos and instability that accompanied the slave raids delayed some and precluded other responses to a drought that affected the whole of Central and Southern Africa in varying degrees of intensity and duration.[51] In the Valley it lasted for two full planting seasons, from January 1862 to March 1863. The rainy season of 1861–62 stopped abruptly in January 1862.[52] The subsequent failure of munda crops planted in November 1861 led villagers from the south to send a delegation to Mankhokwe demanding that he provide a wife for Mbona.[53] This was in August 1862, when other Mang'anja, like the fugitives at Mathiti, were already eating earth and wild plants such as the fruit of the mbvunguti sausage tree.[54] Mankhokwe did reluctantly provide a wife for Mbona, but the slave raids ruled out the other response to drought: the raising of dimba crops.

The slave raids had by this time entirely changed the settlement pattern of the Valley and disturbed the dual agricultural system based on the cultivation of the mphala and dambo. The linga village fortifications had collapsed under Chikunda firepower. Some villagers had taken refuge in the caves of Mounts Malawi and Thyolo: "People had fled from war in the valley, to the summit of the mountain [Thyolo]," wrote Rowley in late 1862.[55] These fugitives were permanently cut off from the life-saving dimba agriculture.

It appears, however, that many more people fled to small islands on the Tchiri River and, particularly, in the marshes. Every small island on the Tchiri from its confluence with the Zembezi to Lake Malawi became a refugee camp or msasa from 1861 on. The Dabanyi and Dinde, which had been scarcely populated in 1859–61, teemed with fugitives toward the end of 1862: "The marsh," wrote Waller, "is most singularly altered since last year: then there was not a soul to be seen, now there are *msasas* throughout it." Procter was more specific when he noted, "Lower down the Elephant marsh [we] passed a great number of fugitives from Matikinya."[56] People fleeing from the Chikunda and Yao raids in the Highlands occupied the islands above Chikwawa.[57]

Very little cultivation could be carried on on these tiny islands. The fugitives were also afraid of crossing over to the mainland to raise crops on the munda. Like the inhabitants of the area around Mount Morumbala in the south, the Mang'anja of the Valley were too insecure to undertake extensive cultivation. They had "no confidence. A large field would be to offer a temptation to marauders and thus by sowing extensively, the whole would be lost."[58] The failure of the November 1862 rains forced some to eat earth.

Death began to take a heavy toll as 1862 neared its end. So many died that only a few were given burial; the occupants of the islands simply threw their dead into the river. When Kirk and Livingstone steamed up the Tchiri between January and March 1863 they were constantly forced to stop the engine of their boat in order to remove human remains from the screw. An average of four to five bodies passed the travelers each day in February.[59] The figure does not include the corpses floating by during the night or those devoured by crocodiles. The reptiles were notoriously aggressive at this time of year, when their regular victims—fish—were spreading out into the marshes.

The scene on land was even more frightening. At the onetime prosperous Mikolongo village, an average of ten persons were dying of starvation each day in March 1863.[60] Every village along the fifty-mile road from Chikwawa to Mikolongo was littered with unburied bodies:

> The famine had done its work; the land was without inhabitants. . . . The villages were left standing, but not a single human being was found alive in them; skeletons were everywhere—in the path and in the villages. It was horrible.[61]

Horror was what also greeted Livingstone when he took a short walk from the mission station at Chikwawa:

> Wherever we took a walk, human skeletons were seen in every direction, and it was painfully interesting to observe the different postures in which the poor wretches had breathed their last. A whole heap had been thrown down a slope behind a village. . . . Many had ended their misery under shady trees—others under projecting crags in the hills—while others lay in their huts, with closed doors, which when opened disclosed the mouldering corpse with the poor rags around the loins—the skull fallen off the pillow —the little skeleton of the child, that had perished first, rolled up in a mat between two large skeletons.[62]

Kirk did not have to look for a graveyard in order to obtain specimens of Mang'anja skulls to send to England. He simply strolled around the mission station in order to get what he wanted.[63] The Mang'anja were on the brink of extinction when the first rains came in March 1863.

Rowley estimated that by February 1863 "war and famine had done their work, and ninety per cent. of the Manganja were dead; save in our immediate neighbourhood, the land was a desolation."[64] At mid-1863 the Valley was a mere ghost of what it had been four years earlier. All was somber and frightfully silent:

> It made the heart ache to see the wide-spread desolation; the river-banks, once so populous, all silent; the villages burned down, and an oppressive stillness reigning where formerly crowds of eager sellers appeared with the various products of their industry.[65]

The slave raids accomplished in the Valley what the conquistadors and other colonial plunderers had done in the Americas: crippled the pre-existing political economy in order to pave the way for Western imperialism.

The early 1860s are the only period in the recorded history of the Valley when disruptions in human social relations closely paralleled those in Mang'anja interactions with nature—when chaola froze human history. Chaola reduced the Mang'anja's ability to control nature through the labor process. Vegetation began to claim for itself the empty spots left by human beings soon after the first rains of March 1863. "Now," lamented the sober-minded Kirk, the "grass is high, [and] the people are gone."[66] And with the bush also came wild animals. Game became conspicuous everywhere. Animal populations may not have increased dramatically, but they now enjoyed greater freedom of movement: "As the people perished the wild-beasts increased upon us . . . they wandered about more, because there were no inhabitants to check them."[67] The European missionaries at Chikwawa fought a losing battle as they tried to protect their diminished flock of goats against leopards and hyenas that preyed around the station every night.[68] Far to the west, elephants freely grazed the abandoned fields. The era of the slave trade anticipated the story of ecological distortion that became a common theme in Africa's colonial history.

The Mang'anja's loss of control over nature coincided with serious strains in their relations with one another. A well-documented example of the latter concerns the conflicts over the semiperennial munda crops such as gonkho sorghum and dimba maize that sprouted on their own following the rains of March 1863. Few people showed much interest in the self-grown crops[69] until they reached maturity, when "owners" emerged against "thieves." But the same famine that created thieves had also killed or disabled the dispensers of village justice, the elders. The result was a truly Hobbesian "war of all against all" as owners took the law into their own hands. They applied *nkhono* medicine, which was to ward off potential thieves from the fields,[70] and when the medicine failed to achieve the desired effect men started sleeping in the fields and shooting poisoned arrows at anyone who came to reap the fruits of nature. Some victims, like the woman who had a poisoned arrow lodged deep in her liver, did survive.[71] But many more perished and were thrown into the river to feed the crocodiles. As the only power at Chikwawa, the missionaries spent their last days litigating cases of theft at a rate that the departed or incapacitated Mang'anja elders had never done before.[72]

The subversion of the legal system was part of a larger story that affected other aspects of Mang'anja social life, including ukapolo servitude. The late Walter Rodney's thesis that the external demand for captives stimulated internal slavery better fits the conditions that had prevailed in the Valley prior to 1860 insofar as the Mang'anja—in contrast to their foreign conquerors like the Kololo—were concerned.[73] Death from starvation and malnutrition must have undermined the demographic basis of ukapolo (as in all famines, children suffered the most from malnutrition and its attendant diseases).[74] Some akapolo perished from eating poisonous roots and berries given to them by their masters for experimentation. Famine also forced many masters to sell their akapolo dependents—their "children"—for food to slave dealers from places such as Sena.[75] There were also those akapolo who took advantage of the general instability to desert their masters in the same way that many Portuguese-owned slaves at Thete did.[76] Mang'anja masters must have also found it difficult to maintain their control over akapolo given the dislocations in the wider communal relations that had buttressed their power as users.

The slave raids physically dismembered village communities and created a situation of generalized insecurity that affected Mang'anja women differently from men. Rowley described the plight of the majority of the eighty-four captives rescued by the British at Mbami in July 1861:

> It was found that more than half of them had no homes to go to; they had seen their homes destroyed in the cruel wars which these slavers had kindled and were keeping up; women had seen their husbands killed, little children had seen their parents killed; they were utterly destitute and desolate.[77]

The destruction must have traumatized women more deeply than men since women rather than men constituted the nucleus of the desolated villages—the rightful owners. The breakup of the communities amounted to a direct assault on the physical and demographic components of their power and authority. And as the primary target of those Portuguese officials and prazo barons who traded their captives for ivory in the interior, women became more vulnerable than men. For the first time, Mang'anja women looked for protectors.

There were, however, not many Mang'anja men or women who could effectively protect other Mang'anja against the marauders. Mankhokwe was the only Mang'anja ruler in the whole Valley who, largely because of the strategic location of his village on an island, survived the chaola without losing too many of his subjects.[78] His Mang'anja rivals during the first phase of the slave trade had all been eliminated by 1863. Chibisa and Tengani had been murdered by the marauders.[79] The uprooted and "floating" women (and men) of the area subsequently turned to non-Mang'anja men who were themselves armed with guns like the marauders. The position of Mang'anja women weakened not so much in relation to their own men as in relation to foreigners. The original balance of power between Mang'anja women and men tipped in favor of only those Mang'anja men who, like the ankhoswe guardians and village headmen, collaborated with non-Mang'anja conquerors.

2.2. The Rise of a Precolonial Peasantry: The Political Context

There were four main groups of well-armed foreign men in the Tchiri region at this time. The first consisted of Yao settlers and slave dealers who confined their operations to the Highlands.[80] The second was made up of the members of the Universities Mission to Central Africa, whose arrival at Magomero in the Tchiri Highlands in July 1861 coincided with the first peak of slave raiding.[81] The raids and famine made preaching impossible and forced the missionaries to move to Chikwawa in May 1862, together with the refugees they had accepted in their camp. Before they finally left the Valley for England in late 1863, the missionaries had cooperated with, collided with, or merely witnessed the activities of two other groups of non-Mang'anja men. The first of these groups were the followers of Matekenya who dominated the area lying between the Tchiri-Zembezi confluence in the south and the Tchiri-Ruo confluence in the north. To the north of the Tchiri-Ruo confluence were Kololo migrants who had settled at Chikwawa since November 1861.

The fifteen or sixteen men whose descendants in the Valley are known today as the Kololo or Magololo originally came from Bulozi (or Barotseland) in what is now the western province of Zambia. They were among the 112 porters impressed by the Kololo king, Sekeletu, in 1855 to serve Livingstone on his journey to England through the east coast.[82] Livingstone subsequently left the porters at Thete, where they lived by selling their labor to the Portuguese as elephant hunters, gold diggers, firewood collectors, ivory carriers, canoemen, and entertainers until the missionary's return from England in 1858.[83] As Livingstone's employees, the men received cloth and firearms as their wages. And it was with these guns and their broadened vision of labor power[84] that the Kololo left Livingstone's expedition to settle at Chikwawa in November 1861. Many of them had been to Chikwawa four times since January 1859.[85]

The rise of the Kololo to power depended on many factors, the most significant of which was the instability created by the slave raids and famine. Armed with guns, the immigrants exploited the chaos to gain a following from the local Mang'anja and Yao fugitives. They emerged from the famine weakened but still in better shape than any of the local Mang'anja communities. Between 1867 and 1870, the immigrants dislodged Mankhokwe from his headquarters at Mbewe-ya-Kumadzi, murdered the impotent successor to the lundu paramounts at Mbewe-ya-Mitengo, and founded six independent chieftaincies under Chiputula, Kasisi, Katunga, Maseya, Mlilima, and Mwita (see Figure 2.1).[86] Their headquarters were all located along the Tchiri River from Mathiti Falls in the north to Mbewe-ya-Kumadzi in the south.[87] The northern frontier was occupied by Kasisi, who installed himself at Mathiti. Chiputula established his first capital at Mbewe-ya-Kumadzi in 1867 and, about ten years later, pushed the southern Kololo frontier to Chiromo on the Tchiri-Ruo confluence.[88]

The consolidation of Kololo rule in the early 1870s put an end to slave raiding in the northern section of the Valley and established the political conditions for the emergence of a peasantry in the region. The chiefs succeeded, in various degrees, to reduce the autonomy of the Mang'anja, which speeded up the integration of the region into the expanding capitalist world economy during the era of legitimate trade. The onslaught against Mang'anja independence took different forms. For example, the chiefs waged a successful war against the Mbona cult, which they interpreted, quite correctly, as a hotbed of Mang'anja resistance. At the same time, they encouraged the village-centered nyau

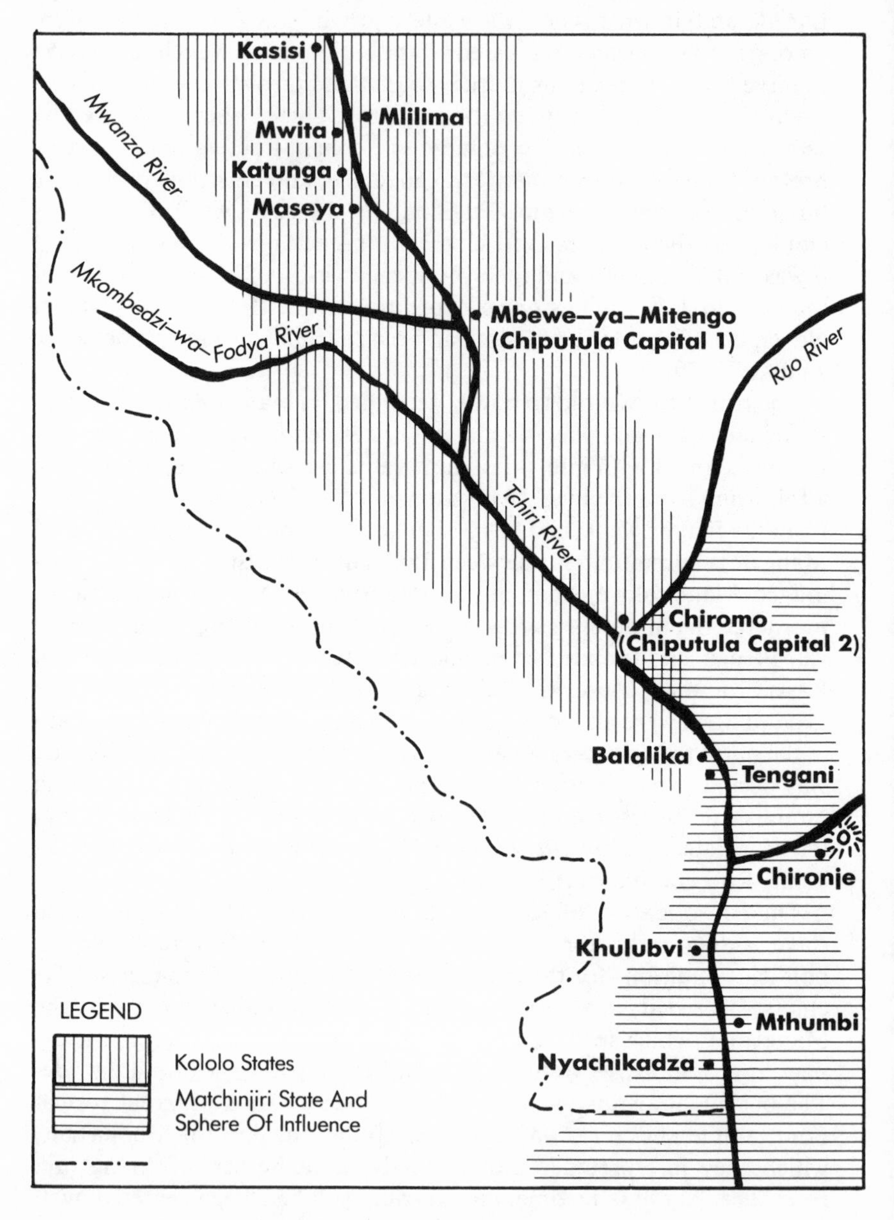

Figure 2.1. Map of Kololo and Matchinjiri Areas (approximate)

cults, which strengthened their control over other local institutions such as the chinamwali initiation schools. Politically, the Kololo reserved the right to dismiss uncomplying headmen, which led to the dismissal of many female headpersons, who were almost invariably replaced by the chiefs' male Yao retainers from the court. Both old and new headmen were charged with new responsibilities, particularly the collection of tribute. The chiefs demanded tribute in foodstuffs and in labor. Every headman had to supply his Kololo chief with men to build the chief's palace, to work the large royal fields known as *magala,* and, from 1875 on, to act as porters (*amtenga-tenga*) for European missionaries and traders.[89] It was through these labor services that the northern Mang'anja supported Kololo mercantile activities and lost their autonomy as political agents and as producers.

> It is assumed that there no longer is, or that there has never been, a local population, i.e. a social body who resisted to the arbitrary creator. It is presupposed that family groups . . . neighbourhoods, villages, groups of villages, local cases of arbitration, etc., briefly that all the local institutions can be reduced to the will of one fama [supreme ruler] or another, presented as supreme and absolute creator of institutions.[90]

The story was slightly different in the southern section of the Valley.

The occupation of the southern part of the Valley by the Chikunda followers of Matekenya under the leadership of his son Paul Marianno III beginning in about 1863 did not bring stability to the area. The region went through a series of political crises, including Chiputula's repeated attacks and the Portuguese occupation, which led to the Matchinjiri uprising of 1884.[91] The conflicts undermined the ability of Matekenya's followers to protect or impose effective control over the Mang'anja of the area. The Mang'anja entered British colonial rule in 1891 virtually independent of either the Matchinjiri or the Portuguese who had tried to succeed them.

None of the men and women I interviewed in 1980 recalled a tradition to the effect that the Matchinjiri had appointed village headmen even in areas like the Dinde Marsh and its surroundings, where Matchinjiri rule had been formally acknowledged. The recognition took the form of tribute giving, which was at all events a very irregular affair.[92] Oral testimonies recorded to the north of the Dinde consistently deny that the Mang'anja ever paid tribute to the Matchinjiri.[93] The Tenganis, in particular, emerged from the disasters of the mid-1860s virtually independent. The struggles against the Portuguese and the Kololo, especially Chiputula, appear to have forced the Matchinjiri into tactical alliances with the Mang'anja rulers. Much of the west bank that became British territory had at best been a Matchinjiri sphere of influence.

Thus, in contrast to the negative response that the Kololo received from the local population in their conflict with the British in the wake of the murder of Chiputula by an Englishman in February 1884,[94] the Matchinjiri (who fought the Portuguese later that year) received grassroots support from the population. The Mang'anja paid dearly for their cooperation with the Matchinjiri. Gouveia's army looted their villages and raped their women; he survives as a villain in Mang'anja folktales.[95] In contrast, the transformation of the Matchinjiri from plunderers in the 1860s to ineffective colonists in the 1870s and, finally, to allies in the 1880s is graphically preserved in the region's popular myths and history. Chagunda, who led the anti-Portuguese insurrection, emerges simultaneously as the man who directed the restoration of the Mbona shrine at Khulubvi following its destruction by Matekenya in 1863 and as the Third Person of the Mang'anja Holy Trinity. His equals are Mbona, the Father, and Chitundu, the Spirit of Wind:

> Chagunda, who used to live in the Matchinjiri country, his equals [*anzache*] are Mbona at Nsanje and Chitundu at Gorongozi. When [the spirit of] Chagunda seizes a person, s/he would say: "You have wronged my brother-in-law, Mbona, because you have not given him a new wife."[96]

Chitundu was, according to Schoffeleers, the commander of the Zimba mercenaries employed by the lundu of the late sixteenth century in his conflicts with the Portuguese of Sena.[97] During the 1880s the Matchinjiri did to the "higher" Mang'anja institutions such as the Mbona cult what the Kololo did to "lower" institutions such as the village-centered nyau secret societies.

2.3. The Rise of a Precolonial Peasantry: Economic Forces

The differences in their religious and political histories notwithstanding, the northern and southern sections of the Valley went through broadly similar economic changes during the last quarter of the nineteenth century. The period witnessed the transformation of previously independent producers into a partially subordinated class of peasants.[98] As in many parts of Africa, this process hinged on two closely interrelated trends in the local economy.[99] The first coincided with the erosion of many branches of the old nonagricultural sector, which tended to marginalize the Mang'anja mbumba community as a unit of production and deepened the dependence of the rural population on the world market for part of its reproduction. The second trend was characterized by the development of commodity relations in agricultural products. From the late 1870s on, rural cultivators in the Valley intensified their agricultural activities and adopted new crops like sesame in response to market demands. These changes had the effect of strengthening the position of the banja household as the principal unit of agricultural labor in a new demographic context in which the Mang'anja competed for local resources with new immigrants from the Lower Zembezi.

2.3.1. Nonagricultural Production and Exchange

The erosion of the nonagricultural sector in the Valley was by no means a unilineal development. The period immediately following the era of the slave trade saw remarkable initiatives in salt production and ivory hunting. Like salt production, ivory hunting in the northern section of the Valley took place in the context of tributary relations. Kololo chiefs responded to the increasing international demand for ivory by mobilizing their Yao retainers and by protecting the local game reserves. Chiputula placed sentinels along the Dabanyi Marsh against the Chikunda and other poachers, while Kasisi and Mlooka protected the Mwanza Valley elephant haunts.[100] The few non-Kololo allowed to kill animals in these reserves were required to hand over one tusk of every elephant they killed—the ground tusk—to the owner of the territory. The chiefs reinforced the ruling more strictly after the arrival of the Scottish traders. The ivory economy left its imprint on nearly every Kololo foreign policy during the era of legitimate trade.

Study of the ivory economy under the Kololo suggests one reason why it was the least-developed sector of the Mang'anja economy. The economy depended heavily on the rulers' ability to control labor. Tall grasses in the Dabanyi Marsh rendered elephant hunting hazardous even for those who hunted with guns.[101] Transporting the ivory to the east coast was an equally difficult business. The constant outbreaks of hostilities between Chiputula and the Matchinjiri virtually closed the easier Tchiri route to Kololo ivory traders, who consequently followed the longer and more dangerous land route to Indian Ocean markets such as Chisanga, Ibo, and Quelimane.[102]

The chiefs themselves or their Yao retainers led the caravans to the east coast. The actual carrying was sometimes done by captives obtained from the Ngoni in exchange for salt or through raids mounted in non-Kololo areas. The ivory, like some of the captives, was traded for alcohol, cloth, guns, and gunpowder.[103] Given the difficulties of hauling ivory to the east coast, the Kololo warmly welcomed Scottish traders on their arrival in the country in 1876.[104] It was not long, however, before the chiefs clashed with the countrymen of Livingstone, their former master, over several issues related to the ivory trade.

The Kololo demand for firearms in exchange for ivory was one of the issues that set them on a collision course with Scottish traders at an early date. The Europeans were reluctant to go along with the demand, fearful that the guns might be turned against them one day. The Scotsmen also refused to sell alcohol to the Kololo, having seen for themselves the mischief the Kololo could commit when under its influence.[105] Disappointed and angry, the Kololo resumed taking their ivory to the east coast.

In order to recover the lucrative local market, the Scottish members of the African Lakes Company devised a plan according to which the company leased guns and powder in return for one tusk of every elephant that the Kololo killed.[106] The plan proved unworkable. Some Kololo chiefs, like Kasisi, would take the gun, offer one tusk for sale to the company, and retain the other as tribute. As a result of this and other irritations, especially thefts of company property, Kololo relations with the Scotsmen deteriorated fast until the two parties almost went to war in 1884, following the murder of Chiputula by a former employee of the African Lakes Company by the name of George Fenwick.

Chiputula had commissioned Fenwick to sell his ivory and sesame seeds on the Lower Zembezi. When Fenwick returned from the errand he quarreled with the chief, who was dissatisfied with the goods the white man had brought in exchange for the ivory and sesame seeds. Fenwick lost his temper and shot the chief in the head. The sons and followers of the dead chief retaliated by killing the murderer, sinking a ship belonging to the company, and closing the Tchiri River to British traffic.[107] But the incident did not become a widespread revolt for two main reasons. Some Kololo rulers exploited the event to win influence among the remaining chiefs and with the British.[108] Still more significant was the failure of Chiputula's sons and followers to gain the support of the Mang'anja. The latter had no love for the dead tyrant.[109] The Mang'anja must also have viewed the conflict as a mere brawl between members of the same class of exploiters. The Kololo had always paraded themselves as black Englishmen. Events soon proved the Mang'anja correct. The British quickly mended fences with the Kololo—with the exception of the "rebel" Mlauli—when threatened by Portuguese imperialism. The Kololo joined the British in opposing the Portuguese military expedition that arrived in the Matchinjiri country in 1889 under the leadership of Major Serpa Pinto.

As in the Kololo-controlled north, the ivory trade in the Matchinjiri country also bypassed the Mang'anja indigenes. Unlike in the north, however, ivory hunting and trading never became a royal monopoly. Tributary relations apparently did not play a key role in ivory hunting and trading. The economy depended rather on personal enterprise, new techniques and technologies of production, and the political weakness of the Matchinjiri that made the region, if only by default, more open to the international economy. The ivory trade thrived against a backdrop of large population movements into and out of the Valley, including the slave traffic to the Lower Zembezi.

The rise of the Kololo to power in the north forced slave dealers to restrict their operations to the south. The southwestern section of the Dabanyi Marsh, which acted as a buffer zone between the well-consolidated Kololo chiefdoms in the north and the troubled Matchinjiri polity in the south, was among the most vulnerable areas to attack from the Lower Zembezi. The traditions of the area are fresh with names like Belshior, Nyaude, Mello, and above all, Doña Luisa, the holder of prazo Gwengwe. Doña Luisa emerges as the bête noire in the memories of the Mang'anja.[110] Almost all the female captives who are remembered by name are said to have been kidnapped by dealers operating on her behalf. The mother of the wife of headman Nguluwe was one of Luisa's victims.[111] It is clear from these and other sources that the Zembezi traffic in human beings persisted well into the early twentieth century.

With the slave dealers also came professional elephant hunters who dominated the ivory trade in the region from the 1870s on. From the Dabanyi down to the present-day Malawi-Mozambique boundary in the south, one finds families and village groupings that identify themselves as Chikunda, Manyika, Mwenye, Phodzo, and Zimba. The Zimba maintain that their ancestors hailed from the region extending from Thete in the southeast to Zimbabwe in the northwest.[112] Although Zimba migrations into the Valley clearly predated the nineteenth century, those who today still identify themselves as Zimba appear to be descendants of nineteenth-century immigrants.

Closely following the Zimba were the Chikunda. The earliest Chikunda to have settled in the Valley were fugitives, fleeing from the Lower Zembezi when their masters, the prazo holders, started selling them into slavery. Like the Khwama from the Zembezi delta, the majority of the first Chikunda immigrants became part of the Mang'anja population. Members of the second migratory wave, triggered by Portuguese attempts to "pacify" the Zembezi region in the late nineteenth century, still maintain their separate identity. Edward Young, who had returned to the Valley in 1876 after an eight-year interlude in Britain, met some of these Chikunda at Chikwawa in 1877. They had left the Zembezi after the death of their master, Belshior.[113] Chikwawa was not, however, an attractive place for the Chikunda at the time. Many of them had clashed with the Kololo even before the latter rose to power. Chikunda immigrants were drawn to the more politically open south, and the area south of the Dabanyi Marsh therefore entered British colonial rule with a large Chikunda segment, including the descendants of Matekenya's followers.[114]

To the Chikunda one must also add small pockets of Mwenye, Manyika, and Phodzo settlers. A spokesman for one of the Manyika families around the Dinde Marsh told the writer that his ancestors had come to the area as soldiers under Gouveia, who put down the Matchinjiri uprising of 1884.[115] More peacefully portrayed are the migrations of the Phodzo, the mkhombwe hippo hunters, who constitute something like a caste. Livingstone had first met mkhombwe hunters on the Zembezi between Sena and Thete in 1858.[116] There were then hardly any Phodzo communities in the Tchiri Valley itself. The Phodzo started penetrating the area in large numbers only after the 1860s. Young encountered numerous Phodzo settlements along the Tchiri River in 1876. Their presence became even more conspicuous at the peak of legitimate trade in the 1880s.[117]

Chikunda, Phodzo, and Zimba ivory hunting and trading did not rely on tributary labor. The hunters were private entrepreneurs who were welcomed by Mang'anja rulers partly because of their expertise. Some of the migrants enhanced their position in the local community by marrying the daughters of important Mang'anja families. Those who came as individuals usually settled within the main Mang'anja villages. Others who came with their families and with a following generally established their own *nthemba* village segments, where they maintained the patrilineal system of descent and virilocal marriage.[118] Their hunting activities were predicated on a division of labor that made agriculture the primary responsibility of women. Hunting was not, in other words, subordinated to the labor requirements of the agricultural economy, as it was among the Mang'anja. A typical hunting party, made up of several experts and some assistants recruited from the patrilineage, would spend weeks or even months away from the village. Hunting could be a year-round activity.

Unlike the Mang'anja, who, according to Rowley, would not molest an animal, Zimba professional hunters confronted their victims directly with the *demu* ax.[119] A hunter would cling to the leg of an elephant with one hand while chopping the tendons of another leg with his other hand until the animal fell down. The gun never replaced this technique among the fierce Zimba as it did among the Chikunda, many of whom entered the Valley after acquiring firearms either independently or when in the service of the prazo holders as hunters, long-distance ivory traders, slave dealers, or warriors. The Chikunda were in this regard the real competitors of the Kololo, whose only advantage over the former was their ability to mobilize tributary labor.[120]

Phodzo mkhombwe hunters, for their part, posed no threat to the Kololo or, for that matter, any other group of elephant hunters. Phodzo hunting activities were directed toward the hippopotamus. They killed the animal with a *chidamba* or *chibutha* iron harpoon that was "inserted in the end of a long pole, but [which] being intended to unship, . . . is made fast to a strong cord of milola, or hibiscus, bark, which is wound closely round the entire length of the shaft, and secured at its opposite end."[121] The actual killing was a high-risk operation that could not be compared with any of the treacherous Mang'anja techniques of snares and pitfalls.

> Two men in a swift canoe steal quietly down on the sleeping animal. The bowman dashes the harpoon into the unconscious victim, while the quick steersman sweeps the light craft back with his broad paddle; the force of the blow separates the harpoon from its corded handle, which, appearing on the surface, sometimes with an inflated bladder attached, guides the hunters to where the wounded beast hides below until they dispatch it.[122]

After removing the teeth, the hunters would sell part of the meat to the villagers in the vicinity and smoke the rest to take home at the end of the expedition.

Marketing was not a problem for the Phodzo, Chikunda, and Zimba hunters in the south as it was for the Kololo in the north. There were ivory dealers all along the Zembezi and the southern portion of the Tchiri River.[123] Although the details of this highly individualized trade are still obscure, there can be little doubt about its profitability or significance in the history of the area. The trade contributed to the multiethnic character of the former Matchinjiri territory. Some of the hunters and traders were already on the verge of converting their economic power into political hegemony when the ivory economy collapsed throughout the Valley toward the end of the century.

Three developments help explain the collapse of the ivory trade in the Valley. The first had to do with the opening of the area following its declaration as part of British Central Africa in 1891 to British, German, and other European hunters, who had until then acted mainly as buyers from African producers. The effects of the indiscriminate killing, which made ivory one of the leading export commodities from the region during the 1890s,[124] became obvious by the end of the century. There were hardly any elephant herds left in the area. Those that escaped the European raids had migrated to safer haunts. The colonial regime subsequently enacted a number of regulations designed to attract new herds. The rules converted part of the Dabanyi Marsh into a game reserve and disarmed African hunters, including the Kololo.[125]

The other two factors were closely connected. The steep decline in the level of the Tchiri River from the 1880s drove hippopotami away from the area while at the same time it exposed the formerly inundated areas of the marshes to both human habitation and an intensive and prolonged agricultural cycle. The resulting increase in the region's population shifted the ecological balance against all types of wild game. The Tchiri Valley entered the twentieth century with a much more restricted nonagricultural base than it had had before.

Particularly relevant for the history of the formation of the peasantry was the decline in the cloth, iron, and salt industries. Unlike cloth making and ironworking, however, salt production made a strong comeback after the period of the slave raids. After ivory, it became the second most important export commodity from the Kololo-dominated north. Soon after taking power, Chiefs Chiputula and Maseya began to centralize the salt economy in their respective territories. The chiefs appointed their own manufacturers and extracted tribute from independent producers. Every independent distiller in the Dabanyi was required to hand over about a tenth of her product.[126] Salt was then in high demand among the Yao and Ngoni, who bought it from the chiefs in exchange for foodstuffs, goats, and even slaves.[127] But the external demand for salt began to decline in the late 1880s as a result of two related factors. British "peace" made it easier for the Ngoni and

Yao to obtain locally manufactured salt in other areas, such as Lake Chilwa. Second, there was an influx of imported salt. Locally produced salt could not compete with the cheaply manufactured salt: "This industry is failing to compete with imported salt," bemoaned one official at the turn of the century.[128] Kololo chiefs responded to the decline in demand by loosening their control over production, which set in motion the third or modern phase in the history of salt production in the Valley.[129]

The most significant difference between the salt economy of the mid-nineteenth and twentieth centuries is in the area of underlying social relations. In particular, neither the mbumba nor the mudzi community was able to reassert itself as the principal unit of labor organization after the Kololo intervention. Salt production has since the turn of the century been largely an individual affair, conducted within the village.[130] It is poor and elderly women who today manufacture salt, especially during periods of food shortage. They sell the salt on local markets and use the money to purchase foodstuffs and imported cloth as well as hoes.

The initial weakness of the iron industry in the economy of the 1850s made it an easier target for merchant capital during the era of legitimate trade. The demise of ironworks appears to have occurred in two stages.[131] The first witnessed the end of smelting (ng'anjo) activities. Foreign iron scraps obtained from European settlers replaced locally smelted iron at an early date. The transformation seems to have been faster in the south than in the north, where remnants of ng'anjo furnaces can be seen to this day.[132] At the same time, it was in the south that the chipala smithies were preserved longest. The art of ironmaking was kept alive not so much by the Mang'anja but by the immigrant Mwenye artisans from the Lower Zembezi.[133]

The Mwenye, who, like the Phodzo, are something of a caste, trace their origins to the pre-Portuguese marriages between African women and Arab and Persian Muslim traders around Sena in contemporary Mozambique. Their migrations to the Tchiri Valley must have been of greater antiquity than those of other immigrants discussed so far. They came to the Valley after many centuries of experience with imported iron and have continued to make hoes and other metal implements and ornaments, such as rings, on the chipala furnace long after ironworking had become obsolete among the Mang'anja indigenes in both sections of the Valley. By World War I Mang'anja elders were telling British officials that their ancestors had never manufactured iron hoes, knives, or arrows.[134] They were saying the same about cloth making.

Cotton cultivation and weaving made a brief comeback after the slave raids and famine in the Kololo north. Travelers to the area during the mid-1870s saw cotton plots measuring up to three acres. The chiefs were then employing their slaves and other dependents in cloth making.[135] That was, however, the last time the cotton economy was mentioned. Imported calico came to dominate all Kololo transactions with Europeans. Indeed, the chiefs who had both ivory and dependent labor to sell to the Europeans became so well stocked with cloth by the 1880s that they started demanding other articles like firearms in their dealings with European traders. Ordinary Mang'anja villagers were also acquiring imported cloth by selling their labor power (mainly as porters), fowls, foodstuffs, firewood, and sesame seeds. Peasants who had none of these commodities to sell resorted to bark cloth in the 1880s[136]—a clear indication that the old industry had collapsed. In his report on colonial activities in the country during the first three years of British rule, Harry Johnston remarked how the cultivation of cotton

> was once probably almost universal and an excellent strong native cloth was made from it. The introduction of European calico has practically killed the native manufactures and the cultivation of cotton is now almost abandoned. Curiously enough the native-manufactured cotton cloth is far superior to the European introduction and the pattern occasionally woven a hundred degrees higher in taste than the execrable Manchester criterion.[137]

The indigenous cloth Johnston referred to in the passage was in all likelihood the beautifully dyed material made into scarves worn by women in the *mabzyoka* spirit possession cult (see Chapter 4). The scarves were made by Mwenye specialists in the southern section of the Valley for ceremonial purposes long after the total collapse of the manufacture of their secular counterpart among the Mang'anja of both the north and south. There was no living Mang'anja who claimed knowledge of cloth making during World War I, when the scarcity of imported calico forced poor women to wear bark cloth.[138] Merchant capital had eroded part of Mang'anja economic independence in a process that tended to marginalize the mbumba and mudzi communities as units of material production.

2.3.2. Transformations in Agricultural Work Patterns

> [The] Manganjas, MaChinkas, and Ajawas have willingly paid homage to this semblance of stability, and the population is now exceedingly large and likely to increase.[139]

As the mbumba and the mudzi became increasingly irrelevant as organizers of social labor, the banja household assumed new agricultural tasks. The expansion and diversification of agricultural work, which took place against a backdrop of political change in the north and significant ecological shifts throughout the Valley, formed the second part of the story of the rise of a precolonial peasantry in the region.

Peace and security under the Kololo led to a quick and sustained agricultural recovery in the north from the late 1860s. Mang'anja cultivators abandoned the tiny islands and inaccessible hilltops to reoccupy the area dividing the dambo from the mphala, where the Kololo had established their strongholds. The Mang'anja were once again able to exploit the advantages of dimba and munda cultivation fully.[140] The results were impressive to Edward Young, who had witnessed the devastating effects of chaola at the height of the famine of 1862–63. All was "peace and plenty," Young declared after entering the northern section of the Valley in 1876.[141] This prosperity continued undisturbed throughout much of the remaining quarter of the century.

The south did not enjoy such a speedy or sustained recovery. Slave raiders from the Lower Zembezi continued to disturb social peace during the 1870s. When the raids coincided with the Matchinjiri wars, the results could be catastrophic. Chiputula's campaign against the Matchinjiri in 1877 uprooted many villagers, forcing them to live, according to one eyewitness account, "in bye-nooks and corners."[142] Seven years later, in 1884, the area became the battlefield of the Matchinjiri revolt against the Portuguese. Portuguese armies under the notorious Gouveia left a trail of destruction. So vindictive were the Portuguese toward the Mang'anja for the support they had given to the Matchinjiri that Gouveia's army uprooted maize and pumpkins and threw them into the Tchiri River.[143] In fact it appears that the war disturbed what had probably been the beginnings of agricultural recovery similar to that which had taken place in the north since the late 1860s. The hostilities certainly slowed the most important agricultural transformation of the late nineteenth century: the shift to the cultivation of sesame seeds (*chitowe, umphedza,* or *ukaka*) as a cash crop.

This shift, which represented the first and most significant popular response to the demands of the capitalist world economy, appears to have started simultaneously in the north and south during the late 1870s.[144] The main difference is that in the north production was initially monopolized by the Kololo rulers. Sesame oilseeds are mentioned as one of the items that Chiputula entrusted to George Fenwick, the

Scottish trader who later killed him. In the south it was ordinary peasants who initiated production. When the Portuguese planned to tax the Mang'anja in 1883, they had sesame seeds in mind. Every adult was to be levied fifty pounds of the seeds, a pregnant woman twice that amount.[145] Hence the support that the Matchinjiri leaders of the anticolonial struggle received from the Mang'anja.

Sesame production increased considerably following the imposition of British armed peace and of taxes on the local population.[146] Production spread to the Upper Tchiri Valley and the northern tip of Lake Malawi, although it was the southern section of the Lower Valley that produced the bulk of the crop exported from the new colony. In 1897, when oilseeds ranked third among the colony's exports (after ivory and coffee from the Highlands), the "Lower Shire District," which coincided with the Matchinjiri sphere of influence, contributed about 70 percent of the total output.[147] It was already difficult for the British colonizers to recruit wage laborers from the district.

The greater popularity of sesame production in the southern vis-à-vis the northern section of the Valley depended on significant changes in local systems of production and easy access to markets. Growers in the north were almost entirely dependent on the African Lakes Company for the sale of their produce, and there were times when the company refused to take all the seeds offered for sale.[148] Peasants in the south enjoyed a diversified market much in the same way as did the ivory traders. Some growers took their crop in dugout canoes to such markets as Mopeia, where Indian, Dutch, and other European merchants bought the seeds in exchange for cloth, hoes, and other foreign goods. Others sold their product to itinerant traders, especially Indians, who also purchased foodstuffs for their own consumption and for resale on the Lower Zembezi and the coast.[149] The availability of a surplus of foodstuffs indicated the strength of the second agricultural transformation of the late nineteenth century: changes in the pattern of agricultural work.

The region's confrontation with merchant capital and political change constituted only one set of forces behind the transformation of rural work schedules beginning in the late 1870s. The other set of events was largely ecological. The level of the Tchiri River began to fall steadily in the 1880s in response to a similar trend in the volume of Lake Malawi.[150] The change, which in due time drove hippopotami out of the area and aborted British plans to turn the Tchiri River into the main artery of the colony's transportation system, exposed the previously inundated marshes for an extended period of cultivation. The new flood season lasted no more than two months, so that growers could work their dimba gardens from as early as late February (instead of June or July as had before been the case) until December (see Chapter 4). Growers could plant many more food crops consecutively than they had done in the past and, for the first time in recorded history, they could raise dimba cotton. The availability of the dambo for extended cultivation also became a major force in the demographic transformation of the Valley since the early 1890s.

2.4. Demographic Change, 1895–1925

The demographic configuration of the Valley changed dramatically during the three decades between 1895 and 1925. The overall population of the region rose from 22,500 in 1895 to 91,000 in 1925 as a result of natural increase and especially immigration.[151] The great majority of the new settlers were an assortment of peoples from the Zembezi region. Some had been uprooted from their homeland by the Portuguese wars of "pacification," but many others had been drawn to the Tchiri Valley by the prospect of extended and productive dimba farming, just as the presence of elephants and hippopotami had attracted ivory hunters and traders during the era of legitimate commerce.

The new settlers entered the Tchiri Valley in small family groupings under such ethnic designations as the Chikunda, Mwenye, Phodzo, Sena, and Tonga.[152] Immigration reached a peak during World War I, when the Makombe uprising of 1917 in Mozambique sent thousands of Tonga fugitives into the Valley (see Chapter 3). It was from this period that the term Sena, which initially referred only to the Chisena-speaking settlers from around the town of Sena on the Zembezi River, came to be used as a blanket name for all the immigrants who trace their origins to what are today the Sofala and Thete provinces of Mozambique and eastern Zimbabwe.

Sena immigrants were not evenly distributed in the Tchiri Valley. They were concentrated within and along the Dinde and Dabanyi—the former Matchinjiri sphere of influence, which, between 1891 and 1922, the British administered as the Ruo (Chiromo) and Lower Shire districts (see Figure 3.1). In 1921 the two districts carried an estimated population of 80,148 between them (39,502 in Ruo and 40,646 in the Lower Shire). The immigrants, who then made up some 30 percent of the population of the Valley, constituted 25 percent of the Ruo and 50 percent of the

Lower Shire districts.[153] They had almost entirely avoided the Kololo-controlled northern section of the Valley, which until 1922 was administered as the Chikwawa section of the West Shire District.

In 1921 this section had a population of only 11,441, which was predominantly Mang'anja.[154] The establishment of British peace in the Tchiri Highlands since the 1890s had brought the immigration of Yao and Mang'anja from that region to a halt. The only new immigrants who entered the area in any sizable numbers after 1891 were the Lomwe (or Anguru) from Mozambique, who were an offshoot of a larger migratory wave that hit the Tchiri Highlands during the first three decades of British rule.[155] In the Lower Tchiri Valley the Lomwe occupied the western slopes of the Thyolo escarpment in northeastern Chikwawa District. Like the Sena, the Lomwe avoided the western part of Chikwawa, which comprised over three-quarters of the district's land area, because it did not have reliable sources of drinking water. The two main rivers of the region, the Mwanza and Mkombedzi-wa-Fodya, stop flowing during the dry season. The area also carried a large population of wild animals and the tsetse fly. None of these hazards existed in the southern part of the Valley and, particularly, the Lower Shire District (see Chapter 7).

The north-south demographic contrast became more striking after the abolition of the central or Ruo District in 1922. In 1925 the new Chikwawa District, consisting of the Chikwawa section of the former West Shire District and the northeastern section of the Ruo District, had a population of 27,954 spread over 1,897 square miles—or 14.7 persons to a square mile. In sharp contrast, the 747-square-mile Port Herald District, which from 1922 on included the former Lower Shire District and the southern section of the former Ruo District, carried approximately 63,294 people, or 94.8 persons to a square mile.[156] Nearly half of this population was Sena. The region had for all practical purposes lost the Mang'anja character it had had in the mid-nineteenth century, which further complicated British attempts to control the region's labor force.

The ways in which demographic change and the new work schedules impinged on the problem of labor control for the British colonizers must be understood in the context of the survival of many elements of Mang'anja society from before the time of the slave trade. The greater availability of the dambo for food cultivation did not, for example, diminish the significance of munda agriculture in rural strategies for survival. Peasants continued to give as much attention to munda cultivation as they had in the past, which exacerbated the problem of labor distribution between the old munda and the new dimba regimes—particularly during the wet season from December to April, when growers continually weeded their munda fields and guarded crops against birds and other predatory animals, and when the majority of poor peasants also divided their labor time between production and the search for food in order to feed the work force.

Reliance on the hoe as the primary instrument of agricultural production was another feature of the pre–slave trade economy that contributed to the conflict between the peasant and capitalist sectors. As in many other parts of the Third World, merchant capital in the Valley did not revolutionize the technology of production. No structural change in the technological base accompanied the transformation of formerly independent cultivators into peasants. Labor power underwrote every significant shift in the peasant's relationship to nature.

Finally, there were significant continuities in the systems of labor recruitment. Unlike in some parts of West Africa, petty commodity production in the Valley did not lead to the reemergence of slavery, mainly because of the relative weakness of ukapolo servitude in pre–slave trade Mang'anja society. Ukapolo servitude had been so peripheral to the local system of control that there was no attempt to revive it in any form. The Mang'anja did not, for example, try to reduce to dependent laborers the thousands of refugees who flooded their territory from Mozambique from the 1890s. The majority of the immigrants became independent cultivators in their own right. Moreover, although rendered irrelevant as a unit of production as a result of the erosion of the nonagricultural sector, the Mang'anja mbumba community retained its pre–slave trade invisibility in agricultural work. Kinship did not provide the peasant of the Valley with a source of cheap labor, as much of colonial anthropology has assumed. The banja continued to be the primary unit of agricultural production. It shouldered the old and new labor demands, although, as Chapter 4 will show, it never became the locus of property relations or undermined the role of the mbumba in land distribution. Rural resistance to colonial policy on cotton cultivation, wage employment, and labor tenancy was doubly determined by the survival of key elements of Mang'anja society dating from before the era of the slave trade as well as by transformations in patterns of labor usage.

Part 2
The Problem of Labor Control

The Lower Shire District supplies no labour to the coffee planters in the Shire Highlands because living as they do on the navigable Shire River most of the population is occupied in boating work and the oilseed trade, and they are able to earn more money . . . than they could do by going to work in the Shire Highlands. . . .

—Alfred Sharpe, 1897

The Chikwawa native works much better for himself than he does for other people. At his own village he will get up at dawn, work hard until 9 or 10 oclock, rest in the heat of the day, and then put in one or two useful hours of work in the evening.

—District Commissioner for Chikwawa, 1934

3

Resistance to Capitalist Colonial Labor Regimes, 1875–1923

> There is room and to spare for English emigrants to settle on and work the virgin soil of the still untilled land of Ham.[1]

> The Amanganja are . . . physically . . . poor and unfit for hard work and are also inordinately lazy—ready to put up with any inconvenience and even suffer death from starvation in preference to undertaking steady work.[2]

> In any historical society, the problems of power and order receive at least an approximate solution through the medium of political institutions and processes.[3]

3.1. Change and Continuity in Local Politics

Demographic change defined the human context of a struggle for labor control that was otherwise economic and political in nature. The ability of the British rulers to divert labor from the food economy depended on their capacity to deploy the indigenous elites, whose internal struggles reflected the precolonial process of political differentiation discussed in the first chapter.

The task of organizing British hegemony through the use of local elites was relatively easy in the northern section of the Lower Tchiri Valley. There, three decades of Kololo rule had more or less frozen the process of political differentiation by 1891. The Kololo occupied the chieftain positions in their respective territories and relegated all Mang'anja rulers to the subordinate position of village headmen. The Kololo, and not the multitude of Mang'anja headmen, signed the treaties that transferred sovereignty to the British crown in 1889–91.[4] It was to the Kololo that the British looked for local allies in subjugating the peasantry.

The south presented a different picture. There was no single group of rulers that monopolized political power. The failure of the Matchinjiri—and later the Portuguese from whom the British formally took the area—to impose their hegemony resulted in stiff political competition among the Mang'anja and between the latter and the non-Mang'anja settlers, particularly the Chikunda and Zimba ivory hunters and traders. Instead of finding a discrete group of local leaders on each of whom to confer the title of chief, the British were faced with many contenders for the positions. There were more than twenty such contenders in the Lower Shire District, from whom the British selected at least eleven.[5] To the principle of hereditary rule that guided their selection of chiefs in the north, the British added that of proven loyalty in the south.

The political map was even more complex in the Ruo District, which had acted as a buffer zone between the strong Kololo states in the north and the fledgling Matchinjiri state in the south during the last half of the nineteenth century. This was a no man's land in which the process of political decentralization had produced at least 182 "chiefs" by 1910–13. They in turn ruled over 648 "headmen," which gave an average of 3.56 headmen for each chief. The future principal headmen, Mlolo and Makhwira (the latter the son of Chiputula), thus found themselves on paper the equals of forty-nine chiefs in their section of the district.[6] And unlike conditions in the Lower Shire or the Chikwawa section of the West Shire District, in which all the recognized chiefs were Mang'anja or Kololo, respectively, in the Ruo District the Mang'anja leaders and the one Kololo chief (Makhwira) ruled side by side with Chikunda, Zimba, and other "foreign" chiefs.[7] Ethnic affiliation had long ceased to be a barrier to political power in this district.

Some of the chiefs had emerged from the ethnically diverse substratum of village headmen, which included not only the descendants of the Chikunda, Phodzo, and Zimba hunters of the nineteenth century but also individuals who had been in the service of the British administration and local planters. They were self-made individuals who successfully competed with the Mang'anja for political power.

> There is no chief in Bangula now Nyanga the old Manganja Chief of this part having lost his influence. . . . Noteworthy heads of villages in Bangula are Jackie, carpenter to the B.C.A. Com. [British Central Africa Company]; Abdullah kapitao [leader, supervisor] to B.C.A. Com. . . . Peter Zuze an excellent kapitao usually in the employ of the Boma [government] . . . lastly Rosinya (Sinyara), head of a clan of Achikunda women of loose morals, who seems to be thought rather a great personage by the local natives.[8]

The British would find it difficult to suppress the forces they had helped unleash when they decided to formalize their "consumption" of traditional power through the application of the District Administration (Native) Ordinance of 1912.

The effect of the ordinance was contradictory. It initiated few if any real changes in British relations with the local population. Headmen continued to mediate colonial relations in the Ruo and Lower Shire districts, just as the ordinance recognized the status quo in the Chikwawa District. The British appointed as principal headmen all the Kololo chiefs (or their descendants) who had signed the so-called treaties and who had since 1891 been ruling as British chiefs. These were Kasisi, Katunga, Maseya, Mlilima, Mwita, and William.[9] Every Mang'anja politician in the area continued to serve as an ordinary village headman.

The ordinance did, however, lay the legal basis for important changes in the relations among the ruling elite and, ultimately, between the elite and the peasantry in the Ruo and Lower Shire districts. In the latter district it reduced the number of chiefs, now known as principal headmen, from eleven or more to seven: Chataika, Chimombo, Chiphwembwe, Ndamera, Ngabu, Nyachikadza, and Tengani.[10] These were all Mang'anja who ruled over both Mang'anja and non-Mang'anja headmen.[11] The reduction was even more drastic when the ordinance was finally applied to the Ruo District in 1919 after much opposition from European settlers. Only 4 of the 182 or so chiefs were recognized as principal headmen. They were Tengani and Ngabu on the west bank, and Makhwira and Mlolo on the east bank.[12] Following the abolition of Ruo in 1922, Mlolo's area, like Tengani's section in the district, formed part of the Port Herald District. Similarly, Makhwira joined the other Kololo in the new Chikwawa District, which initially incorporated the Mang'anja Ngabu merely as a group village headman. Everyone else who ruled as chief until 1919 became an ordinary village headman. The ordinance placed a formal cap on the process of political differentiation in the south, just as the Kololo had done in the north a half century earlier. By relegating every non-Mang'anja to the position of headman, the ordinance created the conditions for ethnic politics in the south. That ethnicity became a major political force only after 1930 (see Chapter 7) resulted largely from the fact that none of the British-appointed principal headmen in the area exercised real control before the 1930s.

The standard view that the British in Nyasaland did not make use of the indigenous political leadership before the Native Authorities Ordinance of 1933 has some validity.[13] The District Administration (Native) Ordinance conferred few if any powers on principal headmen. There

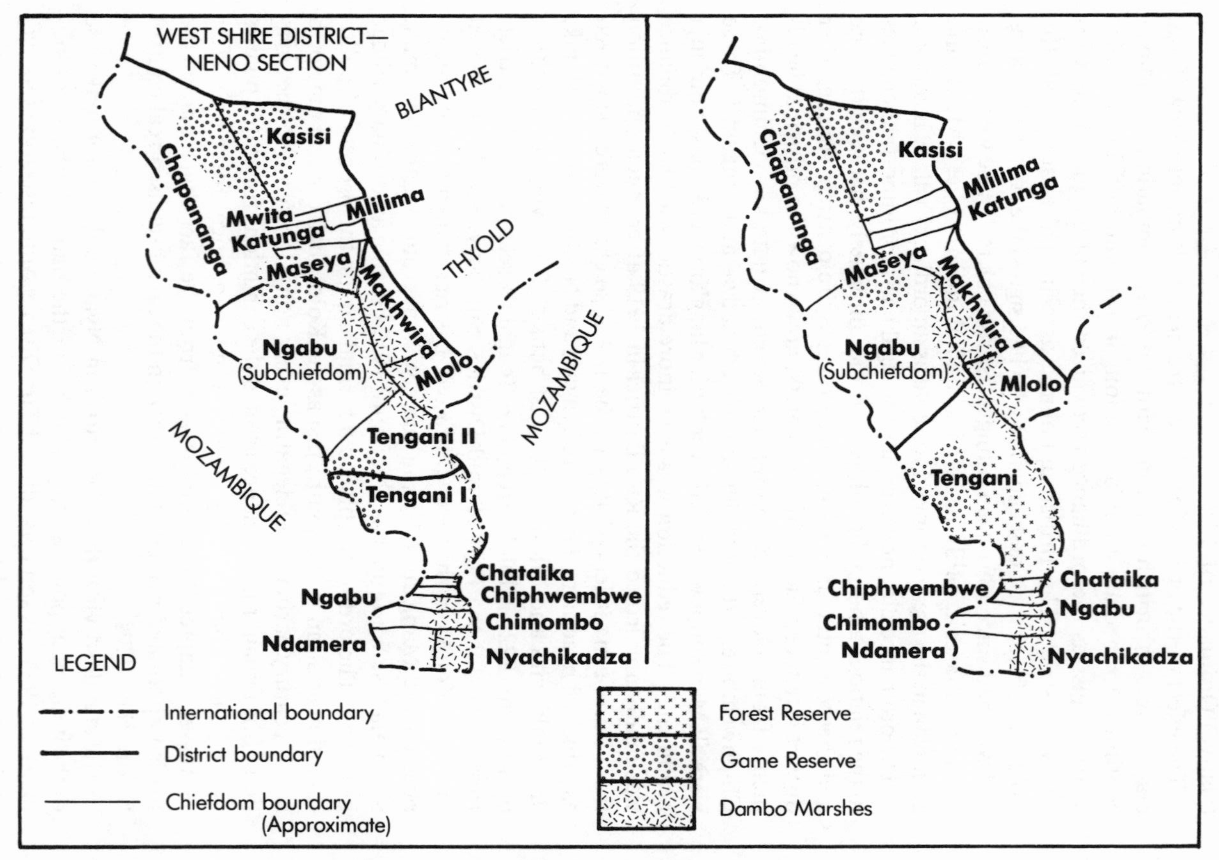

Figure 3.1. Administrative Units, 1912, 1922

was, for example, no provision in the ordinance that allowed principal headmen to dismiss their village headmen. The latter were directly responsible to the collector, as district residents or commissioners were aptly called at the time. Those chiefs who did not already enjoy extensive powers gained next to nothing from their appointment as principal headmen. On the contrary, the ordinance limited the authority of those rulers who, like the Kololo, had previously ruled with few external constraints.

The argument for direct British rule prior to the 1930s cannot, however, be sustained if by "traditional authority" one includes village headmen.[14] British control depended from the beginning on the active participation of village headmen, especially in the more politically fragmented south. The application of the District Administration (Native) Ordinance of 1912 simply confirmed this dependence and inadvertently unleashed new local forces even in the Kololo-controlled north.

The ordinance accomplished this contradictory feat both by what it said and by what it left unsaid. It failed to substantiate the formal hegemony of principal headmen. Headmen were directly responsible to the district resident rather than the principal headmen in all matters relative to the development of the colonial relation, including maintaining law and order in the villages, recruiting labor for both private and public works, reporting serious crimes, and tax collecting.[15] Village headmen did not have to refer to their respective principal headmen in those matters which fell directly under the jurisdiction of the collector.

In addition to these new tasks, headmen continued to shoulder traditional duties, which remained unspecified by the ordinance. These included the distribution of old and virgin land, a service for which they received customary tribute in the form of beer, foodstuffs, and even money.[16] In addition, headmen settled all intravillage and domestic disputes that were not so grave as to attract the attention of the British, a service for which they also received appropriate rewards. There was no issue affecting the peasantry and its relationship to the colonial regime that did not in one way or another fall within the jurisdiction of the village headmen.

The extent to which their old and new responsibilities brought headmen into conflict with their respective principal headmen or with the British was largely the outcome of precolonial political struggles. Village headmen in the north were more likely to clash with principal headmen than were their counterparts in the south. For fear of antagonizing the Kololo, whose power originated outside British colonization, British administrators usually tried to reach village headmen through their respective principal headmen regardless of the actual provisions of the law.[17] For their part, Mang'anja headmen took every opportunity to exploit the ambiguities of the ordinance to their advantage. They tried in particular to reclaim some of their traditional prerogatives that had been usurped by the Kololo. These included the right to stage nyau and other initiation rituals, to extract tribute from salt and palm wine distillers, and to administer the *mwabvi,* or poison ordeal. The administration of the mwabvi, which was banned by British law, allowed Kololo rulers to retaliate against ambitious headmen with the explicit support of the British administration.[18] The situation was different in the southern districts.

With their principal headmen only formally in power, village headmen in the south interacted much more directly with British administrators. These interactions were, needless to say, fraught with tension. A major source of conflict resulted, quite predictably, from the colonial policy of village consolidation, which was aimed at easing the problem of control. To discourage village fragmentation—the material expression of the process of political differentiation—the British decided to compensate village headmen on the basis of the number of taxes the latter collected. For every one hundred taxes collected (about £15 during the late 1910s and early 1920s), headmen received 10*s*. Those headmen who had fewer than fifteen taxpayers

> did not receive remuneration as an endeavour is being made to prevent the small collection of huts being started by families & called villages; and to put them where they exist under the control of the village headman of the largest village in the neighbourhood.[19]

The provision proved more complex in its operation than its designers had anticipated. In order to increase their share of tax revenues, village headmen opened their villages to settlers from Mozambique, which went against official colonial policy on immigration.[20] Moreover, the resolution of intravillage conflicts such as accusations of witchcraft, which signaled that the large community had exhausted its resources, especially land, tended to defeat the campaign for village consolidation. A section of the village community (nthemba) would break away with or without the consent of the headman.[21] Either way, the leader of the breakaway nthemba would need the support of an established village headman in order to get his own tax register (*kaundula*) from the district resident.[22]

But possession of a kaundula would formalize the independence of the new headman only in his official relationship to the British. In many other matters he would remain a junior headman to the man who helped him secure the kaundula.[23] The precolonial process of political differentiation thus continued into the twentieth century, very much to the consternation of local British officials.

At a more fundamental level, the continuities in the precolonial patterns of political alliances and conflict expressed the local origin of the position of headmanship. Unlike most principal headmen in the south, a village headman owed his position to his community rather than to the British administration. The village headmen were in this respect much like the Kololo, whose authority also did not originate from the British conquest. In most cases the British merely confirmed an individual chosen by his community as village headman. For fear of adverse political repercussions, the British found themselves constrained when faced with the decision to depose a popular village headman. Village headmen were more "independent" and sensitive to local opinion, including, among the Mang'anja, the views of the officially disenfranchised group of women making up the matrilineage. Village headmen tried everything they could to balance the interests of their respective communities with their role as representatives of the colonial regime. The resulting conflict, which L. A. Fallers has ably demonstrated for the Busoga of colonial Uganda,[24] became a central force in the capitalist colonial attempts to divert labor from the household economy.

As this and the next chapter will show, village headmen were neither the selfish collaborators of Marxist theology[25] nor the foolhardy rebels of nationalist propaganda. They were human beings who made compromises. Headmen in the Valley dutifully fulfilled their responsibilities as tax collectors and reaped some material benefits from that role; hence the remarkably high record of tax payment noted for the region (see Chapters 4 and 7). But if this strengthens the argument for collaboration, the evidence for resistance is equally rich. "It was the rarest thing," complained a seasoned administrator, "for a headman to bring in a native for punishment for breach of ordinance . . . headmen are afraid of becoming unpopular."[26] More significantly, headmen promoted peasant cotton agriculture against the interests of other segments of the capitalist colonial enterprise. Peasant cotton production guaranteed the collapse of the estate economy and impeded the development of the colonial version of wage labor—the real sequel to slavery.

3.2. Wage Labor: The Colonial Sequel to Slavery

> Local employers have always declared the Amanganja to be lazy and unwilling and his reputation for work has been thoroughly bad. They . . . are more loth to leave their homes and labour afield or submit to discipline than many tribes.[27]

> The local natives are not well suited for transport work [and] the bulk of the carriers come from Angoniland.[28]

> It was also pointed out that, from reports received, the [working] conditions then existing at Chindio left much to be desired, and that the word "Chindio" was anathema with the natives of this District.[29]

The history of wage employment in the Valley highlights two general themes in the rise of the working class in Africa. The first concerns the political and economic forces that released rural labor for capitalist colonial exploitation.[30] Second, this history constitutes an argument for the possibility of an uncoordinated resistance to transform the day-to-day conditions of the workplace.[31]

Mainly because of their location next to the Mamvera Rapids, which blocked navigation on the Tchiri River about fifteen miles to the north of Chikwawa township, the Mang'anja of the northern portion of the Valley were among the first peasants in what is now Malawi to get involved in wage labor. After having intermittently served Livingstone as guides and amtenga-tenga (singular *wamtenga-tenga*) in 1859–64, they came to handle on a regular basis all the traffic going to and from the Scottish stations started in 1875 in the Highlands (Blantyre) and on the northern tip of Lake Malawi (Livingstonia). They hauled European goods to Blantyre and to Matope, a port on the Tchiri River about sixty miles above the Mamvera Rapids. Matope was linked to Lake Malawi by boat service.[32] The northern Mang'anja also rowed canoes that took European travelers down to the Zembezi River and the Indian Ocean.

The drop in the water volume of the Tchiri River beginning in the late 1870s dashed British dreams of using the river as the highway to their settlements in the north[33] and shifted the main labor recruitment zone from the northern to the southern portion of the Valley. Chiromo on the Tchiri-Ruo confluence replaced Chikwawa (or Katunga) as the main port of entry to British Central Africa by the 1890s. There were at least fourteen steamers belonging to the African Lakes Company, the African Flotilla Company, the Zambesi Traffic Company, and the Free Church of Scotland (Livingstonia Mission) operating from

Chiromo in 1899.[34] The Mang'anja and Sena of the southern portion of the Valley thus found themselves servicing the new water transportation network in addition to portering European goods and their owners between Chiromo and Blantyre or Matope. It was not until the mid-1920s that some of these functions were taken over by the Blantyre-Beira railway system.

Inadequate financing and competing capitalist interests made the construction of the privately owned Blantyre-Beira railway a protracted project that lasted over three decades, from 1904 to 1936.[35] Local labor was in high demand throughout this period. The completion of the Blantyre-Chiromo section of the railroad in 1908 only reduced the need for porters between the two points. Wamtenga-tenga porters were still needed to haul goods between different points in the Valley during the dry season when large vessels could not make it to Chiromo.[36] More workers were required to load and unload cargo from ships at ports like Port Herald and Chiromo, to cut firewood and bring it to the river stations for use by paddle steamers, and to serve as domestics on the steamers.[37] Finally, there were the hundreds and thousands of men and women employed in railway construction work.[38] It was the undercapi-

9. Wamtenga-tenga porters, 1922

talized railway companies—the Shire Highlands Railway, the Central African Railway, and the Trans-Zambesi Railway—that were primarily responsible for the unpopularity of wage labor and for intensifying the role of the state in labor recruitment.

State intervention remained central to the rise of wage labor in the Valley[39] not only because of the increased labor requirements of the food economy but also because of the development of sesame and cotton as cash crops. Wage labor competed with petty commodity production as a response to the crisis in precapitalist accumulation occasioned by European conquest and the demise of the nonagricultural sector. Peasants turned to wage labor only when their sector of the economy was in serious trouble. Prior to World War II there were only two periods when capital had a field day in terms of labor supply.[40]

The first coincided with the five years from 1918 to 1923. This was a period of serious economic and social crisis. The end of the war, in which over two thousand men from the area had served as porters, was followed by epidemic outbreaks of Spanish influenza and smallpox.[41] The effect of these epidemics was particularly devastating in the south, where the Duladula floods of 1918–19[42] forced the inhabitants of the marshes to take refuge in crowded msasa tents on the mphala drylands. The floods were not completely over before a serious drought hit the land for three consecutive seasons (1920–23). The result was the catastrophic famine of 1922–23, known as Kherekhe or Mwamthota.[43] The disasters seriously undermined food and cotton production, which had formed the basis of resistance against wage employment and labor tenancy. Peasants turned to European employers in search of money with which to purchase food and to pay their taxes.

The other period of economic disaster that worked to the advantage of European labor extractors extended from 1930 to 1933. The failure of the cotton market adversely affected food supplies given the close relationship that had developed between the two since 1907 (see Chapters 4 and 5). Hungry and without money, peasants flocked to European employers, including the dreaded railway companies and estate holders. Supply exceeded demand to the extent that British officials had to guard local labor against migrants, who had until then sustained the capitalist colonial labor regimes in the area. There was also a sharp increase in the number of local men seeking employment outside the Valley during the two crises.[44]

The search for local workers was always an uphill battle for European employers when the economy was relatively healthy. They could not depend on the forces of rural differentiation for a steady supply of labor.

Under the institution of chikamwini bride-service, Mang'anja boys did not need cash in order to procure wives. Among the Sena, partly because of low wage levels, the elders were generally able to retain boys within cotton agriculture, which generated much of the money used for the *chuma,* or bride-wealth. By satisfying these needs and by acting as a reliable source of primitive accumulation, cotton agriculture, like the absence of bride-wealth among the Mang'anja, robbed the colonial regime of what John Lonsdale and Bruce Berman call the "hidden pillar of the early labour supply."[45] Only the children of poor peasants in agriculturally marginal areas worked for wages during the peak agricultural season from December to March. They used their wages to purchase food during this period, which also happened to be the "months of hunger." Denied the support of their children at this critical juncture in the agricultural cycle, such families ran the risk of never being able to break the vicious cycle of seasonal food shortages and poverty. The ability of most peasants to break the cycle even by such dubious strategies as mortgaging unharvested cotton (see Chapter 4) guaranteed that political intervention always remained central to the process of freeing labor from the peasant economy.

A study I coauthored with Allen Isaacman has shown that economic forces played a negligible part in the rise of wage labor during the nineteenth century.[46] The availability of porters was always keyed to the dominance of tributary relations. On the one hand, Kololo chiefs supplied workers only to those Europeans with whom they were on friendly terms. On the other hand, working for the Europeans was for the Mang'anja an integral part of their social existence as a conquered people. Headmen who failed to supply the chiefs with workers were summarily dismissed. The commission and presents the chiefs received from European travelers and from their subjects, respectively, became an essential element in the reproduction of tributary relations. The Kololo, who had fought for the free circulation of labor power when they themselves were oppressed workers under Livingstone and other employers, never permitted the development of free labor after taking control of the Valley.[47] British imperial control changed only the terms of the struggle; it never undermined the role of politics.

A financially insolvent colonial regime headed by Harry Johnston had little choice but to turn to taxation as a means of raising revenue and driving labor power from the peasant to the emerging capitalist sector.[48] In 1892 Johnston imposed a 6*s.* tax on every male and female adult in the Valley and the Highlands, and reduced the duties of the few Britons who were in the region to tax collection. The public outcry that the high tax rate caused (6*s*. was the official equivalent of a two-month wage) forced Johnston to halve the rate and to change the unit of taxation from the individual adult (poll tax) to the household—the so-called hut tax.[49]

Under pressure from European employers, especially estate holders in the Highlands, the colonial state hiked the tax rate to 12*s*. in 1901, although there was no corresponding increase in the wage level.[50] More significant, it was stipulated that any head of a household who worked for a European for at least one month in a year could qualify, upon producing a certificate signed by the employer, for a 6*s*. tax rebate. The rebate system continued until 1921, although the tax rate kept changing.[51] Colonial officials, including well-meaning missionaries, could thus justify the violence that accompanied the search for laborers. Force was directed against defaulters who could otherwise fulfill their tax obligations by selling their labor power. After it had become clear that peasants would surrender nothing more than the thirty days stipulated by the tax regulations of 1901, the colonial government invented another provision to bail out European employers. A worker had to sign a contract obliging him to remain in employment for a period of at least six months. Employees who returned home before completing six months were to be forcefully taken back to their masters.[52] Labor-hunting expeditions mounted by the regime thus came to have two main targets: the tax defaulter and the deserter.

Direct and forceful state intervention was necessary on two main grounds besides the competing labor demands of the peasant agricultural economy and the general irrelevance of wage labor in local processes of accumulation. The first had to do with the indifference, if not active opposition, of village headmen to wage labor. Village headmen had no compelling reason to engage actively in labor recruitment. They were remunerated on the basis of the taxes they collected rather than on the number of laborers they turned over for public or private works.[53] Headmen actively supported the state in labor recruitment only when, as during the economic hardships of 1918–23 and 1930–33, their subjects had no other means of earning tax money. When other means of earning money for taxes were available to their subjects, headmen proved to be unreliable agents of the colonial regime on the labor issue.[54] Sena headmen were especially constrained in their support for the colonial state. The majority of their subjects had fled Mozambique precisely as resisters to forced labor (*ntarato*) in that country.[55]

The second major reason that necessitated direct intervention in labor recruitment had to do with working conditions themselves. The history of wage labor in Nyasaland—as in neocolonial Malawi—is a textbook example of the tendency of capital to accumulate on the basis of absolute value and to completely externalize the cost of labor reproduction. Extremely low wages and intolerably inhuman working conditions have always characterized wage labor in the country. The wages paid to porters impressed by the Kololo were so low that they could not even sustain tribute relationships,[56] which was one reason why chiefs often joined their subjects in resisting wage employment. Later, European employers rarely gave the stipulated minimum rate of 3*s.* a month. As late as 1906, when the annual "hut" tax amounted to 12*s.*, employers were paying what they termed "the magnificent wage of 6d per month."[57] An employee would have to labor consistently for two full years in order to raise enough money for a year's "hut" tax.

Moreover, although the labor code of 1903 required all wages to be paid in cash, employers like the railway companies routinely paid their workers in hoes and cloth.[58] Railway companies also defied the law requiring employers to feed their workers or give them money to purchase food. Men and women were worked twelve hours a day without food or rest. Employers also found every pretext for withholding the wages of their employees when they were due.[59] Laborers who for one reason or another failed to show up one day were stricken off the payroll for the month. People saw no significant difference between ukapolo servitude and wage labor, which they called *uzungu,* slavery under the white man. They tried everything in their power to withhold labor even in the absence of organizations designed to articulate worker interests.

The discussion of the role of the Kololo as labor recruiters has so far been one-sided. In emphasizing the chiefs' attempts to subordinate wage to tributary relations, this summary has necessarily neglected the ways in which the Kololo also helped the development in their subjects of a sense "of what constituted appropriate conditions of employment."[60] Indeed, one may argue that during the nineteenth century Kololo ex-porters performed some of the functions of labor union bosses. As recipients of a portion of their subjects' wages,[61] the Kololo negotiated for wage increases. When European employers would not give in to Kololo demands, the chiefs took strike action. Katunga, for example, in 1883 prohibited his subjects from working for the African Lakes Company.[62] The chiefs surrendered their right to determine the working conditions of their subjects, particularly the right to organize strike action, only after accepting British "protection." Thereafter, resistance became diffuse, amorphous, and leaderless, which also turned out to be a source of its strength.

As a form of popular opposition, total withholding of labor from local employers took many variations. Hiding was one common strategy that peasants perfected with the implicit and explicit support of their headmen. Rumors of an impending recruitment squad from district headquarters sent tax defaulters and deserters into the bush and across the border into Mozambique. They would stay in hiding until the raiders had left the area.[63] As time went by, peasants developed what might be called formal techniques of hiding, the best documented of which was provided by the *nomi*.

The nomi were youth clubs that had been introduced in the Valley by the Sena.[64] Boys and girls from one or several villages would form a nomi society whose primary function was to render agricultural services in return for payment in cash or in kind. The earnings were used to stage a lavish feast at the close of each individual nomi club, the duration of which usually coincided with the agricultural cycle. While the club remained in operation, its male and female members slept in a *gelo* (Chimang'anja *gowelo*) communal dormitory within a compound called a *palasa*. In the palasa members held their meetings (*nthango*) after work in the evening. The meetings were also attended by married men (but never married women) who held titular positions in the nomi.

Because the working members were by virtue of their age tax exempt, married men took shelter in the palasa whenever the British raided the villages for recruits. It was nearly two decades after the British took control of the area before they discovered the strategy.[65] The result was predictable. There was an all-out campaign against the nomi, which as we shall see in the next chapter, survived only because of the staunch support that the clubs received from headmen at a time when the agricultural economy needed precisely such forms of labor.

The tax obligation required peasants to take more positive forms of total withholding. It demanded in particular that they be able to produce tax receipts when they were found by labor recruiters. The result was an array of strategies for earning cash without getting involved in wage labor. Peasants sold their produce and brewed beer even at times of acute food shortages, which in 1913 provoked a typically racist commentary from one European observer:

> Instead of working one month and getting a rebate of 4s., he wastes grain to make beer and pays his 8s. tax. How native-like![66]

The sale of grain was increasingly replaced by cotton, the primary earner of tax money in the Valley: "The growing of crops for sale is the chief means of obtaining money in the district and labour for payment is practically nonexistant [*sic*]."[67] The popularity of cotton agriculture in the area was directly related to the unpopularity of the wage labor regime. Resistance implied accommodation.

Finally, there was always the possibility of emigration. Conditions of work in Nyasaland were so deplorable that villagers left not only for South Africa and Southern Rhodesia, but also for Mozambique. The exodus of male labor from the Valley reached its peak during the troubled years 1918–23 and 1930–33, when the local economy was in bad shape. The south tended to lose more men than the northern section, partly as a result of the prevalence of the system of chuma bridewealth among the Sena. Young Sena boys joined the taxable male population in seeking employment outside the country during such periods.[68] But the railway companies had earned themselves such a bad reputation that their recruiters "hardly obtained a man" even during a hard year like 1931.[69] Not only did the paucity of employment opportunities disgorge so much of the male labor force from Nyasaland; conditions of work within the fragile capitalist sector also contributed to the trend. Employers of African labor guaranteed that the Mang'anja and Sena remained a population that "prefer[red] to go and seek [work] independantly [*sic*] and [did] not wait to be recruited" for internal purposes.[70]

Growers who for one reason or another could not totally withhold labor from the Nyasaland exploiters surrendered it only partially. Wage laborers would work for a definite period of time during the dry season and quit as soon as they either qualified for the tax rebate or earned enough money for a specific project. The resulting seasonal fluctuations in labor supply necessitated the contract provision that bound workers to their employers for a minimum of six months. But the law had little positive effect in the absence of serious economic disaster. Workers habitually deserted their employers when life in the village was tolerable. The men employed by the Trans-Zambesi Railway Company in Mozambique braved the two-hundred-odd miles from Dondo to Port Herald on foot in open defiance of the contract law.[71]

One can only guess how such men behaved at the workplace. There is very little direct documentary evidence on day-to-day expressions of discontent generated by the labor process itself. The scattered references to the topic, such as the quotations that open this section, suggest patterns of resistance similar to those developed by black miners in early

Southern Rhodesia[72] and by slaves in the American South:

> Side by side with ordinary loafing and mindless labor went deliberate wastefulness, slowdowns, feigned illnesses, self-inflicted injuries, and the well known abuse of livestock and equipment.[73]

The porters pressed into European service by the Kololo consistently refused to carry oversized baggage, which they left at the chiefs' courts.[74] They also ran away with European property as they negotiated their way to Blantyre through the crooked slopes of the Thyolo escarpment.[75] Incidents of pilfering became so common and serious in subsequent years that they attracted the attention of the highest colonial officials.[76] Together with other acts of defiance, the pilfering helped the Mang'anja and Sena earn their reputation in European circles as two of the "laziest tribes" in the colony, "tribes" that were physically unfit for hard work.[77]

Through their continued refusal to submit to the white man's work discipline in a thriving cotton economy, the Mang'anja and Sena were in the end able to wear out the racism of their oppressors. Some perceptive officials were able to distinguish the Lower Tchiri villager as someone who worked hard in his (or her) gardens, but who also took every opportunity of withholding labor power from European employers.[78] Struggle forced the British to understand that there was nothing inherent in the physical constitution of the Mang'anja or Sena that made them bad workers when they labored for others. A large part of the problem of labor control originated in the labor process itself.

The discovery—not an insignificant one in the context of colonial racism—that the Mang'anja and Sena were rational human beings who cared how they spent their labor time had once forced nineteenth-century travelers to make fifty pounds the standard weight for all packages carried by porters recruited by the Kololo.[79] Later, colonial attempts to re-recruit deserters so taxed the meager resources of local officials that some began to question the legality of the force used to hunt down workers who had broken the contract. They brought the matter to the attention of the chief secretary, who found the practice to be illegal and unjustified.[80] He joined those administrators who had called for improvements in the conditions of employment, especially in the railway companies. The latter had to improve the terms of work for their employees or forfeit state support in labor recruitment.[81]

There is sufficient evidence to indicate that necessity encouraged some employers to comply with the chief secretary's directive, which came at a time when the increasing ability of many villagers to pay their taxes through cotton cultivation made it unnecessary for many government officials to look to wage labor as a source of revenue. Burdened by their other responsibilities, district administrators welcomed the chief secretary's ruling on the subject. They rejected employers' requests for man-hunting campaigns in the villages:

> From . . . statements made by natives, who suggested that this form of labour supply resembled the "prazo" system, further demands for labour found in this manner were refused.[82]

And when such assistance was given, it was usually qualified. Employers were told to respect the decision of those employees who did not want to remain at the place of their work for six months. The usual contract period ranged from one to three months during much of the 1920s and 1930s.[83]

Even more significant than the trend toward the enforcement of existing provisions was the change in the attitude of some British rulers. For the first time they felt the need to take "the point of view of the native" in considering the labor demands of European employers. They discovered, for example, that wage labor was not a relevant factor in the local systems of accumulation. "The only inducement . . . for him to go away to work, is that he has to find money to pay his tax. . . ."[84] Otherwise, there was no urge for the peasant to become a wage laborer. Cotton agriculture, rather than wage labor, was the high road to primitive accumulation in the peasant sector. The British also became more sensitive to the cruelties of the workplace, noting in particular how some employers withheld the wages of their workers for any pretext: "The chief trouble of the District natives is that they will not work regularly, and unfortunately many employers do not pay their wages when due . . . when the month's work is finished."[85] Another administrator noted that working conditions at the Central Africa Railway Company at Chindio on the Tchiri-Zembezi confluence "left much to be desired" and that "the word 'Chindio' was anathema with the natives of this District."[86] To the old theme of the naturally indolent Mang'anja or Sena worker officials now added that of the cruel, irresponsible, and super-exploitive European employer.

There were two discernible developments resulting from these changes. Some employers took steps to improve the working conditions of their employees, if only in order to get the cooperation of government officials in recruitment.[87] The railway company responsible for the Chindio depot was reported to have erected "brick buildings for native labour . . . placed a European in charge used to Nyasaland labourers, [and] considerably improved the feeding and other conditions with regard to labour. . . ."[88] The other development was for employers to avoid recruiting workers from the Valley. The region's laborer had become "too expensive" because, with district commissioners very much out of the recruitment exercise, employers had to engage private recruiters. The latter had to be paid and, if the place of work was outside the Valley, given money for transportation in addition to the cost of moving the workers. Employers were particularly discouraged by the fact that, after paying all these costs, they were not sure the laborers would "stay on for 3 months." Thus, companies operating outside the area turned to the Mang'anja and Sena only after all "local supplies had been exhausted."[89] The Tchiri Valley was not the place for the unscrupulous employer, just as it frustrated European settlers who, contrary to Livingstone's dreams, looked down on work as soon as they were on the African continent.

3.3. The Rise and Fall of Settler Cotton Agriculture

> If he works for anyone else, however, he still likes to knock off early, without thinking of doing any more work later.[90]

The stiff competition for African labor that developed between the Nyasaland plantation regime and mining capital should not disguise the common ancestry of the two.[91] Settler[92] agriculture in Nyasaland owed part of its origin to the expansion of mining capital based in South Africa and the Rhodesias. A significant proportion of the land that was later put to the cultivation of such crops as coffee, cotton, sisal, tea, and tobacco in Nyasaland was initially acquired by firms that, like the British Central Africa and British South Africa companies, held major interests in the mining economies of South Africa and Southern and Northern Rhodesia. Most of the acquisitions that preceded the imposition of British rule in Nyasaland in 1891 were driven mainly by the prospect of striking rich mineral resources to the north of the Zembezi.[93] The subsequent discovery that the territory did not have exploitable mineral resources turned companies and individual speculators to agriculture.

In turning to agriculture, landowners found strong support in the colony's British administrators, particularly Harry Johnston, the first commissioner or governor. Johnston shared the European myth of the lazy African who, employing "backward" and destructive farming methods, could not be expected to develop the colony's agricultural resources. The only useful role the peasant could play in Nyasaland's agriculture—now recognized as the colony's economic backbone—was to provide cheap labor to the European landowner. Johnston did not therefore hesitate to ratify European claims to land that had been acquired by the most dubious methods. By 1894 he had formalized the alienation of over 3.75 million acres, which represented some 15 percent of Nyasaland's arable land, leaving thousands of Africans landless and doomed to become tenants and squatters on privately held estates.[94]

European cotton agriculture spread to the Valley by default rather than by design. Unaware of the experiences of the Anglican missionaries in 1861–1863,[95] the colonial state introduced cotton in 1902 as a crop to be raised by European settlers in the Tchiri Highlands. But a series of crop failures resulting from a combination of bad cultivation techniques[96] with an unfavorable climate compelled the colonial regime to redirect its European allies to the Upper Tchiri and the Lower Tchiri valleys. The cotton planters found in the Lower Tchiri Valley the African Lakes Company, the British Central Africa Company, and a number of other European concerns that had unsuccessfully tried to raise coffee since the mid-1890s.[97] State support and the discovery that the Valley was as unsuitable to crops like coffee as the Highlands was to cotton became the two main forces behind the history of settler cotton agriculture during its initial phase from 1905 to the outbreak of war in 1915.

Companies that had already owned land or unsuccessfully attempted to raise coffee took the lead in cotton agriculture. Following the example of the Oceana Company, which opened the first recorded cotton estate in the Valley in 1905 at Kaombe on the western fringes of the Dabanyi,[98] the African Lakes Company revived its former coffee estates in the Lower Shire District for cotton growing. The British Central Africa did the same at Misanje estate in the Lower Shire District and at Makhungwa, Maperera, and Mitole in the Chikwawa section of the West Shire District. An incomplete census taken in 1910 shows that the three firms had been joined by companies such as the British and East Africa Company at Masenjere (Ruo District) and by a wide assortment of individual planters. The latter included G. Boby at Phanga, A. K. Mahomed at Ngabu, Tessiore at Nyathando, and H. Werth at Chikonje, all in the Lower Shire District; J. Fiddes at Mkhate in Ruo District; and J. Dickie at Chirala and Tsapa in the Chikwawa section of the West Shire District. The Kaombe estate in Ruo District had changed ownership from the Oceana Company to H. Haverfield before it was eventually taken over by J. Dickie.[99] "At no time in the past history of Nyasaland," wrote the director of agriculture with satisfaction in 1910, "has such a large area of virgin land been opened in a single season as at present, for cotton, and it is anticipated that the European cotton acreage alone will exceed 20,000 acres."[100]

State support, which until then had been limited to easing the terms of land acquisition and labor recruitment, took a new form beginning in 1910. Colonial officials successfully negotiated for loans to be given to the emerging landlords. Thus, acting on behalf of the Imperial Treasury, the British Cotton Growing Association, formed in 1902 for the explicit purpose of stimulating cotton agriculture in the colonies in order to reduce Britain's dependence on American cotton, advanced a total of £16,970 to European settlers between 1910 and 1913.[101] The result was a sharp increase in the number of applications for land during the last years of the first phase.[102]

There were two principal forces acting in favor of the plantation system during its second phase, which lasted until the end of the Mwamthota famine of 1922–23. In the first place, in addition to providing European employers with cheap labor at unprecedented levels,[103] the dismal performance of the peasant economy was taken as incontrovertible evidence for the supposed inherent inability of African cultivators to work their land. The catastrophes shook the belief of men who, like the representatives of the British Cotton Growing Association, had entertained the possibility of smallholder production coexisting with the estate economy. The other factor had to do with the rise in world demand for cotton and the fall or uncertainties in tobacco prices during the war period.[104] The two forces helped solidify the alliance between the emerging class of landowners and the colonial state and propelled a sharp increase in applications for land.[105]

In 1918 J. S. J. McCall, the director of agriculture, responded to the cotton "rush" by setting aside fourteen five-hundred-acre plots of land for alienation in the Dinde Marsh. He brushed aside local opposition to the alienation of the most fertile land in a crowded district, arguing that European farmers had as much if not more right to the Dinde as the Tonga fugitives, fleeing from the Makombe uprising of 1917 in Mozambique. It was also his opinion that the alienation of their land would break Mang'anja and Sena reluctance to work for Europeans.[106] Governor George Smith was more forthright. He reiterated Johnston's dream of colonial "development" through capitalist enterprise when he wrote to the Colonial Office in 1920:

> I feel . . . it is to the European and European capital that we must look for any considerable and rapid expansion in the growth of cotton in Nyasaland, the native continuing in a large degree to fund the labour.[107]

There was little in the local economy to contradict this view of the proper role of the "native" in capitalist colonial enterprise. A census taken in 1921 shows that African labor was supporting 94 cotton estates in the Valley out of a total of 364 estates put to cotton and other crops throughout the country. Of the 94, 24 were in the Chikwawa section of the West Shire District, 29 in the Lower Shire District, and the remaining 41 in the Ruo District. The last district was second only to Blantyre in the number of estates owned by Europeans and Asians.[108]

European and Asian planters had come to the Valley with a ready-made system of exploiting African labor. This was the notorious *thangata* system,[109] which had been developed by tea and tobacco estate holders in the Highlands in contravention of the only two clauses contained in Johnston's certificate of claims (land deeds) that sought to give a minimum of security to tenants. The provisions denied landlords the right to extract rent from Africans residing on the land at the time of its transfer. They also gave newcomers to the estate the option of paying their rent in cash or labor. But with the tacit consent or indifference of an administration that saw plantation agriculture as the only solution to the country's financial problems, the regulations became a dead letter by 1900. Landlords demanded rent labor from all their tenants. Every head of a tenant household was required, sometimes together with his dependent children, to work for the landlord from January to March.[110] The colonial regime did not merely tolerate landlords' defiance of the original clauses. In order to ensure the availability of tenant labor outside the busy agricultural season from January to March, the labor code of 1903 granted tenants the "option" of paying their taxes to the state by working an extra month for their landlords.[111]

Thangata generated greater and more successful resistance than wage labor. The success of resistance depended on the same forces that undermined wage labor: the continuities in precolonial patterns of political conflict, demographic change, the vitality of peasant cotton agriculture, and, in general, the increased labor requirements of the food economy. These forces came to outweigh every advantage that landlords enjoyed, including state support. Tenants were defending nothing less than their physical survival. Thangata threatened their physical reproduction more directly than wage labor.

Landlords needed the labor of their tenants most during the critical phase of the agricultural cycle from December to March, when the labor demands of dimba cultivation merged with those of the munda on the mphala drylands. This was the time when growers of munda gardens weeded their fields, replanted where mchewere, gonkho, or maize failed as a result of drought, and guarded their crops against birds and other predatory animals. From the 1880s on, January to March became the time when cultivators opened their dimba fields, which required back-breaking work. Moreover, many villagers had to split their labor between cultivation and the search for food in order to maintain themselves during the "months of hunger." Tenancy consequently produced the sharpest conflict between the labor demands of the domestic and the capitalist colonial regime. The term uzungu, slavery under the white man, was applied to wage labor only by extension. It was originally used to denote the labor demands of the plantation regime. It would have required more physical violence than the British were capable of mastering, and a different economic and demographic context than the one that prevailed in the area, in order for landlords to replicate the thangata system of the Highlands. Resistance breached the foundations of the thangata system and secured the demise of estate production.

Tenants withheld their labor either partially or totally (permanently), depending on specific historical circumstances. High population densities in many parts of the Lower Shire and Ruo districts limited the chances of total withholding in the form of intradistrict migrations throughout the 1910s. Tenants in such areas were more likely to pay their rent labor and to deny their landlords only the extra month of work that could have exempted them from paying the hut tax. They contested the extra labor by securing tax money through the sale of fish, foodstuffs, and even their labor power on the open market during the dry season. To these strategies they later added cotton growing in the gardens provided for food crops on the estate, selling the cotton on the public market.[112] Some landlords tolerated the practice, but many others did not. They discouraged the trend directly and indirectly. Landlords forced their tenants to sell them cotton at prices that were well below those prevailing on the public market. When this provision proved unenforceable, many landlords simply prohibited independent tenant cotton growing on the estates unless tenants paid a 2*s*. rent on the gardens in which they grew cotton.[113] The prohibition led some tenants to borrow land for cotton cultivation on Crown (public) Lands[114] and strengthened the resolve of many others to break the chains of uzungu permanently.

There is only one recorded instance in which an entire community refused to pay rent labor. This was in Ruo District,[115] which suggests that population pressure in the area with the highest concentration of private estates closed the door for more viable patterns of resistance such as intradistrict migration. The incident also implies a high degree of unity among the villagers and the relative strength of their headmen vis-à-vis landlords at a time when the future of the plantation regime was still undecided in the minds of many local British administrators. The subsequent commitment of the colonial state to the cause of plantation agriculture left little room for this pattern of resistance. Desertion became the only effective form of total withholding. The eagerness of village headmen on Crown Lands to receive new taxpayers made land availability the only major factor determining the frequency and nature of flights from the plantation regime.

Frustrated tenants in the sparsely populated Chikwawa District found it easier to desert their landlords both as individuals and in groups. These were typically intradistrict migrations that went largely unnoticed by most colonial observers. That they were a frequent occurrence can be deduced from both oral evidence and the greater reliance of the estate holders in the district on imported labor (see the following discussion of Lomwe labor). The demographic situation in the district was such that an estate that had started with a large number of Mang'anja tenants often found itself empty after a short period of time. There were only 834 tenants living on abandoned freehold estates in 1931, notwithstanding the new favorable terms of occupancy resulting from the collapse of estate production.[116]

It was much more difficult to organize intradistrict group flight in the more densely populated Lower Shire and Ruo districts. The few recorded instances of internal flight were restricted to the movements of individual households, as when the Kandeya family fled J. Sinderam's estate in the Dinde Marsh during World War I.[117] Group flights were characteristically interdistrict or international. The three hundred families who in 1908 vacated A. K. Mahomed's estate in the Ngabu chiefdom of the Lower Shire District sought refuge in Mozambique.[118]

Although they were more or less equally restricted in their ability to organize intradistrict group migrations, disaffected tenants in the Ruo District enjoyed the advantage of sharing a common border with the lightly settled southwestern section of Chikwawa District. They did not have to cross the international boundary in order to escape the tyranny of the plantation regime. Dickie at Kaombe and other landlords in the area lost most of their tenants west to Chikwawa during and after World

War I when, on the one hand, the colonial administration pursued an aggressive pro-settler policy and, on the other, peasant cotton agriculture was becoming increasingly popular on the Crown Lands. As a former tenant from Kaombe estate recalled:

> We had grown tired of uzungu . . . so we packed up and went to live on the land of the Boma where we started growing cotton for the first time. That was where we learned how to cultivate cotton that we could ourselves sell on government markets. All the money was ours, and we said to ourselves, indeed, we were wasting our time by working for the white man [*mzungu*]. It is better to continue living here, and so we did.[119]

The director of agriculture was absolutely right when in 1917 he saw the alienation of more land as the only effective weapon against the population's reluctance to work for Europeans. The Mbenje and Ngabu areas of southwestern Chikwawa started to be populated as they received more disgruntled tenants from many parts of the Ruo District, including the east bank. Risking the dangers of predatory animals (see Chapter 7), the new population strengthened Ngabu's claims to principal headmanship, which were formally recognized in 1926.[120]

Individual and group acts of defiance became the single most important cause for the failure of the cotton plantation regime in the Valley. Other causes such as absentee landlordism, fluctuations in world prices, and climatic vagaries were significant only to the extent that they exaggerated the problem of labor control.[121] Tenant desertions and the unwillingness of "free" peasants to labor under uzungu undermined the one structural advantage that settlers in the Valley enjoyed over their counterparts in the rest of the country: the fact that, living closer to the Indian Ocean, they—like peasant producers—received higher prices for their crops because of the lower costs that purchasing companies incurred in transporting the product.[122] High transportation costs constituted a major impediment to the development of both settler and peasant cotton agriculture in areas of the country that, like the Upper Tchiri, were otherwise as agronomically suitable for the crop as the Lower Tchiri Valley.[123] Rural resistance proved to be the major bottleneck in the latter region.

Flight, rent boycotts, and other acts of defiance critically subverted the plantation system designed by landlords in collaboration with the colonial state. Without a reliable tenant population under their control, landlords came to depend on wage laborers for much of the work on their estates during the critical growing season. Competition for labor with other European employers on the open market proved to be an uphill struggle, given the irrelevance of wage employment to Mang'anja and Sena patterns of differentiation. The only time that local labor met the demands of estate production was during the crisis of 1918–23.[124] Otherwise, planters—like other employers in the region—were only relieved by migrant workers from the Ngoni-dominated Ntcheu District and, in particular, the Lomwe from Mozambique, thanks to the brutality of Portuguese colonial domination. The planters who in 1917 boasted of making a net profit of 1*s*. on every pound of cotton they exported managed to do so only because of the availability of Lomwe workers.[125] A significant portion of the Lomwe who settled in northeastern Chikwawa and Ruo districts entered the Valley as wage earners on European and Asian estates both before and after the crisis.

The economic crisis came to a halt with the late rains of March 1923 that sent peasants to their fields of cotton and food crops. Dimba crops were ready by August and the scourge of famine was over. The next harvest was so large that one observer who had followed the events of the previous four years could not believe what he saw:

> a native population, suffering from the physical strain of under-nourishment as the result of the recent famine and reputed to be the laziest and least ambitious in the Protectorate, has been able to grow one of the largest food crops on record and has at the same time greatly increased the acreage planted to an economic crops [*sic*]. These results have been achieved in spite of floods that were serious owing to the length of time during which the water remained on the ground.[126]

The Mang'anja and Sena were reputed to be the laziest people in Nyasaland because they did not easily surrender their labor to local planters and other European employers. They were the least ambitious because they did not emigrate to neighboring countries to the same extent as did other peasants in Nyasaland.

The recovery strengthened resistance to the plantation regime. The district commissioner for Port Herald recruited "with the greatest difficulty" some two hundred boys to work on A. H. Sabattini's Chipolopolo estate near Chiromo. To make the boys complete their contracts, the commissioner had to send policemen to live with them.[127] Planters who could not secure state intervention on their behalf were helpless. Instead of seeing well-cleaned estates, the director of agriculture was greeted in late 1923 with plantations that were, in his words:

> overgrown with weeds owing to the difficulty of obtained [*sic*] labour—Mr. Boby's cotton estate in particular presented a pathetic sight and although there were large numbers of able-bodied natives in the vicinity . . . , he could only obtain four children for work on his estates.[128]

These were the children of the poor who, unlike the "large numbers of able-bodied" adults, had furnished the ukapolo system of slavery in the precolonial era. Mang'anja and Sena adults had rarely furnished the system in peaceful times and were not to become victims of the white man's slavery after 1923.

There were two other factors that complicated the problem of labor control for European employers in the period immediately following the Mwamthota famine of 1922–23. The first had to do with the fact that employers operated on a reduced local population base. The Valley, especially the Chikwawa District, began its economic recovery with a net population decrease that was probably much higher than many administrators were willing to admit.[129] The immigrants who fled to the Valley from areas that had been hit harder by drought and famine, such as the Thete province of Mozambique, did not offset population losses resulting from death through starvation, the Spanish influenza and smallpox epidemics, and permanent emigration.[130] The departure of some temporary immigrants, who must have sold their labor to local planters during the famine, exacerbated the effects of the population losses. The two demographic trends combined to raise the value of the region's traditional source of foreign labor: the Lomwe migrant. Lomwe labor became so indispensable to the settler economy that local officials relaxed or ignored all immigration restrictions in order to attract the migrant workers:

> All chiefs have been informed that it is not the Government policy to discourage Anguru [Lomwe] from entering the country. Mr Feready's Anguru labourers (at Ngombwa estate [on the] Chiromo border) apparently require especially reassuring [*sic*] on this point and I shall visit him shortly for this purpose.[131]

This was a desperate move to save a fledgling economy in the face of the second development of the post-Mwamthota era: the emergence of the large peasant grower, the *zunde* holder, who came to challenge the planters' monopoly on Lomwe labor. And for reasons that will be analyzed in the next chapter, zunde holders became so successful in attracting migrants that some administrators initially thought Lomwe immigration had come to a sudden stop.[132] The time had come for the colonial state to reconsider its policy toward landlords.

The final decision came in August 1923. A tour of inspection made in June of that year by the new director of agriculture, E. J. Wortley, in company with the cotton specialist had revealed the meaning of rural resistance to uzungu: many estates that were "overgrown with weeds" lay alongside a "greatly increased" acreage of well-looked-after peasant gardens planted with both food and cotton crops. Wortley and the cotton specialist were unanimous in reaching the decision that

> in future the Lower Shire District (and parts of the Chikwawa District) should be regarded mainly as a Reserve for Natives and that Europeans or Asiatics should not be allowed to acquire further tracts of land except in very special circumstances. . . . *European efforts to develop this area of the Protectorate have been conspicuously unsuccessful.*[133] (emphasis added)

Colonial agricultural policy was neither monolithic nor static. The only nonnegotiable feature of imperial control was the principle that each colony contributed to the development of the mother country, as by providing the latter with raw materials. The actual methods used to draw out surplus from the colonized society were subject to practical realities as interpreted by the men on the spot.

The decision to close the Tchiri Valley to European farming did not come as a real surprise to anyone familiar with the diversity of official attitudes to European cotton agriculture in the colony. Government support for the plantation system had never been as consistent or as unanimous as suggested by some of the policy statements and official actions examined up to this point. There were officials who were less sanguine, if not at times hostile, to cotton planters and who left the doors open for a peasant alternative. S. Simpson spent much of his tenure as the colony's first cotton specialist from 1905 to 1908 encouraging peasant rather than estate cotton production. Disgusted by what he saw of European cotton agriculture in the Highlands, he decided to distribute cotton seeds to African cultivators in parts of today's Mulanje District, the Upper and Lower Tchiri valleys.[134] The move initiated a dual agricultural policy in the colony. With its right hand the colonial administration supported the plantation system while its left hand left open the possibility of peasant cotton production, if not as an alternative then as a supplement to the estate sector.

J. S. J. McCall, who arrived in Nyasaland in 1909 after Simpson's departure and who was charged with the responsibility of establishing a Department of Agriculture, which he headed until 1921, was the very embodiment of official ambivalence to plantation cotton agriculture.[135] The man who in 1918 decided to sell African land in the Dinde Marsh to European farmers and in 1920 prevailed on Governor Smith to adopt a strong pro-settler stance[136] had started off his career by antagonizing the planter community. Soon after taking office, McCall successfully lobbied for passage of probably the first agricultural ordinance of the country, which allowed African growers to pay their hut tax in cotton. Heads of household who produced thirty-six pounds (in the Valley) or forty-two pounds (elsewhere in the country) of seed cotton "and sold it to a European" were entitled to a 3*s.* tax rebate, "the same as if they had worked one month in European employment." The buyer was supposed to give the seller a labor certificate "in recognition of the fact that he has worked in his own cotton garden."[137] Working in the garden exempted peasants from harassment by labor recruiters. "It is very desirable," McCall wrote at the time, "that natives should have their own cotton gardens (rather than work only on estates belonging to Europeans)."[138] He derided the enraged planters by asking them to purchase machinery and stop relying on unaided human labor power,[139] and he regretted that so much money had been spent on European farmers: "if the Cotton-growing Association had spent the same money as they have spent on advances to planters in erecting ginneries and aiding the native cultivation . . . a much larger cotton Industry would be established in the country."[140] In a debate about the disposal of the cotton that tenants grew in the fields of food crops on the estate, McCall took the side of the tenants. Tenants were not obliged to sell their cotton to their landlords unless they had entered a contract to that effect. Moreover, unless he had provided seeds to his tenants, a landlord who wanted to buy cotton at the public market had to purchase a license like any other buyer.[141]

The shift in McCall's attitudes toward the European cotton planters during 1918–22, when the peasant sector was in distress, did not bring about a united pro-settler sentiment in all colonial circles. The British Cotton Growing Association in particular kept the debate alive, arguing that from its experience in tropical Africa, peasants made more successful cotton growers than planters. Lord Milner at the Colonial Office bought the idea, and in 1920 he questioned the basis of Governor Smith's belated espousal of the view that the future of cotton agriculture in the country rested in the hands of European planters.[142] When Wortley decided to close the Valley to European cotton agriculture in 1923, he knew he had important allies in the colonial administration.

The main weakness, as well as strength, of the pro-peasant argument was that it did not have philosophical or ideological support, as the opposing pro-settler sentiment did. European settlers did not have to work as hard as peasants in order to prove that they were indispensable.

There was an entire ideological support, in the form of European racism and the belief in the superiority of capitalist over noncapitalist production, that magnified the significance of any kind of success that settlers made as cotton growers.[143] African performance had to outdistance that of the settlers by large margins before the peasants could make significant holes in the alliance between the state and European enterprise, which was what they finally did in the aftermath of the Mwamthota famine. Their brilliant performance forced colonial officials to reexamine the history of the plantation system. It was a pathetic record characterized by bad farming practices that invited all sorts of plant diseases,[144] utter incompetence at labor recruitment, and defaults on loans made by the British Cotton Growing Association.[145] Planters had, in brief, failed as cotton producers;[146] they had failed the colonial state in its historic mission as an "instrument of the metropolitan bourgeoisie."[147] No ideology could clean up the record, and colonial officials had to accept if not the principle, then the glaring reality of a more productive peasantry who underwrote metropolitan accumulation. Landlords had undermined the material base of the ideological support of their enterprise.

Without the assistance of the government, planters found it impossible to survive against the backdrop of a vigorous peasant cotton regime. The director of agriculture's declaration marked the beginning of the third phase in the history of cotton plantation agriculture in the Valley. The period lasted until 1930, when all pieces of leasehold land in Chikwawa District were, with one exception, returned to the colonial state to become part of the African Trust Lands (formerly known as Crown Lands).[148]

The earliest casualties in the spate of estate foreclosures toward the end of the 1920s were, as expected, the smaller plantations held on the standard twenty-one-year lease.[149] The foreclosures of such estates proceeded much faster in Chikwawa than in Port Herald District, where there were still eighteen leaseholds embracing 3,529 acres in 1933.[150] Many of these were located in the former Ruo District, which had the highest concentration of privately owned land. There is no evidence, however, of any European production on these estates by the 1930s. Settler production had ceased here as it had on the freehold land belonging to such large landowners as the British Central Africa Company in Chikwawa and Port Herald districts. The seven freehold estates that survived in Chikwawa District produced less than half a ton of seed cotton in 1931.[151] All that remained of the old regime were, in the words of one commissioner, "roofless houses standing in a wilderness of grass and bush or a piece of drerlict [*sic*] farm machinery lying by the road side."[152] The detailed notices of foreclosures of the late 1920s became, in the annual reports of the 1930s, casual statements to the effect that there was no European agriculture in the district. The colonized had voted with his feet against Harry Johnston's program of exploiting African labor through capitalist agriculture.

In order to make some money out of their property, owners of freehold land started inviting peasants from the African Trust Lands to settle on the plantations. A former tenant who once fled Dickie's Kaombe estate described the transformation as a change of heart on the part of the landlord.

> We lived on Crown Land for two or three years. Then the same white man, the same European who had forced us to leave his land because of thangata, felt sorry: "The people who have fled away," he said to himself, "are the owners of the land. They are now on Crown Land. . . . What shall I do? No, I will ask them to come back. . . ." He then called us back to our old villages.[153]

The tenants would pay their rent in cash rather than labor, and the old ban on cotton cultivation was lifted.

> Rent will be in cash from now onward. But how shall they find the money? They will be allowed to grow cotton in their gardens on the estate. I will buy the cotton, take part of the money as rent, and return the rest to them. We started growing cotton on the estate and killed money.[154]

The quotation is an outline of a kind of sharecropping arrangement whose operation clearly demonstrates the erosion of the power of landowners in the region. Their privileges were successfully challenged by every other class, including the peasantry, with the support of the state. Colonial policy had completely reversed itself by the 1930s.

The collapse of the plantation system encouraged some officials to enforce some of the legal provisions designed to protect the rights of tenants. One such provision, contained in the Natives on Private Estates Ordinance, required landlords to buy whatever produce their tenants offered them. Failure to take the produce could exempt tenants from paying rent.[155] Favorable to the landlord when there was a market for the produce, the legislation proved an economic burden when market conditions were otherwise. At such times, landlords would improvise all sorts of special arrangements in order to avoid taking a crop that they could not sell at a profit. Thus, at the height of the Depression in 1931, landlords in Chikwawa tried to impose such an arrangement on their tenants. The latter rejected the proposal and the district commissioner upheld the boycott.[156]

The increase in cotton prices from 1934 on brought another challenge to the weakened landlords. Their eagerness to take all cotton grown on their land drew strong opposition from the British Cotton Growing Association, which since 1923 had exercised a monopoly over peasant cotton throughout the area. The association successfully lobbied against the provision that gave exclusive rights to landlords over cotton produced by their tenants. There was no one to defend the rights of landlords, and tenants were given the option of selling their cotton on the public market.[157] The era of the powerful landlord was gone forever. In a bad year, tenants would dump their cotton on an unwilling landlord; in a good one, they would turn to the highest bidder—hence the popularity of the once hated European estates.[158] The number of tenants on freehold land nearly trebled, from 834 in 1931 to 2,340 in 1938.[159] Some of the new occupants were people who had deserted the estates when landlords were a power to reckon with. But rural struggle had by the late 1930s effectively obliterated the differences between private and public land in the Valley at a time when thangata was crushing the landless in other parts of the country, especially the Tchiri Highlands.

The Nyasaland regime was not the obedient servant of European enterprise that many writers have made of colonial states in Central and Southern Africa.[160] As Lonsdale and Berman have correctly argued, any state in a class-divided society has to "act on behalf of the social order as a whole."[161] Nyasaland's rulers did not relentlessly pursue the interests of capital. They forced railway companies to improve the working conditions of their employees and abandoned cotton planters whose labor demands compromised the legitimacy of the state in the eyes of the oppressed. In so doing, the British implicitly acknowledged the fact that tenancy threatened the reproductive cycle of the peasantry and that wage labor was not a vital force in the Mang'anja and Sena systems of differentiation and accumulation.

Although it corroborates the standard arguments against the "development of underdevelopment" paradigm—and such regional variations as the rise-and-fall hypothesis[162]—this chapter raises several comparative issues that the new literature, or revisionist interpretation, has not adequately addressed. Revisionists are wrong in downplaying the role of the colonial state as an "instrument of the metropolitan bourgeoisie." They ignore the fact that the colonial economy was an "articulated economy" precisely because of its inherent relationship to metropolitan capital. The Nyasaland regime abandoned cotton planters not only because their labor demands conflicted with the state's role as the guardian of social peace. The state disengaged itself from the plantation system mainly because the latter had failed to produce cotton for the British textile economy. In striking a new alliance with the productive peasantry, the state changed the methods rather than the nature of its mission. The British came down hard on the villagers when peasant production stagnated during the 1940s against a backdrop of increased metropolitan demands for raw cotton (see Part III). The colonial state was a subordinate system that coped with its internal contradictions in response to the mission that had given birth to it.

The revisionist position that capitalist colonial domination rested on "the contradictions within the peasant sector" does represent a clear improvement on the crudities of underdevelopment theory.[163] Yet like the latter, the new argument sees these contradictions almost exclusively in terms of the social conflicts between the different segments of the rural population. It does not postulate a contradiction between the structures of control and work as a factor in the circulation of labor power between the peasant and the capitalist sectors of the colonial economy. It does not leave room to theorize that the nature of work itself may affect the ability of dominant groups in either the peasant or capitalist sector to extract the labor of their subordinates. By contrast, this chapter has shown that a social junior was not necessarily a "good" worker. The conditions of work may affect the ability of dominant groups to control their social juniors and subordinates. Peasants in the Valley resisted tenancy and wage labor not only because the one threatened their reproductive cycle and the other was irrelevant to local patterns of differentiation. They also resisted as workers responding to specific labor conditions.

Finally, this chapter shows, in the activities of village headmen, that as in slave societies,[164] resistance in a colonial setting implied accommodation. Village headmen protected their subjects against uzungu while dutifully serving the colonial state as tax collectors. Similarly, one cannot understand the success of peasant resistance to the demands of the territorially based dominant classes—European employers and planters—without appreciating the depth of the rural population's submission to the metropolitan demand for cotton. This chapter makes sense only in the context of the next chapter. Under imperialism, the colonized could negotiate the terms but not the reality of capitalist domination.

4

The Ultimate Compromise: Peasant Cotton Agriculture, 1907–1939

> It is customary for some Europeans to say that the native is lazy. That idea is born of the fact that the native does his work whilst the European is still a-bed, resting during the heat of the day. Anyone who rises *early* will bear me out. Natives have a great knowledge of agriculture and are clever at choosing soils.[1]

> Women play an important part in extending the cotton industry in Africa, both from the point of view of cultivation and importation, by inducing the men to grow cotton for sale so as to have the necessary cash for the purchase of bright Manchester cloths in which they delight.[2]

The strength of Mang'anja and Sena resistance to the labor requirements of the territorially based dominant classes was directly related to the depth of their submission to metropolitan demands for cotton. But like resistance, accommodation was a preeminently political fact. It depended on the ability of colonial rulers to make important concessions. British officials did not only abandon the dream of a white Tchiri Valley. They also gave up their feeble attempts to regulate the work of peasant cotton agriculture. The Nyasaland regime was not the unyielding state of underdevelopment theory, nor was it the autonomous agent of revisionist interpretation. Although it constantly changed its methods, it never lost sight of the mission that had given birth to it. Having been denied a role in production, British officials seized control of the market. They successfully used the market in order to extract surpluses from African growers and to ensure the steady flow of cotton to the mother country.[3] They managed the conflicting interests of cotton sellers and buyers in such a way as to guarantee the hegemony of metropolitan over local cotton buyers. On the other hand, rural success in keeping the state out of production became a major factor in two different but related developments. The first, which will be detailed in the next chapter, relates to the negative impact of cotton agriculture on the food economy and on the region's soil structures. The second concerns the failure of the cotton economy to initiate radical changes in existing systems of control. Peasants domesticated "cotton money" so that it strengthened institutional channels of labor control and disguised the limited changes in the content of the relations of age and gender.

4.1. The Land, Work, and Workers of Cotton Agriculture

> Roughly speaking a native's time is occupied as follows: *January and February:* Clean gardens of weeds, reap early maize, prepare cotton gardens and plant maize; *March and April:* Plant and clean cotton gardens, guard machewere, reap machewere, guard mapira and plant maize; *May and June:* Cultivate cotton, plant beans and maize. Prepare potatoe gardens; *July and August:* Cultivate cotton, maize and potatoes. Reap mapira, commence to reap cotton. *September:* Reap cotton, plant and cultivate maize. Prepare new gardens. *October:* Reap cotton and prepare new gardens. *November:* Prepare all old main gardens for maize and millet. Plant millet and dimba maize. Reap potatoes. Uproot old cotton. *December:* Plant main millet gardens. It will thus be seen that there is no period of the year when the Lower River native is not occupied with some work in his garden.[4]

The work schedule outlined in this quotation was anything but what the state had tried to impose. According to a Department of Agriculture blueprint of 1909 which was originally developed for estate agriculture, cotton was to be a munda crop, planted as were food crops during "the first month of the rains" in November. Growers were also required to open new fields reserved exclusively for cotton. Long ridges were to be made in the cotton fields.[5]

Few if any peasants ever followed the department's directives, which sought to subordinate food to commodity production and to allow the state control over rural work schedules.[6] It is indeed doubtful if many ever heard about the instructions that were given to headmen at the time the latter received seeds for distribution. There was no compelling reason for the unconquered headmen—who also lived by working the land—to enforce the regulations. On the contrary, they had every reason to disregard the rules. Not only did the blueprint interfere with the labor requirements of food cultivation, but attempts to enforce the regulations might have compromised the headmen's efforts to popularize cotton production as an alternative to tenancy and wage labor. Moreover, land scarcity in the south precluded the possibility of opening new fields reserved exclusively for cotton. Instead, peasants invented their own techniques and refashioned the precolonial schedules of raising cotton.

Like their ancestors during the mid-nineteenth century, cultivators of the early colonial era planted cotton on the munda in March and April, after harvesting maize and mchewere millet, and reaped it in September and October.[7] But the fact that unlike their ancestors the new growers raised cotton in the same field as food crops[8] created one difficulty. Although planted at the same time in November as maize and mchewere millet, gonkho sorghum did not mature until June or July. Well over six feet when fully grown, gonkho shaded the shorter cotton when the latter was beginning to shoot flowers. The resulting paucity of cotton yields led some cultivators to phase out gonkho, with adverse consequences for the food economy that peasants were otherwise trying to protect (see Chapter 5). Gonkho was the most heat-resistant crop grown in the area.

Munda cotton, in its various planting schedules,[9] represented only a small fraction of the region's overall contribution to peasant-grown cotton in Nyasaland before the outbreak of World War II. By far the greatest part was grown on land that no colonial expert had considered suitable for cotton: the dambo marshes. The initiative in dimba cotton agriculture came from Sena immigrants in the Dinde. They planted their cotton in the same field and at the same time as food crops after the floods had receded in February.[10]

The earliest reference to the practice dates to the year 1909, when a frustrated colonial official complained that peasants ignored the Agriculture Department's instructions by planting their seeds on the dambo in March instead of the munda in November.[11] The following year the people of the Nyachikadza chiefdom in the Dinde took the greater part of the cotton seeds distributed by the state. Contrary to all expectations, they produced 100 of the 130 tons of seed cotton that the African Lakes Company and the colonial state bought on behalf of the British Cotton Growing Association. The harvest was declared

> a striking proof of the wealth hidden in the soil and proves that the native who wishes to become wealthy need not go outside the Protectorate but may settle at home with his family and friends.[12]

The prediction turned out to be one of the few colonial prophecies that ever came true. Production doubled during 1911–12, when the state withdrew the tax rebate it had extended to cotton growers since 1909.[13] Cotton agriculture was nearly established when a severe drought hit the land the following season.[14] European planters pointed to the subsequent fall in peasant cotton output as proof of Africans' inability to raise cotton and develop the country (see Table 4.1). They were proven wrong.

Production rebounded after the drought. The drastic drop in the level of the Tchiri River during World War I (see Figure I.3, page 6) exposed more dambo for cultivation, and dimba cotton farming began to spread to the Dabanyi. Cotton output kept rising from 1915 to 1918 despite the withdrawal of many able-bodied men from agriculture into the war effort[15] and the flight of many others to neighboring countries like Mozambique in order to escape recruitment as porters. Women grew cotton as they attended their food crops.[16] Production fell only from 1918 to 1923 as a result of the drought, the high floods of the 1918–19 season (known as Duladula or Mmbalu), and the influenza and smallpox epidemics that first broke out among the men returning from the war.[17] As soon as these calamities and the resulting famine (Mwamthota or Kherekhe) were over, peasants returned to their fields with an enthusiasm that quicky killed any competition from the estate sector. The Sena-dominated south, with its extensive dambo areas, maintained its edge over the predominantly Mang'anja north, where cotton was grown chiefly on the munda.

A garden census taken in 1925 showed that over 97.6 percent of all peasant households in the Port Herald District grew some cotton. The corresponding figure for Chikwawa was 76.6.[18] When in the following year the whole Valley contributed 83.6 percent of all the peasant-grown cotton exported from the country, about two-thirds came from the Port Herald District. Europeans interested in the cotton trade were quick to admit that the peasant in the Port Herald District was probably the most exploited grower in the whole colony:

> The Port Herald District has been the mainstay of the Protectorate for years, and the natives have done more for the country than all the others put together . . . they have had the least done for them.[19]

Even when prices fell to the floor during the Depression, peasants in the Valley continued to grow cotton when others gave up the enterprise entirely.[20] Cotton from the Valley accounted for 98.5 percent of Nyasaland's total exports at the height of the Depression in 1932. As in 1926,

Table 4.1 Peasant Cotton Export Figures, 1906–1939
(Seed Cotton in Tons)

Year	Port Herald	Chikwawa	Ruo	Total Tchiri Valley[a]	Total Nyasaland	Valley Exports as a Percentage of Total Exports[a]
1906–7	10	–	–	–	62	–
1907–8	10	0	–	–	19	–
1908–9	41	2	–	–	130	–
1909–10	120	1	13	134	220	60.9
1910–11	310	8	60	378	692	54.6
1911–12	131	40	313	484	962	50.3
1912–13	4	7	5	16	744	2.2
1913–14	200	75	439	705	1,198	58.8
1914–15	264	100	293	656	867	75.7
1915–16	311	20	97	428	815	52.5
1916–17	216	117	238	571	944	60.5
1917–18	216	197	186	599	1,070	56.0
1918–19	56	103	155	314	365	86.0
1919–20	77	50	93	220	300	73.3
1920–21	20	128	69	217	315	68.9
1921–22	3	119	9	131	375	35.0
1922–23	253	4	[b]	257	387	66.4
1923	477	75		552	747	73.9
1924	732	128		860	1,367	63.0
1925	1,692[c]	454		2,156	2,909	74.1
1926	1,266	571		837	2,197	83.6
1927	779	352		1,131	1,387	81.5
1928	1,377	889		1,131	2,486	91.1
1929	1,809	1,248		3,057	3,505	87.2
1930	2,315	2,418		4,733	5,448	86.9
1931	1,126	1,040		2,166	2,477	87.4
1932	1,974	682		2,556	2,698	98.5
1933	2,013	821		2,834	3,080	92.0
1934	2,870	2,074		4,944	5,377	92.0
1935	3,776	3,079		6,855	9,737	70.4
1936	2,600	2,349		4,949	6,389	77.5
1937	2,123	1,167		3,290	7,380[d]	44.5
1938	1,472	2,345		3,817	8,034[d]	47.5
1939	455	829		1,284	3,168[d]	40.5

[a] The totals for the Valley and the percentages have been computed on the basis of the figures for Chikwawa, Port Herald, Ruo, and Nyasaland, which are found in the Department of Agriculture files, Malawi, National Archives, Zomba.

[b] Ruo was abolished as a district in 1922.

[c] Other sources give 1,678 as the figure for the year.

[d] The national figures for the years 1937–39 were originally given in lint cotton and have been converted to seed cotton on the information that three pounds of seed cotton from the country averaged one pound of lint cotton.

10. Harvesting cotton, Chikwawa District, 1959

two-thirds of the area's output once again came from Port Herald. The pattern remained unchanged until 1939, when much of the dambo became permanently inundated. By this time some Sena growers had established themselves as rich peasants or zunde holders.

Zunde owners were growers with holdings that ranged from two to three hundred acres or more and who employed wage labor.[21] A few of these were government employees who used their salaries, which in 1917 ranged from 25*s*. to 30*s*. a month, to employ others to cultivate cotton.[22] Because the Valley did not have a resident agricultural officer from 1922 to 1930, when the cotton economy was at its peak, it is difficult to establish the number of zunde holders during this period. According to a garden census taken in 1932, when the total number of gardens had dropped 9,429 from those planted the previous year (with a corresponding decline of 8,409 in the number of growers), "large gardens" represented 6 percent of all cotton gardens in the Valley.[23] Their owners included such widely known individuals as Amtamigu, Fatchi, and Nyamkhaka in the Dinde and Khembo, Madani, and Sanjama in the Dabanyi.[24] They outdid European and Asian estate holders in competition for the labor of the village poor, the youth in nomi societies, and, in particular, Lomwe migrants from Mozambique who were paid 6*s*. a growing season.[25] In 1929 Amtamigu was reported to have made £100 from the sale of his cotton.[26]

It is not difficult to understand why the dimba regime became popular and successful. The dambo was by far more fertile than the mphala. Each flood season brought to the dambo a rich residue of nutrients that compensated for its intensive cultivation. As the director of agriculture noted in 1915:

> The land in the Ndindi [Dinde] Marsh will always give exceptional results irrespective of variety, as compared with the lighter soils. . . . Every effort should be made to develop the Ndindi Marsh area, as the economic possibilities are enormous, and the depreciation of soil fertility practically negligible owing to the fresh deposits received by the annual floods etc.[27]

A sample of forty cotton gardens taken in Port Herald District in 1932 revealed a marked difference in productivity between the dimba and munda systems, as Table 4.2 shows.[28]

Table 4.2. Dimba and Munda Productivity

	Munda	Dimba
Average acreage	0.9	1.4
Average yield in lbs/acre	310	623
Highest yield in lbs/acre	647 (0.4)[a]	1,256 (0.6)[a]
Lowest yield in lbs/acre	189 (1.7)[a]	168 (1.9)[a]
Largest garden in acres	1.8	2.9
Yield in lbs/acre	334	507
Smallest garden in acres	0.25	0.42
Yield in lbs/acre	406	965
Percentage of first-grade cotton	78	86

[a]The figure in parentheses is the actual acreage of the garden.

Moreover, the practice of intercropping sharply reduced the amount of land and labor time needed for cultivation. It answered two fundamental features of Mang'anja socioeconomic organization: the irrelevance of the mbumba matrilineage in agricultural production, and the absence of an institutional framework for converting into dependent laborers the thousands of Lomwe and Sena refugees who had entered the Valley since the late nineteenth century. The Lomwe ended up as wage laborers on European estates and on the zunde, whereas the Sena not only established themselves as independent producers, but a few among them embarked on the fateful road to rural capitalism. No one knows where zunde farming would have led the Valley had it not been aborted by the Depression and the loss of the dambo to permanent inundation in 1939.

Unlike the double-field system favored by colonial experts, intercropping on the dimba and the practice of raising cotton on the munda after the harvesting of maize and mchewere greatly moderated the land and labor requirements of cotton agriculture. The two cultivation systems did not require drastic readjustments in the existing channels of labor recruitment or division of labor. Ordinary wives and husbands worked their cotton fields together as they looked after their food crops. They met the extra labor requirements of cotton growing by strengthening control over their dependent children. There was, as a result, a clear trend toward the revitalization of those institutions that had channeled youth labor toward agricultural production. These included chikamwini bride-service arrangements, the chigunda or chilere youth gardens, and the nomi youth labor associations. The nomi reached the peak of their popularity during the first cotton boom of the late 1920s (see section 4.3). Boys and girls above the age of ten would join their age-mates in the afternoon after working with their parents in the family field in the morning. They offered their services to anyone who was able to pay in cash or kind, giving the nomi a flexibility that made its services accessible to many ordinary growers. Village elders defended the associations against the charges brought by missionaries to the effect that the nomi undermined schoolwork and Christianity. For the elders the associations were a fundamental aspect of agriculture (*ulimi*) itself.[29] And just as the Mang'anja used chikamwini to create cotton growers out of their prospective sons-in-law, the Sena strengthened the connections between the chuma bride-wealth and agricultural work. Thanks to the capricious nature of wage labor in the country, it became more attractive for many boys to work with their parents in the fields in order to generate the cash needed for bride-wealth. Thus, while the content of these institutions was being transformed (chikamwini generating cash), their formal features were left intact if not actually reinforced through the tentacles of merchant capital.

4.2. Peasants, Merchants, and the State: The Marketing System, 1910–1930

Driven out of the sphere of production, the Nyasaland colonial regime seized control of the market. The human investment it made in this activity was so huge that it invited criticism from individuals who, like

H. C. Ducker of the Empire Cotton Growing Corporation, were more interested in issues relative to cotton production:

> Attempts to improve the grade, and consequently the price, by sorting the crop after picking, and to enforce this sorting by official "classing" before the crop goes to the buyers appear to me to be an attempt at a short cut to the desired object which defeats its own end. These attempts are in no way constructive, in improving the native crop, they imply the assumption of a responsibility by Government which is properly the buyer's business, and they take up a lot of valuable time on the part of the A[gricultural] O[fficer]s and supervisors which would be far better spent on constructive work in the villages and fields.[30]

Although valid, the criticism misses the point. By assuming the responsibilities of buyers, the colonial state was actually performing functions proper to itself. These were the collection of revenue and the policing of contradictory class interests: the interests of the peasantry against merchants on the one hand, and those of local against metropolitan capitalists on the other. Thus, although it had no role in production, the Nyasaland colonial regime did become a force in the process of class formation and the reproduction of the peasantry.

The colonial regime started regulating markets for peasant-grown cotton in 1910, when it passed an ordinance empowering the Department of Agriculture to establish markets in all the major cotton-growing areas of the country.[31] The state authorized the department to levy fees from cotton buyers. Initially, every buying firm or "principal" had to obtain a 10*s*. license in order to purchase cotton and to pay 3*d*. for every one hundred pounds of seed cotton it bought on the market.[32] The rates for both license and market tolls were revised from time to time until 1934, when the schedule was completely revised (see Chapter 6). The government justified the taxes by reference to its role as an arbitrator between buyers and sellers.

The state was represented at all cotton markets by members of the Department of Agriculture and the local administration. They were to ensure that the cotton sellers brought to the market had been properly graded as grade one, two, or three. The staff were also responsible for weighing the cotton before growers took it to the buyers.[33] Traders were required to pay the stipulated minimum prices. After selling their produce, peasants had to show their earnings to government officials. As a former female grower recalls:

> There were government officials at every market. They were responsible for weighing the cotton. If your load weighed 29 [pounds], the kapitao

> [government supervisor] would record the weight on a piece of paper and hand it to you. From there you would go to sell the cotton to the buyer of your choice. Any Indian who wanted to purchase your cotton would simply look at the piece of paper . . . and give you the money. After receiving the money you should not, however, simply leave for home. You had to show the money to another kapitao. If the Indian trader had cheated you, the kapitao would demand reimbursement.[34]

The narrator forgot to add that no male grower could leave the market before paying his "hut" tax to the collectors, who were placed at all such markets. Colonial paternalism appears to have shielded the peasantry from being grossly defrauded by merchants. Indeed, in some marketing seasons before the British Cotton Growing Association was granted a monopoly in 1923, growers had been able to take advantage of the fierce competition among buyers by mixing their cotton with stones and other foreign substances.[35]

Before the British Cotton Growing Association became deeply involved in the country's cotton economy, the colonial regime had pursued a laissez-faire policy toward local capitalists. The state had, for instance, allowed planters to operate ginneries without interference. The Department of Agriculture had seen no reason for intervention because, so the argument went, unlike in Uganda, Africans in Nyasaland did not own hand gins.[36] But the department had to reverse itself soon after the British Cotton Growing Association erected ginneries in the Valley and other cotton-producing areas of the country. The association pressured the state to pass an ordinance that shut down many ginneries operated by local Europeans and Indians. The rationale behind the law was that undercapitalized ginneries were turning out inferior cotton seeds that were later passed on to the peasantry for sowing. The association was particularly interested in limiting the number of ginneries operating in the Valley, which was the heartland of the cotton economy. It was easier for local merchants to obtain permits for establishing ginneries outside the Valley. There were only three ginneries (one of which was owned by the association) in the Valley by 1912 out of a total of eighteen for the country.[37]

After winning the battle for ginning rights, the British Cotton Growing Association turned to cotton markets that had until then been dominated by Indian traders. Here the association wanted nothing short of a monopoly in order to curtail what it termed "Indian malpractices." The state came under heavy pressure from the association's local and Manchester management. An agreement was subsequently signed in

1923 that made the Manchester-based firm the sole buyer of peasant cotton in the Valley.[38]

According to the terms of the agreement, the local association manager and the director of agriculture were to determine and announce the minimum prices for the season at the time of seed distribution. Seeds were to be given free of charge. The most attractive clause of the agreement, however, was the provision that the state would receive 50 percent of the annual profits made by the association, but not suffer any losses.[39] Although passage of the legislation represented another victory for metropolitan capital, the use to which the state put its share of the profits demonstrates the limits of colonial paternalism.

Throughout the negotiations for the contract, the director of agriculture had hoped that part of the state's windfall money would be channeled into peasant production. He had in mind the possibility of creating a price stabilization fund to be used when world prices for cotton fell to the bottom.[40] The governor and local treasury opposed the idea from the beginning, but they allowed the proposal to reach the Imperial Treasury. Winston Churchill, who was then secretary of state for the colonies, scoffed at the idea as smacking of liberalism, which had no place in colonial economic relationships. The cotton trade, he argued, was to stand or fall on its own feet, in response to the immutable laws of supply and demand.[41]

The case was closed, and the director of agriculture found it impossible to employ a resident agricultural officer to post to the Valley at an annual salary of only £150 in 1923, when the government's share of association profits amounted to £7,259.[42] Thus for seven years, when it was reaping high profits, the Nyasaland government was barely aware of the intricate cultivation techniques that peasants were developing. Moreover, the lack of a price stabilization fund and the association's refusal to honor its written commitment to stabilize prices during the Great Depression of the early 1930s became a primary factor in the failure of zunde farming in the Valley.[43]

As Chapter 5 will show, the Depression did not only paralyze zunde cotton agriculture. It also highlighted the conflict between poor peasants and Indian merchants whom the British Cotton Growing Association had driven out of the open cotton market since 1923.

Much of the scheming done by the association was principally targeted at Indian cotton buyers, who had dominated the cotton market since the early 1910s. Unlike their European competitors, who came and went with the marketing season, Indians controlled the market at its very roots: the village. As shopkeepers, they contributed to the decline of the old Mang'anja nonagricultural sector. They ran retail and wholesale shops throughout the Valley, particularly in the rich cotton areas of the Dabanyi and Dinde (during the late 1930s, after many of them had gone out of business because of unfavorable economic conditions, there remained nearly ninety shops operated by Indians in the Port Herald District alone).[44] The shops carried a wide range of consumer goods tailored to rural tastes and needs. These included sugar, salt, paraffin (kerosene), and most important, cotton cloth (in 1939 Indians imported 1,008,496 yards of calico into Port Herald District, over 50 percent of which was cloth for women).[45] Much of the money that growers received from the sale of their cotton ended up in Indian hands.

Backed by these commercial ties, Indians had managed to outdo their European competitors at cotton markets. They provided customers with bags to carry cotton to market. They also gave money to village headmen, who in return would influence their subjects' choice of a buyer at the marketplace.[46] Finally, Indian merchants attracted sellers because, in addition to cash, they gave *bayira,* or presents of hoes, sugar, salt, and other items. As a group, they would form a ring, making sure that the state-stipulated minimum price remained the actual price regardless of any rise in the world demand for cotton.[47]

Indians retained their grip on the peasant cotton economy even after their expulsion from the market in 1923. They entered the two areas of the rural economy most neglected by the state and its European allies: foodstuffs and credit. The collapse of the credit system during the Depression will be explored in full in the next chapter. At this point, it is only necessary to note how Indians provided substantial amounts of credit to poor peasants in anticipation of cotton sales.[48] Before they were forced out of the open cotton market, Indian creditors had demanded to be repaid in cotton, which led many British observers to complain that Indians were indirectly employing Africans to grow cotton for them.[49] Although valid, the accusation missed another important aspect of the credit system. By making loans available to peasants, Indian merchants were performing a crucial service for metropolitan capital. The loans, like credit cards among laborers in contemporary America, made it possible for rural workers to meet their basic needs without realizing the full extent of their exploitation. Growers took credit to the extent they did because merchant capital did not pay the full cost of their labor.

A significant proportion of the credit was neither in cash nor in imported commodities, but in foodstuffs. Indians bought at miserable prices whatever foodstuffs peasants could afford to dispose of at harvest time.[50] The traders consumed some of the food, exported some, and retained the remainder (which they sometimes augmented with imports from the Highlands) for sale at exorbitant prices to the local population during times of scarcity.[51] Poor peasants were compelled to take the food on credit. Thus, after paying their taxes to the state, such peasants spent much of the balance of their cash income in repaying debts to Indian shopkeepers, who would again entice them to take new credit for cloth and other goods—a vicious circle of indebtedness that many growers were unable to break, as events during the Depression demonstrated.

There is a need, therefore, to qualify the idea of prosperity one often finds in colonial and even peasant recollections about the cotton era. Usurious Indian activities both underpinned the appearance of prosperity and disguised the reality of rural exploitation by metropolitan capital. Moreover, as the next chapter will illustrate, the high mobility in foodstuffs affected some of the critical decisions that peasants made in regard to food production and the management of productive forces, particularly the ecosystem. The ways in which these inconsistencies interacted with the equally contradictory developments in production relations constituted the dynamics of the colonial history of the Valley.

4.3. Control and Uses of Cotton Money

> A Headman or a Capitao who takes to cotton growing as a business soon leaves the grass hut, builds himself a house of sun dried brick with a proper wooded door on hinges, buys glass, makes a window and gradually acquires such utensils as enamel basins, plates, etc; and begins to take a pride in his dwelling, enjoying a measure of comfort and health he could never acquire as a paid labourer.[52]

> There is no doubt that one of the reasons why the natives in this district are so pleasant is because they have never been closely in touch with civilization.[53]

The average household in Chikwawa District earned £2. 3*s.* 6*d.* from the sale of its cotton in 1929.[54] Thus, after paying the annual hut tax, which amounted to 6*s.* at the time, a family was left with only £1. 17*s.* 6*d.* to spare for other uses. Rural "prosperity" under these circumstances depended not so much on the availability of expendable income but more on the household's ability to borrow against its cotton before the harvesting season. The phrase "cotton money" will therefore be used to cover both earned income and borrowed cash, goods, and services.

The payment of the annual hut tax constituted the first use of cotton money in monogamous households. Tax collectors were planted at all cotton markets and, as indicated above, no male head of household could leave the market without fulfilling his obligations to the state. The use growers made of the remaining balance became a subject for negotiation between the wife and her husband. Out of this struggle was born the custom that gave wives in monogamous households the right to a piece of cloth. The purchase of a new cloth for and by the wife became the second important use of cotton money in these domestic settings.

A wife's right to a piece of cloth at the end of an agricultural season represented the triumph of the principle that a free adult worker has a right to the product of his labor. Conversely, it represented the fact that, except for the situation in polygamous zunde households, petty commodity production did not develop as a male enterprise in the Valley for four major reasons in addition to the weaknesses of the process of rural stratification (to be discussed later in this section).

11. Husband and wife grading cotton in the home, Chikwawa District, 1959

The first reason had to do with the fact that unlike their counterparts elsewhere on the continent, Mang'anja and Sena men did not become the recipients of colonial extension services and advice.[55] The Nyasaland regime was too poor and too involved in the marketing phase of peasant cotton and the labor demands of estate production to render any services to male (or female) growers in the colony. The state was able to introduce European sexism only to the extent that it held male growers, when present, responsible for the hut tax. Rural resistance only reinforced the state's irrelevance in matters relative to smallholder production.

The second reason that compromised men's ability to turn cotton against their women relates to the failure of the colonial cultivation blueprint of 1909 or, put differently, to the success of peasant opposition to the requirement that cotton be raised as a "pure" crop unmixed with food crops. The adoption of a pure cotton culture on the polygamous zunde household led, as we shall see shortly, to the emergence of commodity production as a male enterprise. The key link in this development was the differentiation between female and male labor along the dichotomy between subsistence and cash crop cultivation, respectively.[56] The popular work schedules adopted in the Valley forestalled such a division of labor and reinforced the precapitalist notion that equated actual work with control in the relations between free adult producers.

The third factor implied in the literature on cocoa production in West Africa concerns the availability of new processing technologies that were monopolized by men.[57] But as noted in the foregoing section, the ownership of the one processing technology that men in the Valley might have monopolized—cotton gins—was restricted to European settlers and later to metropolitan firms such as the British Cotton Growing Association. One sector of Mang'anja and Sena producers was denied the chance of turning cotton money against another sector from this end of the cotton economy.

Fourth, colonial marketing policies inadvertently undermined men's attempts to exploit their women from the point of exchange. At the beginning of the cotton era when there were few markets in the area, some husbands took advantage of their role as carriers and sellers of cotton. They spent the balance after payment of the hut tax in beer drinking and other forms of entertainment on their way home from the market.[58] The establishment of cotton markets throughout the Valley after 1910 curbed the practice. Wives made it a point to accompany their husbands, often carrying their own loads.[59] The practice was subsequently popularized by the colonial regime, whose eagerness to collect revenue led to the establishment of a string of cotton markets throughout the area after 1910. Tax collectors who were planted at all these markets were not supposed to tamper with the money women received from the sale of their loads—an understanding that during the Depression led men to avoid the cotton market altogether in order to evade tax payment.[60]

Women's memoirs attest to their active participation in the marketing phase of the cotton economy. Elderly women I interviewed in 1980 remembered more about the disposal of their cotton than about many other aspects of the cotton economy. They vividly described how they had carried cotton to the market, the heated negotiations they had entered with buyers, the counting of money, and how the latter ended up in an Indian shop buying cloth:

> Thonje [cotton] was grown . . . extensively in these gardens. People sold it to a white man at Kungaecha, Morgeni [Morgan]. Even if you had cultivated only a small plot of this size, and were able to fill only three or four *misekete* [reed crates], you would return with your pouch full of silver. Then [take the money] to a shop, you would get a large piece of cloth, so large indeed that you would have to fold it several times in order to wear it. There was then no woman who could wear a piece bought for five shillings.[61]

There is an unmistakable sense of satisfaction and pride weaving also through women's music about the cotton era. The reality of capitalist exploitation surfaces only in their memoirs about the Depression, when there was no money to purchase cloth, the symbol of their success as producers.

Cotton agriculture took on a different meaning for female heads of households, whose composition kept changing during the colonial era. Young wives married to nontraceable or nonreturning husbands (*machona*) comprised only a small percentage of the group prior to World War II, when a buoyant cotton economy acted as an effective brake on male labor emigration. The largest component of the group was then made up of elderly spinsters, divorcées, and widows—de jure heads of households. Cotton agriculture redefined their relationship to men, including the absent husband, mainly as a consequence of its influence on their relationship to the colonial state. Like adult men, these women were also liable to the annual hut tax.[62]

For these women, as for men, cotton production became the only reliable source of tax money and the only basis for their survival as

12. At the cotton market, Chikwawa District, 1959

an independent group. Other sources of income, such as casual labor for the rural rich, were unpopular because they interrupted food cultivation, which cotton did not under the prevailing techniques of cultivation. Single women, like other producers, looked after their cotton as they tended their food crops. They paid their taxes promptly, which led observers such as E. Lawrence, who worked in the Valley as an agricultural officer, to dispute the widely held colonial view that women in Nyasaland were nothing but "poor and suppressed" creatures[63]—a view that has unfortunately become the only lesson most feminist scholars have learned from colonial records. The comments made by the all-male councils of village headmen during the Depression, when female heads of households were unable to pay their taxes,[64] bear out the conclusion reached by Lawrence: cotton money considerably mitigated the effects of capitalist colonialism on certain categories of women.

The history of female workers in Sena polygynous households, in which the common husband maintained a zunde field, cautions against generalizing Lawrence's observation. Cotton agriculture had the potential of alienating female workers on the zunde through a system of labor allocation that confined female and male growers to subsistence and petty commodity production, respectively.

Much of the work on the original zunde had been done by the husband himself; he called on the labor of his wives only during the peak seasons of weeding and harvesting. As the cotton field of the rich polygynous husband in colonial Nyasaland, the zunde came to employ the village poor, the youth in nomi labor associations, and, in particular, Lomwe migrant workers,[65] which made zunde holders competitors of European and Asian planters on the labor market. Zunde holders generally won the competition despite their more limited financial resources. For one thing, many of them had relatives who recruited the Lomwe on their behalf in Mozambique. For another and more important reason, they could fall back on the services of their wives when there was a temporary decline in the world demand for cotton.[66]

Each co-wife maintained a field of maize, mchewere millet, and gonkho sorghum with the assistance of her dependent children. Co-wives also took turns in preparing food for the common husband and his laborers, who generally lived on the farm for the entire growing season.[67] Husbands sometimes also used the food grown by their wives as payment to laborers when the world demand for cotton fell or when foodstuffs became scarce in the home areas of the workers. But despite their role as the reproducers of the zunde labor force, co-wives had little if any say in the uses of the money made by their common husband. Their contribution remained indirect and was in many cases ignored by the male owner of the cotton garden. He gave them cloth as he saw fit. Many co-wives were guaranteed only inferior cotton that fetched dismally low prices during good cotton years and was rejected altogether by merchants when the market was depressed. As one sympathetic district commissioner complained, buyers

> must realize how unpopular they are with the women when they buy a small quantity of the lower grades of cotton or refuse to buy it. They must know by now that the husband sells No. 1 cotton and gives the lower grades to his wife (or wives) to sell and to make what she can. If she can't sell it she is not pleased.[68]

Rather than clothe the wives they already had, zunde holders spent their cotton money in paying bride-wealth for "many new wives."[69] Like the old wives, the new wives would also become, as the late Chief Ndamera accurately put it, "a permanently alienated labor force."[70]

Submission to oppression formed only part of the story of the zunde household. The other part is about co-wives who struggled against their subordination under the zunde regime in several ways. There were some who sought to cut their ties to the strengthened zunde system by demanding divorce. Many of the divorce cases that came to the attention of the colonial administration during the cotton era were initiated by women, which jostled against the Victorian upbringing of one district administrator:

> Owing to the strong-mindedness or obstinacy of native women I am quite convinced that it is utterly useless for the Court to order a woman to return to her husband when she demands a divorce. She may have little adequate reason for leaving him but it is a sheer waste of time to order her to live with a man when she has declared her intention of leaving him.[71]

Some of the money used in returning the original bride-wealth must have come from independent cotton growing, which constituted a major breach of the traditional zunde economy.

Zunde women tried to reduce their material dependence on their husbands by diversifying their production. They raised cotton in the same fields and at the same time as food crops. They marketed the whole crop themselves and used the income to meet their own and their children's needs.[72] The ability to clothe themselves must have lowered the level of interwife rivalry common in situations in which women are completely dependent on a common husband. Indeed, in good cotton years co-wives, who did not have to pay the hut tax, raised sufficient money to give to their common husbands when the latter needed extra cash for such projects as the purchase of cattle (the rise of the cattle economy is discussed in Chapter 7). And in keeping with the notion that the labor of a free adult bestows rights to a product, the village system of justice came to recognize female contributions to property acquired through a wife's labor. A co-wife could successfully claim part of the property in the event of a divorce.[73]

In addition to new forces such as independent cotton cultivation and the divorces it facilitated, zunde holders also had to contend with traditional forces. More conspicuous among the latter was the mabzyoka cult, a series of rituals performed for women with prolonged psychophysiological illnesses.[74] The rituals, which featured drum beating by male professional drummers, were supervised by a female doctor, known as a *nyahana.* The ceremonies could last a week or more, depending on the speed with which the responsible spirit[75] seized the patient and transmitted its wishes, which varied from one case to another. In some cases they amounted to nothing more than a goat offering. In more elaborate instances, in which the cure constituted the transformation of the patient herself into a nyahana, the spirit could demand a medicine kit and related paraphernalia for use by the new doctor.

The missionaries of the South African General Mission (now known as the Africa Evangelical Fellowship) first spotted mabzyoka ceremonies around the Dinde Marsh in 1900.[76] The cult later spread to the Dabanyi Marsh and its vicinity, following the trail of Sena immigrants.[77] Like Christianity and the many local variants it gave birth to, mabzyoka competed with a wide spectrum of indigenous cults and movements, ranging from the Mbona cult under female or male mediums and the village-centered rain-calling cults that had been led by female mbudzi mediums to the myriad of household-oriented cults of affliction. The historical relationships among these religious movements is a fascinating but difficult subject that Matthew Schoffeleers has diligently started to unravel.[78]

Mabzyoka must have meant different things to the male drummers, nyahana doctors, and female patients vis-à-vis their husbands in different historical contexts. Having a prolonged illness that required the rituals must have vindicated male ideas about the supposed weaknesses of women, as is suggested by the music recorded during the early

13. Mabzyoka spirit possession dance, with nyahana doctor wearing a hat, 1902

1970s, when the cult was being challenged by new male-controlled Pentecostal movements.[79] But one can also read the popularity of mabzyoka during the heyday of the cotton economy as one indication of the intensification of domestic struggle within the Sena marriage setting and, in particular, as a socially accepted mechanism that set limits to the process of male accumulation.

Mabzyoka was a very expensive undertaking. During the entire period of its performance, the household had to prepare great quantities of food grown by women to feed the large gatherings of people who attended the ceremonies. More important, the husband had to pay the male drummers and the nyahana, usually in cash.[80] The husband came out a loser in economic terms regardless of whether the rituals transformed the wife into a nyahana doctor, which was a highly specialized, well-respected, and well-paying profession among the Sena. Whatever its exact relationship to the cotton economy and the tensions it precipitated in the zunde household, mabzyoka must have slowed down men's ability to acquire new means of production. The cult must have also contributed to the absence of any development of private property rights in land among African growers.[81]

Successful as competitors of European and Asian planters on the labor market, zunde holders relied on the Mang'anja land tenure system for access to land. The survival of the old system of land tenure in the political context described in Chapter 3 undermined men's ability to turn cotton money against their women by transforming the latter into a segment of the landless class.[82] Pressures on land generated by population increases and cotton agriculture did not create a landless class in the Valley. They merely heightened the Mang'anja's sense of attachment to their ancestral land and contributed to the cohesiveness of the mbumba matrilineage as a social group (see Chapter 7).[83] With its role as an organizer of labor greatly diminished by the demise of the old nonagricultural sector, the mbumba sustained itself economically as a custodian of ancestral land. The formally disenfranchised Mang'anja female elders continued to play an important role as distributors and as guarantors of the fertility of land within the reconstituted village communities. Thus, the challenges of the capitalist colonial economy notwithstanding, Mang'anja female elders were able, like their male counterparts, to exercise many of their precolonial prerogatives over the labor of the youth.

Feminist scholars ought to pay more attention than they have done so far to the issues, if not the conclusions, raised by Meillassoux, Dupré and Rey, and Terray about the so-called domestic economy or the "lineage mode of production."[84] By making social age the centerpiece of their analyses (see Chapter 1), they underscore the commonsense understanding that in rural Africa, as in many other peasant societies, gender relations are realized only through the intervention of age. Women (and men) do not face the same kinds of challenges throughout their lives. Gender differentiation has had a great deal to do with one's social age in many peasant societies. Any analysis of the impact of capitalist colonialism on women that ignores social age must be conceptually incomplete. The strength of women's resistance to domination in the Valley during the cotton era was in many important ways related to the weakness of the struggles of the youth. If not always in reality, the capitalist colonial economy strengthened the structural position of the seniors. It definitely revitalized those precolonial institutions that had facilitated the appropriation of youth labor.

Youth labor became the target of two different economies during the first four decades of this century. There were the labor requirements of cotton production that, although largely integrated into the schedules of food cultivation, still represented an increase in the household's overall workload. The other sphere had both economic and noneconomic components: wage labor, school education, and Christianity in general. That both the secular and religious European entrepreneurs sought after the labor and minds of the male rather than female youth narrowed their competition (and alliances) with the elders in the struggle for Mang'anja and Sena boys.

When their system of control was largely intact at the turn of the century, Mang'anja elders did not feel as threatened by wage labor as did their Sena counterparts. There was no intrinsic relationship between money and the Mang'anja chikamwini system. Mang'anja boys did not have to earn cash in order to obtain wives. Regardless of the time they spent as wage earners or the amount of money they brought to the village, Mang'anja boys could not avoid chikamwini if they wanted wives. Chikamwini guaranteed Mang'anja elders control over their male juniors at a critical stage in the life cycle of the latter. It was Christianity, with its pretensions as a superior moral code, and European education, which could turn boys and girls into the masters and teachers of their parents within the colonial structure, that constituted a greater threat to the Mang'anja system of control during much of the cotton era.

Mang'anja seniors responded to the threat in several ways. They lengthened the period of chikamwini service during which a prospective son-in-law became, in the words of one informant, a D-7 tractor, felling the largest trees in preparing cotton fields for his mother-in-law.[85] There was also a distinct trend toward the revival of chigunda or chilere farming undertaken by the youth in the afternoons after they had helped their parents in the family garden.[86] The small plots also came to carry cotton that was sold in the name of the parents—the registered growers.

The money resulting from cotton sales served many purposes, the most significant of which was the financing of female chinamwali and male nyau initiation rituals.[87] The ceremonies accomplished at least two ends. They allowed the transfer of cotton money from the lower to the higher grades of elders, including headmen and chiefs who controlled the initiation schools. Kololo chiefs in Chikwawa turned a deaf ear to the complaints by Catholic missionaries against the nyau.[88] For ordinary Mang'anja elders, the rituals provided a special occasion for inculcating the youth with the cultural values that were being attacked by colonialism and Christianity. High among the values that the ceremonies helped uphold were respect for elders and love for agricultural work. African schoolteachers, who had themselves gone through the same process of socialization, took the struggle against modernity to the classroom. They called on their pupils to step up their contribution to agricultural production, just as popular songs among the Sena ridiculed those boys who went to the cities for wage employment.[89]

14. Nyau masked dancers, 1960s

Sena elders could not have been as indifferent to wage labor as their Mang'anja counterparts. The relationship between the chuma bride-wealth and wage employment was intrinsic. In the absence of local sources of money, the Sena could easily have turned to wage labor, as they did during the crises of 1918–23 and 1929–33. Sena mothers and wives had already lost their dear ones to South African mines at the turn of the century when the local economy was in distress.[90] If left unchecked, the trend could have given the youth unprecedented "opportunities for establishing social relationships . . . outside the framework of" the dominant social relations.[91] Sena elders had every reason to encourage cotton agriculture.

Thanks to the inhuman working conditions that characterized wage employment in Nyasaland, Sena elders did not have to put up an extra-ordinarily strong fight in order to retain their boys within peasant production. A small increase in the amount of bride-wealth money was sufficient to lure boys away from the capitalist sector. While bride-wealth rates ranged from 10*s.* to £6 during the 1910s, Europeans were paying their employees 1*s.* 6*d.* a month.[92] A young man would have to be in regular employment for a period of up to five years in order to obtain a wife. By contrast, if he remained home and cultivated cotton with his parents, the family could raise the chuma within one or two seasons.[93] Moreover, he could do this while enjoying some of the village attractions, such as the nomi, that were openly encouraged by elders.

A labor pool at the service of anyone who could pay them, nomi clubs were also a form of social entertainment. At the close of each agricultural season or the life cycle of an individual club, members organized lavish feasts that broke the monotony of village life. The youth enjoyed good food, music, and dance for a week or more outside the normal village controls. Moreover, as an image of the larger society in their internal organization, nomi associations provided the youth with a unique training in their future roles. Every member had a "spouse" throughout the agricultural season. The "husbands" and "wives" were supposed to exchange some of the privileges enjoyed by adults, including sexual favors.

When cotton agriculture reached one of its earliest peaks in the mid-1920s, nomi clubs sprang up everywhere in the Valley. They attracted the attention of European missionaries who denounced the associations for fostering immorality, for demoralizing "the young life of the villages," and for cutting "the very nerve of [the] Gospel and school-work."[94] The headmen who were supposed to support the allegations took a different stand. They told district commissioners that the accusations were ill founded. The gelo dormitory in which boys and girls slept during the nomi sessions was not an integral part of the organization. The trouble with the missionaries, charged both Christian and non-Christian chiefs, was that they based their assessment of the nomi on "inaccurate information" passed on to them by teachers who had "no proper knowledge" of the associations, which were otherwise an "excellent agricultural" institution.[95]

No sensible colonial administrator could dispute the views of the elders and chiefs—the "true representatives of native feeling and sentiment"—at this historical juncture. Unlike their predecessors who had at the turn of the century tried to repress the nomi for concealing potential labor recruits, administrators in the 1920s could find no compelling reason to support the missionaries. The clubs provided a significant portion of the labor needed for cotton production and contributed to tax revenues. The pragmatic British administrator thus found himself on the side of the chiefs in opposition to the missionaries:

> The chiefs pointed out that Nomi dances only took place for 3 or 4 months in the year during the hoeing season and was of real assistance to people in getting their gardens hoed. They thought it did not interfere nearly as much with education as was supposed, but that it was often made an excuse by people and children who were . . . lazy and did not wish to attend school.[96]

The nomi flourished until the same elders withdrew their support following the decline of peasant cotton agriculture.[97]

There is ample evidence indicating that the elders ultimately triumphed over both the European missionary and the employer of wage labor. Labor emigration from the Valley remained at insignificant levels throughout the 1920s and 1930s.[98] Similarly, missionary education made little headway in the area, which apparently pleased many colonial officials who in one memorandum after another commended village elders and chiefs for the excellent job they did at turning the youth into "law-abiding and peaceful" citizens.[99] Agricultural prosperity and the practices it supported acted as a powerful force against modern influences that elsewhere "corrupted" the youth. "Many a young man," wrote the district commissioner of Chikwawa in 1934, "is dissuaded from irresponsible tendencies, and becomes a respectable family man and of necessity a useful producer" of cotton.[100] Still more revealing was the conclusion reached by the district commissioner of Port Herald. In his annual report for 1935, he underscored the point that there was no "gulf between the older and younger generations which is noticeable elsewhere."[101] Petty commodity production had invigorated tradition and revived in the minds of some European observers the image of the Noble Savage.[102]

Chapter 7 will show that this is not an accurate representation of social reality in the Valley. The apparent continuities in formal institutions disguised significant shifts in the content of the relation of social age. For example, chikamwini allowed Mang'anja parents-in-law to extract money from their sons-in-law while the institution retained its formal precolonial features. The revitalization was directly related to the intensification of the conflict between social juniors and their seniors. But because of their focus on the competition between elders and the European employer and missionary, the sources create the impression that all was harmony between elders and youth. It is difficult at this stage of research to document the internal conflict or the nature of youth resistance in accommodation.

The report that Mang'anja boys of no more than sixteen years surprised the administrator at Chikwawa in 1929 by their eagerness to pay their first hut tax is of great significance.[103] The money used in payment of their first tax came from the sale of cotton raised on their chigunda gardens. The report suggests an element of resistance on the part of the youth. By paying their first taxes, the boys were trying to establish themselves as independent producers within the village structure. That this search for emancipation was fraught with ambiguity is also clear. By establishing themselves as independent heads of households, the youth exposed themselves more directly to capitalist colonial domination. Moreover, the changes that followed World War II were such that the youth of the 1930s would in their old age be left more with the symbols than the reality of social adulthood.

Part 3
The Limits and Contradictions of Rural Struggle

The definition of resistance as political response nonetheless draws attention to a break — a qualitative leap — in the continuum of resistance in accommodation and accommodation in resistance.

— Eugene Genovese, *Roll, Jordan, Roll*

When natives put forth special efforts in one direction it means a corresponding falling off in some other direction and I am of opinion that anything which tends to distract the natives' attention from the proper cultivation of their food crops is not likely to contribute eventually to their real benefit.

— District Commissioner for Port Herald, 1916

Mother-in-law help me
Help me with this job
Of bringing up children.
I am pregnant and I carry a young child at my back.
When is your son coming back from Wenela?
Once I'm tired, I shall go back to my parents' home.
I shall leave you this young one to look after,
And I shall go with my pregnancy.

— Song collected in Nsanje District, 1987, by Stanley Namandwa

5

Structural and Conjunctural Strains in Food Production and Supply, 1907–1960

> It is well to remember that wherever the laws of nature are unbalanced by favouring and increasing the number of individuals of any Order in a restricted area the diseases and insects parasitic on the Order are always favoured.[1]

> The price which is paid in any year is not settled by the Gvt. It depends on whether a commodity is plentiful or scarce. . . . I want to help you to grow good crops so that you may have money with which to buy food and clothes and may become more prosperous.[2]

Despite its tendency to conserve the precolonial structures of social control, cotton agriculture significantly altered the nature of the food economy. The evidence suggests a strong correlation between the success of cotton agriculture and such long-term changes as soil depletion, the spread of new plant diseases and pests, and the decline in gonkho production. The colonial relation limited the ability of rural producers to completely subordinate the labor and land demands of cotton to those of food cultivation.

The extent to which structural distortions in food production actually impinged on the problem of food supply depended on such contingent events as droughts, floods, locust plagues, and fluctuations in the world demand for cotton. A vigorous cotton market often shielded the peasantry from the worst effects of both structural and conjunctural strains on food production. A weak world demand for cotton could complicate the problem of food availability for the poor, as the events surrounding the Great Depression show. The collapse of the market in 1929–1933 exaggerated and brought to full light the effects of the growing pressures on the system of production, transformations in the patterns of rural inequality, unfavorable colonial agricultural policies, and the conflict between petty commodity producers and merchants. The Depression also provided a concentrated glimpse of the crises that would follow the permanent inundation of the dambo after 1939.

5.1. Market Constraints

> The Govt. has not deceived you in this matter. I did not know that the price of cotton was going to be low.[3]

The above quotation is part of a long message that Governor S. T. W. Thomas sent to cotton growers in Nyasaland in 1930, the second year of the Great Depression. The crunch had highlighted several structural inequities of the cotton market, including the tendency of capital to externalize the costs of production and government policies that effectively prevented African growers from realizing the benefits of any upward trend in world demand for their produce.

There were powerful forces that denied cotton growers the full benefits of increased world demand for their product.[4] These pressures included the policy adopted by the colonial state throughout much of the cotton era of setting a minimum price—the lowest price cotton buyers were legally required to pay producers—for all grades of peasant-grown cotton.[5] If the policy ever achieved the noble objective of protecting growers from being cheated by unscrupulous traders,[6] it did so at a cost. The assumption that market forces would in a good season drive prices above the stipulated minimum[7] proved to be unfounded. The largest and preferred buyer, the British Cotton Growing Association, was never prepared to enter into healthy competition with other traders. Considering the association a philanthropic rather than a commercial enterprise, the management was always ready to quit the market when competition threatened to push up prices. Buying at a higher price than the guaranteed rates would, the management argued, deplete the association's limited resources and make it impossible for it to purchase the country's cotton during a depression, when there would be no one else to take the cotton.[8] The association bought little cotton under such conditions,[9] leaving its Indian competitors to dominate the market. The latter did so not so much by raising prices as by exploiting their multiple relations with the peasantry (see Chapter 4). Instead of raising prices, Indian buyers would give "presents" of hoes, salt, or sugar and, as a group, form a ring—a kind of cartel—making sure that the prices guaranteed by the state remained the actual rates given to growers.[10] They played this game so skillfully that the British Cotton Growing Association used to employ Indians to purchase cotton on the association's behalf when world demand was on an upward trend.[11] This was in the period before the association gained monopoly buying rights in 1923.

The monopoly contract undermined seasonal and annual pressures toward higher producer prices. It brought an end to the era of confrontation between the state and the British Cotton Growing Association on the question of prices. Government officials no longer insisted that minimum rates should reflect upward trends in the cotton market, as they had periodically done in the past.[12] Nor did the association repeat its earlier unilateral attempts to depress prices below the stipulated minimum in response to seasonal fluctuations in the Liverpool value.[13] There was no reason for doing so. A major clause of the contract made the association party to all official deliberations leading to the determination of the minimum rates for each season.[14] The two parties came closer than they ever had before on the need to stabilize producer prices. Raising the minimum, they agreed, would jeopardize the cotton economy since peasants did not understand the dynamics of market fluctuations. A fall in producer prices preceded by a steady rise would discourage growers to the point that they would give up cotton cultivation.[15] Gone were the days when officials like the director of agriculture had argued that "the native should in common with other growers [namely, planters] reap their [*sic*] legitimate share of the profits accruing from the increased price."[16] Instead, colonial officials became as interested as the Cotton Growing Association in keeping minimum prices at low and relatively stable levels. A key clause to the monopoly contract entitled the state to 50 percent of the profits that the association realized in any year. Allowing the association to make as much profit as the market permitted would raise the government's share of the windfall money which would, it was maintained, be used to subsidize producer prices in the event of a slump.[17] The highest price paid for first-grade seed cotton thus remained 2.5*d.* during the first five-year contract, which expired in 1927—two years before the beginning of the Great Depression, which revealed another dynamic force working against any trend toward higher producer prices.

In opposing any increase in the minimum prices, buyers such as the British Cotton Growing Association almost invariably referred to the exorbitant freight rates charged by the transport companies serving the country.[18] In 1911 the African Lakes Company charged a total of £11 3*s.* 7*d.* on a ton of cotton from Karonga to Liverpool. Only £3 7*s.* 11*d.*, or 27 percent of the total, covered the cost of the more competitive water route between Port Herald and Liverpool. The remainder was spent on internal haulage from Karonga to Port Herald, a distance of about seven hundred miles that involved a myriad of transport networks: lake steamers from Karonga to Fort Johnston (Mangoche), riverboats from Fort Johnston to Matope, porterage from Matope to Blantyre, and railroad from Blantyre to Port Herald.[19]

The completion of the railway system linking Blantyre to the Indian Ocean port of Beira in 1922 did not improve the situation, contrary to the expectations of many officials and merchants.[20] For a variety of reasons that would require a separate study,[21] the privately owned railway system (the Central Africa Railway, the Shire Highlands Railway, and the Trans-Zambesi Railway) serving the colony proved to be a greater impediment to economic development than the more cumbersome porterage and river transport networks it replaced. Merchants had paid £6 5*s.* to get a ton of tobacco from Nyasaland to London via Chindio on the Tchiri-Zembezi confluence by boat. The Central Africa Railway Company, which linked the colony to Chindio from May 1915, raised the freight rate to £10 15*s.* 1*d.*[22] Similarly, the completion of the Trans-Zambesi Railway line between Port Herald and Beira (which replaced the Port Herald–Chindio system in 1922) raised freight rates astronomically. It had cost £3 7*s.* 1*d.* to send a ton of cotton from Port Herald to Liverpool in 1911. By 1930 merchants paid £3 19*s.* 7*d.* to send the same ton just from Port Herald to Beira—and not on to Liverpool. The railway system serving Nyasaland was the most expensive in Central and Eastern Africa, as Table 5.1 illustrates.

A merchant using the Nyasaland Railway system paid between 4.05*d.* and 4.60*d.* a mile to transport one ton; his counterpart using the Rhodesian system paid between only 1.175*d.* and 1.16*d.* The corresponding figure on the Ugandan network was less than a penny. The British Cotton Growing Association estimated that in 1930 Nyasaland's railways swindled 18.77 and 40.66 percent of the money that cotton sellers at the Chiromo market would have received for first- and third-grade cotton, respectively.[23] Peasants paid for the higher transport costs. Railway development did not, as Bridglal Pachai asserts, constitute "a most positive contribution by the British Government."[24] It was a millstone tied to the neck of colonial and postcolonial Nyasaland which strangled the development of agriculture, as traders correctly reminded the government before, during, and after the Great Depression.

Table 5.1 Freight Rates on the Nyasaland, Ugandan, and Rhodesian Railway Systems, 1930–1931

Railway System	Mileage	Weight (lbs)	Rate
Rhodesia			
Pounsley–Beira	234	2,000	£1 2*s.* 11*d.*
Rusape–Beira	267	2,000	£1 5*s.* 10*d.*
Uganda			
Kalindini–Kisumu	587	2,240	£2 8*s.* 3*d.*
Nyasaland			
Port Herald–Beira	236	2,000	£3 19*s.* 7*d.*
Chiromo–Beira	266	2,000	£4 19*s.* 0*d.*
Port Herald–Chindio	218	2,000	£3 15*s.* 7*d.*
Chiromo–Chindio	248	2,000	£4 15*s.* 0*d.*

Sources: For the rates between Kisumu and Kalindini, Port Herald and Chindio, and Chiromo and Chindio see British Cotton Growing Association (BCGA) Manager to Chief Secretary, July 21, 1930, S1/956/30, Malawi National Archives (MNA), Zomba. A document found in the same file gives £5 13*s.* 8*d.* as the freight rate for two thousand pounds of lint from Port Herald to Beira, and £2 17*s.* 10*d.* for the Limbe–Port Herald section. For the Rhodesian system, Port Herald to Beira, and Chiromo to Beira see BCGA Manager, "The Native Cotton Industry," Nyasaland, 1931, A3/2/56, MNA.

The world Depression of 1929–33 dramatized the vulnerability of an economy that had become dependent on a single cash crop, undermined the legitimacy of the colonial regime in the eyes of an outraged peasantry, and weakened the bargaining position of the country's rulers vis-à-vis metropolitan corporations. Responding to an angry public, the governer ordered the chief secretary to plead with the manager of the Nyasaland Railway for a reduction in freight rates. Lower rates would, the government believed, induce reluctant merchants to buy cotton, especially in the northern belt that included such districts as Karonga, Dedza (the southwestern lakeshore), and Blantyre. But the request fell on deaf ears, with the chief secretary rather pathetically reporting that the manager's arguments against a reduction were too strong.[25] This was in July and August 1930.

Rural unrest resulting from the deterioration in world cotton prices the following year (American futures dropped from 6.75*d.* a pound in 1930 to 3.58*d.* a pound in 1931) forced the governor to support the British Cotton Growing Association's application for steep reductions in the freight rates.[26] The association's proposal called for reduced rates on both the Blantyre–Chiromo and Port Herald–Beira sections of the railway system. Sensing that the railway management would not give in to both demands but still hoping for the best deal, the government supported a reduction in the rates between Port Herald and Beira—a distance of 236 miles. The railway management turned down the proposal.[27] It was willing to reduce the rates only for the shorter Blantyre–Chiromo section, which covered a distance of about eighty miles. It reduced the freight rates for seed cotton from 2.14*d.* to 1*d.* a ton-mile and for lint from 7.7*d.* to 2*d.* a ton-mile.[28] The government had no choice but to take the offer and, together with the British Cotton Growing Association, put forward £17,000 in order to raise cotton prices in the northern belt from 0.25*d.* to 0.50*d.* a pound.[29]

The state also emerged as the weaker party in its alliance with the British Cotton Growing Association. The three-year contract, signed in 1927 after the expiration of the first contract, was due for renewal at the height of the Depression in August 1931.[30] But facing no competition, the association kept everyone guessing as to whether or not it would renew the contract. The association was not prepared to renew the contract without a reduction in freight rates.[31] The association's management instead bombarded the government with letters recounting the great contributions it had made to the colony's economy, citing cotton production figures, the profits realized by the state, and the money disbursed to peasants and other parties in the country, such as the railway companies, to prove its case. The letters almost invariably ended with quotations of the sums of money the association had lost in the country. Everyone had benefited from its activities except the association itself.[32] The state was in no position to question some of these claims since most of the letters were replies to frantic officials urging the association to draft another contract on whatever terms so long as it ensured the purchase of peasant cotton.

When the association eventually decided to buy after the announcement of the new freight rates between Blantyre/Limbe and Chiromo, it did so on terms most favorable to itself. It turned down the offer for a new contract but insisted that it be allowed to set cotton prices without any government interference: 0.625*d.* a pound for first-grade cotton in the Valley and 0.25*d.* elsewhere in the country. It also reserved the right to further reduce these rates. In addition, the association demanded certain concessions from the state. The government was to do the actual purchasing in the northern belt and to pay for all transportation costs as far down as Chiromo or Port Herald.[33] The government was, in other words, to provide free steamer and railway transport as well as porters to carry cotton from the markets to river and railway depots. All these concessions were gratefully granted and, in a note that illustrates the degree to which state autonomy had eroded in the face of powerful metropolitan corporations, the chief secretary advised all district commissioners in cotton-growing areas:

> As regards labour for loading, bagging, &c., His Excellency has also promised that the District Commissioners will help so far as they properly can, and where in any case it appears that there is a shortage of labour the British Cotton Growing Association should not be informed that no labour is available until it is certain that there are no tax defaulters that could be used for the purpose.[34]

Few officials would have accepted this kind of blackmail in ordinary times. But not so in the early 1930s. The state had to trade its autonomy in order to rescue its embattled claims to legitimacy among an embittered peasantry.

The immediate political fallout of the market crunch varied from one region to another and between producers of different cash crops in the same region. Popular resentment among cotton producers in the Valley was more muted and fragmented than it was among groundnut growers in the same area and among cotton producers of the northern belt. Cotton production in many areas of the northern belt had been inspired by the colonial state in its eagerness to maximize its share of association profits. District commissioners had come under heavy pressure from the central government to devote their time to cotton propaganda.[35] They had supervised every aspect of the cotton economy, from the teaching of production techniques to the announcement of prices which, following the association monopoly in 1923, was made in advance at the time of seed distribution. The legitimacy of the state became linked to its ability to maintain prices at the promised levels. Cotton growers in the region rightly interpreted the drastic fall in prices as a breach of contract on the part of the state.

> I think that [the] Government will, in the minds of the natives, be held entirely responsible for what they will call this treachery & I personally shall be too ashamed even to attempt an explanation to the Lakeshore Chiefs, more particularly as there does not appear to be any explanation for District Commissioners not having been warned.[36]

Chiefs and the Roman Catholic Bishop Mathurin Guillemé joined the angry district commissioner for Dedza in urging the state to honor its promise by subsidizing the prices offered by the British Cotton Growing

Association.[37] The future of the cotton economy and the very legitimacy and prestige of the state were at stake.[38] The district commissioner staunchly defended the idea of subsidies to peasant producers on the grounds that "European planters are already in receipt of advances from Government. . . ."[39] The heat generated by the outcry drove the state to such desperate actions as courting the association to the point of losing its integrity.

Only the groundnut market created a politically explosive situation in the Valley. Like cotton agriculture in the northern belt, increased groundnut production in the Valley during the early 1930s was encouraged by the state for three main reasons. The Depression exposed the vulnerability of the economy's exclusive dependence on cotton, and local officials were determined to break with the monoculture syndrome by encouraging groundnuts as a cash crop. Second, they were particularly interested in replacing Indian merchants who had until then dominated the little trade in groundnuts with "accredited" traders – a circumlocution for European merchants.[40] Finally, there was the widespread perception among colonial experts that some mphala lands had become unsuitable for cotton cultivation. Such lands, they argued, could best be utilized through groundnut production.[41] The three forces together resurrected a cash crop economy that had gone moribund since the mid-1910s.

Marketing, rather than agronomic factors, had stifled the production of groundnuts as a cash crop in the Valley. Yields on even those soils that were regarded as exhausted were quite high.[42] Moreover, like most other crops raised in the area, groundnuts did not require a separate field. A typical munda crop, groundnuts were interplanted with many crops on the mphala. The planting and harvesting seasons ranged from November to February and April to July, respectively.[43] Furthermore, groundnuts often proved more resilient to infestation by pests and diseases that devastated other crops and were, according to some observers, capable of restoring the nutrients used up by other crops. Despite these advantages, however, groundnuts had failed to establish themselves as an alternative cash crop.

Unlike cotton, groundnuts did not have a metropolitan patron like the British Cotton Growing Association. Their production attracted only the lower echelons of colonial officialdom, particularly the field agriculturalist and district commissioner who, impressed by the quality of the nuts grown in the southern part of the Port Herald District, had started to organize marketing facilities for the crop during the mid-1910s.[44] But the subsequent development of cotton aborted the initiative. The state concentrated all its lean human resources on the lucrative and metropolitan-sponsored cotton trade. Those peasants who grew groundnuts during the 1920s enjoyed only one outlet for their surplus crop: the Indian trading network. Production stagnated until the failure of the cotton market and the assumed degradation of the mphala revived colonial interest in the crop:

> This industry [groundnut cultivation] is to be fostered. Every effort has been made to encourage its extension in those mphala-land areas which do not do greatest justice to cotton cultivation.[45]

The well-intentioned local keepers of British "peace" were soon to regret their action.

A low-keyed campaign that was sensitive to the political repercussions of an inadequate market for the crop, and that also made it "clear on every possible occasion that the groundnut crop is not intended to replace cotton," produced a heavy harvest in 1932.[46] But there was no European to take the crop. The local agent of the African Lakes Company was still waiting for a reply from Glasgow to his request to buy ten tons when peasants were ready to dispose of their produce.[47] The district commissioner for Port Herald had no choice but to send the growers to the vilified Indian merchants.[48] Disappointed by the prices offered by the Indians, many peasants stopped growing groundnuts the following season. Over 50 percent of those who had cultivated the crop in 1932 stopped production in 1933, so that when the agent of the African Lakes Company finally received permission to purchase ten tons in 1933, he had great difficulty filling the consignment.[49] And to complicate matters for the district's British administrators, the agent offered only 1*d.* for two or three pounds of shelled nuts—less than £2 per ton—when on the London market the same ton fetched between £11 and £12.[50] Popular discontent hardened the next season when the African Lakes Company, now joined by two other European firms, demanded four pounds of shelled nuts a penny:

> Early in the opening of the market displeasure at the price was evinced and several growers took their produce away when the price for their weighed load had been announced.[51]

Some of the angry growers took their produce to Mozambique and others returned to the local Indian merchants.

Increased production since 1932 had played into the skillful hands of Indian shopkeepers. They not only reduced their prices to as low as six pounds a penny, but they also converted the bayira system of giving "presents"—hoes, salt, sugar, and so on—into the primary medium of exchange.

> Not only is the native given an absurdly low price for his produce but he is generally forced to take cloth instead of cash.[52]

Peasants decried the barter system, contrary to the opinions of some colonial observers. They forced chiefs who had supported the administration's campaign for groundnut production to confront the white man with this question: How are our people to pay their taxes when they are paid in cloth instead of money?[53] The district commissioner for Port Herald did not have an answer. He subsequently toned down the campaign for groundnut production to a level necessary only to maintain a minimum of interest in the crop:

> Owing to the lack of marketing arrangements . . . it was not thought advisable to press this as a cash crop and at the meeting previously referred to the Chiefs were told the natives must please themselves as to the amount they grew as there was no guarantee of a market.[54]

Peasants had lost confidence in the whole system, and no amount of persuasion by the district administration and chiefs like Tengani could compel them to sell their produce to the local European buyers.[55] Whatever surplus they grew after 1935 went either to Mozambique or into Indian hands.[56] The black market resumed until the 1950s, when proper marketing facilities were organized. Meanwhile, cotton alone continued to decide the fate of the peasantry in an economy in which subsistence had become tied to the operation of the market.

Popular resentment among cotton growers in the Valley was muted, fragmented, and even deflected. For one thing, state intervention in the cotton economy had been limited to control over the marketing system. The state had played little or no role in the process of production as a result of rural resistance. For another, there were always buyers ready to take the cotton grown in the area even under the depressed conditions of the early 1930s.[57] It was less expensive to send cotton from the Valley than it was from other parts of the country. Not only was the distance between the Valley and Beira shorter, but traders who sent cotton from the area had to pay only for the cost of transporting their merchandise by rail. They did not incur the additional expense of transportation to the railway stations. Like the ginneries, most cotton markets in the area were located near the river ports and railway stations to which the growers themselves carried their produce. That is why the minimum rates set for the Port Herald market were always higher than those obtained at any other market in the country. The British Cotton Growing Association paid 0.625*d.* a pound for first-grade seed cotton in Port Herald District in 1931. The corresponding figure in the northern belt was 0.25*d.* because of higher transportation costs.[58]

Thus, instead of precipitating a direct confrontation with the colonial state, the Depression only brought to the surface the internal contradictions resulting from the dominant position of cotton agriculture in the local economy and the absence of an alternative source of money.

> There is no probability of the Nyasaland native giving up the crop entirely, especially in the case of the Lower River grower who has no alternative cash crop to grow.[59]

The steep decline in the number of growers and gardens in 1932 proved to be a temporary phenomenon.[60]

A garden census taken in 1933 revealed another aspect of the strength of the cotton economy in the region. Only zunde holders dropped out of cotton agriculture in large numbers because they were unable to pay their laborers. Of all zunde holders who had grown cotton in 1932, 61.3 percent abandoned the enterprise in 1933. During the same period, however, the number of small gardens rose by 50 percent. Poor peasants and women, for whom cotton was the only source of cash income, responded to the decline in prices by increasing output. The number of independent female growers rose by 600 percent from 1932 to 1933. The dramatic increase also reflected attempts on the part of male growers to evade taxation through the "no cotton garden and no money" formula.[61]

The rather dramatic increase in the number of independent female cotton growers, like the drop in the number of zunde owners, gives a double significance to the Depression in the social history of the Valley. It both dramatized the existing contradictions and provided a special window into the future. The increase in the number of independent female growers was directly related to the parceling of the large zunde holdings among co-wives and to the flight of able-bodied men into wage labor. Arrested temporarily by the recovery of the cotton market from 1934 on, these two trends were to characterize the changing economy after the 1930s. Agriculture would cease to be the chief source of rural wealth. It would be replaced by cattle raising among the rural rich and by labor emigration among the majority of the able-bodied male population. As during the Depression, only the poor and women would expend their labor in agriculture. Peasant and gender differentiation would parallel the distinction between agriculture and nonagricultural production, including wage labor. The Depression provided a concentrated glimpse of the future in addition to highlighting the existing relationships between social differentiation and poverty.

The coincidence of the market crunch with a locust invasion from late 1932 (see section 5.2) exploded the myth of prosperity. The depressed prices for cotton removed for the majority of the peasantry the supplementary source of food supplies that had cushioned the effect of such natural disasters. Everywhere there were complaints about food shortages. In the northern section of Port Herald alone over fifty thousand people were on the brink of starvation by March 1933.[62] Many people were driven to live on wild fruits, while others went to the Highlands to work for food.[63] Summarizing the state of affairs in his chiefdom during 1931, Tengani

> complained about the taxes and the difficulty in finding money. He stated that his people were very poor and that there was great trouble in his section.[64]

The more abrasive Mlolo advised white men to pack up and leave the country if they could not help those who had neither the money nor the opportunity to take credit.[65] Many died as a result of starvation and resulting diseases.[66]

Like the rural rich who could afford to purchase foodstuffs on the market, a significant number of able-bodied men escaped starvation by seeking wage labor in countries like South Africa and Southern Rhodesia. The people who suffered the most from the failure of the cotton market were children and the growing number of female heads of households. Chapter 7 will explore the long-term implications of their plight during this period against the background of the transformations following the floods of 1939 (known as Bomani, which means to push, drive out, or unsettle). At this point it is only necessary to outline the issues as they evolved during the early 1930s. The fall in cotton prices undermined the position of single women in relation both to men and to the colonial state.

The Depression made it impossible for many single women to pay their taxes to the colonial regime.[67] They had no other means of earning money and became a problem for the British administration, which was forced to grant tax exemptions to some women. Of the 5,736 persons granted temporary and lifetime exemptions from the tax burden in Port Herald District in 1933, 1,189, or 20 percent of the total, were widows.[68] Tax relief was given against the explicit advice of the local male politicians, who recommended that such women be encouraged to remarry so long as husbands were liable to a single tax regardless of the number of wives they had.[69] The Depression eroded the economic base of female independence, and many single women found it extremely difficult to make ends meet despite their increased efforts at cotton cultivation. Elderly spinsters were hit particularly hard. They continually moved across the international boundary seeking assistance from relatives in Mozambique.[70] They became the targets of accusations of witchcraft, which reached an unprecedented number during the Depression. The accusations took place against a backdrop of many deaths, incidents of grave desecration, and the Mchapi witchcraft-cleansing movement that reached the Valley in 1933.[71] The Depression imposed severe strains on social life throughout the Valley.

There were serious disruptions in patterns of rural differentiation. The Depression brought zunde farming to a halt while at the same time it undercut the credit system that had tied the peasantry to Indian merchants. Without cotton money, peasants were unable to pay their previous debts and to reestablish creditworthiness. They could not take more credit as they had done in the past. On the contrary, they were instead taken to court by the merchants, which served to deflect rural anger away from the colonial regime toward Indian moneylenders. Indian mercantile activities once again shielded the colonial state from the full consequences of the inequities of the cotton market. Class warfare took precedence over political agitation.

As the Depression deepened, Indian traders, some of whom had as much as £600 worth of book debt, took their debtors to court to recover their money.[72] Difficult cases not resolved by headmen and chiefs found their way to the district commissioner. Of the fifty-two civil cases that the commissioner for Chikwawa tried in 1930, most concerned debts:

> Owing to the lower price paid for cotton this year natives found that they could not meet their obligations . . . consequently the Indians have invoked the and [*sic*] of the Boma and it appears that they rely on the Boma to recover their outstanding debts.[73]

The story was the same in Port Herald District, where conditions were much worse:

> The want of money in the District has been reflected in the number of summonses which have been taken out by Indian Traders against natives.[74]

Many creditors came out of litigation with nothing more than court orders for the accused to fulfill their obligations. There was no money to spare for traders. In other cases, traders were forced to take cotton in lieu of money.[75]

The issue of indebtedness, which was no doubt fought much more fiercely at the village level than the records would permit us to see, came to occupy so much of the attention of district administrators that they considered passing a law that would ban the practice of granting credit altogether:

> I look forward to the day when *all credit* by Shopkeepers to natives . . . is made a criminal offense. The Shopkeepers encourage the natives to become their debtors so that they can keep their custom, and the natives in many cases live beyond their means because of this.[76] (emphasis in original)

It is doubtful, however, if such legislation could have ever worked. The roots of the problem lay deeper than mere greed on the part of the traders or improvidence on the part of the peasants. The problem arose from the tendency of merchant capital to reward labor at below the cost of reproduction. The failure of the market in 1929–33 only exaggerated this tendency; it also compounded the problem of food availability resulting from stresses in the system of production.

5.2. Old and New Tensions in Munda Agriculture

> As you are aware Cotton is the most important export crop of Nyasaland and the Government Revenue and the general prosperity of the Colony are very largely dependent on the success or failure of the Cotton Crop.[77]

> There is a definite tendency . . . for machewere to usurp the position of importance given to [gonkho] in certain areas.[78]

Munda agriculture during the 1930s suffered from a combination of old and new threats, contingent and structural events. The former included an invasion of the red-winged locust (*Locusta migratorioides*), or *dzombe*. The severest of its kind since the turn of the century, the plague entered Chikwawa in September 1932 from the sparsely populated areas of the Thete Province of Mozambique.[79] From northwestern Chikwawa the swarms headed south and east until they reached every corner of the Valley by January 1934.[80] They remained in the area until 1938, having in the meantime multiplied in number and done enormous damage to nearly every munda crop.

A continental phenomenon that afflicted many other parts of Africa at the time, the plague bore the stamp of the changes that man had exerted on the environment. The fliers found shelter in those sections of Mounts Malawi and Thyolo that the local Mbona cult had placed beyond cultivation,[81] in the Lengwe Game Reserve created by the colonial state, and in abandoned sisal estates.[82] They lived and laid their eggs in the bushes during the dry season when there were no crops in the surrounding fields. Once the growing season was on, the hoppers would leave the forests about nine o'clock in the morning and return in the evening after having made havoc on munda crops.[83]

> Over miles and miles of the foot-hill country there is nothing to be seen but short mapira stumps. . . . Maize, even the dead ripe cobs, all the millets without exception, pigeon pea, groundnuts, cotton . . . and all pulses with the exception of cowpea (Vigna spp.) have been reported at one time or another as being completely destroyed.[84]

The damage became more extensive the next season as a new generation of wingless hoppers joined members of the older generation. Early-planted crops began to suffer as much as the late-planted ones.[85] The result was devastating. It was estimated, for example, that the predators devoured 90 percent of all crops, including cotton, by February 1935.[86] Severe on gonkho sorghum, the attacks intensified the activities of predatory birds, which ate up everything left by the swarms.[87] Famine became imminent in many parts of the Valley, particularly the southern portion:

> Locusts caused an immense amount of damage in the five sections south of Port Herald in the first three months of the year. Those furthest south suffered most. Maize and machewere planted and replanted were attacked time after time by swarms and a serious shortage of foodstuffs appeared to be invetable [*sic*].[88]

Though serious, the food shortage did not develop into a famine. The recovery of the cotton market in 1934[89] made imported foodstuffs accessible to many growers. The recovery also slowed down the rate of male labor emigration, and at the same time attracted back to agriculture some former zunde holders.[90] With every sector of the peasantry once again interested in cotton agriculture, the war on the invaders intensified. People dug trenches and burned the bush surrounding their fields in order to eliminate the hoppers and leave the fliers at bay.[91] The invasion slowly lost its momentum and became restricted to a few localities by 1938, releasing local energies for struggles against the more regular natural enemies of munda production, particularly drought.[92]

According to one estimate, droughts of varying intensity either delayed or killed young plants around February every five to seven years during the first three decades of this century.[93] Actual records show that munda farming suffered from rain shortages in 1900–1901, 1907–1908, 1911–13, 1920–23, 1927, and 1933–34.[94] These were the droughts that attracted the attention of European observers, and there is no reason to rule out the possibility of underreporting. There are not many areas in Malawi where insufficient or delayed rains have threatened the reproduction of the peasantry as constantly as in the Lower Tchiri Valley. That the Lower Tchiri has at the same time been one of the most densely populated regions of the country stands out as testimony to the people's resourcefulness in limiting the effects of the treacherous environment.

As during the nineteenth century, peasants responded to the poor performance of munda agriculture by intensifying their efforts at dimba cultivation throughout the colonial era. The drought of 1907–1908 forced every able-bodied inhabitant of the marshlands to open a garden of sweet potatoes (*mbatata*) in November 1907. They were subsequently joined by their counterparts from the mphala and from the hill country such as Lulwe. The latter built temporary msasa tents in the marshes, where they lived on fish while tending their gardens of sweet potatoes.[95] The potatoes were ready for picking by August 1908, when the migrants returned to the hills, carrying the crop and forming what one European observer aptly called the "Sweet Potato Road" linking the dambo with the hills.[96] There were few deaths resulting from what was by all accounts a serious drought.[97]

Two consecutive seasons of poor rainfall from 1911 to 1913 brought the people of the lowlands and the hills still closer together in their struggle for survival.[98] The twelve inches of rain that fell between November 1911 and April 1912 proved insufficient for raising sorghum or maize.[99] Peasants once again turned to the marshes, where they planted sweet potatoes that were ready for harvesting by October

1912.[100] They lived on the potatoes while looking for rains, which did not come in November as expected except in mountain areas like Chididi. Thus, in a reversal of what had happened in 1907–1908, the inhabitants of the marshes were saved by foodstuffs from the hills.[101] Most people worked for food because the failure of the cotton crop reduced the purchasing power of many growers.[102]

An improved cotton market for three consecutive years after 1923 made the drought of 1927 a mere footnote in the history of the region. Only the missionaries of the South African General Mission who lived outside the main cotton-producing area took note of it.[103] Elsewhere Indian mercantile activities sheltered the peasantry from the effects of the rain shortage. Only the protracted drought of 1920–23 precipitated the Mwamthota or Kherekhe famine that killed many people, especially in Chikwawa District, between 1922 and 1923.[104]

Evidence on Mwamthota shows that although severe and widespread,[105] the drought played a secondary role in the genesis of the famine. Mwamthota was the culmination of a chain of sociopolitical and other natural disturbances that had been in the making since the outbreak of World War I. These included the Duladula or Mmbalu floods that destroyed the Dinde and killed many of its inhabitants in 1918–19;[106] the outbreak of influenza and smallpox epidemics that ravaged the entire Valley from 1918 to 1923;[107] the war economy, which weakened food and cotton production and led to serious shortages in cloth and iron hoes;[108] the virtual collapse of the cotton market in 1920;[109] and the rather irresponsible response of the central government to the growing crisis from 1921 on. Officials in Zomba not only refused to grant tax exemptions to the needy, but they also stood firm against the idea of famine relief until September 1922, when peasants were already starving.[110] The failure of the munda crops (as well as dimba crops in the Chikwawa District) in 1921 and 1922 simply compounded a crisis that was to a large degree rooted in forces outside the agricultural system itself.

Mwamthota left an indelible mark on the social structure of the Valley. The region emerged from the famine demographically weakened. The influx of the Nyungwe from the Thete Province of Mozambique at the beginning of the drought did not offset the enormous population losses resulting from starvation, malnutrition, and permanent emigration.[111] Some of the people who went to the Highlands in search of food never returned to the Valley. The ideological repercussions of the famine were equally remarkable. As during the Great Depression, the disasters of 1918–23 formed a fertile ground for revivalist movements aimed at returning to the ways of the ancestors.[112] Imperialism had failed in its claim as the harbinger of "civilization." The British had permitted the economy to return to the stage of food gathering and collecting.[113] But, as with all great human tragedies, Mwamthota twisted the ideological thrust. The dearth of cloth and hoes during the crisis contributed to the myth that now denies the arts of cloth and hoe making to the Mang'anja of the precolonial era.[114] The Mang'anja of the twentieth century should thank the British for introducing the two commodities. Finally, Mwamthota marked the end of the experimental period in colonial cotton agriculture. Peasant cotton production became the way of life in the Valley from 1923 on. It killed estate production and became doubly integrated into the food economy, affecting the distribution as well as the cultivation of foodstuffs.

By raising cotton in the same munda gardens as, but after the harvesting of, maize and mchewere, peasants extended the munda cycle beyond its original limits. Peasants started planting cotton in March and April, when the harvesting of maize and mchewere would have slowed down work on the munda; they kept weeding cotton until July, when all munda cultivation would have come to a close with the harvesting of gonkho; finally, they picked cotton from August to October, when none would have worked on munda fields under the old agricultural system.[115] Popular work schedules differed from those advocated by the colonial state at the beginning of the cotton era only to the extent that the local techniques avoided concentrating agricultural work during the brief rainy season from November to March. They did not entirely do away with the problem of labor distribution between munda cotton and other forms of rain-fed production.

The ways in which peasants dealt with the problem of labor distribution was largely a factor of market forces. The output of cotton from peasant producers was directly related to the amount of labor time devoted to cotton culture, especially during the weeding phase. A poorly weeded field almost always guaranteed poor cotton yields. In good market years traders paid dismally low prices for second- and third-grade cotton, and in bad ones they rejected such cotton altogether.[116] There were strong pressures for growers to pay more attention to the cotton crop after cotton money had become an important medium in food transactions.

The effectiveness of market forces can be understood only in their larger political context. As was argued in Chapters 3 and 4, the success of rural struggle against wage labor and tenancy implied, of necessity, villagers' ability to submit to the demands of metropolitan capital for dead labor in the form of cotton. Successful resistance to both wage/tenant labor and cotton cultivation would have reduced the Nyasaland regime into anything but the subordinate colonial state it was founded to be. The mission of the Nyasaland state was, like that of any other colonial state, to expedite the process of metropolitan capital accumulation:

> We quite appreciate the difficulties of the situation, and recognize the fact that under existing conditions food must take priority over Cotton. At the same time we must point out that Liverpool stocks are getting very low, and if Lancashire Mills are to continue working cotton must be imported either from the United States or elsewhere. . . .[117]

Thus, despite their sincere belief that food should take precedence over cash crop production, colonial officials were often forced to lead vigorous campaigns for cotton cultivation.[118] The campaigns brought home to the peasants the fact that as a colonized people, they had to participate in one or another form of the cash economy, and that the success of resistance to wage employment depended on their submission to the metropolitan demand for cotton. They could not withhold their labor completely from both wage labor and commodity production without breaching the colonial relation. The diversion of labor time from food to cotton cultivation was above everything else a political fact.[119]

The diversion of labor from food production became so obvious by the early 1930s that district commissioners, who were otherwise supposed to propagate cotton agriculture, began to get worried by the trend:

> Much has been done to improve cotton growing but practically nothing with regard to the far more important food crops. When I came back to the District after 4 years of absence I was very struck with the lack of progress in the production of food crops. In some respects things have changed for the worse.[120]

The monthly agricultural reports of the 1930s shed some light on how things had changed for the worse. The reports show that the conflict between cotton and food production on the munda had developed to the detriment of one particular crop: gonkho. Unlike mchewere or maize, gonkho continued to demand the attention of the cultivator until July, when cotton had to be weeded for the last time. Labor-deficient households had to choose between saving the gonkho from birds and letting weeds choke the young cotton. Many growers during the early 1910s might have resolved the conflict in favor of gonkho.[121] But after cotton had established itself as a factor in the system of food supply, many cultivators "chose" to protect cotton. They neglected bird scaring so that seed-eating birds destroyed, according to one estimate, as much as 25 percent of the gonkho harvest every year.[122] This was during the Depression, when many poor peasants intensified cotton production in order to make up for the fall in prices. The dramatic increases in cotton production during the Depression were made at the expense of gonkho cultivation.

Gonkho lost the competition for local labor on another ground. Rising well above six feet, it overshadowed the dwarfish cotton in its early stages of growth. The overshadowing suppressed the fruiting laterals[123] so that cotton intercropped with gonkho tended to yield a disproportionately high percentage of poor fiber. The two cultures were incompatible: "the native having discovered for himself that mapira and cotton do not thrive together."[124] The discovery led to a marked decrease in gonkho cultivation in some parts of the Valley. In such areas cotton subsequently became a pure crop, thriving alone on the munda without the interference of any other crop.[125] The colonial state had lost the campaign for a pure cotton culture only to the extent that growers continued to resist raising cotton in a separate field during the wet season.

The elimination of gonkho cultivation in some areas and its decline in others accorded additional significance to the less heat-resistant but early-maturing mchewere and maize in the local food system. Growers who had dimba fields intensified maize cultivation under two different systems, to be discussed in the next section. Those who did not have such gardens continued to depend on the old munda mchewere[126] and maize crops, which exposed the food economy to the dangers of drought, especially after mphala soils had lost their original fertility. A perceptive district commissioner for Port Herald rejected the standard colonial interpretation of hunger as the consequence of peasant laziness or improvidence. Instead, he blamed cotton for the recurrence of food shortages in the district.

> It is not so much that natives planted less food as that maize was largely planted in soil more suitable for Mapira [i.e., gonkho]. Natives like to plant cotton and food-crops in one garden and this cannot be done with Mapira which remains on the ground too long.[127]

But cotton had become so vital to the local and national economy that colonial experts never considered gonkho a viable option in their strategies for improving the food situation in the area. The plans called for a new food crop that was both early-maturing and heat resistant.[128] Gonkho met the second criterion, but failed the test on the basis of the first criterion. As a late-maturing crop, it conflicted with the labor requirements of cotton the king. Neither the British nor the peasantry were at this time ready to tamper with the conditions of cotton cultivation.

The dominance of the cotton economy at the level of labor allocation was only one structural strain in the system of food production. There were two other trends that troubled agricultural officers working in the Valley during the 1930s: soil erosion and the spread of pests that, unlike the red-winged locust, had become endemic to the area. Pests such as the red bollworm (*Diparopsis castanea*), the stem borer, *nantusi* clipper ants, red and black amaloid beetles, *mphombo* grasshoppers, leaf eaters, and leaf rollers attacked different munda crops every year in different parts of the Valley. For instance, the stem borer wreaked so much havoc on the gonkho crop in 1931 that many growers abandoned whatever the moths had left to seed-eating birds.[129] The attacks contributed, according to one officer, to the decline of gonkho, while soil erosion threatened the survival of munda agriculture itself in areas like northeastern Chikwawa and in much of Port Herald District from the colony's boundary with Mozambique in the south to Chiromo in the north.[130] Erosion was held responsible for undermining the efforts of many growers in the two areas to increase the cultivation of maize and mchewere millet as substitutes for the declining gonkho culture.

It is difficult to determine the nature, causes, and effects of the two problems on the basis of the existing evidence. No systematic attempt was made to understand either problem. All we have are the opinions of field officers, some of which were better informed than others, but none dominating the field to the exclusion of others. For reasons that will be fully explored in Chapter 6, colonial officials at this time disagreed on most aspects of the issues, including the role played by local cultivation techniques in the two developments. Although many saw ratooning as the principal cause of the propagation of the stem borer, there were others who linked the pest to climatic factors.[131] Officials also differed widely in their assessment of the results of such practices as heavy seeding, according to which peasants mixed between twenty and thirty seeds of millet and sorghum before sowing them in a single hole.[132]

Colonial opinion was equally divided on the question of soil erosion. Some officers did not consider it a major problem even in the two areas identified above.[133] A few went so far as to question the very existence of the problem. They agreed, as anyone with eyes could only do, that northeastern Chikwawa and the southern portion of Port Herald District below Chiromo were subject to storm erosion. The two areas were bounded by mountains: northeastern Chikwawa by the western slopes of the Thyolo escarpment and Port Herald by the southern extension of the Kirk Range. These were also among the most densely populated regions in the country. Population pressure had forced peasants to work the same fields every year and to encroach on the slopes of the mountains, which became virtually denuded of their original vegetation by the late 1910s.[134] The two areas faced the danger of being damaged during the rainy season. Torrential rains could create gullies and widen the streams flowing to the Tchiri River. The Chigumukire Stream crossing the main road from Chiromo to Port Herald was only one foot deep and three feet wide in 1927. The heavy rains of 1931 deepened the rivulet to twenty and widened it to fifty feet.[135]

None seriously contested the argument up to this point. Disagreements arose with regard to the second part of the argument, namely, that storm water must also have carried away the topsoil of the flat mphala lying between the hills and the Tchiri River on which most peasants raised their crops. The dissenters pointed to two facts. First, the mphala soil was highly permeable; it could easily absorb running waters from the hills.[136] Second, the popular methods of cultivation, like intercropping and scatter planting, acted as a manmade barrier against sheet erosion.[137] Objectors concluded their arguments with a call for investigation, which was never undertaken. The subsequent ascendancy of the Malthusian interpretation, which formed the intellectual background to colonial intervention after the 1930s, did not rest on a new or scientific understanding of the problem. It represented a pragmatic reaction to the strains in cotton agriculture, resulting in part from the increased attacks on munda cotton by the red bollworm.

Found only to the south of the equator, the red bollworm was the principal enemy of cotton culture in the Valley. The moths attacked bolls, buds, and flowers and sometimes also acted as a tip borer by entering terminal growing points.[138] If infected while still young, the bolls and buds of the cotton plant would subsequently drop off. No other pest, including the stainer, undermined the cotton output of the Valley as much as the red bollworm.[139]

Agricultural officers working in the region detected the bollworm as early as 1909.[140] Yet the central government took no action to understand the etiology of the pest until the late 1930s, despite the importance of cotton to the economy of the country. The result was that local officials grappling with the problem on a day-to-day basis advanced their own control measures on the basis of their understanding of the bionomics of the pest. Many advocated a change in planting dates so as to effect a clear dead or close season separating the cotton crop of one year from the next.[141] Implied in what came to be known as the time-of-planting proposal was the assumption that cotton stalks infected in one season carried the pest into the next season. Local work schedules made transmission easy. The combination of dimba with munda cultivation meant that there were cotton stalks standing somewhere in the Valley from November (in those few places where cotton was planted as a pure crop at the beginning of the rainy season) to October (where the late-planted dimba culture dominated).

Although most officials accepted this reasoning[142] and the need for a change in planting dates, they remained divided on the question of the timing of the dead and planting seasons. For reasons to be explored in the next chapter, some advocated early planting, others late planting.[143] The debate continued with no clear resolution until the early 1950s, well after officials in Zomba had commissioned an investigation into the problem.[144]

Like the final report published in 1945, the preliminary findings made public by the government entomologist, C. Smee, breathed fresh air into the debate.[145] Smee and his colleagues raised the discussion above the level of cultivation techniques by analyzing the bionomics of the pest. "The most important factor," they argued, "is a prolonged pupal diapause during the dry season which enables it to survive in numbers from one season to the next and renders it *independent* of alternative host plants"[146] (emphasis added). The pest did not, in other words, need cotton stalks in order to survive and multiply between seasons. The pupal diapause took place in the soil, some ten to fifteen centimeters deep.[147] Cultivation techniques had nothing to do with this most important link in the pest's chain of reproduction. The red bollworm thrived in the northern belt, where peasants planted cotton as a pure crop at the beginning of the rains and where a clear dead season was automatically maintained.[148] The study went further to conclude that climatic conditions played a major role in determining regional variations "in the time of beginning, and the duration of, the diapause."[149]

The studies faulted local agricultural systems only to the extent that they exacerbated the level of infestation. This was because the "severity of the attack in any year depends largely on the relationship between the peak period of moth emergence and the state of development of the crop at the time." The earliest planted crop that started fruiting in March or April suffered the least damage for two main reasons. First, it was attacked by moths of the first two generations only. Moreover, the infestation took place when members of the second generation were still young and weak and most cotton plants had fully established themselves. Hit hardest was the late-planted crop that started fruiting around May, when "the ratio of moth eggs to fruiting points is always unduly high." It was still in its early stages of development when it became the target of the combined attacks by the fully grown flying caterpillars of the first, second, and succeeding generations prior to the commencement of the long pupal diapause.[150]

Whatever their intellectual value, the findings of the entomologists had little effect on the way the state subsequently handled the problem of the red bollworm. For financial reasons officials did not follow up the implications of the conclusion that local systems of production merely exaggerated but did not create the problem. They continued to focus their attention exclusively on production techniques in their search for a solution. Moreover, the timing of the intervention had little to do with the alarms raised by the findings. The state began to take action only in the late 1940s, after the permanent inundation of the dambo had drastically reduced cotton output in Port Herald District.

5.3. Dimba Agriculture: From Boom to Bust

> These dimbas are more than a second line of defence and their annual value to the populace and to the district cannot be overstressed.[151]

> The flood plain of the Shire river together with the various madimba areas through which it flows have been heavily inundated and water now stands many feet deep over an extensive area of valuable land which normally would be under various crops. The loss to cotton land acres has been considerable and the maize crop has suffered severely in many instances.[152]

Before the dramatic events described in the second quotation had taken place, no argument could have persuaded Nyasaland's rulers in Zomba to pursue one major implication of the campaign for early planting: the elimination of dimba cotton. The cotton economy in the leading cotton-growing district, Port Herald, depended on the survival of the dimba culture. The regime had proven highly resilient to most diseases and pests that afflicted rain-fed agriculture, including the dreaded red bollworm.[153] Dimba production and the prosperity of cotton agriculture were inseparable.

In addition to producing the best cotton from the area, dimba agriculture bore the brunt of the old and new strains in the munda system. Most dimba crops were resilient to attacks by locusts and other pests that devastated munda farming. During the early 1930s dimba production also absorbed the effects of the drop in cotton prices. Squeezed between a failing market and a faltering munda regime, growers looked to the dambo for survival:

> Through the Lower River the dimba gardens are in excellent condition and very much larger areas have been planted this year than ever before. From the north end of Chikwawa to the south end of the Lower Shire maize, sweet potatoes, beans (phaseolus and vigna spp) and pumpkins (maungu, matanga and mphonda) are yielding well or give promise of doing so.[154]

Sweet potatoes gained more significance after the 1930s following the failure of maize, which, together with mchewere, had enjoyed great popularity since the early 1920s as a result of the decline in gonkho culture.

Mchewere usurped the position of preeminence formerly given to gonkho[155] only in those areas without extensive dambo land, for although as a fast-ripening crop mchewere fit the cotton-growing schedule, it could not survive drought and was moreover subject to most diseases and pests affecting munda agriculture. Growers who had access to dimba plots looked to maize as a more viable substitute for gonkho. An acre in the Dabanyi Marsh yielded on the average three thousand pounds of maize. The corresponding figure for the Dinde was two thousand pounds.[156]

One reason for the remarkable difference in productivity between the Dabanyi and the Dinde marshes may have arisen from the fact that maize in the Dinde competed with cotton. A garden census taken in 1933 revealed that 66.2 percent of all cotton grown in Port Herald District was raised in the Dinde.[157] The maize was planted in alternate rows with cotton.[158] If the practice had ever threatened cotton, as some field officers believed it did in the mid-1910s,[159] the tables were reversed by the 1930s. Not only were the average maize yields in the Dinde low, but in order to accommodate the labor demands of cotton many peasants did not raise another maize crop after harvesting the first, which was planted at the same time as cotton.[160] This was in sharp contrast to the practice followed in Chikwawa District, where only 33.9 percent of cotton fields were on the dambo.[161] There peasants raised several consecutive maize crops within a single season, very much as their ancestors had done in the mid-nineteenth century.

> In the Chikwawa District where, to a large extent, maize takes the place of mapira . . . there are some very fine dimba (low-lying heavier soil) gardens. Most of the late planted crop [maize] will be ready towards the end of the month of October.[162]

The maize fields in the district were also looked after much better than the millet gardens on the mphala.[163] Economic change since the turn of the century had reemphasized the centrality of the dimba regime in the reproductive cycle of the peasantry. Its collapse after 1939 was bound to have enormous sociopolitical consequences.

Having reached its lowest recorded levels during 1913–15, when prerainy season (December) depths plunged to between one and two feet,[164] the Tchiri River started to accumulate water steadily until the drought of 1920–23 briefly interrupted the trend. The new levels the river reached immediately after the drought remained relatively constant up to 1933. Serious floods affecting the entire dambo were a rare phenomenon and were highly prized, notwithstanding the damage they often did to human life and early-planted crops. They left enough moisture to support dimba crops against drought in the absence of *chiperoni* rains—light showers that fall in the dry season in July and August.[165] This pattern, which had been in effect since the late 1890s with only minor seasonal variations, began to alter in 1934 as a result of an unexpected increase in the level of Lake Malawi.

The year 1934 confounded many contemporary observers: the river reached a record depth of seventeen feet, ten inches at the beginning of March and dropped by only four feet by the end of the month.[166] Falling on an inflated water system, the rainy season of 1934–35 quickly drove up the level of the Tchiri River to nineteen feet by January 1935.[167] For the first time January rather than March became the wettest month, and the waters did not leave the marshes until August, which was usually the driest month.

More dambo was lost to flooding in 1936 after Lake Malawi overflowed the sandbar separating it from the Tchiri on the northern end of Lake Malombe.[168] Colonial observers who had welcomed the floods of 1934 as a force in the regeneration of the dambo began to grow apprehensive:

> The steadily maintained flow of a heavy volume of flood waters is commented upon. The increase in average level for the month at no less than 5 feet and 7½ inches is a very striking feature also.[169]

Their fears materialized when the river hit the twenty-foot mark in January 1938 and ruined over twenty-five hundred gardens.[170] The volume was so large the following year that the river reversed its course on meeting the equally engorged Dziwedziwe tributary in Mozambique territory. The result was the famous Bomani floods that ruined an estimated 120,000 acres and drove every inhabitant of the Dinde and Dabanyi into temporary refuge on the higher mphala on either side of the river.[171] Four years later, in 1943, it was estimated that the swamps had extended some five miles into what had previously been a mphala zone.[172] The floods of 1945, 1947, and 1952 interrupted a general trend toward the desiccation of the marshes during the second half of the 1940s and early 1950s.[173] The deluge of 1957 permanently reversed the trend, dashing any hope for the revival of a full-fledged dimba regime and reaffirming the dominance of the munda agricultural cycle, which has limited much food and all cotton cultivation to mphala land.

With the flood season extended from December to June, the inflated Tchiri River ruled out the possibility of raising dimba cotton. The end of dimba cotton had started already in 1938:

> As previously suggested the dimba cotton may be discounted for the current year as it can only form a very small percentage of the total acreage. The cotton together with the maize is waterlogged and ill attended.[174]

Peasants who tried to raise cotton on the drier parts of the marshes the following season were in for a disappointment. The Bomani floods washed away the fields. By 1940 it became obvious that the era of dimba cotton agriculture was over. The Valley was joining other areas of the country where cotton was grown exclusively as a munda crop. The proponents of early planting as a method of curtailing the red bollworm did not have to legislate the elimination of dimba cotton after the floods.

Port Herald District felt the consequences of the collapse of dimba cotton more severely than Chikwawa. Dimba agriculture had formed only a small percentage of the total cotton output of Chikwawa. Its collapse did not entail a drastic restructuring of the dominant farming practices of the region. Instead of reshaping, the permanent inundation of the marshes expanded munda cotton production as a result of the influx of immigrants from both the Dabanyi and the Dinde marshes. The migrations, which eventually made Chikwawa a more populous area than Port Herald,[175] converged on the Ngabu chiefdom of the district. An area that villagers had until then tried to avoid on account of the presence of wild animals (see Chapter 7), the chiefdom enjoyed one advantage over other regions of the district: its fertile makande soils, which proved to be as suitable for cotton as the lost dambo. The immigrants exploited the rich soils, transforming Chikwawa into the leading cotton-growing district in the Valley and in the country as a whole. The former backwater emerged from the Bomani floods with a more dynamic and successful cotton economy, as the figures in Table 5.2 show.

Table 5.2 Peasant Cotton Export Figures, 1940–1960
(Seed Cotton in Tons)

Year	Port Herald	Chikwawa	Total Tchiri Valley	Total Nyasaland	Valley Exports as a Percentage of Total Exports
1940	1,017	1,230	2,247	3,520	63.8
1941	648	691	1,339	2,901	46.1
1942	1,806	4,025	5,831	7,691	75.8
1943	780	1,331	2,111	3,411	61.8
1945	1,245	2,837	4,082	5,161	79.0[a]
1947	2,538	2,606	5,144	6,910	74.3
1948	1,989	4,853	6,842	8,137	84.0[a]
1949	537	54	591	1,424	41.5[a]
1950	5,227	100[b]	5,327	5,742	92.7
1951	855	715	1,570	2,368	66.3
1952	851	4,927	5,778	7,704	75.0
1953	491	6,912	7,403	9,730	76.0
1954	961	4,142	5,103	7,177	71.1
1955	565	6,148	6,713	8,589	78.1
1956	566	1,617	2,183	3,288	66.3
1957	548	3,034	3,582	4,288	83.5
1958	661	4,048	4,709	5,513	85.4
1959	519	8,447	8,966	10,029	89.4
1960	1,873	9,153	11,026	12,515	88.1

Sources: Nyasaland Protectorate, *Annual Report of the Department of Agriculture,* 1940–60. The figures for some years include tenant-grown cotton (see Chapter 3): 506 in 1940, 396 in 1941, 1,141 in 1942, 497 in 1943, 687 in 1945, 745 in 1952, 623 in 1954, 202 in 1956, 346 in 1957, 608 in 1958, 731 in 1959, and 1,051 in 1960.

[a]The original figures for these years are in pounds.

[b]I arrived at this figure by subtracting the figure given for Port Herald from that given for the Valley.

The dominance of the munda cycle spelled unmitigated disaster for Port Herald, which has since become the country's "dead south." The expansion of the marshes reduced the amount of mphala land available for cultivation in this densely populated district. Moreover, although one may argue about the exact nature and extent of soil depletion in the area, there can be no doubt that the mphala of the post-Bomani era was a different land than the one that had sustained cotton agriculture at the turn of the century. Three decades of intensive cotton and food cultivation must have distorted the soil's original structure and productivity. Cotton had definitely promoted the propagation of all sorts of diseases and pests that became more conspicuous if not actually more severe in their attacks after the inundation of the marshes had reduced the amount of mphala land. Infestation by the red bollworm was reported to have seriously curtailed munda cotton production in the district in 1945, 1947, 1948, and 1951.[176] Subsequent measures adopted by the colonial state to save the tottering cotton economy proved counterproductive. Ill conceived and high-handed, they drove many growers, especially the wives of migrant laborers, out of cotton agriculture altogether.

The combined effect of the above trends can be seen in Table 5.2. Cotton export figures dropped from 3,776 tons in 1935 (see Table 4.1, p. 137) to a mere 648 tons in 1941. A revival of dimba-grown cotton during the second half of the 1940s as a result of a drop in river levels was arrested by the exceptionally high floods of 1952 and 1957. Port Herald, once the center of cotton agriculture, entered the 1960s as one of the least significant cotton-growing districts of the country.

Chapter 7 will show that the decline of cotton cultivation in the district was also directly related to the food crisis that has plagued the area since the 1940s. The inundation of the marshes stalled all dimba food production in some areas; in others, food cultivation became confined to a few high grounds within and on the fringes of the Dinde. Production on such islands always remained a precarious undertaking. The longer flood season allowed the cultivation of only early-maturing crops like sweet potatoes against the constant danger of annual flooding. Floods killed sweet potatoes on such land in 1945, 1947, and 1952.[177] Dimba agriculture lost its significance in the overall economy as major food crops, in addition to cotton, came to be grown exclusively on the mphala. In turn, the dominance of the munda cycle exposed the food economy to the perennial threat of drought, plant disease, and pests. In 1941 the stem borer reduced the mchewere crop by 40 percent in some areas and by as much as 100 percent in others.[178]

Together with the failure of cotton agriculture, the attacks helped deepen the food crisis that formed the background to colonial intervention after 1939. Unable to collect taxes from a hungry population, the district commissioner for Port Herald was left with little option in 1941 but to urge the central government to start work on the soil conservation scheme that had been under discussion since the late 1930s:

> It is necessary therefore that work should be provided for natives in the southern part of this district to enable them to pay tax this year or early next year. Considerable and necessary works can be undertaken in connection with soil conservation in this district. . . . My object in writing is to ask that they may be carried out sooner, both for the purpose of saving the tax position this year and for providing a means of earning money for food.[179]

Hunger and the shortage of money forced a reluctant district commissioner to accept the unpopular task of supervising a centrally planned conservation project. Nyasaland's rulers may have entertained many conservationist ideas. They did not, however, translate such ideas into action until they were forced to do so by the events of the post-Bomani era. Colonial agricultural policy was profoundly reactive.

6

Reactive Colonial Attempts to Restructure a Distorted Economy, 1930–1960

> The native methods of cotton cultivation appear to suit the Lower River conditions better than the methods employed on the experimental station judging by the yield per acre obtained from both.[1]

> They appear to be very backward and listless; agriculturally, at all events. . . .[2]

> An extensive, low efficient, system of agriculture is to be replaced by a more intensive and efficient system, which will have its repercussions not only on cotton growing but also on the production of food and other cash crops. Without such a development the economic future of the Lower River would be far from bright.[3]

For all its dramatic political and economic consequences in Nyasaland, the Second World War does not constitute a watershed in the agricultural history of the Valley. The two watersheds that divide the history of the region in this century are the Great Depression and the Bomani floods of 1939. The Depression highlighted the contradictory position of the state as a regulator of conflicting class interests at the marketplace. The experience led to the passage of the sweeping Cotton Ordinance of 1934, a pack of inconsistent legislation that drew the state more deeply into the cotton market.

Colonial records of the 1930s imply that the war did no more than provide a political and ideological context for state intervention in peasant production in the Valley. The dynamics of intervention had a local origin. The collapse of dimba agriculture after the Bomani floods of 1939 threatened an end to the historic role of the Valley as the center of the cotton economy in Nyasaland. It weakened the position of those colonial experts who, for expediency rather than ideological commitment, had argued for the status quo. They subsequently joined hands with the interventionists, whose influence grew with each crisis in the economy. Hypotheses about the ecological effect of the prevalent cultivation techniques, which many experts had rightly challenged during the 1930s, became firm scientific knowledge by the late 1940s, when the object of state intervention was to harmonize conflicting trends within and between the physical and social conditions of peasant production. Colonial experts had gone to the Valley to correct a situation, and it was only as they were doing this that they became carried away by conservationist ideas and ideologies that were floating around the colonial world.

6.1. Reorganizing the Cotton Market After the Depression

> Attempts to improve the grade, and consequently the price, by sorting the crop after picking, and to enforce this sorting by official "classing" before the crop goes to the buyers . . . are in no way constructive, in improving the native crop, they imply the assumption of a responsibility by Government which is properly the buyer's business.[4]

The Great Depression sharply revealed the contradictions inherent in the state's position as a regulator of the conflicting relations between cotton sellers and buyers. It had taught the British how dangerous it was for the state to create the impression that it was in control of market forces. The fact that despite this revelation the state did not succeed in disengaging itself from the cotton trade represented, quite ironically, another outcome of the lessons of the Depression. The actions of the British Cotton Growing Association had weakened every argument for monopoly and strengthened the determination of those officials who wanted to throw the market open to competition. But by placing cotton growers at the mercy of unscrupulous traders, competition drew the state deeper into the marketing phase of peasant cotton agriculture.[5]

As the market began to recover in 1934, the administration passed the second most comprehensive cotton bill since the ordinance of 1910.[6] Although section 43 of the ordinance envisaged the possibility of a monopsony, the prevailing mood in the country was decidedly against monopoly. Granting a monopsony to the association had not helped the situation during the Depression. The bill sought to improve rather than change the situation that had existed since 1931, whereby all merchants, including the dreaded Indians, could compete with one another.

So strong was antimonopoly sentiment among the country's rulers that Governor Smith was ready to antagonize the supporters of the association in the Colonial Office.

The world demand for cotton was so high in 1934 that the Cotton Growing Association, which had long been used to a protected market, could not compete with new cotton buyers such as the Liverpool-Uganda Company. The association consequently turned to the state with an application for monopoly rights in the Southern Province, which included the Lower Tchiri River.[7] As usual, the letter was a long litany of the benefits that had accrued to the country as a result of the association's past operations. It warned the state of the dangers that "unscrupulous" traders posed to the cotton economy. Finally, in order to make the offer more attractive to the deficit-ridden administration, the association promised to pay the government *4d.* on every 112 pounds of seed cotton bought under the agreement.[8]

The application received a mixed review from the director of agriculture, but the governor's deputy, K. L. Hall, sent a favorable recommendation to the Colonial Office.[9] In order to accommodate the interests of new and prospective buyers, Hall recommended that the British Cotton Growing Association be granted monopoly rights in the Southern Province as it had requested, leaving the western lakeshore region and the Northern Province exclusively to the Nyasaland Cotton Company and the Liverpool-Uganda Company, respectively. The Nyasaland Cotton Company in the lakeshore region was to establish a ginnery at Salima and promote cotton growing along the newly completed Blantyre-Salima railway extension. The agreements would last five years from 1935.[10]

As one might expect, officials in the Colonial Office found the revenue-raising clause of the Cotton Growing Association offer so attractive that they proposed to grant "monopoly rights over the whole Protectorate" to the association.[11] But with the experience of the Depression still fresh in his mind, the governor rejected the proposal[12] and, after much wrangling, the entire market was thrown open for competition.

There were only a few minor changes to those provisions of the ordinance of 1934 which regulated relations among buyers. In 1938 the state introduced the auction system, according to which a buyer could bid the whole cotton crop brought to a particular market.[13] It is doubtful, however, that the system, which had been tried in the Valley in 1921–22 but had to be abandoned because of its unpopularity among the peasantry,[14] was repeated during the war when the government purchased cotton on behalf of the British Ministry of Supplies. This practice, necessitated by war conditions, set the precedent for the Cotton Marketing Board that was set up in 1951.[15] The activities of the Board and its relations with cotton-buying firms such as the British Cotton Growing Association lie beyond the purview of this study.[16]

Open competition did not lessen the role of the state in the marketing system. On the contrary, it deepened colonial intervention in the conflicts between cotton sellers and buyers and renewed the controversy over ginning rights. As indicated in Chapter 4, pressure from the Cotton Growing Association during the mid-1910s had forced the state to reverse its earlier policy, which had allowed European planters to operate their own ginneries. The issue subsequently went underground as European cotton agriculture foundered and the association won exclusive rights over peasant-grown cotton. The association had ginned all the cotton it purchased from 1923 to 1931. The advent of new buyers revived the old issue. Many buyers wanted to erect their own ginneries if only in order to avoid the high ginning rates demanded by the association. They also argued, quite correctly, that because ginneries also served as distribution centers of cotton seeds, the association enjoyed real as opposed to legal buying advantage. Many growers believed that they had to sell their cotton to the owner of the ginnery from which they had received seeds.[17]

Still reeling from its defeat on the issue of monopoly buying, the Cotton Growing Association fought hard to stop the erection of rival ginneries. Using the same tactics and threats that it had employed during the 1910s, the association argued that undercapitalized ginneries would produce inferior seeds that would be passed over to growers and lead to a deterioration in the quality of the country's cotton exports. It also pointed out the fact that the existing ginneries were operating below capacity. Creating more ginneries would be a costly economic decision for the country. The government would incur unnecessary expense in transporting cotton seeds from a ginnery located in a non-cotton-growing area to areas where they were needed for planting.[18]

Official reaction to the arguments of the association was less consistent at this time than it had been during the 1910s. The association was fighting not only against a group of unorganized local Europeans, as it had done during the 1910s. It was also fighting against another London-based conglomerate, the British Central Africa Company, which, to complicate matters, was a major shareholder of the powerful Nyasaland Railways.[19] The Cotton Growing Association had to concede another defeat. The British Central Africa Company received permission to erect a ginnery at Makande and was able to make a profit out of the operation despite the fact that the area did not grow any cotton. Favorable arrangements with the Nyasaland Railways made it possible for the British Central Africa Company to purchase cotton in distant places like the Lower Tchiri Valley and rail it to Makande and back to the Valley for export at a lower cost than any other company could do with cotton that was bought and ginned in the Valley.[20]

To the extent that the British Cotton Growing Association still maintained its ginneries at Port Herald, Chiromo, Fort Johnston (Mangochi), and Vua in Karonga, the real losers in the war for ginning rights were the small traders. As the director of agriculture manipulated zoning rules that tallied certain cotton-growing areas to particular ginneries[21] in order to broaden the boundaries from which the British Central Africa Company could draw cotton for its ginnery at Makande, the Cotton Bill of 1934 tightened the conditions for licensing new ginneries.[22] Few cotton buyers could qualify for ginning licenses under the new regulations. Many settlers, some of whom owned gins that were now banned, were accordingly infuriated.[23] But their anger did not move the director of agriculture. Colonial marketing policy continued to be heavily biased against local entrepreneurs, just as the new ordinance did not diminish the role of the state in the relations between cotton sellers and buyers.

The presence of many cotton buyers created new problems concerning the pricing system, cotton grading, and touting. Open competition among traders opened a floodgate of old and new forms of touting. Some buyers tried to attract customers by providing them with bags for carrying their cotton to market and by bribing village headmen.[24] Village headmen were given money to influence their subjects' choice of a buyer at the market. Other merchants and their agents purchased cotton in the villages at night, which saved peasants from the need to carry their produce to market. Those growers who reached the marketplace were treated to such attractions as "dumpy figures" placed next to an agent's shed and loud music played on the gramophone.[25] Indeed, as one woman reportedly told a government official, it was more difficult to sell than to grow cotton during the mid-1930s.[26]

Although it made buying agents less attentive to the quality of the cotton they were offered, competition did not guarantee higher producer prices. Knowing that they would lose by purchasing badly graded cotton, buyers perfected the strategies for cheating peasants. Some posted a higher price than the official minimum, but made sure that in weighing they "knock[ed] off a few" pounds.[27] Another common strategy was to purchase at high prices at the beginning of the day and lower the rates after the first sellers had spread the news about the prices.[28] That way merchants were able to beat their rivals and to make up for whatever losses they might have incurred by buying cotton that was improperly graded or mixed with foreign substances such as stones.[29]

In order to curb these and other abuses, the state enacted a series of amendments to the Cotton Ordinance of 1934 in 1936, 1938, 1946, and 1951. The amendments of 1936 and 1946 addressed the problem of touting in several ways. One provision limited the number of agents a principal buyer could employ at any market. No license holder was permitted to have more than four agents (including himself) in one market. It also became illegal for a licensed buyer to use permits issued for one market at another market. Consequently, the Department of Agriculture stopped issuing cotton-buying licenses. Merchants could get the licenses only from district commissioners, who together with other government officials were to ensure that only those buyers with locally issued permits purchased cotton at particular markets.[30] Finally, it became a criminal offense for any buyer or his agents to purchase cotton outside the officially designated marketplaces and market hours, which ran from sunrise to sunset on weekdays.[31]

Other amendments grappled with the problem of pricing at two levels. The first concerned the formula to be used in determining the official minimum rates.[32] After much wrangling, it was decided in 1938 to base local minimum prices on the value of "American Middling 3 months futures," although it is not clear from the record whether and for how long the formula was employed.[33] Colonial sources are clear only on the attempts made to resolve the second aspect of the pricing problem: ensuring that traders paid the official minimum prices. Traders were required to display on blackboards the prices they were going to offer each day. In order to eliminate the practice whereby buyers offered high prices to early arrivals and lower prices to latecomers during the same day, the government demanded that any changes be recorded on the blackboards.[34] Buyers were also required to issue receipts to their customers indicating the amount of cotton purchased and the money given. The seller would show the receipt to a government representative before leaving the marketplace. All buyers had to hand over copies of their transactions to the Department of Agriculture at the close of each market season.[35] From 1951 on it became illegal for any merchant to give a price that was "higher or lower than the price for the time being fixed" by the director of agriculture.[36] Finally, other revisions to the Cotton Ordinance of 1934 dealt with the closely related problem of grading. Some of the provisions in this category sought to discourage buyers from taking improperly graded cotton, whereas others, especially those of 1938, tried to redefine and refine the existing grading standards.[37]

It is difficult to assess the effectiveness of the regulations passed after the British Cotton Growing Association lost its monopoly buying rights. The impression one gets from the sources is that the flurry of legislation did not do much to improve the position of the grower vis-à-vis the merchant. The Department of Agriculture did not have the personnel needed to enforce the new rules. The continual enactment of new rules and amendments is an indirect proof of their ineffectiveness. It is nonetheless clear that however ineffective these legal provisions were, they undermined the position of officials such as H. C. Ducker who stood for "open" markets.[38] These officials lost to paternalists like W. H. Evans, a well-known cotton dealer in the lakeshore region, who believed in the necessity of tightly supervised or "closed" markets.[39] Peasants, the paternalists argued, had more confidence in government agents than in private buyers. The state was drawn more deeply into the marketing phase of peasant cotton agriculture while at the same time other developments entangled it in the still more problematic issue of production.

6.2. Uncoordinated Intervention and Accommodation

> This suggests that previous conclusions were hastily arrived at & formed without sufficiently substantiated evidence (figures) to work upon or without investigation of the possibilities obtaining to December & January sowings.[40]

> The position of cotton as a native crop on the Lower Shire is somewhat complicated, and it is easy to see how various schools of thought have arisen, especially since the shortage in the late rains of the past season or two have tended to control insect damage on December planted cotton on the Port Herald Experimental Station.[41]

The Nyasaland Legislature passed the sweeping Cotton Bill of 1934 after the Department of Agriculture had taken over the Nyachiperi Experimental Station near Port Herald Township in 1931.[42] Established in 1910 for the purpose of serving the European planter community, the farm was closed in 1922[43] — a year before the state officially withdrew its support for estate farming in the Valley. In 1923 the governor rejected the proposal for the state to use part of its share of the profits made by the British Cotton Growing Association to employ a resident agricultural officer who would also conduct experiments at the station. The farm had nearly collapsed when the Empire Cotton Growing Corporation, a research consortium, took it over in 1925 under the supervision of H. C. Ducker.[44] But Ducker, who was in charge of two other stations at Domira Bay and Makwapala, lived in Zomba, and no experiments were conducted at Nyachiperi until the arrival of E. Lawrence as an employee of Empire in 1930.[45] Lawrence had spent the previous year studying agriculture at Cambridge University. The Department of Agriculture appointed him in 1931 as the first agricultural officer in the Valley since the departure of N. D. Clegg in 1922. His official duties included the study of cotton and of "native food crops with a view to their improvement & use in rotations with cotton, native cash crops, study of local system or systems of agriculture with special reference to soil erosion."[46] Intervention in the peasant economy was to expand beyond the market into what Marx called "the hidden abode of production."

Lawrence and his successors, especially Frank Barker, who came to the Valley in 1932 or 1933,[47] made every effort to fulfill their duties as defined by the director of agriculture. For example, Lawrence tried, without much success, to institute communal grain stores that were to function as food reservoirs and as sources for planting seeds.[48] For his part, Barker addressed the problem of the red bollworm and other insects by stepping up the campaign for early planting[49] and early stalk uprooting that had started before the closure of the Nyachiperi Experimental Station in 1922.[50] Attempts were also made to combat soil erosion on mphala lands. Beginning in 1931 European officers themselves or their African assistants—the native agricultural instructors (*akapitao-a-malimidwe*)—made several trips to the Chididi hill area to teach peasants how to construct contour ridges (*mitumbira*).[51] Rules were also made to ban the cultivation of mountain slopes and riverbanks.

Lawrence complemented these measures with three projects or proposals. The first involved the creation of village forest areas designed to check erosion and to supply villagers with firewood.[52] The second proposal called for the planting of belts of grass at one-mile intervals, running parallel to the mountains in the west and the railway line in the east, all the way from Bangula in the north to Port Herald township in the south. The grass belts were to prevent storm water from carrying away topsoil to the Tchiri River.[53] Finally, Lawrence tried to encourage villagers to move from the "congested" southern part of Port Herald

District to the lightly populated area between Thangadzi and Mkombedzi-wa-fodya rivers on the west bank.[54]

A combination of political, economic, and ideological forces worked together to undermine the spate of interventionist activity during the 1930s. As Chapter 7 will explore in detail, rural resistance stymied the resettlement project, whereas government's reluctance to spend its limited financial resources was largely responsible for the death of the grass-planting proposal. Then there were the more intriguing questions about the feasibility and effectiveness of the proposed projects. Officials in Zomba were equally unclear about the nature of the problems that were to be attacked. They did not see any justification for launching an all-out campaign against the region's techniques of production in view of two facts. The first and more important was that local techniques continued to yield the largest percentage of the country's cotton exports. The second was that expert opinion was highly divided on the nature of the techniques (see Chapter 5), partly because of the complexity of the situation itself[55] and partly because of the absence of any detailed studies on the relationship of local techniques of production to the various problems affecting munda agriculture. Barker did not, for example, get much official support in his efforts to combat the red bollworm.

As documented in the previous chapter, most officials agreed on the need for a "dead" or "close" season separating one cotton crop from another, but there was no consensus on when to institute the close season and, by implication, when planting should start. The result was the famous planting-time controversy, which divided colonial experts into two warring factions. The first was led by Ducker, who argued for late planting. According to his proposal, the optimum planting time should fall between late January and late March and the dead season should start from mid-November.[56] Any land that, like the lighter mphala, could not be profitably used for cotton cultivation under this schedule should be put to other uses, such as food or groundnut production.[57]

An entirely different schedule was proposed by Barker, the most articulate proponent of early planting. Peasants should plant cotton at the beginning of the first rains in early December and maintain a dead season from October on.[58] Any piece of land, such as the low-lying dambo, that could not fit this schedule should be dropped out of cotton agriculture. Cotton could be saved from the ravages of the red bollworm only by a complete transformation of existing work schedules.

Barker failed to impress his fellow experts and, through them, his superiors in Zomba. No one in 1935 was willing to accept the contention that his plan was based on the results of experimental work at Nyachiperi.[59] Data collecting at the farm had started only in the 1931–32 season,[60] and the results of the findings were inconclusive, as Barker himself was sometimes forced to admit: "It is most unfortunate that we have no really conclusive data to work upon other than that obtained during the last two seasons. . . ."[61] Two years later, in 1936, his critics pointed to a more serious problem with the research conducted at the station. The light soils at the farm had become unrepresentative of the common mphala lands as a result of changes in rainfall patterns since the late 1920s. Data collected at the farm could not be used as a basis for prediction for the entire Valley.[62] Ducker subsequently attributed the high incidence of red bollworm infestation in 1936 to the success of Barker's campaign for early planting in some areas of the Valley. The combination of early planting in some localities with late planting in others eliminated, according to Ducker, the unregulated dead season growers had maintained before.[63] Other critics such as the local manager of the British Cotton Growing Association, J. A. Lee, dismissed the link between the red bollworm and the absence of a dead season. The pest was found in the area long before the prevailing techniques of production had become firmly established. In 1936 it devastated cotton raised outside the Valley, where growers planted early and where a prolonged dead season was maintained automatically.[64] Lee anticipated the findings of the investigative teams commissioned by the government to study the problem. The red bollworm did not depend on cotton stalks in order to reproduce itself from one season to another. Local cultivation techniques contributed to the intensity but did not create the problem itself.[65]

It is important not to exaggerate the significance of expert opinion in shaping colonial agricultural policy. As we shall see in the next section, the findings of the investigative teams made little difference in policy measures adopted from the late 1940s onward. The absence of such knowledge during the 1930s was not a critical factor either. The inertia of the country's rulers in Zomba was economic and political in origin. Like the cotton cultivation blueprint of 1909, Barker's plan was bound to ignite rural opposition. Planting cotton at the same time as food crops at the start of the rainy season would intensify the problem of labor allocation between food and cash crop production. No politician in Zomba was ready to impose such an unpopular work schedule as long as peasants in the Valley were making their share of the wealth of the mother country. Ducker's plan made more sense precisely because it was not a program of action. Built in to the late-planting proposal was the recognition that dimba cultivation could start only after the floods had receded and when the low-lying dambo was out of danger of being reinundated.[66] Forcing growers to end planting in mid-January, as Barker wanted, amounted to eliminating a substantial portion of the dimba cotton regime. Any scientific or pseudoscientific explanation in support of late planting made real sense.[67] It was a plan for the status quo.

Thus, instead of precipitating an uncontrolled wave of interventions, the reopening of the Nyachiperi farm led to a greater appreciation for and accommodation with the local agricultural systems. The same Lawrence who a year later would lay out big plans for dealing with soil erosion not only denied the seriousness of the problem in 1930 but flatly rejected the suggestion that his responsibilities as an employee of the Empire Cotton Growing Corporation included the introduction of new techniques to the area. "Until more is known," he asserted, "about the optimum spacings, etc., for millets, in the district, the Native Agricultural Instructors are not told to advise anything very drastic in the way of change."[68] Two years later, in 1932, he was to challenge the terms of his appointment as district agricultural officer by emphasizing the positive aspects of such practices as heavy seeding[69] and, in particular, intercropping. "It is even possible," he wrote, "that cotton is better for being grown with maize instead of being rotated with maize."[70] Cotton intercropped with maize or mchewere millet enjoyed the benefit of being shaded from the scorching sun.[71] Thus at the Cotton Conference held in Zomba in 1934, everyone agreed that intercropping was a sound practice that should be encouraged in the Lower Tchiri Valley.[72] The task was to improve existing techniques rather than introduce new ones.[73] The director of agriculture summed up the prevailing accommodationist sentiment with reference to the place of the local practices within the larger context of the peasant economy:

> A close study of native methods on the Lower River has shown that the native practice of growing millets, cotton and legumes in the same garden is a sound one when the time at his disposal for agricultural work, his way of living and his fear of hunger are taken into account.[74]

This was in 1933. Five years later, Lawrence castigated the proponents of early planting, reiterated his faith in the judgment of the peasantry, and emphasized the complexity of the physical conditions of rural work: "There is no one optimum planting date in the Lower River that will suit all soils and all seasons. The range of planting [dates] is wide and . . . the native can be trusted to plant at the proper time. Far too much emphasis has been laid on time of planting in the past with absolutely no value at all to the cotton crop."[75] Ducker carried the implications of the argument for accommodation to their logical and practical conclusion. On the one hand, he blamed the failure of the plantation system on the unwillingness of European farmers to learn from African growers and, on the other, advocated late planting and intercropping among cotton producers in the Karonga District.[76] The 1930s were not the decade for uncontrolled interventionism. The community of the colonizers was less monolithic in its thinking about peasant production at this time than it would become later.

6.3. Coping with the Myths and Realities of Soil Erosion and Population Pressure

> Put very briefly, this position is caused by too many people multiplying too fast and attempting by traditional and inefficient methods to derive an ever-increasing standard of living from a limited amount of land.[77]

Colonial intervention in peasant production after 1940 did not represent a completely new development. It had its roots in the contradictory economic trends (see Chapter 5) and conflicting colonial views of the 1930s. The 1940s represented the triumph of one set of economic conditions and ideas that had been largely suppressed during the preceding period. There was no real hiatus between the two periods in the history of the Valley. Nor was the triumph of interventionism after 1940 an inevitable consequence of the economic imperatives of Africa's "second colonization" or of the supposed "maturity" in colonial conservationist thinking. There is no evidence that colonial understanding of the critical ecological problems affecting the Valley made any progress in the two decades after 1940. Interventionists won the debate largely by accident. The inundation of the marshes undercut the material base of the argument for the status quo. There was no dimba cotton to defend after 1940.[78] The end of dimba cotton and the recurrence of food shortages in the absence of any ideological commitment to the status quo formed fertile ground for the interventionist agenda.

The agenda was two-pronged. One aim was to restore fertility to the depleted lands and the second to create new lands for agricultural production. The latter objective was to be achieved by reclaiming the lost lands in the marshes (the Shire Valley Project) and by resettling peasants from "congested" to lightly populated areas. Study of the Shire Valley Project and the resettlement schemes suggests that after they had passed the threshold of their own inertia, colonial planners entered a world of visions and utopias that had no foundation in the economic and social realities of the Valley: colonial policy had become relatively autonomous.

6.3.1. Measures to Conserve the Old Lands

> It is becoming increasingly obvious that this country must make a complete change in its agricultural policy within the very near future unless it is to meet disaster. The population continues to increase and there is as yet no sign that the African cultivator is willing or able to change his ways. . . . A method of mass attack must be found and put into operation quickly.[79]

> The creation of so many new offences under Native Authorities rules in connection with agriculture [has] resulted in an increase in court and office work. . . .[80]

Although many more experts joined the debate on soil erosion during the two decades after the Bomani floods, their conception of the problem did not differ significantly from that of their predecessors. As late as 1955 the director of agriculture, R. W. Kettlewell, lamented the dearth of knowledge about "the biological aspects of the problem and the technical means whereby high yields may be obtained and maintained without impairing the productivity of the soil."[81] The interventionists of the post-Bomani era operated under the same assumptions as those that had informed men like Lawrence during the 1930s. Any piece of land that had more people than it was supposed to carry or that was denuded of its original vegetation was necessarily eroded. The increase in the population of the southern part of Port Herald District as a result of the influx of fugitives from the Dinde automatically qualified the area for soil conservation measures after 1940.[82] There were no significant changes in the nature of the proposals for dealing with the problem, either. The same solutions proposed during the 1930s found their way into the 1940s, regardless of any changes in the dynamics of the problem.

The main advantage that the interventionists of the post-Bomani era enjoyed over their predecessors was political. Instead of an assorted group of village headmen, the planners of the 1940s and 1950s worked with a few powerful native authorities, as principal headmen came to be known after passage of the Native Authorities and Native Courts ordinances, which introduced formal Indirect Rule in the country in 1933.[83]

Like any other piece of legislation, the effect of the Native Authorities and Native Courts ordinances was inconsistent. Indirect Rule placed a final legal cap on the precolonial processes that had tended to deemphasize the role of ethnicity in local political struggles.[84] The ordinances of 1933 perpetuated the ethnic biases of the District Administration (Native) Ordinance of 1912 by recognizing as native authorities the descendants of Kololo chiefs in Chikwawa District: Kasisi, Katunga, Maseya, Mlilima, and Makhwira. Ngabu and Chapananga were the only Mang'anja native authorities in this overwhelmingly Mang'anja area.[85] Likewise, the six native authorities who came to rule over the large Sena population in Port Herald District were all Mang'anja: Chimombo, Chiphwembwe, Ndamera, Ngabu, Nyachikadza, and Tengani.[86] The use of Mang'anja chiefs was to complicate British attempts to restructure the economy of Port Herald District, as we shall see in the next chapter.

A closely related by-product of Indirect Rule that did not in the long run advance the cause of colonial agricultural policy was the revival of "tradition." The native authorities had everywhere greeted the ordinances with great enthusiasm. For the Kololo the legislation constituted another formal recognition of their historical dominance over the Mang'anja. Their Mang'anja counterparts in Port Herald welcomed and used the ordinances to protect their political and, in particular, cultural hegemony against foreign and, in particular, Sena influences. Thus in an unusual show of unity, Mang'anja native authorities pressed the administration to revive the lundu paramountcy—the symbol of Mang'anja political and cultural unity that had been supplanted by the Kololo in Chikwawa toward the end of the 1860s.[87] And with the approval and assistance of the district commissioner, they acted swiftly to restore the Mbona cult.[88] Unknown to the British at the time was that "traditional" leaders would later justify their resistance to colonial agricultural policy in the name of Mbona.

But if Indirect Rule heightened the Mang'anja's sense of their past and traditions, it also had the potential of creating powerful progressive chiefs and allies of British interventionists. The ordinances spelled an end to the era of the rebellious village headman. From 1933 on village headmen came under the direct control of native authorities, who were given wide legislative, judicial, and economic prerogatives. Each native authority maintained his own treasury, whose funds originated from two main sources. The first was in the form of market dues, land rentals, marriage registration fees, and similar moneys that the chiefs shared with the central government.[89] The other sources consisted of court receipts. Under the Native Courts Ordinance, every mfumu was granted warrants to try certain categories of offenses.[90] Finally, every mfumu was empowered to promulgate new rules that he enforced together with those passed by the central government. Most of the soil conservation rules fell under the jurisdiction of the mafumu. Native authorities were to fund all projects related to the conservation of the old lands: "The Native Authority is primarily responsible for the land within his area of jurisdiction and there is no justification for seeking the financial assistance of other tax payers. . . ."[91]

It was primarily because his department could not come up with money that the director of agriculture had rejected Lawrence's plan to plant grass belts between Bangula and Port Herald.[92] Officials settled on storm drains and ridges as the principal methods of combating soil erosion on the hills and on the flat mphala[93] because the two systems were the least expensive. The main responsibility of the state in drainage digging was to provide the technical know-how. Native authorities were to be entirely responsible for the ridging campaign. The government turned down the request for a technical adviser in ridging because, as one official put it, "Every Native knows what box-ridging is and leaving drains and ditches unhoed needs no great intelligence."[94] Implicit in colonial attitudes toward the schemes for restoring fertility to the old lands was the idea that peasants who refused to be resettled in new areas should bear the cost of their resistance. Consequently, the implementation of the schemes came to depend on local forces.

Local events, rather than a carefully laid out plan of action from Zomba, decided the timing of the construction of storm drains in Port Herald District. Hunger and the shortage of money for taxes in 1941 forced a reluctant district commissioner to plead with the soil conservation officer for the immediate commencement of drainage digging in the district.[95] The project would offer employment opportunities to the district and minimize the consequences of food shortage. But the request seems to have fallen on deaf ears. Very little was done on the scheme before 1949, and the few drains that were dug were constructed so badly that some experts feared they would cause greater damage to the land.[96]

The next opportunity for extensive drainage digging came with the countrywide famine of 1949. The famine once again forced villagers to work on the project in order to get maize flour (*ngaiwa*). Storm drains were excavated from the Nyasaland-Mozambique border (which suggests not much work had been done before) to about eight miles to the north of Port Herald township.[97] It is not clear, however, that plans to extend the digging to the chiefdoms of Tengani and Mlolo were completed in 1949.[98] One suspects that very little was done. The work was very unpopular, and the state was too preoccupied with other issues, like ridging, to provide even the technical assistance that was needed for the proper construction of storm drains.

Ridges or mitumbira were earth checks "1 foot to 18 inches high, and with base-width varying with the soil, but varying from 1 to 3 feet"; these ridges ran along "the contour at intervals of 3 to 5 feet."[99] They were supposed to check the water running from the hills in the west. Box ridges constituted what one senior agricultural officer defined as "the next step [after contour ridges] in elementary arable soil conservation." They too were "earth checks raised at intervals between contour ridges and at right angles to" the latter.[100] They were to "stop or restrict the movement of water along these furrows if the planting ridges are not on the contour," as was the case in much of the Valley.[101] According to one estimate, one man could construct 440 to 660 yards of ridges a day on previously unridged ground and between 660 and 880 yards on previously ridged garden. Although some experts warned that if not properly constructed ridges would, like drains, "cause appreciable damage," ridging still turned into "the principal system . . . advocated to control soil erosion in native gardens."[102]

Conceived in the early 1930s if not earlier, the idea of ridging munda gardens was first tried in the mountainous areas of Chididi and Lulwe in 1931 and on the Thyolo escarpment in northeastern Chikwawa in 1937. It was not until after the economic crises following the inundation of the marshes that the system was imposed on growers who cultivated the flat mphala in Port Herald District. The earliest known resolution in this direction was passed in 1944 by native authorities Chimombo, Chiphwembwe, Ndamera, Ngabu, and Nyachikadza, who were known collectively as the Native Authority of South Shire. The resolution required growers of maize, gonkho, and mchewere to ridge and complete ridging their gardens by October 31. Owners of cotton gardens were to complete ridging their fields by December 31 (in 1951 the date was changed to July 31 in order to establish a four-month dead season that was considered a necessary step in the war against the red bollworm).[103] Anyone who failed to complete ridging by the deadline was liable to a fine of 5*s*. or a "sentence of imprisonment for not more than two weeks."[104] Other native authorities followed the lead of the Native Authority of South Shire in subsequent years.

If they ever tried to implement the resolution, the chiefs must have met effective resistance from the peasantry. There were no ridges in the area by 1948 when, in reaction to the serious food shortage of 1946,[105] the British launched a massive compulsory drive for the building of mitumbira throughout Port Herald District.[106] In order to ensure that peasants complied with the regulations, it was decided that native authorities should inspect gardens twice a year, accompanied by akapitao-a-malimidwe and one or two European members of the district administration. The primary purpose of the first tour in November was to warn growers that the chiefs "intend[ed] to carry out [their] words." Heavy punishment was to be inflicted on a few peasants as a warning to others. During the second tour in December the native authorities were to punish "all those who [had] failed to ridge" their gardens.[107]

Excited by the apparent enthusiasm of the native authorities, the district commissioner calculated—very much to the disbelief of his superiors in Zomba—the exact number of defaulters who would be tried, fined, and imprisoned during the first two-week tour. Each native authority was to try ten cases a night. Twenty defaulters would be given a six-month imprisonment sentence and the others would be fined 30*s.* each. Any European traveling with the chiefs was to give advice but not take an active part in the court cases. In particular, the actual sentencing was to be done by the native authority himself. That would make peasants revere and respect the authority of their traditional rulers.[108] The "war of ridges," *nkhondo-ya-mitumbira,* had started in earnest.

Colonial dependence on the native authorities in the implementation of soil conservation and other agricultural rules became a major factor in the redefinition of chiefly power. It would divide Mang'anja ruling houses and create tyrants out of traditional rulers. The redefinition and consumption of chiefly power permitted the central government to concentrate its meager human and financial resources on the Shire Valley Project and resettlement schemes, which promised greater and more effective control over the peasantry.

6.3.2. Visions of Control: The Shire Valley Project and Resettlement Schemes

> Reducing it to its essentials the object must be to create a class of professional farmers with sufficient land to derive a reasonable standard of living. . . . The policy in Nyasaland is to encourage the

> individual, to develop his initiative and to evolve a class of yeoman farmer.[109]

Officials who had remained unmoved by academic arguments about the red bollworm were propelled into action by the economic and demographic disruptions following the Bomani floods. The flooded marshlands expanded to cover the adjoining mphala lands by as much as five miles in the relatively densely populated southern Port Herald District by 1943. The failure of the cotton crop and the level of poverty and malnutrition found among fugitives from the dambo convinced Nyasaland's rulers of the need for action.[110] The Shire Valley Project represented the most direct colonial response to these transformations.

The principal objective of the scheme was to reclaim the inundated marshes for cultivation—to return, in a modified form, to the conditions that had existed before 1939. Other objectives, such as the construction of hydroelectric power stations in the Upper Tchiri Valley and the improvement of navigation on Lake Malawi, were added mainly for the purpose of making the project more attractive to investors: "The importance of the development of Lake Nyasa and Shire River in the progress of Nyasaland, has been stressed by all three experts. . . . The chief advantages however would accrue from the utilisation of the land thereby made available."[111]

With everyone agreed on the need for new agricultural lands, the debate on the Shire Valley Project centered on methods for controlling the flow of the river. Arguing that the river channel was too narrow and shallow to contain a normal amount of floodwater, one group of experts, led by A. E. Griffin, former director of irrigation in the Sudan, recommended that the river "be enlarged or banked, or a combination of both used."[112] Others, such as Frank Debenham, professor of geography at Cambridge, emphasized the relationship of changes in the level of the river to those in Lake Malawi. Any plan to control the river had to deal with the problem of the fluctuations in the level of Lake Malawi.[113]

Elements of the two theories and recommendations found their way into the final report made by the engineers of the Halcrow consulting firm, which the Colonial Office had hired from 1952 to 1954 to do an extensive study of the issue.[114] The outflow of the lake had to be controlled while at the same time the channel of the river was deepened and widened. This work would involve a complicated series of component projects to be undertaken in two phases. The first would focus on bunding the Upper Tchiri River, which would permit more feasibility studies in the lower part of the Valley. Irrigation works designed to reclaim parts of the mphala and the deepening of the channel in the lower part of the river would constitute the second phase of the project. When completed, the Shire Valley Project would retrieve for cultivation about three hundred twenty thousand acres of dambo and, through irrigation, forty-five thousand acres of mphala.[115] The latter would be included in the empty areas earmarked for resettling the region's "surplus" population.

The idea of controlled mass removals from the congested southern Port Herald and northeastern Chikwawa districts was not, as suggested in section 6.2, completely new; it had been in the making since the late 1920s. Between 1929 and 1931, Lawrence had identified two "empty" areas as potential candidates for the resettlement schemes. The first (Area II in Figure 6.1) lay between the Thangadzi Stream in northern Port Herald and the Mkombedzi-wa-fodya River in Chikwawa District. The area was estimated to have between seventy and eighty square miles of arable land.[116] The second area (Area III in Figure 6.2) was that between the Chikwawa–Port Herald boundary and the southern fringes of the Lengwe Game Reserve in Chikwawa. It encompassed some two hundred square miles of land of varying agricultural quality.[117]

The loss of the marshes renewed the idea of resettling peasants, and between 1943 and 1957 four new areas were added to Lawrence's original list. The first, Area I (see Figure 6.1), was located within the Tengani chiefdom. It was supposed to take peasants from the mountains to the west of Port Herald township.[118] The other three areas (see Figure 6.3) were located in Chikwawa District. Highest on the government's agenda at the time was Area IV, which lay on the east bank of the Mwanza River above Kakoma farm (operated by the Nyasaland Farming Corporation from 1948 to 1953). It was to this area that the state tried, in vain, to resettle peasants from Thyolo District and those from Mwamphanzi (northeastern Chikwawa) between the mid-1940s and late 1950s.[119] Another region (Area V) was bounded by the Mwanza River in the north, the northern boundary of the Lengwe Game Reserve in the south, and the Tchiri River in the east. This was the Tomali-Mbewe area, which was estimated to have fifteen thousand acres of land.[120] At the invitation of the Chikwawa Land Use Committee, a group of forty men from Port Herald District inspected the area in 1956 for the possibility of resettlement.[121] Finally, there was the Mpheza-Phwadzi region (Area VI) to the south of the Lengwe Game Reserve,

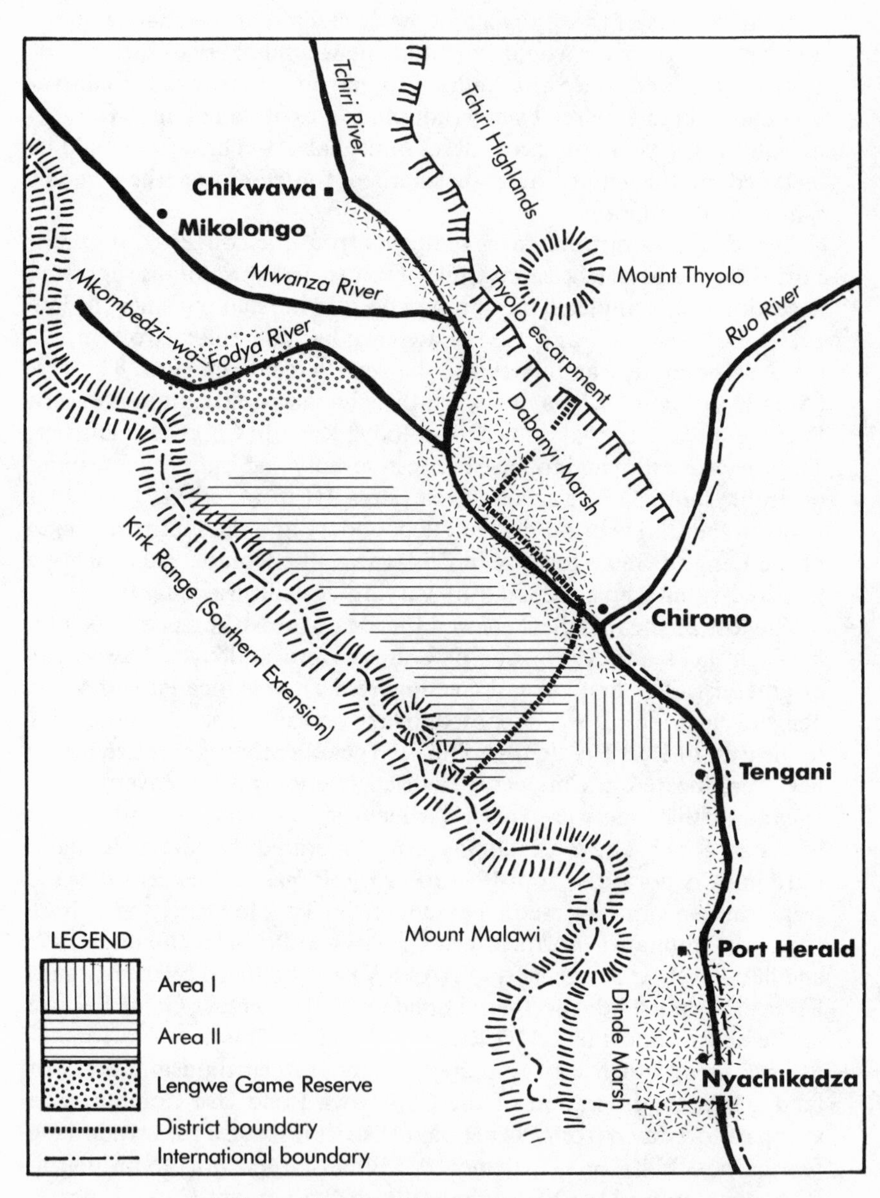

Figure 6.1. Map of Settlement Areas I and II

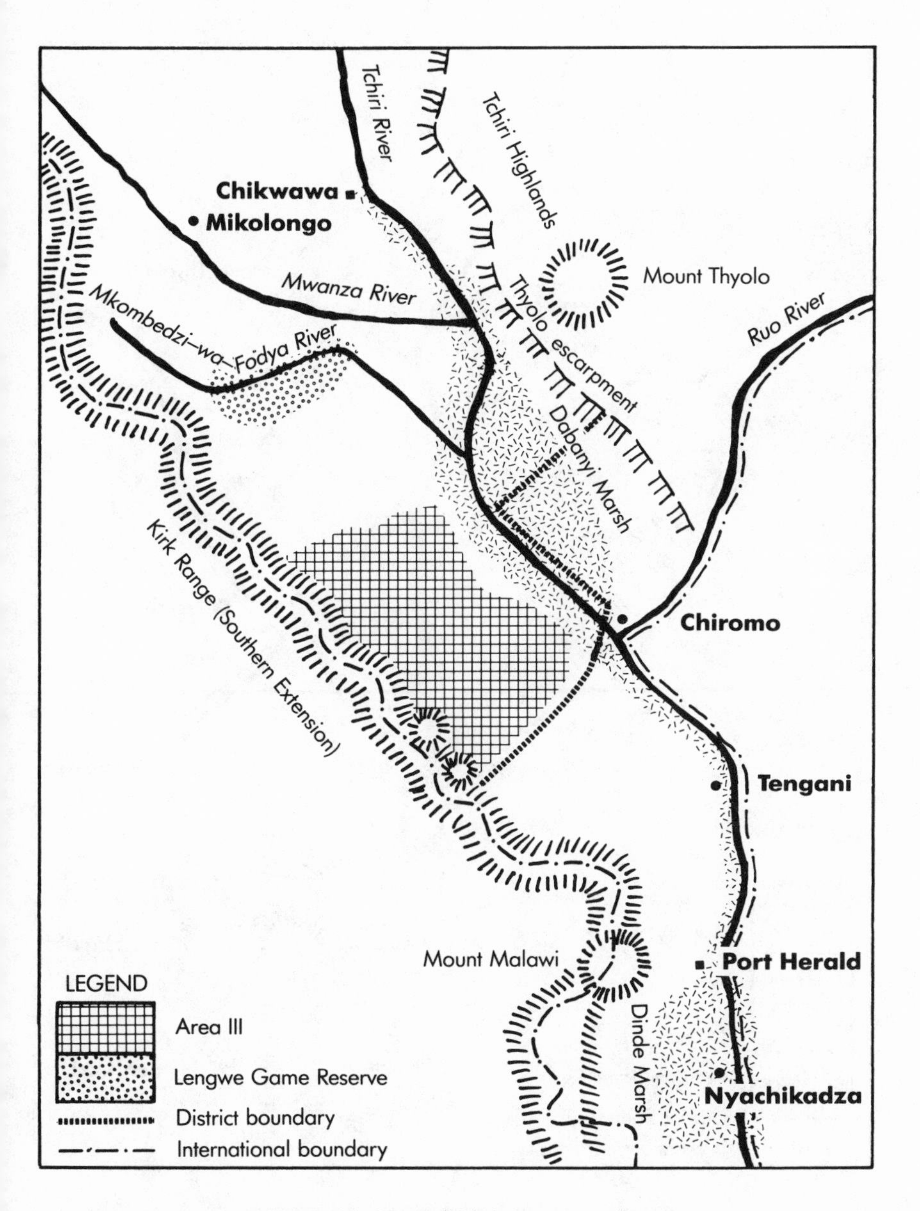

Figure 6.2. Map of Settlement Area III

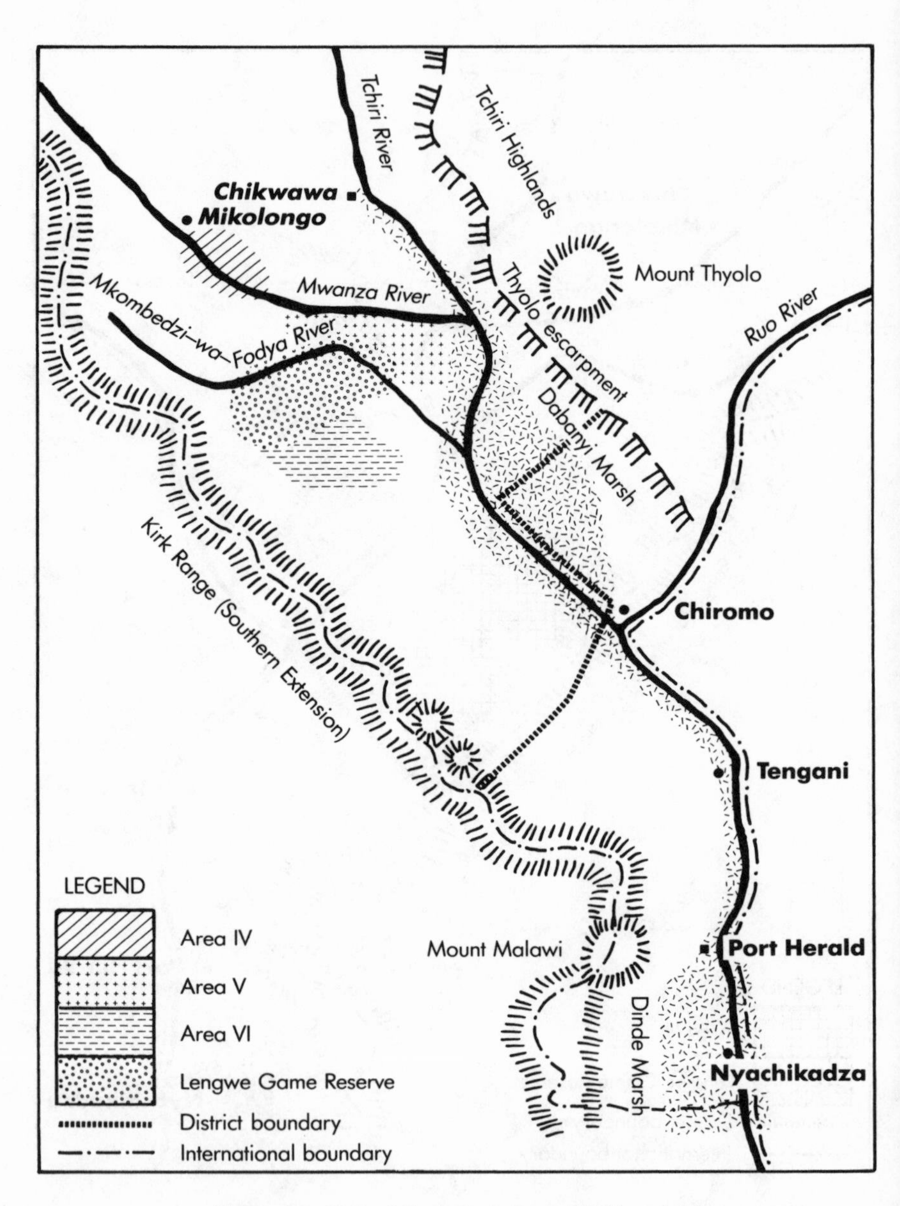

Figure 6.3. Map of Settlement Areas IV, V, and VI

a zone that was often treated as a single unit with Area V.[122] The two units together promised thirty thousand acres, fifteen thousand of which were considered to be very fertile. Peasants were to be moved to the two areas on a five-year plan running from July 1958 to June 1963.[123]

Having started as pragmatists responding to the concrete conditions of the post-Bomani era, the planners of the resettlement schemes, like those of the Shire Valley Project, got carried away by a vision of a completely new agrarian society—a dream world that rested simultaneously on the optimistic predictions of the Halcrow team of engineers and a rather impressionistic understanding of the dynamics of soil erosion, mixed here and there with the conservationist ideologies floating in colonial circles during and after World War II.[124] Unlike Lawrence, who in the 1930s had emphasized the need for caution,[125] the visionaries of the 1940s and 1950s had no place for the possibility of rural resistance. Moreover, fearing that they might lose the initiative in restructuring the region's economy to the peasantry (see Chapter 7), colonial planners were not satisfied with measures that would have given them only limited control. They increasingly came to see the economic crisis as a rare opportunity to "capture" the peasantry. The object of colonial planning became, in the words of Governor G. F. T. Colby, to "revolutionise the whole life of the Southern Province and, indeed, the economic life of the Protectorate as a whole."[126]

Revolutionizing the life of the peasants in the new lands meant above all else reshaping their relationship to nature through the labor process. Those resettled through the government program would have to stop cultivating the hillsides and riverbanks. They would have to respect any hill in the same way as they revered Mbona's sacred grounds on Mount Malawi.[127] Left uncultivated, the hillsides in the resettlement areas would provide a protective cover against the ravages of storm water and form natural village forest areas. Storm drains dug within the forest belt would act as an additional protective measure and as water storage tanks.[128] The Tchiri Valley of the resettlement projects would be a land dotted with hills and rivers covered with luxuriant vegetation.

Revolutionary change was also to characterize the cultivation of the lands below the mountains. Existing methods of munda agriculture would not be allowed in the new areas. Half the land allocated to each settler (which was variously calculated as twelve, eight, and four acres) was to lie fallow at any time of the year. Different systems of crop rotation[129] were to replace interplanting, and every crop was to be raised on ridges. Cotton was no longer to be subordinated to the labor requirements of the food economy. It was to be planted at the same time as food crops on the munda.[130]

Settlers would meet the new labor demands, especially the hard work that went into the opening of new fields, with the help of new instruments of production: tractors, rented from a common pool,[131] and plows drawn by oxen. According to one recommendation, an initial herd of oxen would be acquired on a "revolving herd scheme" like the one used in Europe after the war. The state would give a female ox to a selected group of settlers, who would in turn hand over a heifer calf to the common pool for redistribution.[132] Other planners proposed that the government purchase working oxen, plows, ridgers, and farm carts and place them in a central pool. Peasants would first hire and later purchase the cattle and equipment for their use. A resident veterinary officer would be posted to Chikwawa District in 1958 together with an agricultural officer who would supervise the use of the oxen. The result would be increased cotton production and state revenues.[133]

Nyasaland's planners also saw from the beginning the need to support the new agricultural system with a new village structure. Physically, the new villages were to be located in relation to water supplies, particularly the boreholes that were to be sunk in every settlement area. Village compounds were to be "bunded and grassed" in order to demarcate them clearly from the surrounding fields. Like the private nkhokwe granaries, the houses making up the new communities would be "erected of the latest approved pattern." Each family would have its own trees of mango, pawpaw, citrus, and other fruits. The trees of each household would be separated from other family dwellings by "carefully aligned" roads. As part of the Village Land Improvement Schemes, the settlers' communities would be self-contained, each with its dispensary, a nondenominational school (up to the third standard), a village hall, a cooperative market, and communal famine relief granaries.[134] These islands of "civilization" were to expand on the mphala with the addition of forty-five thousand irrigated acres after the completion of the second phase of the Shire Valley Project, whose primary objective was to reclaim the dambo for cultivation.

Projections of the amount of dambo land that the project would release for cultivation varied from one study to another. E. O. Pearson and B. L. Mitchell estimated a total of seventy thousand acres.[135] The party of federal government officials who inspected the area in 1955 expected sixty thousand acres from the Dinde Marsh alone.[136] The Halcrow engineers raised the figure for the whole Valley to three hundred twenty thousand acres.[137] The possibilities for increased production appeared limitless, and so too were the prospects of introducing radical change in the dimba cultivation system.

The new agricultural techniques on the dambo were to be anything but the intercropping regime that had permitted peasants to subordinate the labor requirements of cotton to the food economy. Regardless of the system of land control that would finally be adopted—a controversial issue, as we shall see shortly—cotton was to be grown in a pure stand. Like munda food crops, cotton would be planted in December (after the dambo had been artificially flooded for one month) and harvested in June and July. Only then would work on food crops begin, which would last until November. The food crops to be raised each season would be determined by a three-year rotational system.[138] Much of the work involved would be done with the help of mechanical devices such as tractors and combines for harvesting and threshing sorghum.[139] The state would have to ensure that this or any other cultivation program adopted was strictly followed. The project "could only be justified if full control is exercised on the crops planted and manner in which they are grown to obtain the maximum output and economic return."[140]

The anticipated economic return was indeed impressive. Working on the basis of Pearson and Mitchell's figure of seventy thousand acres, the agricultural officer for Thyolo District calculated that with only fifty thousand acres put to cotton the area could raise twenty-five thousand tons, which at the current average price of 3*d.* a pound would result in £625,000 a year. Oil extracted from cotton seed would bring in another £360,000. The food crops raised on the remaining acres would be worth £175,000 annually. Thus the income for one year alone would significantly offset the cost of the project, which according to Griffin stood between £0.75 million and £1.75 million, as well as that of the purchase of various instruments of production (one ginnery, one oilseed extracting plant, thirty heavy track-laying tractors, fifty combine harvesters, fifty seed drills, and fifty tractors for intercultivation).[141]

These estimates were later revised to accommodate Halcrow's prediction that when completed the Shire Valley Project would reclaim three hundred twenty thousand acres. According to this estimate, which placed the cost of the whole project at a whopping figure of £17 million, the production of cotton (eighty thousand acres), rice (eighty thousand acres), and food crops (one hundred sixty thousand acres) would result in a combined annual income of £4.82 million.[142] The project would pay for itself within four or five years. Colonial officials—including Governor Colby, who tended to emphasize the sociopolitical rather than the economic benefits—were understandably determined to overcome whatever obstacles stood in their way, including the problem of land tenure and land control.

Although its details were never fully worked out, a new system of land tenure was considered a prerequisite for the success of the resettlement projects on the mphala. "No programme of rural development can be formulated without giving careful consideration to the subject of land tenure."[143] In particular, colonial planners believed that their ability to restructure peasant production depended on the substitution of the old with a new system of land tenure. An outline of the general principles to guide the evacuation of the Port Herald District emphasized the need to grant "security of tenure . . . to settlers" if only in order to avoid the process of land fragmentation.[144] The entire Master Farmer Scheme, which was designed to create and assist capitalist farmers in the resettlement projects and elsewhere in the country, was predicated on the evolution of private property in land.[145] Colonial planners were clearer, although divided, as to what system of land control they would adopt on the reclaimed dambo.

They gave more thought to the question of dambo land tenure for two main reasons. First, they expected dimba agriculture to defray the huge expenses involved in draining the marshes. Second, there was a real fear that peasants who had cultivated the dambo before 1939 would reclaim their rights to the land. To forestall the latter possibility, officials proposed in 1949 that the state or another agency, such as the Colonial Development Corporation, should take control of the land for a period of at least two or three years before measures would be devised to hand it over to the peasants.[146] Others recommended the formation of a Shire Valley Authority, which would acquire legal rights to and develop the dambo. "Local land rights should also not be allowed to interfere with any construction work that may be necessary."[147] All calculations about the economic returns from the reclaimed dambo were based on the existence of such a body. Whichever body finally acquired control, peasants were to get access to the dambo only as tenants.[148] The aim was to create new social relations that would be in harmony with the new productive forces: a colonial approach to large-scale social engineering.

That men like Ducker joined the interventionists after 1940 is a telling example of how the colonizers could band together once their mission appeared to be in jeopardy. The quarrel between the governor of Nyasaland and the Colonial Office over the British Cotton Growing Association's application for monopoly buying rights was about the means and not about the mission itself. Nyasaland's rulers consistently manipulated the cotton market in order to serve the interests of metropolitan capital. Even the weak Nyasaland colonial state was in this respect indeed an "'over-developed' instrument of the metropolitan bourgeoisie."[149]

It would be misleading, however, to assume, as some writers have done, that state intervention had its roots in a set of ideas and ideologies floating in colonial circles during and after World War II.[150] The assumption creates supermen out of men of flesh and blood. Throughout the 1930s, experts such as Barker tried in vain to convince their superiors of the ecological dangers of the Valley's agricultural systems. The colonizers became a community of believers only after confronting a real threat to their position as agents of metropolitan capital. Conservationist ideas were not applied uniformly either in Nyasaland or within the Valley itself. Beyond the resettlement schemes, Chikwawa District remained outside the conservationist agenda even at the height of Africa's "second colonial occupation." Local events made the southern part of the Valley ripe for the kind of social engineering to which many other parts of the colonial world were subjected after World War II.

7

Constrained Peasant Initiatives and Agrarian Change, 1930–1960

> The Lower River District has always been far behind all other areas of the Southern Province in respect to agricultural betterment.[1]

> That the year is passing without any serious debilitation being noticeable is more an example of the unbelievable adaptability of the African to changing environments and his uncanny ability to wrest something from nothing.[2]

> No social order ever perishes before all the productive forces for which there is room in it have developed; and new, higher relations of production never appear before the material conditions of their existence have matured in the womb of the old society itself.[3]

A visitor traveling through the Valley after the floods of 1957 (known locally as Msasila) could see hardly any material evidence of the previous two decades of colonial planning. Planners had abandoned the grandiose Shire Valley Project, and the storm drains dug during the famine of 1949 (known as Thodi) in Port Herald District had collapsed. It was equally difficult to find any trace of the resettlement schemes in Chikwawa District. There were no more than a dozen migrant families occupying the land surrounding the defunct Nyasaland Farming Corporation at Kakoma (Resettlement Area IV). The project to evacuate peasants from Port Herald had produced only thirty-two families in Areas V and VI. The Nyamphota scheme, which involved three villages in their original settlements and for two brief years served as a showpiece of the colonial vision of controlled production, had also come to a dead end. Only the issue of the mitumbira, ridges built to prevent soil erosion, continued to pit the peasantry against the state until 1960 when, in a futile attempt to undermine grass-roots support for the nationalist movement, the dying colonial regime suspended the project.

The conspicuous failure of the British to fashion peasant society in their image did not leave the peasantry "uncaptured." Colonial planning formed an integral part of rural responses to the ecological and economic crises of the post-Bomani era. Failed projects left their mark on the social structure that peasants constructed after 1939. The communities outside the cotton-growing areas of Chikwawa District were in many significant ways really new. They survived on a much degraded land. Women and the elderly dominated the impoverished agricultural sector as men turned to nonagricultural production, including labor migration, which became an important source of wealth in a highly differentiated rural society. Poverty also sapped the vitality of some of the key institutions of social control.

There were also remarkable continuities between the pre- and post-Bomani communities. This chapter will highlight some of the precapitalist elements in the discussion of rural resistance to colonial land reform projects. The schemes failed not only because of the new labor demands they entailed. They foundered also because the changes in the productive base did not exhaust all the "material conditions of the existence . . . of . . . the old society."

7.1. From Centrally Planned Projects to Nkhondo-ya-Mitumbira

> European efforts to develop this area of the Protectorate have been conspicuously unsuccessful.[4]

A combination of ecological, financial, and social forces determined the failure of the centrally planned land utilization programs. Notwithstanding the persuasiveness of his argument, Governor Colby could not raise enough money to fund the Shire Valley Project. Cooperation with officials of the Central African Federation did not go beyond the planning stage. The federal government contributed only £57,000 to the £8 million that was needed to cover the cost of the first part of the first phase of the project.[5] No other organization, including the Colonial Development Corporation, came forward with the balance required to "put a cork in the bottle"—Colby's famous phrase for the works needed to control the Tchiri River.

Unexpected changes in Tchiri water levels proved anyone who had misgivings about the project correct. The entire scheme had been premised on the assumption that the level of the river and of Lake Malawi would continue to fall. But heavy rains at the end of 1956 suddenly reversed the trend. An inflated Tchiri River threatened to sweep away the dam constructed at Liwonde as part of the first phase of the project. The dam was subsequently opened to let the river flow freely and to curtail the possibility of flooding above the bund. The resulting deluge, known as Msasila in the Lower River,[6] killed the prospects of controlled dimba agriculture.

Neither ecological disturbances nor lack of money decided the fate of the resettlement schemes on the mphala. The country's rulers in Zomba were committed enough to the cause of the region's agricultural renovation that they were ready to spend their meager resources on the relatively inexpensive resettlement schemes. Between 1944 and 1956 they allocated at least £17,649 to cover the expected cost of moving peasants to Areas IV, V, and VI. The moneys were to meet the expenses for sinking wells, purchasing materials for the construction of temporary houses, and transporting the personal effects, especially foodstuffs, of the settlers and, when they were not forgotten—which sometimes happened[7]—the people themselves. Indeed, colonial officials were so determined to effect an "orderly occupation" of the virgin lands that they were ready to do what in the estimation of one critic amounted to "spoon-feeding."[8] The grand vision foundered primarily because of rural resistance.

Not unlike their successors in postcolonial Africa, Nyasaland's planners took little or no account of the dynamics of agrarian society in their calculations. They never asked the simple question of why peasants crowded in one part of the Valley and left the other uninhabited. The few hastily executed feasibility studies that were undertaken—usually on the eve of the planned removals—were intended to confirm rather than question the assumed suitability of the new lands.[9] The belief that their superior technical knowledge could solve every agrarian problem led planners to ignore the fund of ecological knowledge accumulated by the peasantry.

Peasants had avoided western Chikwawa, the home of the resettlement projects, for at least two ecological reasons. First, the area had few if any reliable sources of drinking water. The streams that crossed the region from the west were seasonal. Even the Mwanza, the largest river in the area, was not a perennial stream, drying up during the hot season. The well-sinking project, which had started in 1929, did not completely solve the problem. The capacity of the boreholes was limited by the low water table. Moreover, much of the water so obtained was "much disliked for its salinity."[10] There was also the probability that in some areas the water was contaminated with carbon dioxide.[11] The game that roamed the region trekked to the marshes in search of drinking water.

The presence of wild game constituted the second major obstacle to human settlement in the area. The Mwanza Valley and the western outskirts of the Dabanyi Marsh had carried heavy animal populations since the nineteenth century. The region had formed the primary hunting grounds for the Kololo, Chikunda, and European hunters in the late nineteenth century.[12] The resulting decimation of the animal population led to the establishment at the turn of the century of what came to be known as the Lengwe Game Reserve, which separated Resettlement Area V in the north from Area VI in the south. A series of game control regulations succeeded in repopulating the area with elephants, lions, kudu, eland, waterbuck, and other animals,[13] and in turning the ecological balance against the scattered human settlements:

> During the first quarter [of 1932] a lion killed and eat a youth at Beleu village but could not be traced. . . . Lions were active in P[rincipal] H[eadman] Kasisi's section taking many pigs from their kraals. On 13th September . . . Mr. Mortmer . . . killed a bull elephant near the Kakoma River. A leopard caught in a trap near the Lisuli Pool was killed on the 21st July. A wounded lion was killed on 6th July near P.H. Kasisi's village. A wounded lion was killed at Bwalo village, P.H. Kasisi on the 6th August. Mr. D. Thompson killed a bull elephant near the Mwanza river on the 3rd October. Mr. G. Garden was reported to have killed a lion near the Kakoma stream during October. On 22nd November a lion seized and eat a woman at John's village, P.H. Katunga, but could not be traced. . . . A man was seized by a lion within 100 yards of this Hospital on the night of the 10th December, but escaped badly mauled, with his life. He is recovering in Blantyre Hospital. Two lions were killed on the 13th December, one a very large male lion being killed within 150 yards of the Residency.[14]

A group of independent settlers from Port Herald were forced to return to the congested district after being terrorized by the beasts in the neighborhood of Resettlement Areas V and VI.[15]

Study of independent migratory trends after the Bomani floods (see section 7.2.1) indicates that ecological forces were not in themselves powerful enough to deter growers from the resettlement schemes. Peasants avoided the schemes primarily because of the prospect of controlled production. Anyone who joined the schemes faced the ordeal of kuswa mphanje, "the very heavy work entailed in the original clearing and cultivation of the land."[16] Unlike independent settlers in the same region, growers on the government projects could not choose the type of land in which to invest their labor. Nor were they in a position to set the size of their fields. Each household was allocated the same amount of virgin land (up to twelve acres), regardless of the number of workers a family could mobilize. Moreover, while for most peasants in the Valley kuswa mphanje on the munda was a one-time event, the fallow system proposed for the schemes made it a recurrent undertaking. The promise that the state would make mechanical implements and even paid labor available to the migrants failed to convince the skeptical grower, and for good reason. At the pilot Nyamphota scheme, the government tried to solve the problem of overwork by forcing peasants to clear the land under the unpopular *magombo* or communal labor regime.[17]

Peasants resisted the labor regime of the resettlement schemes on two other grounds. The first was the requirement that crops, which would be chosen by the state, were to be raised on mitumbira and that cotton be planted at the same time as but in separate fields from food crops. The order, which generated much opposition among growers who continued to work the old lands, was to be enforced more stringently on the virgin soils of Chikwawa. The state was determined not to allow settlers to implement the traditional farming techniques that had supposedly destroyed the land elsewhere.[18] Finally, peasants found the schemes especially unattractive because of the absence of dimba cultivation. This was due partly to the lack of dambo lands in western Chikwawa and partly to the fact that the labor schedules of the resettlement schemes conflicted with dimba farming, as the disastrous story of the Nyamphota scheme illustrates.

Inaugurated in 1954, the scheme did not involve new settlers. The participants were drawn from three existing villages (Nyamphota, Chipakuza, and Kadinga) on the southeast of Resettlement Area V. The state allocated a large munda to each household and, in order to ease the problem of overwork, forced growers to hire tractors. The money for the rentals was to come from the proceeds of cotton sales. The cotton crop failed. The most fortunate peasants did not earn more than £10. With debts that averaged £7 10*s.* a household, peasants were required in 1955 to do magombo communal work in stamping and clearing the land and to hire tractors again for breaking and plowing the cleared fields. The average plot holder was billed £8 10*s.* for the hire of tractors in this season.[19]

Working from May to November on the munda fields, peasants were left with no time to open dimba gardens in June and July. By December they had nothing to eat when their neighbors "not affected by the scheme" were helping themselves to sweet potatoes from dimba gardens.[20] Nor did they have the money with which to purchase foodstuffs. Instead, they were heavily indebted to the tractor pool. The situation of the Nyamphota peasants deteriorated steadily until January 1956, when the government was forced to cancel a portion of their debts and to provide them with food and "old sacking for clothing." They were "in their present plight as a result of a Government experiment."[21] The project, which had at first served as a showpiece of the colonial vision of controlled production, had to be abandoned in 1956.[22] No rational peasant could trust any scheme conceived in Zomba.

The state failed to win the confidence of the peasantry for another reason besides the plight of the Nyamphota villagers. There was no local political support for the projects. The campaign to "move . . . a whole or part of a village" alienated village headmen. They were afraid of losing "their personal prestige by losing their people."[23] The forty men—including several headmen and chiefs—who were brought from Port Herald to inspect Area V in February 1956 raised no other issue besides "the question of headmanship." They wanted to know in particular if a headman who moved into the scheme would retain his position and under which native authority. The answer they received must have dampened whatever enthusiasm they might have had for the scheme. They were told a headman could retain his position under Native Authority Lundu only if he moved with all his subjects[24]—an impossible condition given the grass-roots opposition to the scheme.

Mang'anja headmen must have also been discouraged by the loose talk in colonial circles about giving freehold titles to land in the resettlement schemes.[25] Private property rights in land threatened the very idea of headmanship as understood by the Mang'anja. No one could be a headman, nyakwawa, without control over land. The survival of many elements of the precolonial Mang'anja social structure was predicated on the persistence of the system of land tenure in which headmen occupied the strategic position as land distributors. Cotton agriculture had failed to turn against Mang'anja women partly because of the continuities in the system of land control.[26] Indeed, pressures on land resulting from petty commodity production and the immigration of the Sena had the overall effect of sharpening the Mang'anja's attachment to their ancestral lands:

> When asked if any of the villages would be prepared to move voluntarily to Chikwawa from the neighbourhood of Port Herald all the headmen emphatically stated that as the nucleus of each village was Mang'anja they did not wish to move from their present location.[27]

No sensible Mang'anja headman would forfeit his position as custodian of the ancestral land for unsubstantiated claims about the material benefits of the proposed schemes.

Without the support of village headmen, the colonial state could not break grass-roots opposition. After nearly two decades of planning, the state had to accept defeat by 1957: "As far as removing surplus population from Port Herald is concerned the scheme has therefore been a failure."[28] Subsequent attempts to move peasants into Areas V and VI produced no more than three dozen families by 1959: "Very few persons have shown any inclination to settle within the re-settlement area."[29] That marked the end of the grand vision of controlled production in the Valley. The men in Zomba should have listened to the advice of some of their officers working in the area.

E. Lawrence, the agricultural officer for Port Herald District in the early 1930s, was one of the officials who had anticipated considerable local opposition. He had viewed his grass-planting project in 1931 as a compromise that would "interfere as little as possible with native agricultural practise."[30] Writing in a similar vein, the soil conservation officer at Chikwawa had warned of the "many disappointments and setbacks . . . before real progress can be made."[31] Although few ever questioned the schemes from a technical viewpoint, many administrators stationed at Port Herald were concerned about their political ("administrative") implications. In 1949 P. M. Lewis deferred his opinion on the proposal to make storm drains by means of mechanical equipment until after consultation with the chiefs.[32] Earlier, M. A. Sharpe had opposed the idea of moving five hundred families from southern Port Herald as "inadvisable from an administrative point of view."[33] But no one in Zomba took the warnings seriously until the 1950s when, after much frustration, officials started to rethink their original agenda.

Colonial agriculture policy toward the Valley had become doubly reactive by the mid-1950s. In addition to the original economic crisis, planners were also responding to the failure of the resettlement schemes and to independent peasant occupation of the "empty" lands. The news that peasants were leaving Port Herald for Chikwawa District on their own raised serious concerns among British planners. They feared that if left unchecked, such movement would result in "a patchwork of unco-ordinated gardens and villages" in which they would not be able "to enforce good agriculture practice."[34] It was partly in order to forestall such an outcome that officials hastily declared large parts of western Chikwawa resettlement schemes. The object was to seize as much land as possible before it fell into the hands of independent settlers. Officials decided against caution because "it is not possible to keep land for settlement free of squatters for any length of time."[35] All "settlement should be properly organized" if the new lands were not to become "indistinguishable from other African Trustland."[36]

Realizing, however, that peasants continued to resettle themselves on the reduced but undeclared lands, officials began to make the resettlement projects so attractive that they effectively lost their original purpose. The retreat took several steps during the second half of the 1950s. After two and a half fruitless years, the chairman of the Land Use Committee recommended that the original cost of the resettlement schemes for Areas V and VI be reduced by half, from £12,000 to £6,025. Neither people nor cattle had moved to the projects during the first phase, which ended in 1958. Only a negligible fraction of the original budget had been spent on resettling three peasants during the first six months of the second phase of the project, which was planned to run from July 1958 to June 1963. The proposed £6,025 would be enough for the period since there would not be any expenses for cattle boys, oxen, or mechanical farming equipment during the first two years of the second phase.[37]

Disappearing together with the idea of a cattle-farming economy was the colonial determination to keep Areas V and VI exclusively for settlers from Port Herald District. The latter had shown no inclination to move into the scheme, and it was decided in 1957 that the project should be "thrown open to all who wish to enter" although, on the request of the district commissioner, peasants from Port Herald would get free transportation until the end of calendar year 1958.[38] Such moves would be voluntary. No one, except the inhabitants of the Thyolo escarpment in northeastern Chikwawa, would be compelled to join the schemes. Compulsion had not worked, and it should be replaced by persuasion and "suitable propaganda."[39] The prospective settlers who inspected Area V in 1956 were explicitly told "they were under no compulsion to move."[40]

It was further recommended that the areas to be occupied by voluntary settlers be thoroughly examined before the moves were made. And in a complete departure from earlier practice, the agricultural officer for the Southern Province required in 1957 that the surveys should incorporate information provided by peasants: "As much information as possible should be gleaned from local Africans as to the soil types considered desirable for cultivation."[41] Rural struggle had reestablished in some officials the kind of respect that their predecessors had shown toward the peasants as managers of their ecosystem and as controllers of their labor power.

The most significant feature of the emerging accommodationist policy hinged on the issue of labor control. In a last-ditch effort to attract settlers, officials abandoned those aspects of labor control that were considered the hallmark of the resettlement projects. A resolution unanimously passed at a meeting held in Blantyre on February 11, 1956, stipulated that "no excessive control over cropping would be enforced."[42] The district commissioner for Chikwawa passed this message to the inspection committee that visited Area V later that month. Members of the committee were told in particular that "there would be no Magombo—i.e., compulsory stumping of land as at Nyamphota."[43] Like the recognition of peasants' ecological expertise, the exclusion of magombo, oxen, and tractors removed the technical and technological foundations of the schemes. The man who was recruited as chief agricultural officer responsible for land settlement, F. E. Luscombe, found his position greatly diminished when he arrived in the country about 1956 "in consequence of the policy decision to permit uncontrolled, as distinct from organized, settlement in the land use sense."[44] There would be no difference between moving into the schemes and into the undeclared lands of the district. The result was an influx of settlers fleeing from nkhondo-ya-mitumbira, the "war of the ridges," in Port Herald District.

A decade of mitumbira legislation enacted by native authorities had produced few tangible results by 1947. The campaign to promote ridge cultivation as a measure against soil erosion had succeeded only in northeastern Chikwawa along the Thyolo escarpment and on Lulwe plateau to the west of Port Herald township. How much of this rather unique accomplishment should be credited to the political leadership in the two localities is not clear from the record. It is evident, however, that with many of their fields located on steep hillsides, peasants may have found it reasonable to adopt contour ridging as a method of checking storm erosion. Growers in the Tchiri Highlands who worked in a similar topographical setting responded as positively to the campaign for ridging. Ridge cultivation has become a permanent feature of the Highlands in spite of the fact that the independent state of Malawi scrapped all colonial regulations that enforced mitumbira. It is also significant to remember the practice of raising mathutu, or mounds, a farming technique in widespread use in some of these areas during the precolonial era.[45] Mathutu may not have been designed to combat storm erosion, but they fulfilled one other stated objective of mitumbira construction: they increased productivity. And like mitumbira, mathutu cultivation was more labor intensive than the popular practice of planting on the flat land.

The story was quite different in the remaining parts of the Valley. Peasants living in western Chikwawa greeted the news about the introduction of mitumbira on the east bank in 1938 with such hostility that the native authorities of the area refrained from passing any legislation on the subject during the 1940s.[46] Policymakers in Zomba gave in to the opposition, hoping to impose the system on peasants who would move into the resettlement schemes. The resignation became a major force attracting independent settlers to western Chikwawa throughout the 1940s. Some of the migrants came from the northeast but most were from Port Herald, where every native authority had passed legislation supporting the campaign since 1938.

The flurry of legislative activity in Port Herald District only heightened rural resistance. District commissioners who, for obvious reasons, were in the habit of exaggerating their achievements when reporting to their superiors in the capital found themselves in a pitiful situation when it came to the question of mitumbira. They would acknowledge the efforts made by the native authorities but had to conclude that "the results are not particularly startling." Others simply admitted the existence of "complete hostility . . . to changes in [the peasant's] agricultural methods."[47] Thus, summarizing the developments of the previous decade in the Southern Province, the senior provincial agricultural officer, A. P. Forbes, commented with evident frustration in 1947:

> The opposition is much greater in the Lower River than has yet been experienced in any of the other areas in the Province where, after preliminary difficulties, the inhabitants gradually took to ridging. . . . The

> failure is obviously not due to lack of drive on behalf of our European staff and certain of the Administrative Officers have given full co-operation. What must be faced is that the African cultivator does not want ridge cultivation.[48]

He went on to ask himself, as all colonial officials did when confronted with failure, whether "there may be sound agricultural grounds, perhaps obscure, for this opposition," and whether his department was "justified from available experimental information in enforcing ridge cultivation."[49]

Commenting on Forbes's status report, Lawrence speculated that there were "many reasons for the opposition" and that it would "take time to overcome them all."[50] He was completely right. The reasons belonged to different categories, which allowed different segments of the population to relate to the resistance. The fact that the new system demanded so much heavy work guaranteed its unpopularity among the growers. Even by the most optimistic colonial calculations, mitumbira rivaled only kuswa mphanje, the opening of new fields, in terms of labor demands. It took an able-bodied man an entire day to construct 440 to 660 yards of ridges on previously unridged ground and between 660 and 880 yards in a previously ridged garden.[51] The coincidence of the campaign with the rise in male labor emigration (see section 7.2) in an economy where men had always shared agricultural work with their women helped undermine the campaign for mitumbira. The extra work fell on women and the elderly. Ridging, conceded one district commissioner in 1943,

> is of course unpopular among natives owing to the hard work involved in the first year. Old men and old women will no doubt be unable to carry out the order to a full extent next year.[52]

The old men and old women did not carry out the order to a full extent the following year either. They did not see any reason for investing so much labor in mitumbira, and they were not alone in their skepticism about the supposed benefits of the technique on productivity and soil structures.

Administrators who tried to implement mitumbira through the native authorities were told at an early stage that peasants did not think the system "desirable on a comparatively flat land."[53] They were not convinced that ridge cultivation would raise their productivity. And research done at the Nyachiperi Experimental Station for five years prior to 1947 proved them right. The experiments showed "no big difference between yields" obtained on ridged and unridged land.[54] On the contrary, there was fear among both the peasantry and the educated elite that mitumbira might actually destroy the land. By loosening the topsoil, it was argued, ridging exposed the land to wind erosion, which posed greater danger on the flat mphala than sheet erosion.[55] Opponents of the system also reminded colonial experts of the possibility that mitumbira might encourage both water lodging and attacks by white ants.[56] Ridge cultivation may have made sense to growers in hilly areas, but it did not appear rational to the peasantry who worked the flat mphala.

In opposing mitumbira, the peasants found support not only among the educated, who articulated the more technical or scientific dimension of the resistance. They were also joined by some native authorities, especially those such as Chiphwembwe and Ngabu, who had been recruited from the ranks of the custodians of the Mbona territorial cult. Their ability to control the local population depended largely on their position in a cult that had developed as one of the principal systems of ecological control.[57] Their opposition to mitumbira was based on the argument that the ridges would impede the movement of Mbona (conceived as a snake) with his annual gift of rain. They subsequently pointed to the drought of 1949, which followed the forceful implementation of mitumbira as evidence of Mbona's anger.[58]

The accusation confirmed what some colonial officials had begun to suspect since the mid-1940s. Not all native authorities were as committed to the "progressive" colonial agenda as suggested by either their structural position in the country's administration or their legislative and judicial activity since the introduction of Indirect Rule.

P. M. Lewis, who administered Port Herald from 1947 to 1953, was among the first commissioners to see a discrepancy between the actual and legal responses of native authorities to mitumbira and other agricultural rules. His predecessors, with the possible exception of A. E. Savage,[59] had read the impressive rules and orders enacted by native authorities as evidence of the latter's undivided commitment to mitumbira. The British had placed all the blame for the failure of the campaign on the "backward-looking" peasantry, and had looked forward to the day when the enlightened chiefs would break the largely uncoordinated opposition.

Nicknamed Tsengoyammadzi (a thorn hidden under the water) because of his ambiguous relations to the population as an administrator and as a man (he was married to an African woman from the area),

Lewis understood the workings of local politics better than any of his European contemporaries.[60] He read the annual reports compiled by the native authorities with skepticism. In particular, he did not believe that every native authority who enacted legislation on mitumbira did in fact support the project. The orders were made for the purpose of impressing European officials:

> Years of this propaganda have broken down the African's expressed hostility to more enlightened methods but this has merely been replaced by invidious lip service which no more raises the hoe than did the old hostility. The greatest exponents of this lip service are the chiefs themselves who at meetings give almost enthusiastic response to new ideas but later fail miserably to produce one example of work accomplished.[61]

Lewis must also have realized the real significance of the growing number of convictions made under the native authorities' agricultural rules. It was not difficult for any chief to convict a number of unfortunate peasants toward the end of the year in a district where, as Savage had once put it, agricultural regulations were "more honoured in the breach than in observance."[62] Taken by other administrators as proof of the chiefs' dedication to the cause of mitumbira, for Lewis the convictions were nothing more than an attempt on the part of the native authorities to keep the British from meddling in the affairs of their territories. Having crossed the watershed, Lewis became determined to confront the problem squarely at the political level.

Lewis was not the first British official to try to solve the area's economic problems by maneuvering the political system. His predecessors had responded to the economic difficulties resulting from the inundation of the marshes by reviving an old plan to amalgamate the southern chiefdoms. In a quick and ill-conceived move the administration had in 1940 united the five southern chiefdoms (Chiphwembwe, Chimombo, Ndamera, Ngabu, and Nyachikadza) in a federation, officially known as the Native Authority of South Shire—the Mtholola court of the oral historian. Deep-seated historical rivalries, personality clashes, and differences of opinion over the new agricultural policies ensured the breakup of the hastily constituted federation in 1946.[63] Lewis was determined to adopt a different strategy. He would bring the chiefdoms that spearheaded resistance to mitumbira and other agricultural reforms under one progressive native authority: a traditional ruler in appearance but British at heart and an autocrat in action.

Pressured to take action on mitumbira before the implementation of his political agenda, Lewis made it known to his superiors that he did not trust the native authorities of the district: "the normal methods of propaganda through Chiefs and headmen was completely useless."[64] He therefore entrusted the responsibility of carrying out the first district-wide compulsory drive for ridging in 1948 to a number of European hardliners. The officers inflicted "heavy punishments" on defaulters, warning peasants that they "would no longer be allowed to continue in their old habits with immunity." In all, about a thousand defaulters were rounded up, charged, and fined anything from 5*s.* to "six months imprisonment without option."[65] The lesson was not easily forgotten. Despite the drought and famine in 1949, up to 50 percent of all growers ridged their fields in those areas in which resistance had been strongest. In others the compliance rate was between 80 and 100 percent,[66] which greatly impressed Profesor Frank Debenham of Cambridge University when he passed through the area later that year.

> Much of [the land] was box-ridged, that is to say one set of ridges was crossed by another so that the general effect was that of a huge waffle-iron, each little "box" ready to hold the rain when it fell and to keep it from running along eroding the parallel trenches.[67]

Lewis was not equally impressed. He looked beyond 1949 and saw no reason for optimism. The success, he admitted, had been "obtained by fear and not willing co-operation."[68] He was especially concerned that the departure of the European taskmasters would spell the end of the experiment in much of the district, with the exception of the Lulwe plateau and the Mlolo chiefdom where the incumbent, Liva, had single-handedly broken resistance to mitumbira and other agricultural reforms.[69] Peasants under the "conservative" chiefs would fall back on their old ways. Chiphwembwe and Ngabu had to be replaced by a permanent taskmaster in order to maintain the momentum of 1948–49. The two chiefdoms had to be handed over, directly or indirectly, to Mollen Tengani, who had through the years established his credentials as the most "progressive" chief of the district besides Liva Mlolo.

Born around 1900, Mollen Tengani was among the earliest converts of the South African General Mission.[70] He succeeded his maternal uncle, Thembzya (Mandebvu) Tengani, in 1936 after having worked as a foreman on the Nyasaland Railways and as a teacher and catechist for the mission. As chief, he fashioned himself in the contradictory images of Indirect Rule. He rewrote the history of the Tenganis to reestablish the chiefdom's historical preeminence in the area during the lundu era.[71] The British would not need to create a paramount chief should they need one. At the same time he left no one in doubt about his qualities as a "modern" chief. As a Christian, he refused to have anything to do with the "devil" Mbona.[72] Instead, he cooperated with the colonial regime in all measures, including advocating mitumbira. He was the only chief who in 1938 had asked the agricultural officer, Carrall-Wilcocks, to force his subjects to grow sweet potatoes on ridges.[73] And although he was not always successful in implementing the new rules because of peasant resistance, the British recognized his effort and rewarded him accordingly. He was the recipient of the King's Medal; was sent to Jeans School at Domasi, where promising native authorities attended crash courses in the rudiments of rural "development"; and participated in several international conferences designed to acquaint chiefs with the objectives of Indirect Rule.[74] His only rival in the district was Liva Mlolo. Unlike the abrasive and assertive Mlolo,[75] however, Tengani was always diffident toward his masters. He credited the British with whatever "progress" had been made in his chiefdom.[76] Even the skeptical Lewis could not seriously question his suitability as a replacement for the recalcitrant Chiphwembwe and Ngabu. His only problem was how to do away with the two chiefs without inciting political unrest among their followers.

The God of Imperialism came to the rescue of Lewis and Tengani before the two had exhausted their faith. Both Chiphwembwe and Ngabu died in 1950.[77] Lewis seized the moment. He gave the two chiefs' families no chance to elect successors. Instead, he handed the chiefdoms over to Njanje Makoko, who had been a subchief of the "conservative" Kapusi Chimombo. In a move that was intended to warn other "conservative" chiefs in the district, Lewis removed the new Makoko chieftaincy from Chimombo and placed it under Mollen Tengani, who was Makoko's son-in-law.[78] When Lewis was transferred from Port Herald in 1953, he left four-fifths of the district under the direct or indirect authority of Tengani. Tengani subsequently installed his son, Edwin, born of Makoko's daughter, as successor to Makoko on the death of the latter in 1957.[79] The manipulation of the matrilineal system of inheritance allowed Mollen Tengani to enforce mitumbira rules more evenly throughout his expanded territory. Nkhondo-ya-mitumbira had started in earnest.

The specifics of nkhondo-ya-mitumbira under the Tengani dictatorship must await another study since the annual district reports for the 1950s are still closed to researchers. The following summary is based mostly on oral sources. Even in this incomplete form, the account raises two important issues. The first concerns the role that colonial agricultural policy played in generating support for the nationalist movement and in raising the political consciousness of the peasantry. Second, the story highlights the potential of Indirect Rule for creating tyrants out of traditional rulers.[80]

Mollen Tengani, the father who, as some critics claim, was bought for £20, and his son Edwin did not disappoint their British masters. They demanded strict compliance with all existing laws, such as the regulations about latrine construction, marriage registration, the ban on the cultivation of riverbanks and hillsides, and ridging. They also enacted new ones, the best remembered being the order that regulated peasant work schedules on a daily and seasonal basis. All growers were expected to be in their fields from dawn to noon and from about two to five in the afternoon during the garden preparation period from about August to November. To enforce the law, the chiefs dispatched their messengers and akapitao-a-malimidwe, not to the fields but to the villages. They were to arrest anyone found "loafing" during "working hours."[81] It was also at this time of year that the Tenganis sought to give teeth to the old rule, passed but rarely enforced by the "conservative" chiefs, that banned the making and drinking of beer.[82] When caught, beer brewers—mostly women—were arrested together with their clients and taken to the chiefs' headquarters for trial. The messengers broke the beer pots or forced the women to carry them to the chiefs' headquarters, where the pots were used as evidence against the defendants. On conviction, offenders were liable to fines of up to 5*s.* or imprisonment sentences of up to six months.[83]

In November and December, the chiefs would themselves make inspection tours of the fields together with their messengers and akapitao-a-malimidwe. They would be led to the fields by the village headman. The gardens were scrutinized for any violations of the rules about streambank and hillside cultivation, the uprooting of grasses and stalks, and, above all else, mitumbira. Growers whose fields were found to have contravened any of these orders were tried in the evening. Those who were convicted and failed to pay their fines were sent to prison—not to the European-supervised prison at district headquarters, but those at the chiefs' capitals.[84] Gone forever were the days when peasants could break agricultural regulations with impunity on the understanding that, as some headmen had told colonial officials, the central prison at Port Herald township was too small to take in all the offenders.[85] Tengani and his son maintained their own prisons, where all sorts of atrocities were committed against those convicted as well as those awaiting trial.

Removed from the central battlefield, the British must have watched the final stage of nkhondo-ya-mitumbira with a mixture of apprehension and satisfaction. Mollen Tengani did succeed in breaking resistance, especially in his original chiefdom. Ridging became as much a fact of life in this area as it was in the northeastern section of Chikwawa, the Lulwe area, and the Mlolo chiefdom. One cannot, however, say the same about the south, including Edwin Tengani's territory. Here, as in the remaining southern chiefdoms, open resistance had only given way to more sophisticated forms of silent opposition. Beer brewers shifted the site of liquor production from the villages to the bush. Makers of *kachasu,* the local gin, would do the initial inconspicuous preparations (mixing sugar with the bran of maize, millet, or sorghum in earthen pots) inside their houses and carry the pots to the bush, especially the marshes, at dawn when the brew was ready for distilling. Clients known for their drinking habits would be informed about the event. The village would be empty when the chiefs' messengers made their rounds during working hours.[86] There are also stories of peasants who feigned madness at the sight of the dreaded messengers.[87]

Nkhondo-ya-mitumbira became a major factor in the independent migrations from the area. In addition to those peasants who left the area permanently, there were others who tried to maintain one foot in Nyasaland and the other in Mozambique. The rule of the Tenganis brought to maturity the trend, already noted in the early 1940s, whereby peasants maintained their houses in Nyasaland and their fields in Mozambique, enjoying the lower taxes of the British colony while avoiding its agricultural reforms.[88] Some male growers institutionalized the practice by reverting to polygamy. They would have one wife in Nyasaland and another in Mozambique, where they did all their farming.[89] Without a field in Nyasaland, they had nothing to fear in November and December when the chiefs rounded up defaulters.

More disquieting to British officials, however, must have been the protest staged by women, especially the wives of migrant laborers. Unable to leave the area, single women sought to limit colonial control over their labor by dropping out of the cotton economy.

> In addition to the low prices, people were forced to clean the gardens, so clean that even if one stalk remained [standing], they would arrest and fine you. [Consequently] we stopped growing cotton; we stopped cotton because if one plant was found standing, they would say, "Why is it there? You should burn everything and nothing should sprout on its own." [They would force you to do this] in your own garden, your own garden. There were African instructors who stood by the government as they received

money from doing that. That was when, you see, people decided to stop, saying "Let us leave everything." That is why cotton growing ceased in this area.[90]

The ruthless implementation of *malimidwe,* new agricultural rules, helped the entry of much of Port Herald District into the postcolonial era as a non-cotton-growing area.

Individual acts of defiance began to merge with the nationalist movement for political independence from the late 1940s. The intellectuals who articulated the technical arguments against mitumbira were members of the Nyasaland African Congress, the predecessor of the ruling Malawi Congress Party. In order to win the support of the peasantry, the intellectuals presented the nationalist struggle as a movement against nkhondo-ya-mitumbira and those who implemented malimidwe, especially Mollen Tengani. The intellectuals had started to challenge Tengani as early as 1948. At a meeting held at the chief's court, they delivered a stinging attack on the proposed draconian measures and won the favor of all the village headmen present. They subsequently visited the headmen "and urged them to exhort their people to show open hostility to the campaign"—an action that led to their being charged with "attempting to undermine the lawful power and authority of Chief Tengani."[91] The trials that followed the charge turned them into folk heroes.

The fact that most of the local intellectuals who opposed Tengani were Sena (see section 7.2.3) gave nkhondo-ya-mitumbira distinct though shifting ethnic overtones that ultimately clouded the class divisions within the anticolonial movement. Whereas Tengani, Mlolo, and other native authorities who in either action or legislation supported mitumbira were all Mang'anja, the majority of the peasantry and a large proportion of the village headmen were, like their educated heroes, of Sena origin. The subjective implications of this objective condition have yet to be explored. That some Mang'anja rulers did see the conflict in ethnic terms is beyond dispute. Vuntade Nyachikadza probably expressed the opinion of the collaborating Mang'anja chiefs when he indiscriminately and contemptuously referred to the local nationalists as *aphajoni,* troublemakers of foreign origin.[92]

When Nyachikadza made this remark in 1959, ethnicity had taken another bent. The coup d'état made by Lewis on behalf of Tengani in 1950 had permanently divided the Mang'anja ruling houses. On the one end, there were Dalesi Ndamera and Vuntade Nyachikadza, who, if only to secure their positions against Mollen Tengani, became staunch supporters of mitumbira. They became small Tenganis and small Mlolos in their respective territories.[93] On the other end were the disinherited followers of Chiphwembwe and Ngabu, who had nothing to lose and everything to gain by allying themselves with the new forces. The traditional anti-mitumbira Mang'anja wing gained more weight after Kapusi Chimombo, who had also lost part of his chiefdom to Tengani, openly sided with the nationalists (Port Herald District was renamed after him during the first years of independence). Tengani was not, for the Mang'anja nationalists, a true Mang'anja. But he could not be a true Sena either. He could only be a bastard—born of a true Mang'anja woman and a Tonga man.[94] He was the creation of a dying colonialism.

Roundly rejected by all relevant forces in the district, the Tenganis became a liability rather than an asset to British officials, who saw the success of the nationalist movement as inevitable. Representatives of metropolitan capital were not ready to radicalize the movement or jeopardize the chances of returning to the country through the back door (as Ngugi wa Thiong'o would put it) because of a soil conservation scheme. Thus, referring to mitumbira regulations in their final report, the members of the Devlin Commission of Enquiry concluded, as the local nationalists had been saying all the time, "All rules are not universally considered to be beneficial, even by well informed opinion." The commissioners further asserted: "We have quite independent evidence that the government was sometimes too rigid about their enforcement."[95] Tengani had gone too far.

The indictment, made after the countrywide anticolonial disturbances of 1959, strengthened the opposition and heightened the dependence of Tengani on the local British regime for his survival in a politically charged environment. Thus, to put down a mass insurrection against him in 1960, he had to rely on the friendship of District Commissioner M. N. Saunders, who called in the Police Mobile Force. Together with the chief's messengers, the force committed innumerable atrocities, the most savage of which was the smearing of the buffalo plant *chitedze,* which causes intense irritation and itching, on the private parts of women.[96] The violence marked the climax of Tengani's alienation. The *Malawi News,* the official organ of the Malawi Congress Party, editorialized:

> Chief Tengani . . . has antagonized himself against all the people in his area. . . . Bitterness and resentment are very strong, they are crying for help . . . that Tengani should be removed and Malimidwe stopped. Unpopularity of Tengani is almost 100 percent. [His] authority . . . had

been flouted and so he had decided . . . to call in [the] P.M.F. to "reinstate [his] power."[97]

The reinstatement proved short-lived. Following the general elections of 1961 that effectively put the Malawi Congress Party in power, the new rulers moved swiftly to remove Mollen Tengani from office in 1962. Edwin Tengani subsequently fled for his life to Mozambique at a time when some of the victims of his own and his father's brutalities were returning to the emerging neocolonial state of Malawi (which gained internal self-rule in 1963, independence in 1964, and republican status in 1966). Peasants had declared their independence from mitumbira during the last three years of Mollen Tengani's rule.

7.2. Responses to Ecological and Economic Crises

The Nyasaland government abandoned its land utilization schemes after they had reshaped rural responses to the economic and ecological crises following the Bomani floods of 1939. The idea that peasants could somehow have escaped state intervention[98] is a loud and politically dangerous myth—the weakest link in the growing chain of revisionist interpretation in African studies. The very concept of a colonial (or postcolonial) peasantry implies a minimum of political if not economic coercion. Rural strategies to escape state intervention in the Valley bore the stamp of the failed plans.

7.2.1. Internal and External Migrations

The two decades following the Bomani floods were a period of unprecedented population movement in the Valley. The first migratory wave, which lasted until the mid-1940s, was largely the consequence of the inundation of the marshes. The migrations followed a predictable pattern. As they had always done in the past, the inhabitants of the flooded Dabanyi and Dinde fled to the mphala sections of Chikwawa and Port Herald districts, respectively. But finding little or no land on the flat mphala in the southern section of Port Herald District, some fugitives from the Dinde were forced to occupy the hills forming the southern extension of the Kirk Range. It was here that the soil conservation officer for Chikwawa found about two thousand fugitives from the Dinde in 1943. They were, according to the officer, poor, "backward and listless."[99] The land was barely able to support the immigrants.

Unable to make a living in the congested south, some fugitives trekked northward to the chiefdoms of Tengani and Mlolo and, eventually, to western Chikwawa. The movement initiated the redrawing of the demographic portrait of the Valley, as Table 7.1 shows.

Table 7.1 Population Growth, 1925–1977

Year	Chikwawa	Port Herald	Total
1925	27,954	63,294	91,248
1931	35,892	81,410	117,302
1945	59,664	66,746	126,410
1966	157,805	101,074	258,879
1977	205,873	113,333	319,206

Sources: Data for 1925 are derived from "Production Per Head of Export Crops," 1925, A3/2/233, Malawi National Archives (MNA), Zomba. For 1931, 1945, and 1966, see J. M. Schoffeleers, *The Lower Shire Valley of Malawi: Its Ecology, Population Distribution, Ethnic Divisions, and Systems of Marriage* (Limbe, Malawi: Montfort, 1968), 5. For 1977 see Malawi National Statistical Office, *Population Census, 1977: Preliminary Report* (Zomba: Government Press, 1978).

Even if the drop in the population of Port Herald between 1931 and 1945 was not as great as the figures suggest,[100] one thing is quite clear: the district made hardly any gains during this period, while Chikwawa nearly doubled its population. And although Port Herald was not the only source of the increased population in Chikwawa, census compilers were correct in emphasizing the effect of the exodus from Port Herald:

> The Port Herald and Chikwawa Districts should be considered together as the distribution of the population in both of them is influenced by the vagaries of the Shire river—the effect has been to flood considerable areas of the Port Herald District, with a resulting movement of the population from the Port Herald District upstream to the drier land in Chikwawa District.[101]

The finding must have helped create the fear among colonial planners that if left unchecked, the independent movements would result in cultivation techniques that had allegedly destroyed the land in Port Herald District.

Colonial agricultural policy played a contradictory role in the internal migrations of the post–World War II era. The typical migrant of the period was not a fugitive from the Dabanyi or Dinde marshes. Migrations from the dambo had stabilized by the mid-1940s. Typically, the new migrant was someone who fled Port Herald District because of nkhondo-ya-mitumbira and the economic crisis. But the same forces that induced migrations also frustrated them. The growing notoriety of Mlolo and Tengani as staunch supporters of malimidwe, including mitumbira, closed the two chiefdoms to resisters from the south. The two chiefdoms were creating their own fugitives, who joined the resisters from the south on the march toward western Chikwawa.[102]

The new migrants found a different western Chikwawa than the one that had received evacuees from the marshes at the beginning of the 1940s. A substantial portion of the area had been demarcated as resettlement schemes and closed to independent settlers. And although colonial planners had not been able to seize the best available land, the alienation narrowed the field of options available to the independent settler. About a thousand villagers who moved to the area at the height of nkhondo-ya-mitumbira in the mid-1950s found much of the land left unclaimed by the colonial state to be inhospitable. Some had to return to Port Herald because, as one official put it, they "were expressing dissatisfaction of [*sic*] conditions prevailing in Chikwawa."[103]

That many others stayed on in the region is evidence of the depressed condition of the economy in southern Port Herald and the willingness of peasants to pay a price for their autonomy. The settlers were ready to wrestle with such ecological hazards as the general scarcity of good drinking water, marauding animals, and the tsetse fly because of the absence of malimidwe in the areas outside the resettlement schemes. And as more immigrants entered the region, the bush began to recede and the ecological balance started to tip in favor of human beings. The Ngabu chiefdom in western Chikwawa, with its rich makande soil, entered the 1950s as the new demographic and cotton-growing center of the Valley. Chikwawa District was able to maintain the high rate of population growth that was first observed in 1945. The census of 1966 put the population of the district at 157,805, against Port Herald's 101,074. The latter district had also lost some of its population to Mozambique since the late 1940s.

The first wave of migrants from the marshes had as a rule avoided moving to Mozambique on a permanent basis because of higher taxes, forced labor, and, from 1938, forced cotton cultivation.[104] Mozambique had until then been a place of temporary refuge for peasants who remained in the marshes. They would cross the international boundary when threatened by high floods and return to Nyasaland as soon as the marshes had become dry. Nkhondo-ya-mitumbira and other agricultural reforms in Nyasaland changed the pattern. In 1947 there were already about one thousand reported cases of people who moved to Mozambique permanently.[105] They were followed by others whose numbers must remain anyone's guess. Living on the fringes of that vast country, many villagers may have found it easier to evade forced labor and compulsory cotton production than the mitumbira regime as enforced by the Tenganis.

Resistance to mitumbira forced many other growers from the southern chiefdoms of Port Herald to return to the marshes during the first half of the 1950s. As was noted in Chapter 5, during this period there was a general trend toward the desiccation of the marshes. The Dinde became attractive because the state never tried to enforce mitumbira on this land. The marshes were not only thinly populated, but the annual floods washed away any ridges constructed during the dry season. Consequently, a string of villages emerged along the bridge of land separating the Tchiri River in the east from the Dinde channel in the west. These communities, which from the perspective of the makers of the colonial agenda resembled marooned societies, had to cope only with the flooding that threw them temporarily to the mphala on either side of the international boundary nearly every year.[106] For many, however, the inconvenience and sometimes the loss of life involved in the seasonal migrations presented a more attractive proposition than living under the tyranny of the Tenganis. It was in these isolated communities surrounded by water on all sides that mphala dwellers took refuge when the Tenganis raided the villages for "loiterers" during working hours.[107] When the marshes were again permanently inundated from 1957 on, some maroons went to Mozambique, others to western Chikwawa, and others to the politically charged and impoverished southern chiefdoms of Port Herald District. The majority of the men who moved to the latter area simply left their wives in the villages. They themselves continued the march across international boundaries as migrant laborers.

Economic change after the Bomani floods broke Mang'anja and Sena "reluctance" to work for Europeans and set the stage for the third phase in the history of male labor migration from the region. The first stage had lasted from the beginning of the century to the end of the Mwamthota famine in 1923. The number of people involved in this stage is impossible to determine, although the dynamics of the process are fairly clear. As shown in the discussion in Chapter 3, the migrations represented one outcome of the encounter between capitalist colonialism and the people of the region. As elsewhere in colonial Africa, the imposition of taxes was a powerful force that "freed" labor from the peasant sector in the Valley. The migrations also formed part of the process leading to the reconstitution of preexisting political and domestic struggles. Many young men left the Valley in order to fulfill their traditional obligations, such as earning the chuma bride-wealth among the Sena.[108] The rate of male absenteeism was always higher among the Sena than among the Mang'anja, who formalized their marriage transactions through the labor services rendered by the prospective son-in-law.

Chapter 3 made clear, moreover, that some of the migrants might have sold their labor power in the country were it not for the extremely low wages and inhuman working conditions prevailing within the colony. Many boys were traveling to Southern Rhodesia and South Africa when Nyasaland's rulers could not get anyone to work on European estates in the Highlands.[109] Finally, the ability of the British to procure labor from the Valley was always an outcome of the state of the agricultural economy. Resistance to internal and external wage employment was at its weakest during the economic crisis of 1918–1923.

The end of the crisis initiated the second phase in the history of male labor migration, which lasted until the Depression of the early 1930s. Few men left the area during this phase, and those who did tended to stay away for very brief periods.[110] Wage labor was not a significant factor in the internal or external relations of the peasantry. The sudden increase in the number of emigrants at the beginning of the third phase during the Depression thus caught the British administration unprepared.[111] The recovery of the cotton market from 1934 on proved to be a temporary respite that came to an end in 1938 when, together with the inundation of the marshes, the fall in cotton prices reestablished labor migration as a structural feature of the economy.

For reasons discussed in Chapter 5, labor migration after 1938 affected Chikwawa and Port Herald districts differently. Fewer men left Chikwawa than Port Herald. No more than one-fifth of the estimated ten thousand men working outside the Valley in the 1939–1943 quintennium came from Chikwawa.[112] Only 390, or 4 percent, of Chikwawa's taxable population of 10,251 paid their taxes outside the country in 1940.[113] Cotton growing in the Ngabu chiefdom acted as an effective brake on the flow of male labor.

The story was quite different in Port Herald District. Men seeking wage labor outside the country were issued 7,208 permits between 1937 and 1940, which, according to the annual report for 1940, "suggests that probably 3,000 to 4,000 [men] are out of the district at any one time."[114] Only 202 migrants were reported to have returned to the district between June and December of 1940.[115] Between 13 and 19 percent of all taxes collected in the district from 1941 to 1946 were paid by migrant laborers working in Southern Rhodesia, which employed most of the men from the Valley.[116] A slight decrease in migration rates during the first half of the 1950s proved a short-term phenomenon. The dramatic increase in the level of the Tchiri River after 1957 threw more men out of the district.

The figures cited above underestimate the situation, as colonial officials conceded at the time.[117] For a variety of reasons, including the attempts by chiefs to regulate the flow of male labor, many taxpayers left the district without identification cards. Still more significant is the fact that the figures do not include the non-tax-paying male youth who became part of the migratory system. Like the Depression of the early 1930s, the failure of cotton agriculture from 1938 on drove many boys from the district. The South African General Mission at Tengani lost about two hundred boys to labor migration in 1938 alone.[118] Many more deserted the school in subsequent years. Boys were also among the first to take advantage of new employment opportunities within the country from the mid-1950s onward. They flocked to Blantyre and Limbe before becoming the staple of the labor force at Nchalo Sugar Estate in Chikwawa District in the early 1960s.[119]

Although critical, economic distress alone cannot explain the dynamics of the process or the forms it took. Political and domestic struggles played their role. Many boys saw wage labor as a form of emancipation from gerontocratic rule. Nkhondo-ya-mitumbira and resistance to other agricultural rules also affected the migration of married men. Cotton agriculture foundered in the 1950s not only because of ecological disturbances such as the inundation of the marshes, the spread of the red bollworm, and the depletion of mphala soil. It also failed because, as suggested earlier, peasants were trying to limit state control over their labor. They gave up cotton agriculture in order to restrict nkhondo-ya-mitumbira to the indispensable food economy. Colonial agricultural policy inadvertently contributed to the failure of cotton production and, by implication, helped "free" male labor power from the peasant sector. It also shaped the forms taken by the migrations.

Realizing the importance of male participation in malimidwe, native authorities tried to adjust the flow of labor to the rhythm of munda production. In particular, men were not allowed to leave the district for employment until after they had prepared their fields and planted them with crops; passes were issued to men desiring to leave the district only at the end of January.[120] Although the chiefs were not always able to enforce the law, its passage constituted an important factor in the history of labor migration. At the very least, the order compounded the problem of quantifying the process, since many men left without the official permit.

Colonial records make it abundantly clear that the connection between the migrations and agricultural reform was not a one-way relationship. The legal and illegal exodus of so many able-bodied men undermined the campaign for mitumbira, as noted in the preceding section. W. D. S. Talbot, who administered Port Herald District from 1953 to 1956, also singled out male labor migration as one of the main reasons for the failure of the resettlement projects. It was difficult, he noted, "to induce families to move because so many men were extra-territorially employed."[121] The projects foundered largely because the extra labor demands fell on women and the elderly, who shouldered the burden of reorganizing the increasingly uncertain food economy.

7.2.2. Restructuring the Forces of Food Production

> A much greater acreage must be planted if this crop [sweet potatoes] is to become an affective [*sic*] reserve against a failure of the sorghum or millet.[122]

With the emigration of men seeking work, the women and the elderly who remained in the villages turned their attention to the food economy. The inundation of the marshes demanded a complete reorganization of the old system of food production in Port Herald District, which is the focus of the following discussion. The same forces that had made Chikwawa the less prosperous district during the 1920s and 1930s guaranteed its general stability after 1939. Neither the increase in the district's population nor the rise of a vigorous cotton economy demanded a radical transformation in the munda regime. The district was large enough to absorb the new pressures during the two decades after 1939.[123] It was the economy of Port Herald that required a complete reorganization.

The inundation of the Dabanyi and Dinde reduced the amount of cultivable dambo in Port Herald District to a few spots on the western fringes of the marshes and, in the case of the Dinde, to the bridge of land broken by rivulets and streams lying between the Tchiri in the east and the Dinde channel in the west. Production on these islands, as on the fringes of the marshes, was unpredictable and restricted. In a good year the dambo was available for cultivation for a period of less than six months, from July or August to November or December. As they had done during the mid-nineteenth century, the long flood seasons eliminated any possibility of growing dimba cotton. Only fast-maturing food varieties could be raised against the perpetual threat of early flooding. Floods destroyed the tiny plots throughout the Valley in 1943 and in one or another locality in the years after 1945. Dimba agriculture had become what the term denotes in contemporary Chimang'anja and Chisena languages: a secondary undertaking, if not so much in terms of the physical reproduction of the peasants, then definitely in terms of their relationship to the capitalist colonial economy. Munda agriculture mediated the latter relationship.

The mphala of the post-Bomani era was anything but the land that had received cotton at the turn of the century. It was very much reduced in extent as a result of the expansion of the inundated areas. In the southern section of Port Herald, the marshes encroached on the mphala by as much as five miles.[124] With the waters also came new settlers from the marshes. The migrations raised the region's population density to 113 persons per square mile by the mid-1950s.[125] Southern Port Herald continued to be one of the most crowded places in Nyasaland. Peasants scrambled for all sorts of land, including the stony hillsides. The soil had deteriorated to the point that one could expect good crops only in a "season of good planting and growing rains."[126] Such optimal years were few and far between. The Thodi famine of 1949 was preceded and followed by many seasons of severe food shortage.[127] When droughts did not threaten, the food economy suffered from attacks by insects and other pests, as was the case in 1943 and 1948.[128] The inundation of the marshes highlighted the structural distortions of the munda regime.

The economy that peasants refashioned in their constrained responses to the changed productive base was diversified and precipitated greater social inequalities. Labor migration, cattle raising, and fishing replaced cotton as the main source of money. As during the mid-nineteenth century, nonagricultural production dwarfed the agricultural economy in the process of rural differentiation. Agriculture became largely confined to the production of foodstuffs, which peasants supplemented with the fruits of nature much more often than they had done during the "prosperous" cotton era, when many villagers were able to purchase or borrow imported foodstuffs.

The Thodi famine, which followed the first district-wide compulsory adoption of mitumbira in 1948, provides a special window into peasants' ability to cope with recurrent crises in the food economy. Villagers survived the famine without much assistance from the state or migrant workers. Their only insurance was their resourcefulness. Some bartered property such as goats, fowls, and earthenware. Some worked the fields of friends and relatives within and outside the Valley. But the majority lived on the fruits of nature—wild sorghum, the *nyezi* (a tuber of the coco yam family), and, more commonly, the nyika water lily bulb.[129] As in the nineteenth century, men traveled in dugout canoes to places such as Guwa in Mozambique, where the nyika was found in abundance. Women without husbands scavenged the less richly endowed local lagoons in the Dabanyi and Dinde marshes. "Whole communities have lived on this root without any other form of food at all for weeks at a time, and the long string of men, women and children returning from the river . . . with heavily laden baskets was," District Commissioner P. M. Lewis reminded his superiors in Zomba, "reminiscent of the cotton markets at the height of the season."[130]

Nyasaland's rulers in Zomba had from the beginning seen the famine as a unique opportunity to procure the cheap labor needed for the construction of storm drains in Port Herald District. Only those peasants who were able and willing to work on the scheme received ngaiwa or maize flour.[131] Others had to buy so-called famine-relief maize at the exorbitant price of 3*d.* per pound, which infuriated the peasantry as well as District Commissioner Lewis. By hiking the maize price, roared an angry Lewis, the central government was putting the "Africans of the district . . . on the same footing as the wage-earner in the Towns."[132] Imperialism was not nearly as farsighted as students of famine relief programs in colonial Africa have suggested.[133] Lewis admitted that much when he wrote that "the European . . . has really had little influence on events" during this—or any other—food crisis in the Valley.[134]

The British were too preoccupied with their resettlement schemes to become useful partners in the inconspicuous but more realistic peasants' attempts to restructure the region's rural economy. Within the food sector, efforts ranged from the replacement of old cereal varieties such as gonkho sorghum with early-maturing types on the mphala, to the completion of the "revolution" in the cultivation of mbatata sweet potatoes (Sena *bambaya*).[135]

The sweet potato, which according to some informants was introduced by the Sena, was originally grown exclusively as a dimba crop in the southern part of Port Herald District. The members of the South

African General Mission were among the earliest European observers to underscore the importance of the crop in alleviating the problem of food shortages. "Many of our women" from the hills, reported Edwin Price in 1907, "are staying at the river, having gone down to put in potatoes on the river bank."[136] They remained there until after harvesting the crop, which they carried up the hills along what one observer called the "Sweet Potato Road."[137]

What happened to sweet potato culture during the 1910s and 1920s remains to be investigated. There were no regular agricultural officers, and the few colonial officials residing in the district were primarily interested in cotton. It was only during the 1930s, after the reopening of the Nyachiperi Experimental Station, that one hears something about the sweet potato. The crop had become more popular as a result of the decline in the cultivation of some of the established cererals such as gonkho on the mphala.[138] Still interplanted with other food crops, sweet potatoes were also grown on the munda at this time. Peasants planted the cuttings at the same time as other munda crops between December and January. They lifted the root in May, which was the optimum planting month on the dimba (in some areas the planting season started as early as April and lasted as late as September). The ideal lifting period for dimba sweet potatoes was October to December.[139]

The records of the 1930s also show that the sweet potato had drawn the dimba and munda cultures closer together than previously. The fact that the cuttings of sweet potatoes could not be stored over a long period of time necessitated, whereas the briefness of the flood season provided, the conditions for the interdependence between the dimba and munda systems. The cuttings that growers used for planting sweet potatoes on the munda in December to February came directly from the dimba harvest. Similarly, the "seeds" used by dimba growers from April onward originated in the munda harvest. Thus, according to the agricultural monthly report for May 1931, "Practically every village throughout the [Port Herald] District is planting up the dimbas with cuttings from the mpala [*sic*]."[140] The inundation of the marshes shattered this interdependence. Dimba growers could no longer rely on the munda culture for seed. The munda growing season ceased in April, several months before the new dimba growing season started in July. The two systems grew apart until the munda culture virtually died out by the late 1940s: "At present [sweet potatoes] are confined almost entirely to dimba gardens, and the people show little inclination to adopt them as a dry land crop."[141]

One reason sweet potatoes ceased to be a munda crop may have to do with the varieties that were grown by the late 1940s. The end of the extended dimba growing season had forced peasants to look for fast-ripening varieties that could fit the shortened dimba season. The efforts had proved a success although, as with other aspects of agrarian initiative, the evidence is thin on such critical questions as the ways in which growers resolved the seed problem. They may have introduced new techniques of preserving seeds or used the few elevated spots in and around the marshes as places reserved exclusively for raising nurseries for the fast-maturing varieties, which mostly came from Mozambique. The new sweet potatoes included *chaina* and *mache,* which have in many places replaced older late-maturing types such as *ropa.* Planted in July or August and lifted before the floods in November or December, chaina, mache, and other varieties have become the main if not the only dimba crops in many places.[142] The drop in the level of the Tchiri River in the late 1940s exposed more land for sweet potato cultivation. "The acreage of land put under sweet potatoes is steadily growing," noted the annual report for the Valley in 1948.[143] Thus, when the central government preoccupied itself with its doomed projects, local officers were encouraging peasants in Chikwawa District to follow the example of their southern neighbors in sweet potato cultivation. The crop had become the most effective insurance against famine in Port Herald:

> 1943 was one of the poorer seasons from an agricultural point of view. Grain crops . . . failed owing to too heavy rains followed by long periods of drought. Locusts destroyed the mapira in the foot hill country. The rice in the river plain was destroyed by floods. High winds almost of cyclone force did additional damage. The mainstay of the people in this area has been the potato, which was planted in great [quantity].[144]

There were few years when the local administration did not sing praises to the life-saving capacities of the sweet potato in the district. Unlike most cereals, sweet potatoes were immune to virtually every ecological hazard besides floods. Locusts could nibble on the leaves but not kill the root.[145] Sweet potatoes also formed an important element in the marketing and food supply system that developed after 1940. Only cattle raising and fishing rivaled the potato culture as an index of what Lewis called "the unbelievable adaptability of the African to changing environments."[146] Notwithstanding the intensions of the colonial planners in Zomba, rural differentiation in Port Herald District rested on the restructuring of the forces of the nonagricultural sector.

7.2.3. The Nonagricultural Sector and Rural Differentiation

> Whatever the relative values of the two modes of civilization might be, there can be no doubt of the ever growing attraction of money and the power it can wield.[147]

The history of peasant differentiation in Port Herald District falls into two distinct phases. The first was associated with cotton agriculture and lasted until the world Depression of the early 1930s. Unlike the situation in some parts of colonial Africa, the process resulted from neither the introduction of new technologies nor the rise of private property in land. The employment of wage labor was what distinguished a minority of rich cotton growers and zunde holders from the majority of poor peasants. Close to becoming capitalist farmers in a model that makes wage labor the distinguishing feature of capitalist development, zunde holders were also the most vulnerable to the vagaries of the international market.

Having outdone their European and Asian competitors in the recruitment of migrant Lomwe labor during the late 1920s, zunde holders were paralyzed by the Depression. Many were forced to postpone the payment of wages in 1930. But 1931 and 1932 brought no relief to the large cotton grower, who subsequently cut down production to a level that he could manage without paid labor. A census taken in 1933 showed a 61.3 percent drop in the number of zunde holders throughout the Valley.[148] Five hundred zunde farms were closed down between 1932 and 1933 in Chikwawa District, which had fewer zunde holders than Port Herald District.

> It is obvious that the large grower is finding cotton growing less profitable in these years of low prices and the writer has come across a number of cases where growers have been unable to pay their employees.[149]

Many laborers took their delinquent masters to court.[150] There were barely a hundred zunde holders left in the Valley by 1936. Many had left agriculture after dividing their large holdings among their co-wives. Another drop in cotton prices in 1938 and the subsequent inundation of the marshes, where most zunde fields were located, wiped out the trend toward rural differentiation based on agriculture. The differentiation of the peasantry would thereafter be linked to changes within the nonagricultural[151] economy, particularly cattle raising and fishing.

Fishing had always been an important male-dominated activity in the economy of the Valley. Unlike other branches of the nonagricultural sector, fishing did not suffer any competition from merchant capital. On the contrary, the fish economy expanded considerably from the late nineteenth century as a result of the introduction of new or Sena techniques, such as use of *kokota* (or *khoka*) seine nets and the *psyairo* "encircling fish fences."[152] The addition of these and other techniques to the old Mang'anja gear[153] helped the professionalization of the fish economy. Sena fishermen drove a thriving trade in dried fish even during the cotton era. It was not, however, until the late 1930s that fishing for export became a major undertaking and attracted the attention of colonial officials.

A combination of internal and external forces stimulated commercial fishing from the late 1930s on. The emergence of Blantyre and Limbe as urban centers provided a new market for dried fish. The two towns came to rival the tea estates in Mulanje and Thyolo districts, which had been the main destination of dried fish from the Valley since the turn of the century. The ability of fish traders from the Valley to compete with their counterparts from Lake Malawi and Lake Chilwa was largely the result of easier communication links established by the railway line between Port Herald and Limbe/Blantyre. Nearly all the fish from the Valley reached the Highlands by train, whereas fish dealers from Lake Chilwa and Lake Malawi hauled their product on bicycles or lorries.[154]

Within the Valley itself, the impetus toward commercial fishing came from two related developments: the rise in the level of the Tchiri and the failure of cotton agriculture. The increase in the volume of the Tchiri River turned the Dabanyi and Dinde into ideal fishing grounds. The failure of dimba cotton had the same effect in the Valley as it did around Lake Malombe, where, according to John McCracken, "many peasants switched their attention to fishing or fish trading."[155] Many peasants in the Valley operated as small-scale but independent fishermen; others sold their labor power to the emerging class of commercial fishermen. Oral sources portray the earliest successful fishermen such as the Fatchis and Khembos as men who had prospered in the cotton economy as zunde farmers. There was a considerable spillover of capital and entrepreneurship from the cotton to the fish (and cattle) economy, although it is impossible to quantify the transfer.

Successful commercial fishing required significant amounts of capital at the beginning. The money was needed to purchase large dugout canoes (*ngalawa* or *mwadiya*) and expensive fishing gear. The latter included the popular kokota or khoka, a flat trawl or seine net, the gill net (*malitchela, matchera, ukonde*), and the psyairo encircling fences. Psyairo were made of reed sheets woven together with palm strings. Some psyairo measured three hundred yards long and three yards tall.[156] Still more expensive than the psyairo was the kokota. Like malitchela gill nets, kokota seine nets were originally made of indigenous fibers (*bwazi*) that were found in abundance in Mozambique among the Lolo. The Lolo made the nets in their country and sold them to fishermen in the Valley.[157] The Lolo were later replaced by Indian merchants who sold imported nylon thread. Fishermen sometimes bought the thread and constructed the nets themselves. But increasingly they came to rely on ready-made nylon nets, especially after manufacturers started to respond to the need for nets with small mesh. The mesh of the nets made by the Lolo ranged from two to three and a half inches, whereas the machine-made nets that became popular in the Valley were as narrow as one and a half inch, capable of catching very tiny fish. Much of the commercial fishing in the Valley involved the use of psyairo, kokota, or malitchela.

One difference between the kokota and malitchela lay in size. A standard kokota was much larger in size than a typical malitchela.[158] The other major difference related to the labor processes characterizing the two instruments of production. Fishing with malitchela was an uncomplicated affair that could be carried on by one man. He would lay the nets, anchored on either end with a bamboo firmly planted in the ground, and leave for home, returning the next morning to harvest the fish.[159] Malitchela fishing was from this perspective not very different from using mono fish traps. The fishermen did not have to induce the fish into the nets, as was the case with kokota fishing.

Kokota fishing was labor intensive. It required a team of workers who cut the underwater reeds and bande grass before the nets were laid down. The nets were erected in a semicircle with the opening facing land. The men would beat the water in order to drive fish from the shallow water into the gate. Later they would bring the two ends of the gate together, forcing the trapped fish to get caught in the meshes. Those not caught in the meshes would be impaled with long momba spears or scooped in baskets.[160] The operation could take several days to complete.

Equally complex was psyairo fishing. The exercise started with the erection of two fences of reed planted across the stream. The object was to dam as long a section of the stream as possible. Hired workers would cut the grass and reeds between the two "walls" before bringing

15. Fishermen landing with their catch, 1960s

the sheets together "until nothing remain[ed] but a seething mass of fish."[161] The workers would use baskets to scoop the fish out of the water. It sometimes took an entire week to complete the operation.

After all the fish had been landed on the ground in the msasa camps that dotted the marshes during the dry season, the owner of the psyairo or kokota would give a portion of the catch to the village headman in whose area the fishing was done.[162] He would also sell some of the fish to villagers from the neighborhood and to traders who had been waiting at the msasa. The remainder would be prepared for sale outside the fishing grounds. Smoking was the most common technique used in curing the popular mlamba fish, which was exported in coffinlike boxes made of reeds.

The Tchiri Highlands imported the bulk of the fish that left the Valley. Demand on the Highlands was so high in the early 1940s that even small traders sent their dried fish there, which tended to raise fish prices in Port Herald District. "It seems almost impossible," complained one district commissioner, "to persuade the average Native that he can make as much profit by selling a small proportion of his produce at a lower price here than what he may expect to obtain for the same produce after it is transported to Blantyre."[163] The administrator was probably right. The unscrupulous management of the Nyasaland Railways must have hiked up freight rates, although apparently this did not prevent traders from venturing to the Highland market. A. W. R. Duly estimated that no less than 305 tons of fish "at a selling price value of £14,500" left Port Herald District in 1945.[164] Four years later, in 1949, the Highlands received 210 tons of dried fish shipped from the Valley. Indian merchants had by this time joined the fish trade, exporting their merchandise not only to the Highlands but also to Southern Rhodesia, where migrant workers from the Valley must have formed a segment of the consumers.[165]

Not all the fish went to the Highlands or Southern Rhodesia. Many small traders and part-time fishermen continued to sell their merchandise within the Valley, as they had done in the past. They operated at such markets as Marka, Mbenje, Port Herald, Chiromo, Masenjere, Dolo, and Ngabu, retailing their product to the local population as well as to traders from the Highlands. The increase in the volume of the fish trade in the 1940s led to the extension of the Port Herald and Masenjere markets, where the colonial administration built rest houses. The native authorities of Thyolo District, from which most of the Highland traders came, contributed some money toward the construction of the rest houses.[166] The native authorities of the Valley responded

16. Food market, 1960s

to the increased fish trade by requiring commercial fishermen to take official permits. Over three thousand such permits were issued in 1949.[167] The fish trade had become a major force shaping both social differentiation and the system of food supply in Port Herald District.

Every market listed above handled, in addition to fish, a wide range of foodstuffs, particularly maize and sweet potatoes. A full-scale market became a microcosm of the structure of inequality emerging in the district. At the bottom of this structure were poor women who sold sweet potatoes that they had either raised themselves or purchased or worked for in the marshes. Their clients were other poor peasants from the neighborhood. One penny bought between twenty-five and twenty-seven tubers,[168] about a tenth of what a healthy woman could carry to the market. With this money the women purchased fish and maize. The maize dealers were traders from the Highlands and middlemen from the Valley itself—*anyamata-a-geni*—who, together with the commercial fishermen, stood at the top of the new village society. The middlemen sold the maize at exorbitant prices, which left a considerable profit margin.[169] The distinction between the poor and anyamata-a-geni became quite glaring during food crises such as the Thodi famine of 1949:

> The gentlemen [*sic*] with long trousers, jacket, pork-pie hat and bicycle, making a living entirely as a middle-man, was able to find food at all times

> with the money in his pocket, while his honester and harder working brother who laboured on the land was left without subsistence should his crops fail from causes beyond his control.[170]

Enormous indeed became the power of the man who made money outside agriculture, as the following account of another sector of nonagricultural production—the cattle economy—demonstrates.

Cattle raising was a relatively new branch of production in the Valley, one of the earliest fruits of merchant capital. The first documented cattle keepers in the area were Kololo chiefs. A number of them received oxen as their wages from Livingstone during the latter's last trip to the region in 1863 (Livingstone had purchased the animals in the Lower Zembezi for the purpose of drawing his carts and wagon from the Mamvera Rapids on the Tchiri River to Lake Malawi).[171] Later, other Kololo acquired cattle through trade and raiding. What happened to these initial holdings is not entirely clear from the record. Late nineteenth-century European travelers do not refer to cattle in Kololo areas. Similarly silent on the subject are early colonial observers. The initiative may have foundered, as some of the earliest references to the topic appear to imply. A census taken in 1929 showed that there were only 148 head of cattle in the entire Chikwawa District.[172] On the basis of a report made in 1931, which breaks down holdings by owner, one can infer that over 50 percent of the animals were owned by Kololo chiefs.[173] It is also clear from the census that the majority of these animals were raised along the Tchiri River, especially on the east bank. The west bank was inhospitable to cattle because of the presence of the tsetse fly.

Thinly populated (the 767-square-mile Chapananga chiefdom had a density of only 8.4 persons a square mile in 1935) and dominated by mopane (tsanya) woodland, much of western Chikwawa has been infested with the tsetse fly since the mid-nineteenth century, if not earlier. In October 1859 Kirk noted the abundance of the fly along the trade route from Chikwawa to Thete.[174] Four years later, in April, Rowley could not bring cattle to Chikwawa "on account of the quantity of Tsetse fly which abound between here & Tete, especially at this season."[175] Subsequent colonial reports confirm the observation, specifying the area on both sides of the Mwanza River between Mikolongo and the Mozambican border as the worst affected.[176] And if the theory that associates the tsanya forest with the fly is valid,[177] the entire belt from the Mwanza River in the north down to the southern boundary of Chikwawa with Port Herald must have carried the fly at varying levels.

There were also persistent reports about the outbreak of sleeping sickness in cattle and human beings in the area since the 1920s.[178] The outbreaks reached alarming proportions during the 1950s, when nine cases of infected persons were reported in 1952 alone.[179] The increase may reflect better reporting at a time when the whole area was being closely scrutinized for resettlement purposes. It may also have been the result of the dramatic increase in the animal population following the extension of the boundaries of the Lengwe Game Reserve in 1936 and the imposition of stricter game control regulations. Whatever the exact effect of these developments, colonial administrators already knew at the beginning of the 1930s that no cattle could be raised on the west bank on account of the tsetse fly.[180] That some twenty years later officials in Zomba ever contemplated the possibility of integrating cattle in the resettlement schemes that bordered the expanded Lengwe Game Reserve confounds anyone with the crudest familiarity with the region. Not Chikwawa but Port Herald was destined to become the center of the cattle economy despite the fact that the animals made their first appearance in the district only at the turn of this century.

The densely populated Port Herald District has been free of the tsetse as far back as documentary evidence goes. Neither has there been any major outbreak of sleeping sickness. Only at Kaombe estate and at Sankhulani were cattle reportedly struck by the disease in 1923.[181] But these two sites are part of the district only from an administrative point of view. Ecologically, Kaombe is an extension of western Chikwawa, whereas Sankhulani forms part of the Highlands. The Ndamera chiefdom on the border of Mozambique in the south is the only area that is representative of the general environment of the district and from which came reports about sleeping sickness in cattle during the 1940s.[182] If the outbreaks in the chiefdom were, like those at Sankhulani, indeed caused by trypanosomes,[183] the parasites may have been transmitted from infected cattle by blood-sucking flies or ticks. There was considerable traffic in cattle and human beings between Ndamera or Sankhulani and Mozambique, where both the tsetse fly and sleeping sickness were common. Port Herald District was otherwise sufficiently free of the disease to permit the development of a cattle economy.

It was not the old Mang'anja aristocracy but European and Indian settlers who introduced cattle to Port Herald District at the turn of the century. Best known among the cattle-owning settlers were the Jenningses at Nyathando (Ndamera chiefdom) and the Deuss family, who maintained large holdings at Muona (Mlolo chiefdom) and Marka

(Ndamera chiefdom). The Deuss family used to produce ghee, which they sold at Chiromo and Port Herald townships in addition to Blantyre.[184] In 1939 there were 847 head of cattle owned by the settlers and 367 owned by Africans.[185] The situation was to change dramatically in the 1940s.

The decline in cotton agriculture laid the conditions for unprecedented growth in the cattle economy. Although there is no statistical evidence, oral information makes cattle keeping, like fishing, another outgrowth of the dying cotton agriculture.[186] Whereas some former zunde holders turned to fishing, others looked to cattle raising. There were still others who combined the two either concurrently or at different phases in their careers. They were joined by a small group of ex-migrant workers. The number of African-owned cattle rose from 1,345 to 4,437 in the period from 1949 to 1955.[187] By 1980 there were, according to some estimates, between seventy-five thousand and one hundred thousand head of cattle in the whole Valley, over half of which were raised in Port Herald District.[188]

Like cotton agriculture, the cattle economy was from the beginning dominated by members of the Sena ethnic group.[189] They later consolidated their economic position politically when they sided with the peasantry in the anticolonial and anti-mitumbira movement against Tengani and other Mang'anja chiefs. Their participation in the nationalist struggle won them most of the important positions in the Malawi Congress Party after the country gained independence in 1964. They have since then successfully used their political influence to promote their economic interests. They have for all practical purposes become the ruling class in the postcolonial Tchiri Valley. They own most of the cattle raised in the region.

Then as now, one of the main attractions of cattle raising in the Valley was that it cost virtually nothing to maintain the beasts after finding the initial capital to purchase them. All one needed was a *khola,* a kraal made of tree poles, and a herdsman. To reduce operating expenses, cattle owners employed small boys as herdsmen. The boys led the cattle from the kraal in the morning for grazing on the mphala or on the dambo during the wet and dry seasons, respectively. Once the beasts were out in the fields, the small, undernourished, and badly paid herdsmen could hardly control the movements of the large beasts.[190]

Left alone the beasts laid the land to waste, destroying peasant gardens with impunity. They undermined the popular strategy of survival through the cultivation of sweet potatoes:

> There are so many cattle these days, so many herds that you cannot see even sweet potatoes in these gardens. Soon after you have planted the cuttings, and long before the vines have started spreading on the ground, cattle are there already to devour them. What is it that gives us famines? Is it not the beasts? There is no agriculture these days. If we eat sweet potatoes, it is only because we are stubborn enough to continually keep watch over the gardens . . . that is why we have *mchete.*[191]

The term *mchete* refers to the color that African skin takes on after exposure to the cold. The phrase *kudza mchete* is used figuratively and means to become very poor and to be without a shelter. Cattle owners indirectly expropriated the land and converted it into grazing grounds—a crude form of exploitation the political basis of which has not escaped poor peasants.

Colonial officials did little to protect the poor against the depredations of the beasts. The British had complained about the absence of cattle in the area, cattle keeping being in their view the sign of rural "progress."[192] Most cattle holders were the fathers of the intellectuals who served the colonial regime in various capacities as teachers, clerks, and tax collectors. They used their position to protect their parents against peasants who complained against cattle both inside and outside the courtroom. The alliance that the intellectuals forged with the peasantry during nkhondo-ya-mitumbira was, as in many other parts of Africa, only tactical. It collapsed soon after political independence was gained in 1964.

Peasants are now even more afraid to speak openly against cattle and cattle owners than they were during the colonial era, when their grievances found an official spokesman in the person of the medium of the Mbona cult. The Malawi Congress Party has silenced the medium, accusing him of political subversion. The few peasants who have dared take cattle owners to court have been flatly told to stop being jealous of their "hard-working" neighbors.[193] The conflict between the poor and the rich has now gone underground, as the former continue their struggle by secretly spearing and stealing cattle—a limited and uncoordinated form of resistance that does not directly challenge the system. The old morality that had penalized the accumulating neighbor and relative has become incompatible with the new forces of class differentiation and the complex transformations in age and gender.

7.3. Change and Continuity in Domestic Struggle

> The influence of these Asena groups on what is now clearly a Mang'anja minority has been profound. Over a period of perhaps 50–60 years they have steadily infiltrated into the District and strict Mang'anja Law and Custom have been modified accordingly.[194]

Rural differentiation, poverty, and ecological change adversely affected many social institutions that had prospered on cotton money during the 1920s and 1930s. The mabzyoka spirit-possession cult was on its way out during the second half of the 1960s, when Matthew Schoffeleers started his anthropological investigations in the Valley.[195] Popular music recorded by Wim Van Zanten during the late 1970s warned co-wives against being jealous and, in particular, against contracting diseases that had in the past required the performance of mabzyoka:

> The polygamist's wives pretend to suffer from eye-diseases
> The eye-disease is ever-lasting
> Washing the face does not clean their eyes. . . .
> The polygamist's wives pretend to suffer from boil
> Their boils are ever-lasting. . . .
> The polygamist's wives pretend to suffer from coughing
> It's a pity when they cough at the market
> Their sputum can fill a pot.[196]

The performer went on to list other insults, making it clear that such women deserved to be divorced. The time when the accumulating husband spent his money on expensive mabzyoka rituals had passed. I did not see a single mabzyoka performance during the period from December 1979 to September 1980 in a district where even a casual visitor would not have missed the drumming that had characterized mabzyoka in the past.

The decline of mabzyoka formed part of a general pattern that has resulted in the displacement of women from positions of power in the public religious arena.[197] The displacement has taken two distinct though related courses. First, there has been a phenomenal increase in the number of Pentecostal churches since the 1970s, all of which are led by men, including ex–migrant laborers.[198] Some of the churches have drawn their followers almost exclusively from women, especially those suffering from the kinds of disease that female nyahana doctors had treated through the performance of mabzyoka. The psychological control of oppressed women and the profits so realized have now gone to the male elite, with implications that have yet to be explored.

17. Mai Menala, one of the last famous nyahana doctors, 1960s

As the ex-migrant laborers and fish and cattle traders introduced Pentecostal churches, Mang'anja men from the traditional ruling families began to displace female mediums in local rain-calling cults. The most revealing example of this process comes from the court of Nyachikadza. There the long tradition of female mediumship came to an end, quite significantly, in 1964, when colonial Nyasaland became independent Malawi. Nsayi Ndakuonetsani resigned her position and was replaced by a man because, as she put it, she had found it difficult to operate "in the world of men."[199] Although more research is still needed to determine the relationship of this trend to what Schoffeleers calls "neo-traditionalism"—the equally male-controlled indigenous-oriented religious movements that oppose "independent" churches—one point is clear. The political disenfranchisement of women that had started under Kololo rule and was subsequently reinforced by the British has now come to coincide with the masculinization of positions of power in public religion.

The displacement of women from the public religious domain took place against a backdrop of significant changes in the institutions that regulated the relations of social juniors to their seniors. Nomi youth labor associations received a serious blow in the early 1930s when some of the newly appointed Mang'anja native authorities joined the missionaries in the campaign against the associations.[200] Exercising their powers under Indirect Rule, the chiefs attacked the associations that, as the missionaries charged, corrupted the youth morally and stood in the way of the Gospel and school education.[201] However, the effectiveness of these measures depended largely on economic forces. The decline in cotton agriculture undermined the material basis of the political support the associations had once enjoyed in the area. Neither commercial fishermen nor cattle owners needed nomi labor services, which left the associations with only one main constituency: the ordinary cultivator, who was too poor to hire paid workers. Furthermore, like the missionary schools themselves, the nomi must have suffered considerably from the exodus of male youth labor into the cities. Duly was observing the combined effect of these developments in the late 1940s when he wrote that "the custom has largely died out . . . over the past fifteen years."[202]

By "custom" Duly meant the old sexually mixed nomi groups whose members had included boys, nubile girls, and a considerable number of married men. In contrast, the few associations that he saw were not only small in size but were also "restricted to young boys and girls who have not reached puberty."[203] Some of these groups would in time become sexually segregated, with the all-female varieties predominating. The older boys and married men would never return to the nomi as laborers during the associations' checkered resurgence in the early 1950s and in the period immediately following independence in 1964. The few grown-up men who joined the female-dominated clubs did so as managers and profiteers (much like the male leaders of Pentecostal churches) rather than as workers.[204] The nomi had lost many of its socializing functions. The city, rather than agricultural work in the villages, prepared the male youth for marriage. Wage labor had become the only reliable source of chuma bride-wealth.

Economic change from the late 1930s onward helped popularize the chuma at the expense of the chikamwini bride-service arrangement. The Mang'anja matrilineal-matrilocal system was under pressure, as Duly found in the late 1940s: "Today, even in the families of the highest chiefs, the payment of bride price is now the generally accepted principle, though . . . succession to office has continued to remain with the descendants of the deceased chief's sisters and these are not always allowed to marry patrilocally."[205] A survey conducted two decades later showed that over 60 percent of all marriages in the Valley had been contracted through the payment of chuma, which gave the husband the right to take his wife to his natal village and to have his children inherit his property.[206]

It is tempting to interpret, as many colonial officials did, the spread of the chuma institution and of the patrilineal system merely in ethnic and demographic terms.[207] Although valid, the idea that the Sena simply carried with them this aspect of their social organization wherever they went would leave the dynamics of the process unexplained. Why was it that the Sena were able to preserve this particular institution? Or why was it so appealing to the Mang'anja that they dropped their own system? It becomes more difficult to answer the latter question when one recognizes that the Sena were a political minority throughout the colonial era. How were they able to impose their institution on the politically dominant Mang'anja?

To answer these questions one must go beyond ethnic and demographic "facts" to their relationship with political economy. A major conclusion reached in Chapter 4 was that the content of the chikamwini system had started to change long before the economic crisis that followed the Bomani floods of 1939. By making their sons-in-law work their cotton gardens, Mang'anja elders received money for their daughters just as the Sena did despite the structural differences between the chikamwini and chuma institutions. Chikamwini appears to have survived in substance only in those areas of Chikwawa District that, in addition to being predominantly Mang'anja, had also been at the periphery of the cotton economy. Elsewhere, the content of the system started to move toward the chuma institution in the 1920s if not earlier. What the economic crisis of the post-Bomani era did was to reveal the underlying contradiction between the appearance and the reality of the Mang'anja system.

The collapse of the cotton economy in Port Herald District left Mang'anja elders with two options. The first was to return to the precolonial economy, in which the labor services of a prospective son-in-law were used almost exclusively in the production of use-values. The other was to continue the trend set during the cotton era, when chikamwini had allowed parents-in-law to extract money from their sons-in-law. The second alternative became irresistible given the strong ties that had developed between the household and the capitalist colonial economy. Mang'anja elders had little choice but to redirect male youth labor into wage employment and to give up the institutional appearances of chikamwini:

> Lately, the [Mang'anja] people found out that they were losing by giving away their daughters without demanding money. [They said to themselves]: We are losing indeed . . . we should also ask for money; we should take money and eat it and make marriage transactions into real business [*malonda*]. So everyone these days takes money and eats it. They are now charging money [for their daughters], which was not the case in the past.[208]

Bridged that way was the gap that had been growing between the continuities in the form and the shifts in the reality of Mang'anja marriage transactions. The next and even more difficult task is to determine the effect of these institutional changes on the content of domestic struggle.

The difficulties arise from three principal sources. First, the continuities in the forms of control during the 1920s and 1930s did not, as Chapter 4 showed, preclude real change in the content of those relations. It therefore becomes problematic to isolate the transformations that occurred before and after the disruptions in organizational structures. This problem is fundamental to the extent that it touches on the issue of stages and periodization in historical reconstruction. The second source of difficulty results from the fact that this study stops somewhere around 1960, before some of the institutional changes provoked by the demise of the cotton economy had fully worked themselves out. Finally, the documentary evidence for the 1950s is less complete than that for the preceding decades. Although rich, the data on agricultural change during the 1950s cannot fully compensate for the annual district reports to which I had no access. Despite their many weaknesses, annual district reports throw more light on village life than any other colonial source for the Valley. For all these reasons, the following discussion must be treated as a series of hypotheses, although for the purposes of clarity they are often presented as definitive findings.

Institutional and economic change since the late 1930s impinged on the struggle between the male youth and their elders much more directly and uniformly than on gender. Not only did the new structure of rural differentiation favor the male youth, but their conflict with the elders had already taken a new turn during the cotton era. The post-Bomani events found a relation that was already in transition.

The clearest indication that elders had lost some of their control over the male youth by the 1940s comes from official comments on labor migration. The reports imply that young men, both married and unmarried, looked to wage labor as a form of emancipation from rural controls. Many never returned to the village and became part of the growing number of machona, the lost ones. Many others turned a deaf ear to pleas for help from their parents or young wives. "It is . . . obvious," wrote one district commissioner for Port Herald,

> that the local native is concerned because of the ease with which young men escape their responsibilities when living outside the district.[209]

Subsequent reports emphasize the powerlessness of the elders: their inability to stem the tide that imposed on them the responsibility for the wives and children of their sons. Unable to reverse the trend on their own, elders turned to the chiefs for help. One native authority after another responded by imposing rules seeking to regulate the outflow of youth labor. Principal among the regulations was, as noted earlier, the ban on emigration during the garden preparation season.[210] That such orders were largely ineffective in controlling emigration is evident from the reports of the period. Young men left their villages very much according to their assessment of the situation. Finally, the few who returned with some money went into the fish or cattle trade, which introduced a class element to the existing age-based conflicts.

It is important, however, not to read unidirectional change into these reports. The relation of age rested on many other forces besides the material economy. The former included the ideological terrain, whose transformation did not always coincide with economic change. Moreover, economic change was not itself without its contradictions. It affected the female and male segments of the youth differently. Young women did not become part of the migrant labor force. They continued their struggle within the village setting, which guaranteed the survival of the nomi and must have given village elders some leverage over the revolting male youth.

Not so much the elders as the wives of the migrants—women of child-bearing age—paid the highest price for the male revolt. As social juniors in the village community, they continued to bear the brunt of the decaying but not necessarily less oppressive gerontocratic rule in its patrilineal variation. Their independence as de facto heads of households had originally depended on the prosperity of cotton agriculture. Like elderly divorcées and widows, young wives had looked to cotton as the principal source of tax money and support for their children. Indeed, if the reaction of the male chiefs to the subsequent plight of these women is any clue, some had come to prize their forced status as heads of households, especially in the matrilineal Mang'anja communities, where they lived with their own families rather than the parents of the absentee husband. Rural poverty from the time of the Depression dramatically altered the equation.

For one thing, there was a significant change in the composition of female heads of households. Elderly divorcées and widows became a distinct minority as the exodus of the male youth turned a large number of young wives into de facto heads of households. In the 1920s female heads of households had represented less than 10 percent of all the cotton-growing households in the Valley. The Great Depression raised the figure to 25.5 percent.[211] For another, the same process that disgorged cheap labor for the capitalist sector drastically reduced the cash-earning potential of female-headed households. It became increasingly difficult to make ends meet in a rural society that had for decades depended on money. District reports on the Depression of the early 1930s are replete with the sufferings endured by formerly self-supporting women. One development, noted in Chapter 5, was for elderly widows and divorcées to move constantly between Nyasaland and Mozambique seeking assistance from their children and relatives.[212] Another development, also noted in Chapter 5, was for single women to step up the cultivation of cotton in order to make up for lower prices. The struggle to remain part of the cash economy was so strong that it threatened food production: "The major portion of the cultivation of the crop [cotton] is carried out by women and young folk whose chief concern is the provision of adequate food supplies each year."[213] The relative disadvantage of female-headed households became obvious during the late 1930s. When male heads of households hauled their cotton to

Mozambique for better prices or abandoned cotton growing altogether for more lucrative enterprises, female heads dumped their produce on the depressed Nyasaland market.

Having received no taxes from these women for two consecutive years since 1930, G. F. Philip, district commissioner for Port Herald, raised the issue with his superiors in Zomba and with the chiefs of the district. He wanted to exempt women from the tax burden. The reply he received from the all-male council of principal headmen (the future native authorities of Indirect Rule) is worth quoting in full. It confirms the idea emphasized in Chapter 4 that women's economic autonomy during the cotton era did not come about without struggle. All men resisted and those in power even more strongly:

> Principal Headman Tengani almost repeats the words of the Chikwawa Chiefs. Councillor Makoko and Councillor Moya state definitely that exemptions to widows for more than a year or two lead to immorality. P.H. Chipwembwe is not quite sure but thinks that most widows could and should re-marry. Headmen think that the idea of a man paying one tax only for all his wives is a good one. . . . When it is explained that all women would become automatically exempt headmen express the fear that many women would refuse marriage. The general opinion of the Council expressed by Tengani is that the law should remain as it is in this respect.[214]

Colonial tax regulations were to be used to the advantage of men. Women continued to carry the tax burden until the report of the Bell Commission of 1937.

Members of the Bell Commission appointed to examine the tax issue must have given in to the pressure of chiefs such as Tengani when they recommended that "the plural tax on additional huts or wives is a bad tax, and should be abolished."[215] On the other hand, single women must have sighed with relief when, acting on the other recommendation of the commission, the Nyasaland regime abolished the tax on female heads of households in about 1940. The commissioners had appropriately argued that any "system of taxation which might lead to women marrying against their will in order to find money for tax is to be deplored."[216] The exemption formalized the displacement of the women of the Valley from the cash economy while at the same time it removed them from the larger picture of colonial enterprise. As nontaxpayers, women subsequently entered colonial reports as footnotes to the records of the evolving legal system or as plaintiffs against their absentee husbands.

The record of migrant workers from the Valley confirms the parasitic view of wage labor in Africa. The young men who rebelled by going to Blantyre or Limbe did not find it easy to survive on the wages they received. Wage labor in Nyasaland, as in contemporary Malawi, never formed the highroad to rural accumulation. Many young men returned to the village in tatters and infected with diseases:

> You have seen a boy from Limbe . . .
> His blanket is a sack . . .
> He has come with big lice which bite and itch
> Go and ask Dolika who went to bed with her husband
> She was bitten in the buttocks by lice from Limbe
> Go and ask Enigetsi who went to bed with her husband
> Her breasts fell off one by one because of lice from Limbe
> When they bite, they itch and it hurts.[217]

Their counterparts who traveled to Southern Rhodesia were not in a better position.[218] Those who managed to save some money, as the oral accounts of the origin of cattle keeping and fishing suggest, represented a very tiny minority. The majority were unable to send any support to their parents or wives:

> Concern has been expressed by the Native Association because of the increasing number of natives absent from the district who either do not support their wives or else remain away for too long a period. It is possible that some form of compulsory remittances to wives will be suggested by the Native Association.[219]

Nothing came out of this proposal, and many women decided to sever their ties to their absentee husbands.

Marriage cases increased by 25 percent in Port Herald District in 1942.[220] Of the 108 cases tried by Chief Mlolo in 1944, the overwhelming majority were divorce lawsuits.[221] And the explanation in all these cases was the same. The cases "appearing under the head marriage were for the most part actions brought for the dissolution of domestic ties either on the grounds of adultery, neglect, or the protracted absence of one party—almost invariably that of the man."[222] The young women had grown tired of their honorary status as wives, a position that brought them neither emotional nor material satisfaction, yet still subordinated them to the parents of their nominal husbands, especially under the patrilineal-patrilocal regime. Indeed, some of the accusations of adultery must have been brought against the young women by their parents-in-law.

As one might expect, colonial records are silent on what became of the young women after they had obtained their divorce papers. Some may have remained single for the rest of their lives. Rural poverty and the need for companionship may have driven others into second marriages. These probably ended up as second or third wives. Duly estimated that 10 percent of all married men in Port Herald District in the late 1940s had more than one wife.[223] Still more revealing is his observation that polygyny was most common "among men of the middle-age," including chiefs. The other category of males that benefited from the failure of marriages between poor young peasants was, according to Duly, men who "have established themselves a good trade in fish or some other commodity," such as cattle, "or who are in good permanent local employment."[224] Poor young women were, in other words, being married to men of a different age group and socioeconomic category. The relations they developed with these men must have been significantly different from those between co-wives and their common husband during the cotton era. They must also have been different from the relations that prevailed between two ordinary peasants of the older generation during the 1940s and 1950s.

The evidence of the 1940–60 period allows nothing more than a broad hypothesis on the relations between ordinary men and women in the post-childbearing age group. The struggles of this category of the peasantry were only remotely related to gender. Ordinary men in this age group were not in a position to take advantage of the newly created reservoir of nubile women. Their relationships with their wives had reached maturity. Adulthood had diminished the relevance of the "female" factor in the social relations of this category of women. They had become more like companions than objects of social control. Like much of the literature on South Africa today, colonial records portray the couples in this age group as resisters to the broad societal changes outlined in the preceding pages. They resented having to accommodate economic trends such as wage labor that tended to undermine their control over the male segment of the youth. They also formed a united front in their resistance to colonial agricultural schemes. "One suspects," wrote one observer, "that the opposition [to the new techniques] very naturally lies amongst the older men, and for that matter amongst the older women too."[225] They represented the bulwark of tradition and guaranteed the survival of many precolonial relations in the postcolonial era.

Two decades of neocolonial struggles have not completely eradicated the tradition of independence associated with this category of women. Unlike most of their male counterparts, the female elders I interviewed in 1980 were unrestrained in their criticism of contemporary rural society (see Preface). They were particularly forthcoming in articulating the relationship between the new political system and their own poverty. They blame the ruling party for permitting, among other things, the irresponsible cattle-grazing practices that have contributed to the ecological degradation initiated by cotton growing at the turn of the century. One wishes they had written this book themselves.

Conclusions

A Simple but Diverse Peasant World: The Lower Tchiri Valley Revisited

1

Primitive civilizations offer privileged cases, then, because they are simple cases.[1]

A careful reader may argue that the story told in the foregoing pages is quite unique. Few regions in Southern Africa have experienced as many ecological shifts and modes of capitalist penetration as did the Lower Tchiri Valley during the period under review. One may therefore conclude that this study has little or no relevance to the ongoing debate on peasants and production in Africa.

I turn the argument for the uniqueness of the Valley the other way around. The Valley is unique in three interrelated ways which enhance rather than weaken its comparative value. First, the history of the region during the century covered by this study combines several stories of different rural economies in Africa. Ecologically, the Valley is a microcosm of the many natural environments that straddle the African continent.[2] The mphala drylands, which in the Valley constitute only a micro-ecosystem, is the dominant natural environment in areas such as the Tchiri Highlands. In other parts of Africa such as northwestern Zambia, the mphala complements the dambo floodlands as it does in the Valley.[3] The dimba and munda agricultural systems, which dominated different periods in the history of the Valley, have prevailed in other parts of Africa although not necessarily in the same relationship as they did in the Valley.[4] Finally, every part of Southern Africa has been subjected to one or another form of capitalist domination. The Valley is unique only in the regard that it experienced all the major routes toward capitalist development and underdevelopment in Africa.

Another feature of the Valley that has added to the comparative significance of this study is the relative "simplicity" of the individual systems that make up the socioeconomic structure and history of the region. The munda agricultural regime of the Valley was a far more restricted system than its counterpart on the Highlands, which did not compete with another major system of land use.[5] Moreover, every major fluctuation in the level of the Tchiri River rejuvenated the dambo and laid the conditions for a new dimba regime. Together with the erratic character of rainfall, the shifts in the water volume of the Tchiri River simplified the Man-Nature relationship in the history of the Valley. The student of the region cannot treat the ecosystem as a mere backdrop. So-called environmental factors left an indelible mark on every phase of capitalist intervention in the Valley.

Each of these capitalist phases was in itself a simple system. Although dramatic, the slave trade and legitimate commerce did not have the long-term effect in the Valley that they did in West Africa, where the two trades flourished for over four centuries.[6] Similarly, plantation agriculture, peasant cotton production, and male labor migration were less developed in the Valley than they were in areas such as the Tchiri Highlands, Uganda, and Lesotho,[7] respectively.

Finally, the collapse of the lundu state in the eighteenth century had left Mang'anja society on the eve of the slave trade a less differentiated social formation than many other societies at a similar stage in their encounter with the West. In the Tchiri Valley the village community represented the highest form and most effective unit of economic and political organization. Instead of a complex set of institutions binding the individual in society, the student of the mid-nineteenth-century Tchiri Valley is confronted with "elementary" relations of age and gender imposing themselves uncluttered at every level of the social fabric. Studying the Tchiri Valley is on this count studying "primitive" structures like Durkheim's religion of the Australian Aborigines.[8]

The third feature that makes the Valley a unique laboratory for anyone interested in comparative studies is methodological. In order to understand the history of the region one has to combine two different methods that are often employed separately.[9] On the one hand, one has to devise simplifying concepts in order to make sense of the interconnections within and between the ecological and economic systems. The labor process is one such simplifying or generalizing concept (see Introduction). On the other hand, the simplicity of each system forces the student to employ another method: to view each component in simpler form. That is to approach the different components for what they are: uncomplicated structures the understanding of which should, however, uncover the inner workings of better-developed systems. Easy to understand because of its simplicity, the plantation system of the Valley did, for example, exhibit all the essential features of the more developed regime of the Highlands. Study of the more primitive systems of the Valley holds the potential of raising fundamental, if not always exhaustive, questions about the process of the formation of the peasantry in Africa.

2

> The active transformation of nature for the purposes of survival might generally be called labour, and in the case of human beings it has certain distinctive characteristics which are absolutely central to the understanding of society.[10]

The first and most general conclusion that links the different aspects of this study is that peasants are, among other things, a class of partially subordinated workers. This means that in order to understand the process of the formation of a peasantry, one has to link changes in market forces, colonial domination, and/or the development of private property in land to changing patterns of rural work. Unlike most of their interpreters who have never had to engage in manual labor, peasants spend a greater part of their brief life spans working with their hands in order to meet basic human needs.

Injecting the notion of work into the definition of peasantry raises two immediate questions about peasants' relationship to land. The first centers around the natural determinants of production. This is, as we shall see in the final conclusion, a complex problem. Let it suffice to point out at this stage that the simplicities of the Malthusian paradigm, which holds environment and population as long-term determinants of African agriculture,[11] do not warrant the recent tendencies to treat the environment as a mere backdrop to the problems of rural production. Man is part of nature itself. What he does to nature as a social agent is as important as what he finds in nature. Issues like soil types, rainfall patterns, crop diseases, and ecological fluctuations like those occasioned by the Tchiri River in the Valley can affect the labor process in many significant ways, as this study has demonstrated. These are the issues which, although often ignored in the literature, constitute the stuff of agricultural as distinct from agrarian history.[12]

The second and closely related problem raised by the definition of peasants as workers concerns the role of technology in the transformation of productive forces. This study has shown that the failure of capitalism to revolutionize the technology of rural production did not condemn peasant productive forces to inertia, as both Marxist and their bourgeois antagonists have assumed.[13] Capitalist and colonial demands made in the absence of major technological breakthroughs highlighted the significance of labor power in the development and underdevelopment of productive forces. Producers in the Valley responded to market forces by continually shifting their relationship to nature through the labor process. They discarded some labor processes such as those that had gone into nonagricultural production while at the same time they intensified and diversified agricultural work against the backdrop of the fluctuations in the level of the Tchiri River. The uneven trends in the patterns of labor usage did not affect only the ecosystem. They also formed part of the story of the emergence of the peasantry as a partially subordinated class from the 1880s onward. The process of peasantry formation was a momentous event that included significant transformations in the Man-Nature relationship. Merchant capital had precipitated the reorganization of productive forces in the absence of new technologies and the colonial state.

The second major conclusion of this study is that one does not need to go beyond peasant studies in order to ask meaningful questions about gender, generational, and other forms of rural differentiation. Familiarity with the feminist discourse, the anthropology of age, and class analysis may sharpen the questions, but the questions themselves are implicit in the study of peasantry formation. As an analytical concept, the labor process "raises the possibility that women and men," the young and elders, the poor and rich, are "engaged in quite different patterns of work." The concept offers a strategic entry into the "question of how power [is] negotiated and exercised in the countryside."[14] But answers to these internally generated questions are necessarily ambiguous. The social position that an individual holds in society does not always accurately reflect his role in material production.

A long historical perspective on gender has illuminated the debate on domestic struggles in at least two ways. First, it suggests the need to reexamine our assumptions about patriarchy as "primal fact." Close analysis of the ideological, political, and economic structures of precapitalist Mang'anja society indicates that the battle between the sexes had not been settled one way or the other by the time of the international slave trade. The nature of women's relationships to men varied widely from one context to another. Thus the prevalence of men as political leaders did not imply generalized male domination, as some students of similarly organized communities have argued.[15] The corollary was also true. The presence of a select group of women in powerful positions of political and religious leadership did not result in matriarchal rule. Women's relationships to men in the Valley were too dynamic and fraught with too many contradictions to be neatly packaged under the concepts of matriarchy or patriarchy.

The study suggests, in the second place, that although capitalism in general tended to dispossess women, different forms of capitalist domination affected different categories of women in dissimilar ways. Thus political change from the time of the slave trade disenfranchised all women in the Valley, but petty commodity production strengthened the struggles of many categories of women, including elderly spinsters and heads of households of the childbearing age group. They successfully used cotton agriculture to defend their right to a life of decency, and their political disenfranchisement became an economic liability only after the conversion of the Valley into a labor reservoir. A disaster for young wives, labor migration did not adversely affect the position of female seniors vis-à-vis their husbands. Male and female elders closed ranks in their resistance to colonial land consolidation schemes and to the socioeconomic developments that tended to limit their control over the male segment of the youth population.

In order to understand the conflict between social juniors and seniors in Mang'anja society one needs to pay as much attention to economic as to ideological facts. For although not determinant, religious ideology constituted the dominant sphere in the local system of control. Religion defined the youth as nonhuman beings and as nonlaborers within the economy of social reproduction; it devalued their labor power within agriculture and, in so doing, made sense of the denial of control of the product to youth.

The subsequent incorporation of this system of control in the capitalist world economy tended to magnify preexisting contradictions between work and control, between content and form, and between the economics and ideology of generational conflicts. For example, the struggle of Mang'anja elders to retain youth labor within agriculture both elaborated preexisting institutions such as chikamwini bride-service and precipitated significant changes in the content of the institution. The revived chikamwini of the cotton era came to serve a very different purpose than it had done during the mid-nineteenth century. It buttressed primitive accumulation despite the continuities in the form of struggle. Thus, when Mang'anja elders finally adopted the institution of chuma bridewealth following the decline of cotton production and the rise of male labor migration, they simply closed the gap between the form and content of their system of youth control against the backdrop of new patterns of accumulation.

The rapid succession of events marking the different modes of capitalist domination and the sharp ecological discontinuities combined to simplify the story of peasant differentiation and class formation in the Valley. Cotton production subsidized rural accumulation for a period of only three decades from the late 1900s to the late 1930s. The typical accumulating peasant (the zunde holder) of the period was a male Sena immigrant who, largely for demographic reasons, cultivated if not actually resided on the fertile dambo in the Dabanyi and Dinde marshes. The interpenetration of demographic and ecological forces gave a distinctively ethnic bias to the process of peasant differentiation in the Valley, as was the case in many other rural economies in colonial Africa.[16]

Another point of comparative interest emerging from study of the period relates to the ambiguity of the position of the rural rich. As a peasant, the zunde holder exploited communal lands and such precapitalist channels of labor recruitment as marriage. But as a capitalist farmer, the zunde holder also employed wage laborers, which heightened his dependence on the world market. The ambiguity determined both the rise and fall of the zunde holder. With a good portion of his income rerouted into the precapitalist sphere,[17] such as the acquisition of new wives and the settlement of domestic struggles, the zunde holder was left with little or no capital to invest in new technologies that might have reduced his dependence on the vicissitudes of nature. The permanent inundation of the marshes from 1939 on paralyzed the zunde holder after nearly a decade of struggle against the fluctuations in the world demand for cotton.

The collapse of zunde farming marked the beginning of a new phase in the history of peasant differentiation in the Valley. Nonagricultural production, particularly fishing and cattle raising, became the new sources of wealth. Some of the original commercial fishermen and cattle owners had been zunde farmers, which explains the retention of the initial ethnic bias in the new process of accumulation. The new era carried the past in another sense. The collapse of cotton agriculture created a cheap labor force that proved indispensable to the success of commercial fishing. It was cattle holders, however, who became the real antagonists of the rural poor. Cattle owners turned communal lands into their own grazing grounds, informally expropriating the land. But it was not until after political independence in 1964 that the rich translated their economic into political might. The two segments of the rural population became self-reproducing classes after the rich captured the state from the British. Political independence transformed the conflict between peasants and the state, which is the third major theme of this study.

Study of rural resistance in the Valley corroborates the view of "peasants as *continuous initiators* in political relations among themselves and with nonpeasants" (emphasis in original).[18] When villagers openly challenged the authority of Chief Tengani in 1960, they were not simply responding to nationalist propaganda. Tengani personified the forces that had eroded their autonomy as producers and as political actors. The revolt represented only one visible expression of peasant struggle to regain the autonomy they had lost since the nineteenth century. Hidden for nearly a century, the struggles came into the open in the early 1940s as a result of the intensification of colonial intervention in rural production.

In the Tchiri Valley, peasants' attempts to control their own destinies as workers provided the most significant link between "primary" and "everyday" resistance on the one hand and the nationalist struggle on the other.[19] The African countryside was not simply at the receiving end of nationalist propaganda, and it did not simply provide the elite with the crowds that disarmed the British. It also generated the agenda and language for nationalist resistance. The local leaders of the Nyasaland African Congress (as the ruling Malawi Congress Party was then known) had to adopt the cause of the grass-roots movement against mitumbira and other land consolidation schemes. Unlike their counterparts in other parts of Africa, these leaders did not have to revive memories of past struggles.[20] In the nkhondo-ya-mitumbira (war of the ridges) they found a political platform that had already united different segments of the rural population against the colonial state.[21]

The history of the Valley also highlights the limits of rural struggle. Under colonialism, rural resistance formed, as did slave struggles in the American South,[22] an essential aspect of accommodation. Resistance and accommodation cannot be separated in the colonial world. Resistance to wage employment or labor tenancy in the Valley succeeded only because of the depth of peasants' submission to metropolitan demands for cotton. Similarly, the success of peasant resistance to the colonial cultivation blueprint that concentrated agricultural work within the brief rainy season implied submission to a work schedule that extended the agricultural cycle beyond traditional limits. Imperialism eliminated the "tribal" cultivator—Hyden's "uncaptured peasantry"—as a meaningful social category.

The idea that accommodation formed an essential aspect of resistance has several implications. It suggests, for example, that the peasant world is in many significant ways not as far removed from the world of scholars as such esoteric debates about peasant "rationality" imply.[23] The peasant world is ultimately a human world. The selective character of rural struggle highlights "the elements of ambiguity, contradiction and conflict" which peasants experience in their daily lives in common with other human beings.[24]

Appreciating these ambiguities also helps us understand the blockages in African agriculture as an integral part of the process of peasantry formation itself. In the Tchiri Valley, peasants accommodated metropolitan demands for cotton by neglecting or phasing out those food crops that extended beyond the rainy season and therefore competed for labor with the late-planted munda cotton. That was how gonkho sorghum came to lose its former popularity in the Valley in spite of the fact that it was the most heat-resistant cereal in this region of frequent droughts. Finding it difficult to combine gonkho with cotton crops, many growers increasingly chose the latter. The decision reflected the operation of many forces, including changes in ideas about food security. The development of a market in foodstuffs, which in the Valley was tied to the cotton economy, undermined the significance of production in the system of food supply. Peasants could use cotton money to purchase imported foodstuffs. Those who did not have money often mortgaged their unharvested cotton. But more significant than these market forces was political pressure. As a colonized people, peasants had either to sell their labor power or to produce commodities; they could not completely resist both without breaching the colonial relation. Under imperialism, villagers could negotiate the terms but not the reality of capitalist domination, as the following discussion of the colonial state (which is the fourth major theme of this study) seeks to demonstrate.

The literature on the colonial state in Africa sits uncomfortably on two contending paradigms. On the one hand, the colonial state is seen as inherently weak and autonomous in relation to specific class interests.[25] On the other hand, the state is perceived as a powerful agent that always acted in the interests of metropolitan capital.[26] Study of the Tchiri Valley does not support either view. The Nyasaland regime was both weak and powerful; it was both subordinate and autonomous.

The Nyasaland regime exhibited all the weaknesses that scholars have attributed to colonial states in Africa. The British gave up their blueprint for cotton cultivation of 1909 when faced with rural opposition. Later, they displayed the autonomy of the state when they abandoned European settlers and forged a new alliance with the peasantry. But these were concessions in the means by which the state pursued its mission; they should not be confounded with the mission itself. In shifting its alliance from European farmers to peasants, the state only changed the method of extracting surplus from the colony. Otherwise the Nyasaland regime stood firm when it came to carrying out the mission that had given birth to it.

The imposition of British armed "peace" made up for the deficiencies of market forces as a factor in the subordination of African producers. Whereas merchant capital had only facilitated, imperialism necessitated a new division of labor in which the production of use-values competed with wage employment, labor tenancy, cash crop agriculture, and a host of informal means of earning cash for taxes and other demands of the new economy. Thus, even those villagers who did not directly participate in money-making activities were indirectly subordinated as workers in their own fields. They absorbed the withdrawal of their husbands, sons, and occasionally daughters from the food economy by modifying their patterns of agricultural work. Imperialism effectively closed the exit option that peasants of the precolonial era had enjoyed. The otherwise weak Nyasaland regime did bring about a qualitatively different epoch in the history of peasantry formation. It was indeed a powerful state despite its limitations.

The Nyasaland regime also proved to be a subordinate state. Even the most liberal wing of the colonial establishment did not hesitate to join the interventionist hard-liners when the decline in peasant cotton output threatened the historic mission of the state as an agent of metropolitan accumulation. Nor did the failure of the various betterment programs to achieve their stated objectives leave the peasantry unaffected. At the very least, the projects undermined the ability of the villagers to cope with the ecological crises that followed the Bomani floods of 1939. By weakening rural resistance to wage employment, the programs drew the village economy further into the tentacles of capitalism.

The fifth and final conclusion of this study addresses the broader theoretical question of how physical processes engage with the social conditions of peasant production.[27] Answers to this question are necessarily ambiguous. Like other workers, peasants unite in a contradictory relationship the physical and mental processes that, for heuristic purposes, scholars isolate as the forces and relations of production.

The assertion that through work peasants combine the forces and relations of production in a contradictory relationship directs attention to two different types of relationship. The first is the relationship of correspondence or convergence. Unlike bees, peasants engage their physical world as social and cultural agents; they create their structures in the mind before they actually construct them in wax.[28] Like salt and iron production, hunting and food cultivation were not simply physical processes. They were also cultural events in which social knowledge, rituals, and taboos formed part of the very instruments of production. The separation between the physical and the mental in human activities is more analytical than real.

Second, the assertion that peasants engage the physical and social conditions of production in a contradictory relationship highlights the possibility of a conflict or divergence within and between the two analytical structures of the economy. This study has shown how, for example, developments in the patterns of labor usage contradicted those in the technological base. It has also documented the discrepancies between form and content, and between the ideology and economics of gender and generational conflicts.

Finally, there is the possibility of a temporal divergence between the forces and relations of production. Cotton agriculture started to degrade the mphala ecosystem from the time of its inception in the first decade of the twentieth century. Yet, because of peasants' access to imported foodstuffs, the Valley experienced a period of relative prosperity for nearly three decades (with the exception of the economic crisis of 1918–23). The social world did not accurately reflect the changing structure of productive forces. It took a contingent event—the flooding of the marshes—to highlight the contradictory trends between the forces and relations of production. However, it was social struggle in the form of the conflict between peasants and the state that ultimately turned the post-1940 ecological disruptions into social events, just as neocolonial struggles since the 1970s have "socialized" the structural distortions of many African economies. It is in this very limited sense that one can speak of the primacy of the relations over the forces of production: whereas structural contradictions create the possibilities for, it is ultimately human beings as social agents who create social revolutions. Human beings seize on the opportunities for change created by structural contradictions. Otherwise, the question of causal primacy remains open-ended. As a part of nature, man cannot conquer nature without destroying himself.

Notes
Bibliography
Glossary
Index

Notes

Preface

1 G. W. Clendennen, ed., "The Shire Journal of David Livingstone, 1861–1864" (unpublished typescript in author's possession); D. Livingstone and C. Livingstone, *The Narrative of an Expedition to the Zambesi and Its Tributaries and of the Discoveries of Lakes Shirwa and Nyassa* (London: Murray, 1865); J. P. R. Wallis, ed., *The Zambesi Expedition of David Livingstone, 1858–63,* 2 vols. (London: Chatto and Windus, 1956); R. Foskett, ed., *The Zambesi Journal of Dr. John Kirk, 1858–1863,* 2 vols. (Edinburgh: Oliver and Boyd, 1965).
2 For a guide to the Livingstone materials in the National Library of Scotland see G. W. Clendennen and I. C. Cunningham, comps., *David Livingstone: A Catalogue of Documents* (Edinburgh: National Library of Scotland, 1979).
3 For a good account of the mission see O. Chadwick, *Mackenzie's Grave* (London: Hodder and Stoughton, 1959).
4 N. R. Bennett and M. Ylvisaker, eds., *The Central African Journal of Lovell Procter, 1860–1864* (Boston: Boston University Press, 1971); H. Rowley, *The Story of the Universities Mission to Central Africa* (1867; New York: Negro Universities Press, 1969).
5 J. P. R. Wallis, ed., *The Zambesi Journal of James Stewart, 1862–1863* (London: Chatto and Windus, 1952).
6 M. Vaughan, "Social and Economic Change in Southern Malawi: A Study of Rural Communities in the Shire Highlands and Upper Shire Valley from the Mid-Nineteenth Century to 1915" (Ph.D. diss., London University, 1981), 15.
7 H. Kjekshus, *Ecology Control and Economic Development in East African History: The Case of Tanganyika, 1850–1950* (London: Heinemann, 1977), 1-25. Kjekshus does not, however, establish the standards he uses for rejecting one set of European accounts (those relating to the slave trade) and for accepting others (those pertaining to peasant production and exchange).
8 E. C. Tabler, ed., *The Zambezi Papers of Richard Thornton: Geologist to Livingstone's Zambezi Expedition.* 2 vols. (London: Chatto and Windus, 1963). Thornton's papers are not particularly useful for the study of Malawi. He did not visit the Tchiri Valley until 1863, the year he died of malaria.
9 The Slave Trade, Foreign Office (FO) 84, Public Record Office (PRO), London. I have not come across British records covering the period from 1867 to 1875. The only British traveler I know of who visited the area during this period was Henry Faulkner, who was murdered on his way to the east coast.

10 The most notable exception to this rule is the unpublished diaries of Frederick T. Morrison, an engineer to the African Lakes Company. The diaries are now in the University of Edinburgh Library.

11 Africa, FO 2, PRO. Johnston's survey is doc. 66 in the collection.

12 The first volume of 1907 also contains a section on the precolonial history of the ethnic groups in each district. District commissioners for the Lower Shire and Port Herald continued to record their observations in this volume until the 1950s.

13 J. M. Schoffeleers, "Crisis, Criticism, and Critique: An Interpretative Model of Territorial Mediumship Among the Chewa," *Journal of Social Sciences* 3 (1974): 74–80; idem, "Cult Idioms and the Dialectics of a Region," R. Werbner, ed., *Regional Cults* (London: Academic Press, 1977), 219–239; E. C. Mandala, "The Tengani Chieftaincy and Its Relations with Other Chieftaincies in Nsanje District, c. 1850–1951" (unpublished paper, Department of History, University of Malawi, 1973–74). The data from these two projects are referenced as SM73/— and T73/—, respectively.

14 Oral testimony from 1976 is referenced M/CK—; from 1980, TVES—/—.

15 E. C. Mandala, "The Nature and Substance of Mang'anja and Kololo Traditions: A Preliminary Survey," *Society of Malawi Journal* 31 (January 1978): 1–14.

16 See TVES7 and TVES8 under Oral Testimonies in the bibliography.

17 I am in no position to confirm the view that traditions about the period before 1850 contain "only incidental references to economic, religious and other social developments" (K. G. M. Phiri, "Chewa History in Central Malawi and the Use of Oral Tradition, 1600–1920" [Ph.D. diss., University of Wisconsin, 1975], 15; see also H. Langworthy, "Understanding Malawi's Pre-Colonial History," *Society of Malawi Journal* 23 [January 1969]: 36–45). I tend to believe that the scarcity of such information is largely due to the questions posed rather than the nature of the traditions themselves.

18 For an academic elaboration of this perspective see S. Miers and I. Kopytoff, eds., *Slavery in Africa: Historical and Anthropological Perspectives* (Madison: University of Wisconsin Press, 1977), esp. I. Kopytoff and S. Miers, "African 'Slavery' as an Institution of Marginality," 3–81.

19 Each of the six zones is profiled in the TVES interview series, nos. 1–6.

20 This evidence seems to validate the claim of D. D. T. Jabavu, a political activist in South Africa during the early 1920s, that men are more "psychologically subjected in the wider society" than women (see W. Beinart and C. Bundy, *Hidden Struggles in Rural South Africa: Politics and Popular Movements in the Transkei and Eastern Cape, 1890–1930* [Berkeley and Los Angeles: University of California Press, 1987], 239).

Introduction: The Labor Process in African Agrarian History

1 A. Sayer, "Epistemology and Conceptions of People and Nature in Geography," *Geoforum* 10 (1979): 30.

2 The following geographical information is taken from J. G. Pike and G. T. Rimmington, *Malawi: A Geographical Study* (Oxford: Oxford University Press, 1965); J. M. Schoffeleers, *The Lower Shire Valley of Malawi: Its Ecology, Population Distribution, Ethnic Divisions, and Systems of Marriage* (Limbe, Malawi: Montfort, 1968); Shire Valley Agricultural Development Project, *An Atlas of the Lower Shire Valley, Malawi* (Blantyre, Malawi: Department of Surveys, 1975).

3 Chap. 3 discusses the problems in navigating the river as a result of the drop in its water volume beginning in the 1880s.

4 The description of soil structures and so on is based on Schoffeleers, *The Lower Shire Valley;* and Shire Valley Agricultural Development Project, *Atlas.*

5 Schoffeleers, *The Lower Shire Valley;* Shire Valley Agricultural Development Project, *Atlas.*

6 Monthly Agricultural Report, August, November, and December 1930, A3/2/200; monthly Agricultural Report, June 1934, A3/2/201, Malawi National Archives (MNA), Zomba.

7 K. Marx, *Capital,* Vol. 1, trans. B. Fowkes (New York: Vintage, 1977), 283.

8 For a critique of this model in the literature on Central and Southern Africa see F. Cooper, "Peasants, Capitalists, and Historians: A Review Article," *Journal of Southern African Studies* 9 (April 1981): 285–314; T. O. Ranger, "Growing from the Roots: Reflections on Peasant Research in Central and Southern Africa," *Journal of Southern African Studies* 5 (October 1978): 99–133.

9 See A. Foster-Carter, "The Modes of Production Controversy," *New Left Review,* January/February 1978, 47–73, for a lucid introduction to the subject.

10 J. Tosh, "The Cash Crop Revolution in Tropical Africa: An Agricultural Reappraisal," *African Affairs* 79 (1980): 79–94. See also A. Isaacman, "Peasants and Rural Social Protest in Africa" (paper commissioned by the joint American Council of Learned Societies–Social Science Research Council Africa Committee and presented at a meeting of the African Studies Association, Atlanta, November, 1989).

11 Tosh, "The Cash Crop Revolution," 80.

12 See, for example, B. Hindess and P. Hirst, *Pre-Capitalist Modes of Production* (London: Routledge and Kegan Paul, 1975), 9–12. The Althus-

serians are of course reacting against another school of thought which, on the basis of Marx's famous dictum that it is not the articles but how they are made that distinguishes one mode of production from another, have argued for the causal priority of productive forces (see n. 13).

13 For a concise introduction to the debate over the forces and relations of production see G. A. Cohen, *Karl Marx's Theory of History: A Defence* (Princeton: Princeton University Press, 1978); R. Edwards, M. Reich, and T. Weisskopf, *The Capitalist System* (1972; Englewood Cliffs, N.J.: Prentice-Hall, 1978), 42–49.

14 J. Copans and D. Seddon, "Marxism and Anthropology: A Preliminary Survey," D. Seddon, ed., *Relations of Production: Marxist Approaches to Economic Anthropology* (London: Cass, 1978), 39.

15 See, for example, E. Boserup, *Women's Role in Economic Development* (London: Allen and Unwin, 1970); J. Goody, *Technology, Tradition and the State in Africa* (Cambridge: Cambridge University Press, 1971). These and other determinisms are reviewed by S. Berry, "The Food Crisis and Agrarian Change in Africa: A Review Essay," *African Studies Review* 27 (June 1984): 59–112.

16 See, for example, M. Vaughan, *The Story of an African Famine: Gender and Famine in Twentieth-Century Malawi* (Cambridge: Cambridge University Press, 1987).

17 G. Hyden, *Beyond Ujamaa in Tanzania: Underdevelopment and an Uncaptured Peasantry* (Berkeley and Los Angeles: University of California Press, 1980), 245–246. See also D. F. Bryceson, "Changes in Peasant Food Production and Food Supply in Relation to the Historical Development of Commodity Production in Pre-Colonial and Colonial Tanganyika," *Journal of Peasant Studies* 7 (April 1980): 281–311. For a cogent critique of this view see S. N. Chipungu, *The State, Technology and Peasant Differentiation in Zambia: A Case Study of the Southern Province, 1930–1986* (Lusaka: Historical Association of Zambia, 1988), 1–17; P. Richards, "Ecological Change and the Politics of African Land Use," *African Studies Review* 26 (June 1983): 1–72.

18 Sayer, "Epistemology and Conceptions," 28–29.

19 For a critique of this myth see G. Arrighi, "Labour Supplies in Historical Perspective: A Study of the Proletarianization of the African Peasantry in Rhodesia," G. Arrighi and J. Saul, eds., *Essays on the Political Economy of Africa* (New York: Monthly Review Press, 1973), 180–237.

20 Marx, *Capital,* 284; K. Marx and F. Engels, *The German Ideology,* ed. C. J. Arthur (New York: International Publishers, 1970), 47.

1. Major Tensions in the Political Economy of the Lower Tchiri Valley, 1859–1863

1 Marx and Engels, *The German Ideology,* 46.

2 Bennett and Ylvisaker, eds., *Central African Journal,* 260; Horace Waller diaries 4:12 (June 12, 1862), Rhodes House, Oxford University.

3 Bennett and Ylvisaker, eds., *Central African Journal,* 308; Waller diaries 4:12 (August 6, 1862); Wallis, ed., *Zambesi Journal,* 92, 95. Tengani, who was the second paramount in the Valley, apparently refused to provide Mbona with a wife (see Rowley, *Story of the Universities Mission,* 224–226).

4 J. M. Schoffeleers, "Trade, Warfare and Social Inequality: The Case of the Lower Shire Valley of Malawi, 1590–1622," *Society of Malawi Journal* 33 (July 1980): 6–24; idem, "The Zimba and the Lundu State in the Late Sixteenth and Early Seventeenth Centuries," *Journal of African History* 28 (1987): 337–355.

5 The following account is a summary of the various writings of Schoffeleers, especially "Mbona, the Guardian Spirit of the Mang'anja" (B.Litt. thesis, Oxford University, 1966); "The History and Political Role of the Mbona Cult of the Mang'anja," T. O. Ranger and I. Kimambo, eds., *The Historical Study of African Religion* (London: Heinemann, 1972), 73–94; and "The Chisumphi and Mbona Cults in Malawi: A Comparative History," Schoffeleers, ed., *Guardians of the Land: Essays on Central African Territorial Cults* (Gwelo, Zimbabwe: Mambo, 1978), 147–185.

6 Rowley, *Story of the Universities Mission,* 244.

7 For Chingwandu, Nkanga, and Tera see Bennett and Ylvisaker, eds., *Central African Journal,* 135. According to this testimony, collected in the Highlands, Mankhokwe, Nkanga, and Tera were juniors (*ng'ono*) to yet another paramount, who is identified only by the title "rondo" (see pp. 183, 278). For Tengani's claim as lundu, see for example, Foskett, ed., *Zambesi Journal* 1:164; Rowley, *Story of the Universities Mission,* 72; and Waller diaries 4:13 (October 29, 1862). For Chibisa see E. C. Mandala, "The Kololo Interlude in Southern Malawi, 1861–95" (M.A. thesis, University of Malawi, 1977), 192–194; and J. M. Schoffeleers, "Livingstone and the Mang'anja Chiefs," B. Pachai, ed., *Livingstone, Man of Africa: Memorial Essays, 1873–1973* (London: Longman, 1973), 111–130. Kaphwiti could have been one of the four lundu paramounts listed by Procter (Bennett and Ylvisaker, eds., *Central African Journal,* 135), especially the unidentified "rondo" who lived near the falls (p. 183).

Mgundo, who according to Procter was a junior to the great rondo, emerges in oral traditions as the Kaphwiti who was murdered by the Kololo (see Mandala, "The Kololo Interlude," 77).

8 See, for example, Wallis, ed., *Zambesi Expedition* 2:335; Schoffeleers, "Livingstone." Chigunda, the chief of Magomero in the Highlands, had twelve villages under him, in each of which he had a wife (Rowley, *Story of the Universities Mission,* 203).

9 Rowley, *Story of the Universities Mission,* 223.

10 Ibid., 224.

11 Ibid. See also Wallis, ed., *Zambesi Expedition* 2:359.

12 E. A. Alpers, *Ivory and Slaves in East Central Africa* (London: Heinemann, 1975), 22–29.

13 A prazo was an estate given by the Portuguese crown to one of its subjects for the purpose of furthering Portuguese imperialism in the Lower Zembezi. But by the nineteenth century many of these estates had become independent, Africanized chieftaincies that resisted Portugal's claim to the region (see A. Isaacman, *Mozambique: The Africanization of a European Institution, The Zambesi Prazos, 1750–1902* [Madison: University of Wisconsin Press, 1972]).

14 Livingstone and Kirk were wrong in thinking that the practice was introduced in the region by the Portuguese, and in assuming the corollary, that in the areas not visited by Portuguese and Chikunda hunters chiefs did not demand tribute in elephant tusks (Foskett, ed., *Zambesi Journal* 1:165, 168–169; Wallis, ed., *Zambesi Expedition* 1:90–91). Perhaps they simply sustained the belief in order to justify their determination not to give in to the demands of local chiefs. The practice represented an extension of the well-established tradition that required lower chiefs to hand over ivory to their superiors in tribute (see Foskett, ed., *Zambesi Journal* 2:357).

15 Foskett, ed., *Zambesi Journal* 1:284.

16 Wallis, ed., *Zambesi Expedition* 1:91. Traders had to wait many days before they could speak to an important chief.

17 Foskett, ed., *Zambesi Journal* 1:181–182, 186.

18 See ibid., 180–181, for more direct methods of monopolizing trade.

19 Ibid., 1:165; Wallis, ed., *Zambesi Expedition* 1:90.

20 Bennett and Ylvisaker, eds., *Central African Journal,* 118–119; Livingstone and Livingstone, *Narrative,* 106, 559.

21 Bennett and Ylvisaker, eds., *Central African Journal,* 118–119; Foskett, ed., *Zambesi Journal* 1:144.

22 Waller diaries 4:12 (June 29, 1862). The missionaries later became so tired of the presents, especially beer, that they tried to stop the practice, first by giving more to those who came to sell their goods than to the present givers, and second, by declaring that anyone except the chiefs who made a present would receive nothing in return besides a thank-you (Bennett and Ylvisaker, eds., *Central African Journal,* 118–119).

23 Foskett, ed., *Zambesi Journal* 1:172; Schoffeleers, "Livingstone."
24 Foskett, ed., *Zambesi Journal* 1:182.
25 Schoffeleers, "Trade, Warfare and Social Inequality," 16.
26 Wallis, ed., *Zambesi Expedition* 2:335. Stewart adds that although "considerable" the population was not "prodigious," as Livingstone tended to portray it (Wallis, ed., *Zambesi Journal,* 47).
27 Foskett, ed., *Zambesi Journal* 1:146; Wallis, ed., *Zambesi Expedition* 1:59, 78; Wallis, ed., *Zambesi Journal,* 86.
28 Bennett and Ylvisaker, eds., *Central African Journal,* 66; Foskett, ed., *Zambesi Journal* 1:168.
29 Wallis, ed., *Zambesi Expedition* 1:79; Bennett and Ylvisaker, eds., *Central African Journal,* 257; Foskett, ed., *Zambesi Journal* 1:146–147; Wallis, ed., *Zambesi Journal,* 90.
30 For estimates on Khulubvi see Bennett and Ylvisaker, eds., *Central African Journal,* 50; Rowley, *Story of the Universities Mission,* 63; Waller diaries 4:5 (May 22, 1861); 4:12 (September 20, 1862). For Mankhokwe see Bennett and Ylvisaker, eds., *Central African Journal,* 70; Wallis, ed., *Zambesi Expedition* 1:79; Wallis, ed., *Zambesi Journal,* 89; Waller diaries 4:5 (July 1, 1861). For Chibisa see Bennett and Ylvisaker, eds., *Central African Journal,* 79. For a description of Tengani's village see, for example, Foskett, ed., *Zambesi Journal* 1:143, 164; Wallis, ed., *Zambesi Expedition* 1:77, 90.
31 Wallis, ed., *Zambesi Expedition* 1:98. See also Bennett and Ylvisaker, eds., *Central African Journal,* 55, 66, 70; Foskett, ed., *Zambesi Journal* 1:142, 164, 178, 183–184, 237; Livingstone and Livingstone, *Narrative,* 105; Wallis, ed., *Zambesi Expedition* 1:77, 79, 88, 89, 97; Wallis, ed., *Zambesi Journal,* 89.
32 A. C. P. Gamitto, *King Kazembe and the Marave, Cheva, Bisa, Bemba, Lunda, and Other Peoples of Southern Africa: Being the Diary of the Portuguese Expedition to That Potante in the Years 1831 and 1832* (Lisbon: Junta de Investigações do Ultramar, 1960), 1:93.
33 J. M. Schoffeleers and A. A. Roscoe, *Land of Fire: Oral Literature from Malawi* (Limbe, Malawi: Popular Publications, 1985), 42.
34 Rowley, *Story of the Universities Mission,* 203.
35 Small gifts such as a chicken were sometimes given in addition to bride-service (ibid., 210).
36 Ibid., 211.
37 Ibid.
38 M. G. Marwick, *Sorcery in Its Social Setting: A Study of the Northern Rhodesia Chewa* (Manchester: Manchester University Press, 1965), 111–167; D. M. Schneider, "The Distinctive Features of Matrilineal Descent Groups," D. M. Schneider and K. Gough, eds., *Matrilineal Kinship* (Berkeley and Los Angeles: University of California Press, 1961), 1–29. See also E. Colson, *Marriage and the Family Among the Plateau Tonga*

of Northern Rhodesia (Manchester: Manchester University Press, 1958); J. C. Mitchell, *The Yao Village* (Manchester: Manchester University Press, 1956); A. Richards, *Bemba Marriage and Present Economic Conditions* (Livingstone, Northern Rhodesia: Rhodes-Livingstone Institute, 1940). According to Marwick, matriliny is different from patriliny only to the degree that women in the former system are more capable of influencing decisions than are their counterparts in patrilineal societies; otherwise the two systems are similarly predicated on the universal principle of male dominance. Marwick thus ignores the bulk of the evidence in his book to affirm the universality of male dominance on the basis of two types of evidence. First, his male informants told him that "women 'lack strength' . . . implying social as much as physical strength" (p. 144). The other evidence is that although Chewa women were able to influence events, they were "not . . . executive officers of the matrilineage" (ibid.). Real power rests in men as it has always done throughout human history.

39 Schoffeleers, "Mbona"; idem, "Oral History and the Retrieval of the Distant Past: On the Use of Legendary Chronicles as Sources of Historical Information," J. M. Schoffeleers and W. Van Binsbergen, eds., *Theoretical Explorations in African Religion* (London: Routledge and Kegan Paul, 1985), 164–188.

40 See C. Meillassoux, *Maidens, Meal and Money: Capitalism and the Domestic Community* (1975; Cambridge: Cambridge University Press, 1981), 28–30, for the role of violence in the process leading to the subjugation of women.

41 M/CK2; TVES1/9; Foskett, ed., *Zambesi Journal* 1:162; Livingstone and Livingstone, *Narrative,* 92, 108, 116; Wallis, ed., *Zambesi Expedition* 1:88, 96–97, 106, 123; 2:247; Marwick, *Sorcery in Its Social Setting,* 144.

42 Bennett and Ylvisaker, eds., *Central African Journal,* 72–73.

43 Ibid., 73.

44 Ibid., 72.

45 Livingstone and Livingstone, *Narrative,* 92, 108, 116.

46 Rowley, *Story of the Universities Mission,* 208–209; Wallis, ed., *Zambesi Expedition* 2:229. See also Livingstone and Livingstone, *Narrative,* 517, for the same among the Chewa of central Malawi.

47 TVES1/13–15.

48 Rowley, *Story of the Universities Mission,* 226–227.

49 Ibid., 224–225.

50 Waller diaries 4:12 (September 20, 1862).

51 Rowley, *Story of the Universities Mission,* 208.

52 Marx, *Capital,* 165.

53 E. Terray, "Classes and Class Consciousness in the Abron Kingdom of Gyman," M. Bloch, ed., *Marxist Analyses and Social Anthropology* (London: Malaby, 1975), 85–135; C. Meillassoux, " 'The Economy' in Agricultural Self-Sustaining Societies: A Preliminary Analysis," D. Seddon,

ed., *Relations of Production: Marxist Approaches to Economic Anthropology* (London: Cass, 1978), 127–157; G. Dupré and P. Rey, "Reflections on the Relevance of a Theory of the History of Exchange," Seddon, ed., *Relations of Production,* 171–208. The following discussion has been partly inspired by E. Genovese, *Roll, Jordan, Roll: The World the Slaves Made* (1972; New York: Vintage, 1976), 25–49.

54 Terray, "Classes and Class Consciousness," 107.

55 Meillassoux, "'The Economy,'" 138.

56 Dupré and Rey, "Reflections."

57 If this had been the only problem, Terray's model could have accommodated the Mang'anja situation in many important ways. The Abron were similar to the Mang'anja in many respects. They were matrilineal and did not use bride-wealth in their marriage transactions. The absence of bride-wealth has allowed Terray to downplay the role of exchange and to make this study consistent with his other studies of the region (see, for example, his "Long-Distance Exchange and the Formation of the State," *Economy and Society* 3 [1974]: 315–345).

58 Dupré and Rey, "Reflections," 193–197.

59 Meillassoux, "'The Economy,'" 138. In his *Marxism and "Primitive" Societies* (New York: Monthly Review Press, 1972), 102, 137–156, Terray does give due weight to ideological forces in his definition of a "mode of production" (or what I would call a "social formation"). But he does not follow out the implications of his definition in formulating the problem of social age, either in this work (pp. 163–176, where he closely follows Meillassoux's theory) or in his "Classes and Class Consciousness" (where he leans more toward the position of Dupré and Rey, "Reflections").

60 M. Godelier, *Perspectives in Marxist Anthropology* (1973; Cambridge: Cambridge University Press, 1977), 180.

61 Like the heading of this section, my formulation of the problem has been influenced by Genovese, *Roll, Jordan, Roll,* esp. 25–49.

62 See the bibliography for a partial listing of Schoffeleers's works on the Mang'anja.

63 Godelier, *Perspectives,* esp. 169–185.

64 Marx, *Capital,* 173.

65 See Godelier, *Perspectives,* 169–185.

66 Schoffeleers, ed., *Guardians of the Land,* 8.

67 Godelier, *Perspectives,* 183.

68 Schoffeleers, "The Chisumphi and Mbona Cults in Malawi."

69 See, for example, Dupré and Rey, "Reflections," 197.

70 Schoffeleers, "The History and Political Role of the Mbona Cult."

71 Genovese, *Roll, Jordan, Roll,* 27.

72 According to the main thrust of Mang'anja and Chewa myths of origin, man once lived in perfect harmony with animals and spirits until he invented fire. The various religious rituals, especially nyau, are supposed to reunify

the three worlds and make communication among them possible (see J. M. Schoffeleers, "The Meaning and Use of the Name 'Malawi' in Oral Traditions and Pre-Colonial Documents," B. Pachai, ed., *The Early History of Malawi* [London: Longman, 1973], 91–103; idem, "The *Nyau* Societies: Our Present Understanding," *Society of Malawi Journal* 29 [January 1976]: 59–68).

73 Rowley, *Story of the Universities Mission,* 203.

74 Children of chiefs were an exception.

75 J. M. Schoffeleers, "Symbolic and Social Aspects of Spirit Worship Among the Mang'anja" (Ph.D. diss., Oxford University, 1968).

76 See, for example, M. Etienne, "Women and Men, Cloth and Colonization: The Transformation of Production-Distribution Relations Among the Baule (Ivory Coast)," M. Etienne and E. Leacock, eds., *Women and Colonization: Anthropological Perspectives* (New York: Praeger, 1980), 214–238.

77 E. W. Chafulumira, *Mbiri ya Amang'anja* (A History of the Mang'anja) (Zomba, Nyasaland: Government Press, 1948), 23–25; TVES1/5, 9–10, 14–16.

78 *South African Pioneer* 18 (November 1915): 174. The system of labor prestation that the missionary describes does not fit the Sena bride-wealth system, as the text of the article wrongly suggests.

79 Schoffeleers, "Trade, Warfare and Social Inequality," 9–10; idem, "The Chisumphi and Mbona Cults."

80 Schoffeleers and Roscoe, *Land of Fire,* 64.

81 Schoffeleers, personal communication, November 12, 1988.

82 W. Rodney, "African Slavery and Other Forms of Social Oppression on the Upper Guinea in the Context of the Atlantic Slave Trade," *Journal of African History* 7 (1966): 431–443. Reactions to the article include J. D. Fage, "Slaves and Society in Western Africa, c. 1445–c. 1700," *Journal of African History* 21 (1980): 289–310; J. E. Inikori, Introduction to Inikori, ed., *Forced Migration: The Impact of the Export Slave Trade on African Societies* (New York: Africana Publishing Company, 1982), 13–60; Inikori, "The Chaining of a Continent: Export Demand for Captives and the History of Africa South of the Sahara, 1450–1870" (unpublished typescript, UNESCO, 1986); P. Lovejoy, *Transformations in Slavery: A History of Slavery in Africa* (Cambridge: Cambridge University Press, 1983); C. Meillassoux, "The Role of Slavery in the Economic and Social History of Sahelo-Sudanic Africa," Inikori, ed., *Forced Migration,* 74–99; and C. C. Wrigley, "Historicism in Africa: Slavery and State Formation," *African Affairs* 70 (1971): 113–124.

83 See, for example, C. Meillassoux, "Female Slavery," C. Robertson and M. Klein, eds., *Women and Slavery in Africa* (Madison: University of Wisconsin Press, 1983), 49–66.

84 TVES1/10; TVES2/4; TVES3/5, 9, 11, 15; Livingstone and Livingstone, *Narrative,* 103, 592; Wallis, ed., *Zambesi Journal,* 189.

85 Even the trade in salt and foodstuffs with the Highlands, which is often cited as a source of captives (TVES1/9–11; TVES2/4) could not reproduce a slave class. Not only were the partners in the trade culturally and politically similar, but the proximity of the two regions placed severe limits on exchanges in human beings (victims had to be led blindfolded at night) and the resulting system of servitude. Most people acquired from the Highlands were pawns to be redeemed later (see Wallis, ed., *Zambesi Journal,* 122, on buying back a "slave").

86 Bennett and Ylvisaker, eds., *Central African Journal,* 181, 374. The practice had become so common by the early 1860s that a boy once offered himself as a "slave" to a woman who had accused him of stealing two eggs (ibid., 90; see also Gamitto, *King Kazembe* 1:99).

87 The most glaring recorded example is that of headman Chepa, who took a girl captive after accusing her mother of merely intending to steal his crops (Bennett and Ylvisaker, eds., *Central African Journal,* 343–344).

88 Rowley, *Story of the Universities Mission,* 211.

89 TVES1/9, 10, 13.

90 Bennett and Ylvisaker, eds., *Central African Journal,* 249–298, 420; Rowley, *Story of the Universities Mission,* 229–232.

91 Meillassoux, "The Role of Slavery," 98.

92 Rowley, *Story of the Universities Mission,* 100.

93 Genovese, *Roll, Jordan, Roll,* 30; TVES1/4, 9, 14; TVES2/4; Foskett, ed., *Zambesi Journal* 1:190. According to Livingstone, Portuguese masters in the Lower Zembezi did not treat their slaves too harshly for fear that they might lose them through flight (Wallis, ed., *Zambesi Expedition* 2:349).

94 TVES3/12; also TVES1/9.

95 TVES1/13; TVES2/4; TVES3/12.

96 Miers and Kopytoff, eds., *Slavery in Africa,* esp. Kopytoff and Miers, "African 'Slavery.'" For some of the critics' views see F. Cooper, "The Problem of Slavery in African Studies," *Journal of African History* 20 (1979): 103–125; M. Klein, "The Study of Slavery in Africa," *Journal of African History* 19 (1978): 599–609.

97 Akapolo in Mang'anja society were valued for both their productive and reproductive capacities. To emphasize only their productive capacities, as C. Robertson and M. Klein do ("Women's Importance in African Slave Systems," Robertson and Klein, eds., *Women and Slavery in Africa,* 3–25), would be to ignore the fact that akapolo had different users even in this weakly stratified society.

98 Bennett and Ylvisaker, eds., *Central African Journal,* 116, 176, 191–193.

99 Rowley, *Story of the Universities Mission,* 256.

100 Kopytoff and Miers, "African 'Slavery.'"

101 TVES1/9; TVES3/12.
102 TVES1/14.
103 Foskett, ed., *Zambesi Journal* 1:210.
104 Terray, *Marxism and "Primitive" Societies,* 95–186.
105 I have no evidence of work teams formed on a contractual basis at this time in Mang'anja history, as was the case among the Guro (ibid., 124–125).
106 K. Poewe, *Matrilineal Ideology: Male-Female Dynamics in Luapula, Zambia* (London: Academic Press, 1981), 12, 33, 120.
107 See, for example, Kjekshus, *Ecology Control,* 80–110.
108 See, for example, M. Vaughan, "Which Family?: Problems in the Reconstruction of the History of the Family as an Economic and Cultural Unit," *Journal of African History* 24 (1983): 275–283.
109 Bennett and Ylvisaker, eds., *Central African Journal,* 383, 398; Livingstone and Livingstone, *Narrative,* 90, 99; Waller diaries 4:13 (October 21, 1862); Wallis, ed., *Zambesi Expedition* 1:75–76. On food collecting in general see Clendennen, ed., "Shire Journal," 12, 146; Livingstone and Livingstone, *Narrative,* 507.
110 The only nonproducer who probably got part of the product was the canoe owner.
111 Foskett, ed., *Zambesi Journal* 1:162; Livingstone and Livingstone, *Narrative,* 453.
112 The Sena word for mudfish is *nsomba,* which is a generic name for fish in Chimang'anja.
113 See chap. 7 for a discussion of Sena techniques. For some of the fish species found in the Tchiri River and Lake Malawi during the twentieth century refer to K. J. McCracken's illuminating article "Fishing and the Colonial Economy: The Case of Malawi," *Journal of African History* 28 (1987): 413–429. For a technical discussion of fishing in the Lower Tchiri Valley see C. Ratcliffe, "The Fishery of the Lower River Area, Malawi" (Malawi Ministry of Agriculture, Fisheries Bulletin no. 3, 1972). The Mang'anja also used a variety of nets, but their use is not fully described by nineteenth-century observers (see, for example, Foskett, ed., *Zambesi Journal* 1:99, 107, 174).
114 Wallis, ed., *Zambesi Expedition* 1:76; see also p. 81; Bennett and Ylvisaker, eds., *Central African Journal,* 400; Foskett, ed., *Zambesi Journal* 1:42, 174; Livingstone and Livingstone, *Narrative,* 99–100.
115 Angling was unproductive when the water was either too hot or too cold (Livingstone and Livingstone, *Narrative,* 90). Rowley noted how "a native would sit by the river all day long angling, and think himself well repaid if he caught a fish weighing four ounces" (*Story of the Universities Mission,* 330).
116 Livingstone and Livingstone, *Narrative,* 402; see also pp. 99–100 and Clendennen, ed., "Shire Journal," 12.
117 TVES1/5, 9, 10, 12, 13.
118 Ibid.

119 TVES1/9.
120 Ibid.
121 Foskett, ed., *Zambesi Journal* 1:152. Kirk noted that teeth weighing above six pounds were considered very good and that the best came from the Tchiri Valley after the extermination of elephants in the Lower Zembezi (p. 106; see also Livingstone and Livingstone, *Narrative,* 422).
122 Livingstone and Livingstone, *Narrative,* 97; Wallis, ed., *Zambesi Expedition* 1:78.
123 Foskett, ed., *Zambesi Journal* 1:169.
124 Ibid., 145.
125 Ibid., 142. See also Bennett and Ylvisaker, eds., *Central African Journal,* 59; Livingstone and Livingstone, *Narrative,* 94–95; Wallis, ed., *Zambesi Expedition* 1:76, 78, 81, 124; Wallis, ed., *Zambesi Journal,* 109, 127, 256.
126 Livingstone and Livingstone, *Narrative,* 94–95.
127 Wallis, ed., *Zambesi Expedition* 2:318. Some traditions go so far as to deny that the Mang'anja ever killed elephants or hippopotami (TVES1/10; TVES3/2, 5).
128 For some of Livingstone's comments on the purpose of his mission and its relationship to British imperialism see Wallis, ed., *Zambesi Expedition* 1:50–53, 80, 126–127, 136–137.
129 F. Monclaro, "Account of the Journey Made by the Fathers of the Society of Jesus with Francisco Barreto in the Conquest of Monomotapa in the Year 1569," G. M. Theal, ed., *Records of South-East Africa,* 9 vols. (1899; Cape Town, South Africa: Struik, 1964) 3:229, 234; J. dos Santos, "Eastern Ethiopia," Theal, ed., *Records* 7:261, 266.
130 Livingstone and Livingstone, *Narrative,* 112.
131 TVES1/15, 16. According to some traditions people brewed beer in order to recruit extra household workers in the process (TVES1/2, 10, 12).
132 Livingstone and Livingstone, *Narrative,* 112.
133 TVES1/13, 14.
134 Wallis, ed., *Zambesi Journal,* 83–84.
135 Bennett and Ylvisaker, eds., *Central African Journal,* 66.
136 Wallis, ed., *Zambesi Journal,* 155. According to other calculations, it took one man two days to complete a piece measuring one and a half yards by three-quarters of a yard, or two men five days to complete a piece measuring three by two yards (p. 162; see also p. 100).
137 For maria see Waller diaries 4:16 (February 17, 1863); for gondo TVES3/5; Wallis, ed., *Zambesi Journal,* 155. Some pieces were dyed and others were not (Bennett and Ylvisaker, eds., *Central African Journal,* 66; Foskett, ed., *Zambesi Journal* 1:240). Still, the impact of merchant capital on the cloth industry was so devastating that some oral historians today deny that the Mang'anja ever made cloth from cotton (TVES1/4, 11).
138 Wallis, ed., *Zambesi Journal,* 83, 87–89, 100–103.
139 It is important to place Livingstone's optimism for the region into perspective. The accounts not only reflect his dislike of the Lower Zembezian

Portuguese society, but more important, they are designed to justify continued funding for his expedition. The expedition's initial goal was to explore Barotseland, which Livingstone had earlier portrayed as an ideal British colony (see his *Missionary Travels and Researches in South Africa* [London: Murray, 1857]). But Livingstone was forced to abandon the project in late 1858 after discovering the Quebrabasa Rapids, which blocked the Zembezi River to all navigation. The Tchiri River and Lake Malawi region took the place of Barotseland in his designs for Central Africa. The immediate results of his writings on the region proved disastrous, as the history of the Universities Mission to Central Africa demonstrates. Livingstone's expedition was finally recalled in late 1863, when his fame was at its lowest ebb among the capitalists who had funded the expedition. It is ironic, however, that one of the greatest critics of Livingstone at this time, James Stewart (who threw a copy of *Missionary Travels* into the Zembezi River, declaring it to be little better than a pack of lies), also became one of his greatest adulators after his death. Stewart was one of the founders of the Livingstonia Mission in northern Malawi.

140 As Horace Waller told Stewart: "Apropos de 'Cotton.' I have firmly stated, and stuck to it, that inasmuch as the country had undergone war, famine and drought and pestilence, sweeping pestilence, and that between the periods of the Dr's first visit to spy it out and yours, there is nothing inconsistent in the two reports that will be made of the country, and that you are not the man to suppose these things go for nothing or that they would be without their effect" (Wallis, ed., *Zambesi Journal,* 226).

141 Ibid., 210–211, 222–223, 225, 227.

142 Livingstone and Livingstone, *Narrative,* 112.

143 The Universities Mission had taken a cotton gin to Magomero on the basis of Livingstone's comments. But there was no cotton to be bought, which led Rowley to declare the gin as one of the "most useless . . . things taken up to Magomero" (*Story of the Universities Mission,* 344; see also chaps. 3 and 4 in text).

144 Wallis, ed., *Zambesi Expedition* 1:94; see also Foskett, ed., *Zambesi Journal* 1:172.

145 Wallis, ed., *Zambesi Expedition* 2:318.

146 Rowley, *Story of the Universities Mission,* 358; Wallis, ed., *Zambesi Journal,* 211.

147 Clendennen, ed., "Shire Journal," 183; Livingstone and Livingstone, *Narrative,* 528; Wallis, ed., *Zambesi Expedition* 1:189.

148 Livingstone's practice of buying raw cotton with calico would have had the potential of invigorating cotton cultivation had it been pursued over a long time (see Bennett and Ylvisaker, eds., *Central African Journal,* 60; Foskett, ed., *Zambesi Journal* 1:149, 170; 2:342, 553; Wallis, ed., *Zambesi Expedition* 2:407; Wallis, ed., *Zambesi Journal,* 211). The expedition bought three hundred pounds of cleaned cotton in three months at about a penny a pound (Livingstone and Livingstone, *Narrative,* 352), which was

the average price paid to peasants in the Valley by the colonial regime during the first half of the twentieth century.

149 About a third of the men Stewart saw in the Dabanyi Marsh wore bark cloth (Wallis, ed., *Zambesi Journal,* 127).

150 TVES1/1, 2, 4, 7, 9, 10, 12. According to some accounts the Mang'anja also extracted salt from the *suludi* tree and from earth taken from anthills (*chulu*) (TVES2/2).

151 Bennett and Ylvisaker, eds., *Central African Journal,* 299.

152 Ibid.

153 TVES1/1, 2, 4, 7, 9, 10, 12.

154 Foskett, ed., *Zambesi Journal* 1:137; Livingstone and Livingstone, *Narrative,* 113.

155 Rowley, *Story of the Universities Mission,* 194–195.

156 TVES1/11, 12.

157 The sources are ambiguous on the social position of the blacksmith and in particular how he recruited men for work in the Highlands. Some accounts imply that blacksmiths were headmen who would have obtained labor on the basis of their political authority (see, for example, Rowley, *Story of the Universities Mission,* 355). Others suggest that the two positions were separate, and that blacksmiths were either dependent on or worked in some symbiotic relationship to those in political power. Procter's eyewitness account supports the second interpretation (Bennett and Ylvisaker, eds., *Central African Journal,* 270).

158 Rowley, *Story of the Universities Mission,* 206.

159 Foskett, ed., *Zambesi Journal* 1:196, 237. As a result, none of the European travelers on whom we depend for information about the period witnessed the smelting process.

160 Foskett, ed., *Zambesi Journal* 1:196; see also p. 178 and Bennett and Ylvisaker, eds., *Central African Journal,* 270.

161 Rowley, *Story of the Universities Mission,* 206.

162 See, for example, TVES1/1, 4. I consider that these accounts reflect the experiences of the First World War, when the lack of hoes led poor peasants to use wooden ones and the government to try to revive the iron industry. Government officials were then told that there was no living Mang'anja who knew how to work iron (see Chikwawa District Annual Report, 1918–19, S1/781/19; Lower Shire District Annual Report, 1919–20, S1/1077/19; Ruo District Annual Report, 1919–20, S1/1041/19, MNA).

163 Chafulumira, *Mbiri ya Amang'anja,* 13–14. These were probably the hoes that were left on the graves of their past users.

164 See, for example, Kjekshus, *Ecology Control,* 80.

165 In a sample of six lists (Bennett and Ylvisaker, eds., *Central African Journal,* 64, 270; Foskett, ed., *Zambesi Journal* 1:192; Livingstone and Livingstone, *Narrative,* 113; Wallis, ed., *Zambesi Expedition* 2:319; Rowley, *Story of the Universities Mission,* 206) the hoe is mentioned only twice (Bennett and Ylvisaker, eds., *Central African Journal,* 64; Livingstone and Living-

stone, *Narrative,* 113). Otherwise, the commonly listed items are anklets, assaigais (for the hand and not for throwing), arrowheads, bracelets, knife blades, needles, spearheads, and brass rings and earrings. The battle ax was not a common tool among the Mang'anja (Foskett, ed., *Zambesi Journal* 1:165).

166 Livingstone and Livingstone, *Narrative,* 113; see also Foskett, ed., *Zambesi Journal* 2:553.

167 Monclaro, "Account"; dos Santos, "Eastern Ethiopia." See also Schoffeleers, "The Zimba and the Lundu State"; idem, "Oral History."

168 They were more interested in hoes, which they almost invariably purchased with cloth, including the garments they received from Livingstone as part of their wages (Livingstone and Livingstone, *Narrative,* 404–405).

169 See, for example, Schoffeleers, "Livingstone," 111–118; Mandala, "The Kololo Interlude," 192–196.

170 Foskett, ed., *Zambesi Journal* 1:172.

171 Bennett and Ylvisaker, eds., *Central African Journal,* 51; Foskett, ed., *Zambesi Journal* 1:143, 164–165, 233; Livingstone and Livingstone, *Narrative,* 76, 96–97; Wallis, ed., *Zambesi Expedition* 1:77–78.

172 Bennett and Ylvisaker, eds., *Central African Journal,* 51; Foskett, ed., *Zambesi Journal* 2:343; Livingstone and Livingstone, *Narrative,* 93, 404–405; Waller diaries 4:19 (September 7, 1863). One or two fathoms of cloth fetched one bag (about thirty-five pounds) of cleaned rice and eight to ten fowls (Rowley, *Story of the Universities Mission,* 70; Waller diaries 4:5 [May 22, 1861]; Wallis, ed., *Zambesi Expedition* 1:77, 88, 105).

173 See, for example, Bennett and Ylvisaker, eds., *Central African Journal,* 176, 185, 277; Foskett, ed., *Zambesi Journal* 1:192; Livingstone and Livingstone, *Narrative,* 90, 113; Rowley, *Story of the Universities Mission,* 179, 194–195; Waller diaries 4:12 (June 29, 1862); 4:19 (August 21, 1863); Wallis, ed., *Zambesi Expedition* 1:104, 2:246.

174 The market in foodstuffs was so limited in its development that the characteristic response to the threat of famine was in the form of population movement to areas where people could cultivate food crops themselves (see, for example, Waller diaries 4:12 [August 26, 1862]).

175 See the sources cited in n. 173 above.

176 Livingstone and Livingstone, *Narrative,* 113.

177 See, for example, Rowley, *Story of the Universities Mission,* 70.

178 Ibid., 71; see also p. 69 and Foskett, ed., *Zambesi Journal* 1:244. Along Lake Malawi a wife openly rebuked her husband for trying to sell a goat in her absence (Livingstone and Livingstone, *Narrative,* 550).

179 Bennett and Ylvisaker, eds., *Central African Journal,* 322.

180 Wallis, ed., *Zambesi Expedition* 1:105.

181 Bishop Charles F. Mackenzie, as quoted in Livingstone and Livingstone, *Narrative,* 500.

182 Rowley, *Story of the Universities Mission,* 71.

183 See, for example, ibid., 203.

184 This is implied by, for example, Rowley's cryptic remark that although a Mang'anja boy had no difficulty in getting a wife, "now and then it happened he had to put up with a woman old enough to be his mother" (ibid., 211).

185 Ibid., 222.

186 See Livingstone and Livingstone, *Narrative,* 464, 471, for other lists of household goods.

187 Livingstone and Livingstone, *Narrative,* 380–381. The graveyard was probably the source of the discarded or misikiri hoes noted by Chafulumira (*Mbiri ya Amang'anja,* 13–14).

188 See, for example, J. Guyer, "Household and Community in African Studies," *African Studies Review* 24 (June/September 1981): 87–137; K. G. M. Phiri, "Some Changes in the Matrilineal Family System Among the Chewa of Malawi Since the Nineteenth Century," *Journal of African History* 24 (1983): 257–274; Vaughan, "Which Family?"; Poewe, *Matrilineal Ideology,* 55–57.

189 Clendennen, ed., "Shire Journal," 184.

190 The nomenclature used here is the correct one. That employed in my earlier writings is incorrect (see, for example, E. C. Mandala, "Capitalism, Ecology and Society: The Lower Tchiri [Shire] Valley of Malawi, 1860–1960" [Ph.D. diss., University of Minnesota, 1983]). For some classic statements on the system refer to Bennett and Ylvisaker, eds., *Central African Journal,* 374; W. B. Morgan, "The Lower Shire Valley of Nyasaland: A Changing System of African Agriculture," *Geographical Journal* 119 (December 1953): 459–469.

191 The main exception was that munda cotton and gonkho were not reaped until July, when most people were busy opening dimba fields. Similarly, dimba rice was harvested at about the same time as mchewere and maize grown on the munda.

192 Livingstone and Livingstone, *Narrative,* 110. Opening a new munda corresponded closely to what Livingstone called "woodland" cultivation.

193 Ibid., 110–111. See also Foskett, ed., *Zambesi Journal* 1:238.

194 Bennett and Ylvisaker, eds., *Central African Journal,* 353; Rowley, *Story of the Universities Mission,* 314. For evidence that the mapira grown at this time was of the slow-maturing variety see Waller diaries 4:16 (December 13, 16, 1863).

195 Livingstone and Livingstone, *Narrative,* 499; TVES1/4, 10; TVES2/2, 4; TVES3/1; Foskett, ed., *Zambesi Journal* 1:146.

196 Livingstone and Livingstone, *Narrative,* 110.

197 TVES3/9, 13, 14.

198 No one who has lived in the Valley would indulge in the controversy over whether or not hunger during this period was a reality or merely a political idiom, as some academics have done (see, for example, Richards, "Eco-

logical Change"; and M. Watts's reply, "Good Try, Mr. Paul: Populism and the Politics of African Land-Use," *African Studies Review* 26 [June 1983]: 73–83).

199 Chafulumira, *Mbiri ya Amang'anja,* 14–15.

200 TVES3/1, 9; Chafulumira, *Mbiri ya Amang'anja,* 14–15.

201 TVES3/1, 9; Chafulumira, *Mbiri ya Amang'anja,* 14–15.

202 Chafulumira, *Mbiri ya Amang'anja,* 14–15; TVES1/5; TVES3/1, 9. See also Wallis, ed., *Zambesi Journal,* 51.

203 Waller diaries 4:16 (December 13, 1863).

204 Bennett and Ylvisaker, eds., *Central African Journal,* 60; Foskett, ed., *Zambesi Journal* 1:258; Livingstone and Livingstone, *Narrative,* 111–112, 587–588; Wallis, ed., *Zambesi Expedition* 1:127; 2:285.

205 Foskett, ed., *Zambesi Journal* 1:258; Livingstone and Livingstone, *Narrative,* 11; Wallis, ed., *Zambesi Expedition* 1:127.

206 Wallis, ed., *Zambesi Journal,* 210–211; Rowley, *Story of the Universities Mission,* 194, 313.

207 Foskett, ed., *Zambesi Journal* 1:181, 185; Wallis, ed., *Zambesi Expedition* 2:318.

208 See chap. 4 for the implications of this fact on the development of the colonial cotton economy.

209 Wallis, ed., *Zambesi Journal,* 211. On the height of the crop refer to Foskett, ed., *Zambesi Journal* 1:252; Livingstone and Livingstone, *Narrative,* 111; Wallis, ed., *Zambesi Expedition* 1:39, 127.

210 Wallis, ed., *Zambesi Expedition* 2:239.

211 Foskett, ed., *Zambesi Journal* 1:240.

212 Quoted in Wallis, ed., *Zambesi Journal,* 210–211.

213 Livingstone and Livingstone, *Narrative,* 528.

214 A. Freeman, "A Preliminary Investigation into Dimba Cultivation in the Lower Shire Valley" (unpublished typescript, Shire Valley Agricultural Development Project, 1973).

215 Chafulumira, *Mbiri ya Amang'anja,* 4–5 (my translation).

216 Foskett, ed., *Zambesi Journal* 1:234–235; see also Wallis, ed., *Zambesi Expedition* 1:124.

217 Wallis, ed., *Zambesi Expedition* 2:318; see also vol. 1, p. 105.

218 Foskett, ed., *Zambesi Journal* 1:210.

219 A. W. R. Duly, "The Lower Shire District: Notes on Land Tenure and Individual Rights," *Nyasaland Journal* 1 (July 1948): 44.

220 Wallis, ed., *Zambesi Expedition* 1:76. Palm wine was made from midikhwa (Clendennen, ed., "Shire Journal," 12, 146; Foskett, ed., *Zambesi Journal* 1:170; Livingstone and Livingstone, *Narrative,* 100–101; Wallis, ed., *Zambesi Expedition* 1:79, 91).

221 G. Jackson and P. O. Wiehe, *An Annotated Check List of Nyasaland Grasses* (Zomba, Nyasaland: Government Press, 1958), 37.

222 Foskett, ed., *Zambesi Journal* 1:207; Livingstone and Livingstone, *Narrative,* 75.

223 Bennett and Ylvisaker, eds., *Central African Journal,* 50, 64.

224 Ibid., 64; TVES1/5; TVES2/4.

225 TVES1/15; TVES3/2; Foskett, ed., *Zambesi Journal* 1:146, 173; Livingstone and Livingstone, *Narrative,* 90; Wallis, ed., *Zambesi Expedition* 1:124. Livingstone identified two types of sugarcane, both of which he thought were of indigenous origin and contained much sugar (*Narrative,* 562, 588).

226 Bennett and Ylvisaker, eds., *Central African Journal,* 49; Livingstone and Livingstone, *Narrative,* 93. Members of the Livingstone expedition traveled to Khulubvi (modern Nsanje township) from the Lower Zembezi to buy rice in June 1859 (Foskett, ed., *Zambesi Journal* 1:209; Wallis, ed., *Zambesi Expedition* 1:104–105). The white rice found in the Lower Zembezi had been imported from North Carolina a few years before (Livingstone and Livingstone, *Narrative,* 406).

227 TVES1/5, 10; TVES3/1, 9.

228 TVES1/5, 10; TVES3/1, 9.

229 TVES1/1, 2, 4, 5, 7, 9, 10; Livingstone and Livingstone, *Narrative,* 457.

230 Foskett, ed., *Zambesi Journal* 1:142; Wallis, ed., *Zambesi Expedition* 1:78, 81. The traps were without the iron spikes at this time. But see also Foskett, ed. (*Zambesi Journal* 1:235), in which Kirk writes that no traps were seen during the January and April trips.

231 During the early 1930s an acre of dimba yielded between three thousand and forty-five hundred pounds of maize.

232 Waller diaries 4:12 (August 26, 1862); see also 4:18 (June 20, 1863); Livingstone and Livingstone, *Narrative,* 102; Foskett, ed., *Zambesi Journal* 1:73; Wallis, ed., *Zambesi Expedition* 1:92.

233 Foskett, ed., *Zambesi Journal* 1:164.

234 Ibid.

235 Rowley, *Story of the Universities Mission,* 358. Rowley makes a similar observation for the people of Mankhokwe's village (p. 87).

236 Vaughan, "Social and Economic Change," 37–60.

237 Livingstone and Livingstone, *Narrative,* 544; see also Chafulumira, *Mbiri ya Amang'anja,* 22. But there is not enough information on these activities during the nineteenth century. For a description of Mang'anja houses see Bennett and Ylvisaker, eds., *Central African Journal,* 49, 79; Foskett, ed., *Zambesi Journal* 1:164; Wallis, ed., *Zambesi Journal,* 251. For a partial description of beer brewing and mat and pot making see Bennett and Ylvisaker, eds., *Central African Journal,* 56; Livingstone and Livingstone, *Narrative,* 76. Stewart's account of the domestic division of labor is too racist to form a useful basis for analysis (Wallis, ed., *Zambesi Journal,* 250–259).

238 Young wives did not generally accompany their husbands to the fields, staying rather in the village in order to prepare food for the family (see Chafulumira, *Mbiri ya Amang'anja,* 24).

239 TVES1/5; Bennett and Ylvisaker, eds., *Central African Journal,* 71; Rowley, *Story of the Universities Mission,* 359; Wallis, ed., *Zambesi Journal,* 166.

240 TVES1/5, 10.

241 Foskett, ed., *Zambesi Journal* 1:42; 2:449.
242 Ibid., 2:449.
243 Livingstone and Livingstone, *Narrative,* 543.
244 Ibid., 543–544.
245 Foskett, ed., *Zambesi Journal* 1:42; Rowley, *Story of the Universities Mission,* 201.
246 Chafulumira, *Mbiri ya Amang'anja,* 16.
247 TVES1/12, 13.
248 The song was recorded by and reproduced here with the permission of Dr. Enoch Timpunza-Mvula. Oral history does of course contrast this harsh picture with that of the kind mother-in-law who brews beer to thank her hard-working son-in-law (see Chafulumira, *Mbiri ya Amang'anja,* 23–24; TVES1/12).

2. From the Slave Trade to the Rise of a Peasantry, 1859–1925

1 Marx, *Capital,* 915.
2 With a few modifications to accommodate the labor process (see Introduction and Conclusions), I adopt J. Saul and R. Woods's definition of peasants as rural producers "whose ultimate security and subsistence lies in their having certain rights in land and in the labour of family members on the land, but who are involved, through rights and obligations, in a wider economic system which includes the participation of non-peasants" ("African Peasantries," T. Shanin, ed., *Peasants and Peasant Societies* [New York: Penguin, 1971], 105). For variations of the same idea see M. Klein, Introduction to Klein, ed., *Peasants in Africa: Historical and Contemporary Perspectives* (Beverly Hills, Calif.: Sage, 1980), 9–43.
3 These accounts include Clendennen, ed., "Shire Journal"; Foskett, ed., *Zambesi Journal* vols. 1 and 2; Wallis, ed., *Zambesi Expedition* vols. 1 and 2; and Livingstone's letters in the National Library of Scotland (NLS), Edinburgh.
4 See in particular Wallis, ed., *Zambesi Journal,* 30–35, 125. Stewart was so disappointed with what he had seen in the Valley and Highlands in late 1862 and early 1863 that he threw the highly structured *Missionary Travels* into the Zembezi River: "The day was bright, hot and clear. In the afternoon I went down the river-bank a short way and threw with all my strength into the turbid muddy weedcovered Zambesi my copy of certain 'Missionary Travels in South Africa.' The volume was fragrant with odours of and memories of the earnestness with which I studied the book in days gone by. How different it appeared now! It was nothing short of an eyesore, the very sight of its brown covers. I do not think it is as the Rev. R— M— is said to have called it, 'a pack of lies,' but it would need a great many additions to make it the truth. Thus I disliked the book and sent

it to sink or swim into the vaunted Zambesi. So perish all that is false in myself and others" (Wallis, ed., *Zambesi Journal,* 190). I will show in the text how far Livingstone exaggerated the conditions prevailing in the Valley prior to 1860.

5 A. Isaacman, *Mozambique;* M. D. D. Newitt, *Portuguese Settlement on the Zambesi: Exploration, Land Tenure and Colonial Rule in East Africa* (London: Longman, 1973); L. Vail and L. White, *Capitalism and Colonialism in Mozambique: A Study of Quelimane District* (Minneapolis: University of Minnesota Press, 1980).

6 These include the oral testimony numbered M/CK6 as well as those recorded by the British between 1859 and 1863, especially in connection with the life history of Chibisa: Bennett and Ylvisaker, eds., *Central African Journal,* 261, 346, 355–356, 362–364, 400–403, 419; Rowley, *Story of the Universities Mission,* 188, 305, 395; E. C. Tabler, ed., *Zambesi Papers* 2:166, 277–278; Wallis, ed., *Zambesi Expedition* 1:92–93.

7 See, for example, TVES3/1, 9, 15.

8 Coimbra had been to Bourbon in 1854, the year the engagé scheme was formally inaugurated. He had been given wines and other goods to be repaid in slaves (Clendennen, ed., "Shire Journal," 103, 167–168; Livingstone and Livingstone, *Narrative,* 25; Wallis, ed., *Zambesi Expedition* 1:48–49, 84–86).

9 The sources give the name of Matekenya's village as Chimwala (Foskett, ed., *Zambesi Journal* 1:115; Wallis, ed., *Zambesi Expedition* 1:49) or Chamo (Clendennen, ed., "Shire Journal," 116–117; Foskett, ed., *Zambesi Journal* 1:71; Wallis, ed., *Zambesi Expedition* 1:104–106).

10 Foskett, ed., *Zambesi Journal* 1:163.

11 See the sources cited in n. 3.

12 See, for example, Foskett, ed., *Zambesi Journal* 1:187–193, 247, 255–256; Livingstone and Livingstone, *Narrative,* 128, 138; Wallis, ed., *Zambesi Expedition* 1:98–101.

13 Foskett, ed., *Zambesi Journal* 1:42–43; Livingstone and Livingstone, *Narrative,* 25–27.

14 Livingstone and Livingstone, *Narrative,* 125–126, 592; Wallis, ed., *Zambesi Expedition* 1:98.

15 Slave prices were four yards of cloth for a man against three for a woman (or two for a girl) (Livingstone and Livingstone, *Narrative,* 125–126; but see also Wallis, ed., *Zambesi Expedition* 2:248).

16 Foskett, ed., *Zambesi Journal* 1:163.

17 Ibid., 179, 183–184, 237; Wallis, ed., *Zambesi Expedition* 1:98 (also pp. 77, 79, 88–89). See Gamitto, *King Kazembe* 1:93, for the prevalence of the linga among the Chewa of the northwest during the 1830s.

18 Bennett and Ylvisaker, eds., *Central African Journal,* 49; Foskett, ed., *Zambesi Journal* 1:163, 210; Livingstone and Livingstone, *Narrative,* 92, 93, 116; Wallis, ed., *Zambesi Expedition* 1:88, 105, 123.

19 See, for example, P. Curtin et al., *African History* (Boston: Little, Brown,

1978), 391–418; Vail and White, *Capitalism and Colonialism,* 16–41.

20 Bennett and Ylvisaker, eds., *Central African Journal,* 82–83; Foskett, ed., *Zambesi Journal* 2:351–353; Livingstone and Livingstone, *Narrative,* 355; Rowley, *Story of the Universities Mission,* 103–104.

21 The resulting disappointment and failure of the mission became one major cause for the criticism against Livingstone's presentation of the region in England.

22 Foskett, ed., *Zambesi Journal* 2:351–357; Livingstone to G. Frere, February 14, 1863, MS. 10779[14], no. 1318, NLS; Wallis, ed., *Zambesi Expedition* 1:183–184.

23 Foskett, ed., *Zambesi Journal* 2:358. Kirk thought Bonga's men had the consent of Chibisa himself (see also Wallis, ed., *Zambesi Expedition* 1:188).

24 Foskett, ed., *Zambesi Journal* 2:359.

25 Livingstone and Livingstone, *Narrative,* 420; Wallis, ed., *Zambesi Expedition* 2:369. See also Foskett, ed., *Zambesi Journal* 2:448.

26 Foskett, ed., *Zambesi Journal* 2:414; Livingstone and Livingstone, *Narrative,* 402–403.

27 Livingstone and others suspected that Matekenya bribed some officials to buy his freedom (Livingstone and Livingstone, *Narrative,* 402–403; Foskett, ed., *Zambesi Journal* 2:414).

28 Clendennen, ed., "Shire Journal," 15; Foskett, ed., *Zambesi Journal* 2:411; Livingstone and Livingstone, *Narrative,* 140.

29 Livingstone to Russell, December 29, 1862, MS. 10715, no. 1307, NLS; Rowley, *Story of the Universities Mission,* 298. The exact location of Matekenya's capital in the Valley is given differently in the sources. Waller has it ten miles below Khulubvi, which roughly corresponds to Mthumbi, the place that some sources identify as Matekenya's capital (Waller diaries 4:19 [September 9, 1863]; see also TVES6/1, 20). For Procter the capital was between Tengani and Khulubvi, at a place called Chiperoni or Chibwata (Bennett and Ylvisaker, eds., *Central African Journal,* 383, 400). Chibwata is the name of a small hill near the Chironje tributary of the Tchiri on the east bank. Some traditions (e.g., TVES4/8) make Chibwata Matekenya's capital, as does the traveler W. M. Kerr (in *The Far Interior: A Narrative of Travel and Adventure from the Cape of Good Hope Across the Zambesi to the Lake Regions of Central Africa,* 2 vols. [London: Sampson Low, Marston, Searle and Rivington, 1887], 2:262–281). From these sources it appears that Mthumbi was either a second capital or the headquarters of one of Matekenya's senior headmen.

30 Foskett, ed., *Zambesi Journal* 2:498.

31 Bennett and Ylvisaker, eds., *Central African Journal,* 380.

32 Ibid., 383; Rowley, *Story of the Universities Mission,* 370.

33 Bennett and Ylvisaker, eds., *Central African Journal,* 383; Clendennen, ed., "Shire Journal," 150; Waller diaries 4:19 (September 8, 1863).

34 Livingstone and Livingstone, *Narrative,* 578; Bennett and Ylvisaker, eds., *Central African Journal,* 378, 468.
35 Bennett and Ylvisaker, eds., *Central African Journal,* 289.
36 Ibid., 105.
37 Ibid., 83; Livingstone and Livingstone, *Narrative,* 357.
38 Livingstone and Livingstone, *Narrative,* 472–473; Waller diaries 4:19 (September 9, 1863); Wallis, ed., *Zambesi Journal,* 231.
39 Chained in large canoes, few captives reached their destination (Livingstone and Livingstone, *Narrative,* 356–357, 406, 593). The drivers also killed captives in order to make an impression (Wallis, ed., *Zambesi Expedition* 1:183). See also Foskett, ed., *Zambesi Journal* 1:192; 2:351, for other cruelties.
40 Rowley, *Story of the Universities Mission,* 106; Livingstone and Livingstone, *Narrative,* 357, 593.
41 Clendennen, ed., "Shire Journal," 15, 101; Livingstone and Livingstone, *Narrative,* 106–107, 406, 593–594. See also Foskett, ed., *Zambesi Journal* 2:411, 414.
42 Livingstone and Livingstone, *Narrative,* 406.
43 Clendennen, ed., "Shire Journal," 54, 73; Livingstone and Livingstone, *Narrative,* 126, 446; Wallis, ed., *Zambesi Expedition* 1:139, 157; 2:306, 346, 407.
44 Livingstone and Livingstone, *Narrative,* 472–473; Wallis, ed., *Zambesi Journal,* 231.
45 Clendennen, ed., "Shire Journal," 97–98; Livingstone to Antonio Talvares de Almeida, July 10, 1862, MS. 10715, no. 1245, NLS.
46 Waller diaries 4:18 (May 29, 1863); Bennett and Ylvisaker, eds., *Central African Journal,* 397; Clendennen, ed., "Shire Journal," 124.
47 Livingstone and Livingstone, *Narrative,* 457, 456.
48 Mandala, "The Kololo Interlude," 105.
49 For a more complete elaboration of this theory see Schoffeleers, "Mbona"; idem, "Cult Idioms." For examples of the population forcing the aristocracy to perform its responsibilities in connection with the cult see chap. 1 (for the 1862–63 period); Port Herald District Annual Report, 1933, NSP2/1/4, MNA (for actions taken during the crisis of the early 1930s).
50 Mandala, "Nature and Substance," 1–14.
51 Bennett and Ylvisaker, eds., *Central African Journal,* 346.
52 Livingstone and Livingstone, *Narrative,* 400; Rowley, *Story of the Universities Mission,* 341.
53 Bennett and Ylvisaker, eds., *Central African Journal,* 308; Rowley, *Story of the Universities Mission,* 223–226, 338–340; Wallis, ed., *Zambesi Journal,* 93, 95.
54 Bennett and Ylvisaker, eds., *Central African Journal,* 333, 377–378; Waller diaries 4:17 (April 17, 1863).

55 Rowley, *Story of the Universities Mission,* 339. This was apparently an ancient practice that fostered the belief that Mbona would miraculously provide the fugitives with pumpkins and rice (see also Waller diaries 4:12 [August 6, 1862]; TVES1/11–12).
56 Bennett and Ylvisaker, eds., *Central African Journal,* 382; Waller diaries 4:12 (September 18, 1862).
57 Bennett and Ylvisaker, eds., *Central African Journal,* 321–331; Foskett, ed., *Zambesi Journal* 2:364; Rowley, *Story of the Universities Mission,* 316–317; Wallis, ed., *Zambesi Journal,* 107.
58 Foskett, ed., *Zambesi Journal* 2:500.
59 Ibid. Nineteen bodies were seen one week in January 1863 (Clendennen, ed., "Shire Journal," 124; Livingstone to Russell, January 28, 1863, MS. 10715, no. 1316, NLS). Eight bodies were seen floating from Mathiti on different days in December 1862, and many more bodies were seen in January 1863 (Bennett and Ylvisaker, eds., *Central African Journal,* 379, 396). By February 22, 1863, Livingstone had counted thirty-four bodies, which he says was probably only a tenth of the total (Clendennen, ed., "Shire Journal," 145).
60 Waller diaries 4:17 (March 4, 1863).
61 Rowley, *Story of the Universities Mission,* 386.
62 Livingstone and Livingstone, *Narrative,* 457–458.
63 Foskett, ed., *Zambesi Journal* 2:516.
64 Rowley, *Story of the Universities Mission,* 384. It is impossible to verify the figure given here. Elsewhere (p. 93) Rowley says that from July 1861 to about March 1863 approximately two hundred persons a day were taken from the Highlands by slave dealers. For the number of dead in the Valley see also Wallis, ed., *Zambesi Expedition* 2:230.
65 Livingstone and Livingstone, *Narrative,* 450. I am quite aware of the danger of proposing what H. Kjekshus (*Ecology Control,* 1–25) has termed the "maximum population disruption theory" resulting from reliance on nineteenth-century European accounts. The precautions I have taken to minimize this possibility are explained in the Preface.
66 Foskett, ed., *Zambesi Journal* 2:595.
67 Rowley, *Story of the Universities Mission,* 384.
68 Ibid.
69 Livingstone and Livingstone, *Narrative,* 457. In the more seriously affected areas like Mathiti above Chikwawa the matured grains fell to the ground and rotted because there was no one to pick them up (Waller diaries 4:18 [May 27, 1863]).
70 Rowley, *Story of the Universities Mission,* 347–348.
71 Livingstone and Livingstone, *Narrative,* 462–463. See also Bennett and Ylvisaker, eds., *Central African Journal,* 373, 396; Rowley, *Story of the Universities Mission,* 306; Waller diaries 4:16 (December 1, 1862; January 16, 1863).
72 Bennett and Ylvisaker, eds., *Central African Journal,* 359–360, 366, 373,

379, 410; Rowley, *Story of the Universities Mission,* 347–348; Wallis, ed., *Zambesi Expedition* 2:237–238; Waller diaries 4:16 (January 20, 29, 1863).

73 Rodney, "African Slavery."

74 Waller described children in Madugu village near Chikwawa in January 1863 as "an awful sight their feet and eyes swollen terribly, their ribs nearly through the skin, and the stomach largely distended. A group was eating roots round a hut . . . another was almost blind with an affection [*sic*] of the eyes very common now" (Waller diaries 4:16 [January 11, 1863]; see also 4:16 [February 4, 1863]).

75 Bennett and Ylvisaker, eds., *Central African Journal,* 176; Clendennen, ed., "Shire Journal," 124; Livingstone to Russell, January 28, 1863, MS. 10715, no. 1316, NLS; Waller diaries 4:16 (January 20, 1863).

76 Nearly 75 percent of the slave population of Thete took to the woods to feed themselves on roots and berries, which brought to a standstill all business in a town that was so dependent on slave labor (Livingstone and Livingstone, *Narrative,* 448–449).

77 Rowley, *Story of the Universities Mission,* 106.

78 Many people took refuge in the village, which consequently grew in size (see, for example, Wallis, ed., *Zambesi Journal,* 89).

79 Livingstone and Livingstone, *Narrative,* 578; Mandala, "The Kololo Interlude," 192–194; Wallis, ed., *Zambesi Expedition* 2:228.

80 See, for example, N. R. Northrup, "Southern Malawi, 1860–1891: A Case Study of Frontier Politics" (Ph.D. diss., University of California, Los Angeles, 1978); Vaughan, "Social and Economic Change."

81 For accounts of the Universities Mission to Central Africa see Bennett and Ylvisaker, eds., *Central African Journal;* Chadwick, *Mackenzie's Grave;* Rowley, *Story of the Universities Mission;* Waller diaries.

82 Sekeletu was a descendant of the Kololo who had conquered Bulozi in about 1840. There were only two members of the Sotho-speaking aristocracy among the 112 men who left Bulozi for Thete in 1855. The others belonged to the subjected ethnic groups such as the Bulozi (the former rulers), Batoka, Basuleya, Basubia, and Mbundu. The men forged their common identity as the Kololo at Thete before fifteen or sixteen of them migrated to Chikwawa in 1861 (M. Mainga, *Bulozi Under the Luyana Kings: Political Formation in Pre-Colonial Zambia* [London: Longman, 1973]; J. D. Omer-Cooper, *The Zulu Aftermath: A Nineteenth Century Revolution in Bantu Africa* [London: Longman, 1966]; Mandala, "The Kololo Interlude," 3–4).

83 For a detailed account of the Kololo immigrants at Thete and under Livingstone see Mandala, "The Kololo Interlude," 1–34; A. Isaacman and E. Mandala, "From Porters to Labor Extractors: The Chikunda and Kololo in the Lake Malawi and Tchiri River Area," C. Coquery-Vidrovitch and P. Lovejoy, eds., *The Workers of African Trade* (Beverly Hills, Calif.: Sage, 1985), 209–242.

84 Isaacman and Mandala, "From Porters to Labor Extractors."

85 It was Livingstone who formally dismissed the Kololo because the porters had gone out hunting elephants in the Linthipe area against the expressed wishes of their master. It is clear that the Kololo had wanted to go their own way. They had grown tired of Livingstone, as had every other member of the expedition, black or white. By 1861 Livingstone was a frustrated man because of the failure of the expedition to achieve its stated objectives. It was being criticized in England, and the era of Livingstone the hero was drawing to a close. Livingstone knew this and became very irritable and impatient with everyone on the expedition. He forced people to walk long distances without rest. He had become a "beast," as Kirk put it. Everyone left him before the expedition was finally recalled in late 1863. The Kololo might also have been attracted to the Universities Mission, especially the affable Bishop Mackenzie, who died early in 1862. Chikwawa proved more attractive to the men than Livingstone had expected. He had hoped the Kololo would find life so difficult at Chikwawa that they would be forced to return to Bulozi. He was proven wrong (Mandala, "The Kololo Interlude," 19–22).

86 Ibid., 59–95.

87 Ibid., 98. Kololo confinement to this small area was mainly the result of Matchinjiri occupation of the southern section and of the presence of the Yao and Ngoni in the northeast and northwest.

88 The exact date is not known, but when the Scottish missionaries and traders came to the region in 1876 they found Chiromo already occupied by Chiputula (W. P. Livingstone, *Laws of Livingstonia: A Narrative of Missionary Adventure and Achievement* [London: Hodder and Stoughton, n.d.], 60–63; E. D. Young, *Mission to Nyassa* [London: Murray, 1877], 29–58).

89 Mandala, "The Kololo Interlude," 121–162; Isaacman and Mandala, "From Porters to Labor Extractors."

90 J. Bazin, "War and Servitude in Segou," *Economy and Society* 3 (1974): 129.

91 Mandala, "The Kololo Interlude," 121–162.

92 TVES4/2, 3, 9; TVES5/6, 8; TVES6/1.

93 TVES4/1, 4–6, 10; TVES5/2; TVES6/2.

94 Mandala, "The Kololo Interlude," 132–135.

95 TVES3/3, 15. See also Kerr, *The Far Interior* 2:263–280.

96 TVES3/3. See also TVES4/1, 6; TVES5/1, 3 for a variant of the same theme.

97 Schoffeleers, "The Zimba and the Lundu State."

98 See n. 2 above.

99 See, for example, Arrighi, "Labour Supplies."

100 Mandala, "The Kololo Interlude," 121–122; H. Faulkner, *Elephant Haunts: Being a Sportsman's Narrative of the Search for Dr Livingstone, with*

Scenes of Elephant, Buffalo and Hippopotamus Hunting (London: Hurst and Blackett, 1868), 285–297.

101 Bennett and Ylvisaker, eds., *Central African Journal,* 408; Foskett, ed., *Zambesi Journal* 1:144–145, 162–163.

102 H. W. Macmillan, "The Origins and Development of the African Lakes Company, 1878–1908" (Ph.D. diss., University of Edinburgh, 1970), 98; M/CK1; TVES2/3.

103 Macmillan, "Origins and Development," 198; M/CK1; TVES2/3.

104 Livingstone, *Laws of Livingstonia,* 60–63; Young, *Mission to Nyassa,* 29–58.

105 J. Buchanan, *The Shire Highlands (East Central Africa): As a Colony and Mission* (London: Blackwell and Sons, 1885), 79–80; Macmillan, "Origins and Development," 197–198. See also Young, *Mission to Nyassa,* 46–47, for Kololo cruelties.

106 Buchanan, *The Shire Highlands,* 94–96; Macmillan, "Origins and Development," 163, 200; Morrison diaries 2 (September 25, October 4–5, 1883), University of Edinburgh Library.

107 A sample of the enormous literature on the subject includes H. H. Johnston, *British Central Africa: An Attempt to Give Some Account of a Portion of the Territories Under British Influence North of the Zambesi* (London: Methuen, 1897), 69; Macmillan, "Origins and Development," 198–206; Morrison diaries 3 (March 7, May 24, 1884); D. J. Rankin, *The Zambesi Basin and Nyasaland* (London: Blackwell and Sons, 1893), 56–57, 74–77, 81–83.

108 Mandala, "The Kololo Interlude," 137–138.

109 Chiputula is remembered by the Mang'anja for his excessive labor demands and cruelty (see M/CK10–12; TVES1/5; TVES2/3; TVES3/9; TVES6/1).

110 TVES1/9; TVES3/9–15. For the vitality of the trade in the Thete region at this time see Kerr, *The Far Interior* 2:125–129; Young, *Mission to Nyassa,* 174, 192, 211, 216; H. H. Johnston, Report on the First Three Years' Administration of British Central Africa, March 31, 1894, FO 2/66, PRO.

111 TVES3/15.

112 TVES3/2, 5, 6, 12; TVES4/10; TVES6/4, 6. See also Lower Shire District Book 1, 1907; Ruo District Book 1, 1907, MNA; Schoffeleers, *The Lower Shire Valley.*

113 Young, *Mission to Nyassa,* 169–170; Isaacman, *Mozambique,* 124–153; Isaacman and Mandala, "From Porters to Labor Extractors," 209–242.

114 Ruo District Book 1, 1907, MNA. There is a Chikunda family at Bangula by the name of Balichoro (Belshior?).

115 TVES5/7.

116 Livingstone and Livingstone, *Narrative,* 38–39. It is impossible to date the migrations of the Mwenye to the Lower Tchiri Valley.

117 Morrison diaries 4 (October 4, 1884); E. D. Young, *The Search After Livingstone: A Diary Kept During the Investigation of His Reported Murder* (London: Letts, 1868), 239–243.
118 Schoffeleers, *The Lower Shire Valley.*
119 TVES3/2, 5–6, 12; TVES4/10; TVES6/4, 6; Rowley, *Story of the Universities Mission,* 323.
120 Isaacman and Mandala, "From Porters to Labor Extractors."
121 Livingstone and Livingstone, *Narrative,* 38.
122 Ibid., 38–39.
123 TVES3/10; TVES4/8; TVES5/9; TVES6/6.
124 Johnston, Report on the First Three Years, March 31, 1894, FO 2/66; M. A. Sharpe, Report on British Central Africa for the Year Ending March 31, 1897, FO 2/127, PRO.
125 Sharpe, Report on the Trade and General Condition of British Central Africa, April 1, 1899, to March 31, 1900, FO 2/307; H. C. McDonald (Collector), Annual Report for Ruo District, 1899–1900, FO 2/307; Sharpe, Report on the Trade and General Condition of British Central Africa for the Year 1900–1901, FO 2/468; Sharpe, Report on the Trade and General Condition of British Central Africa, April 1, 1900, to March 31, 1901, FO 2/470, PRO.
126 Mandala, "The Kololo Interlude," 122–123.
127 *Central Africa: A Record of the Work of the Universities Mission* 4 (1886): 86; H. K. Matecheta, *Blantyre Mission: Nkhani ya Ciyambi Cace* (Blantyre Mission: The Story of Its Origins) (Blantyre, Nyasaland: Hetherwick, 1951), 2; M/CK1, 4–6, 9.
128 Ruo District Book 1, 1907, MNA.
129 TVES1/1–9.
130 Ibid.; TVES3/9.
131 TVES1/1, 2, 5, 10.
132 TVES1/16.
133 TVES1/3; TVES2/1; TVES3/14. There were still some Mwenye who were engaged in ironworking in the late 1930s (*South African Pioneer* 53 [June 1939]: 65).
134 Chikwawa District Annual Report, 1918–19, S1/781/19; Ruo District Annual Report, 1919–20, S1/1041/19; Lower Shire District Annual Report, 1919–20, S1/1077/19, MNA; TVES1/10, 13, 15–16; TVES3/3, 5. See also Chafulumira, *Mbiri ya Amang'anja,* 13–14, for an oral history perspective that emphasizes the weakness of the Mang'anja iron industry.
135 H. B. Cotterill, ed., *Travels and Researches Among the Lakes and Mountains of Eastern and Central Africa: From the Journals of J. Frederick Elton* (London: Cass, 1968), 259, 264–266.
136 Morrison diaries 1 (June 22, 1882); 3 (February 13, June 26, 1884); 4 (September 12, 1884).

137 Johnston, Report on the First Three Years, March 31, 1894, FO 2/66, PRO.
138 TVES3/1, 9, 15.
139 Young, *The Search After Livingstone,* 196.
140 Kerr, *The Far Interior,* 2:257–258; Young, *Mission to Nyassa,* 36–37, 46.
141 Young, *Mission to Nyassa,* 36–37, 46.
142 Cotterill, ed., *Travels and Researches,* 255–256.
143 Kerr, *The Far Interior* 2:264–274; TVES4/2.
144 Morrison diaries 4 (July 25, 1884); Vail and White, *Capitalism and Colonialism,* chap. 2; TVES4/3, 5; TVES5/3.
145 Morrison diaries 4 (September 4, 1884).
146 The question of taxes will be discussed in relation to the problem of labor control in the next chapter. The Lower Tchiri was the first district in the protectorate to be taxed. Harry Johnston justified the move on the grounds that the peasants in the district were used to paying taxes, having done so under the Matchinjiri and the Portuguese.
147 Sharpe, Report for British Central Africa for the Year Ending March 31, 1897, FO 2/127, PRO.
148 Morrison diaries 4 (September 12, 1884).
149 TVES4/3, 5; TVES5/3. See also Vail and White, *Capitalism and Colonialism,* 64–69.
150 See, for example, Johnston, Report on the First Three Years, March 31, 1894, FO 2/66; Sharpe, Report on the Trade and General Condition of British Central Africa, April 1, 1900, to March 31, 1901, FO 2/470, PRO; R. Crossley, "High Levels of Lake Malawi" (unpublished paper, Chancellor College, University of Malawi, 1980).
151 Production Per Head of Export Crops, 1925, A3/2/233, MNA. There were over 10,000 people in the Lower Shire District in 1894 (H. H. Johnston to Secretary of State for Foreign Affairs, January 22, 1894, FO 2/66, PRO). In 1921 the Lower Tchiri Valley as a whole had a population of 91,859, distributed as follows: 11,441 in the Chikwawa section of the West Shire District; 39,502 in Ruo District; and 40,646 in the Lower Shire District (S. S. Murray, *The Handbook of Nyasaland* [1922; London: Crown Agents for the Colonies, 1932], 72–73, 80–85). Each person in the Chikwawa section of the West Shire District represented four in the Lower Shire or Ruo District. Assuming that these ratios also held true in 1894, then there were about 10,000 in Ruo and 2,500 people in the Chikwawa section of the West Shire District; hence the total of about 22,500 for the entire Valley in 1894.
152 Schoffeleers, *The Lower Shire Valley.*
153 Murray, *The Handbook of Nyasaland,* 72–73, 80–85.
154 Ibid.
155 Vaughan, "Social and Economic Change."
156 Production Per Head of Export Crops, 1925, A3/2/233, MNA.

3. Resistance to Capitalist Colonial Labor Regimes, 1875–1923

1 Wallis, ed., *Zambesi Expedition* 1:137.
2 Ruo District Book 1, 1907, MNA.
3 E. Fox-Genovese and E. D. Genovese, *Fruits of Merchant Capital: Slavery and Bourgeois Property in the Rise and Expansion of Capitalism* (Oxford: Oxford University Press, 1983), 208.
4 Mandala, "The Kololo Interlude," 121–162.
5 Lower Shire District Book 1, 1907, MNA. The eleven were Chataika, Chazuka, Chimombo, Chiphwembwe, Makoko, Malemia, Mbangu, Ngabu, Ndamera, Nyachikadza, and Tengani.
6 Ruo District Book 2, 1910–13, MNA.
7 Two of the better-known "foreigners" were Mchenga and Nyembe; Ruo District Book 1, 1907, MNA.
8 Ruo District Book 1, 1907, MNA.
9 Mwita was dropped by 1917, and William's chiefdom was later given to Beleu (a Mang'anja) before it finally came to be known as Chapananga. The only significant Kololo chief who was not recognized by the District Administration (Native) Ordinance was Mlauli. A resister of British imperialism from the beginning, Mlauli was expelled from Chikwawa in 1894 for refusing to pay taxes. He settled in the Neno area of West Shire District (Mandala, "The Kololo Interlude," 121–162; West Shire District Book 1, 1907; 2, 1913–18, MNA).
10 Lower Shire District Book 1, 1907, MNA.
11 Distribution of Mang'anja and non-Mang'anja headmen in the Lower Shire District (as of 1913) and in the Chikwawa section of West Shire District (as of December 1911) was as follows:

	Lower Shire							Chikwawa					
	A	B	C	D	E	F	G	A	B	C	D	E	F
Mang'anja	43	17	35	22	27	30	33	4	19	27	44	42	61
Non-Mang'anja	13	11	19	17	33	38	22	0	6	3	7	2	21

In the Lower Shire sections A–G represent, respectively, Tengani, Chataika, Chiphwembwe, Ngabu, Chimombo, Ndamera, and Nyachikadza (Lower Shire District Book 1, 1907, MNA). In Chikwawa sections A–F represent, respectively, Mwita, Mlilima, Katunga, Maseya, Kasisi, and William (West Shire District Book 2, 1910–13).
12 Ruo District Book 2, 1918–23, MNA.
13 See, for example, B. Pachai, *Malawi: The History of the Nation* (London: Longman, 1973), 181–185.
14 A major source of the presentation of "traditional" authorities as unmitigated collaborators of the colonial state (especially among Marxist scholars)

results from the failure to distinguish between the different layers of the local elites.

15 See, for example, Ruo District Book 2, 1918–23 (November 21, 1921), MNA; Murray, *Handbook of Nyasaland,* 62–63. These duties obviously overlapped with those of principal headmen.

16 In areas such as Port Herald, headmen did not have to refer this issue to the district commissioner or principal headman. Money was given by peasants from the hills who rented dimba plots under the nchoche arrangement (Port Herald District Annual Report, 1924–25, NSP2/1/1, MNA; TVES3/12; TVES4/8; TVES5/6; TVES6/4, 7; Duly, "The Lower Shire District," 44).

17 Chikwawa District Monthly Report, November 1927, NSC2/3/3; Chikwawa District Annual Report, 1931, NSC2/1/3, MNA.

18 Chikwawa District Monthly Report, August 1923, NSC2/3/1; Chikwawa District Monthly Report, February 1926, NSC2/3/2, MNA. Cases against headmen who infringed on Kololo rights to palm wine became known to the British after the latter had imposed new rules on palm wine making (Chikwawa District Annual Report, 1936, S1/66B/37, MNA). It was also in Chikwawa that headmen were often taken to British courts and fined for failing to concentrate villages (Chikwawa District Monthly Report, January 1928, NSC2/3/3, MNA). The fines ranged up to £5, which led some officials to declare the punishment unfair given the meagerness of the monetary compensation that headmen received (Chikwawa District Annual Report, 1927, NSC2/1/2, MNA).

19 Chikwawa District Annual Report, 1926–27, NSC2/1/1, MNA. See also Chikwawa District Monthly Report, June 1927, NSC2/3/3; Chikwawa District Quarterly Report, July–September 1928, NSC2/2/1, MNA. The district commissioner for Port Herald noted that "the practice of unauthorized persons collecting a group of huts round them and calling themselves headmen is being checked and the time has come when these people should be fined" (Port Herald District Annual Report, 1925–26, NSP2/1/1, MNA). For overt opposition to the policy see Chikwawa District Quarterly Report, April–July 1929, NSC2/2/1, MNA.

20 Chikwawa District Monthly Report, September 1925, NSC2/3/2; Ruo District Annual and Monthly Reports, 1920–21, S1/487/20; Port Herald District Annual Report, 1925–26, 1929–30, 1930–31, NSP2/1/1, 3, MNA. But see sec. 3.3 for ways in which British administrators broke the law in order to attract Lomwe migrant laborers.

21 Port Herald District Annual Report, 1931, S1/60F/32; Ruo District Book 1, 1907, MNA; TVES1/6; TVES3/2, 13; TVES4/8; TVES5/6; TVES6/4, 7.

22 Seven headmen interviewed by the writer received their kaundula this way (TVES1/6; TVES3/2, 13; TVES4/8; TVES5/6; TVES6/4, 7). Some headmen received their kaundula because of their special relationship—mostly

as employees—to the British (Ruo District Book 1, 1907, MNA).

23 TVES1/6; TVES3/2, 13; TVES4/8; TVES5/6; TVES6/4, 7. See also Chikwawa District Quarterly Report, July-September 1928, NSC2/2/1, MNA, where a Sena (Chikunda) headman, Ndombo, had for a long time paid allegiance to headman Nyangu instead of Makhwira, the principal headman.

24 L. A. Fallers, *Bantu Bureaucracy: A Study of Integration and Conflict in the Political Institutions of an East African People* (Cambridge, England: Heffer and Sons, 1956), 155-179.

25 See, for example, J. Lonsdale and B. Berman, "Coping with the Contradictions: The Development of the Colonial State in Kenya, 1895-1914," *Journal of African History* 20 (1979): 487-505.

26 Port Herald District Annual Report, 1930, NSP2/1/3, MNA. See also TVES4/9; TVES5/5, 7; TVES6/3, 4 for the unwillingness of headmen to support the state in labor recruitment. Many local administrators welcomed the Native Authorities Ordinance of 1933 because, among other things, it was to end the era of uncooperative headmen.

27 Chikwawa District Annual Report, 1931, NSC2/1/3, MNA.

28 Ruo District Book 1, 1907, MNA.

29 Port Herald District Annual Report, 1927, NSP2/1/2, MNA.

30 See, for example, D. Cordell and J. W. Gregory, eds., *African Population and Capitalism: Historical Perspectives* (Boulder, Colo.: Westview, 1987); C. Coquery-Vidrovitch and P. Lovejoy, eds., *The Workers of African Trade* (Beverly Hills, Calif.: Sage, 1985).

31 C. Van Onselen, "Worker Consciousness in Black Miners: Southern Rhodesia, 1900-1920," *Journal of African History* 14 (1973): 237-255.

32 Buchanan, *The Shire Highlands;* H. Drummond, *Tropical Africa* (London: Hodder and Stoughton, 1888); Cotterill, ed., *Travels and Researches;* A. Hetherwick, *The Romance of Blantyre: How Livingstone's Dream Became True* (London: Clarke, n.d. [1931]); Johnston, *British Central Africa;* Kerr, *The Far Interior;* K. J. McCracken, "Livingstonia Mission and the Evolution of Malawi, 1873-1939" (Ph.D. diss., Cambridge University, 1967); Macmillan, "Origins and Development"; F. L. M. Moir, *After Livingstone: An African Trade Romance* (London: Hodder and Stoughton, n.d.); Morrison diaries.

33 Johnston, Report on the First Three Years, March 31, 1894, FO 2/66, PRO. The situation improved briefly between 1896 and 1901.

34 See, for example, Sharpe, Report on the Trade and General Condition of British Central Africa, April 1, 1899, to March 31, 1900, FO 2/307, PRO. The number rose to about 125 steamers, barges, and boats by 1904; Ruo District Book 1, 1907, MNA.

35 L. Vail, "The Making of an Imperial Slum: Nyasaland and Her Railways, 1895-1935," *Journal of African History* 16 (1975): 89-112; idem, "Railway Development and Colonial Underdevelopment: The Nyasaland Case," R. Palmer and N. Parsons, eds., *The Roots of Rural Poverty in Central and*

Southern Africa (Berkeley and Los Angeles: University of California Press, 1977), 365–395; Pachai, *Malawi,* 138–152. The line between Blantyre and Chiromo was built by the Shire Highlands Railway Company from 1904 to 1908; that between Port Herald and Chindio on the Tchiri-Zembezi confluence in Mozambique, completed in 1915, by the Central Africa Railway Company. The Trans-Zambesi Railway Company constructed the line between the Zembezi River and Beira on the Indian Ocean before 1922. The two-and-a-half-mile-long bridge over the Zembezi River was not finished until 1935, at the time when the northern extension from Blantyre to Salima on Lake Malawi was still under construction.

36 Ruo District Book 1, 1907, MNA. Vessels carrying fifty tons could reach Chiromo only when the river was in full flood. Otherwise, the normal load was between four and eight tons during the four to five months after May.

37 Ibid. A steamer operating on the river at this time had an African crew of between fifteen and twenty men.

38 Lower Shire Railway Construction, MNA (a set of photographs taken during the construction period). A picture taken on August 19, 1904, and an undated picture show women carrying heavy loads of earth on their heads.

39 J. W. Gregory and E. C. Mandala, "Dimensions of Conflict: Emigrant Labor from Colonial Malawi and Zambia, 1900–1945," Cordell and Gregory, eds., *African Population and Capitalism,* 221–240.

40 There are indications of serious stresses in the local economy at the turn of the century. The difficulties appear to have culminated in the Makanandula famine of 1901 (Malawi Congress Party, "Nsanje District Calendar of Events, [1859–1966]," unpublished typescript, 1966; *South African Pioneer* 14 [April, May 1901]: 59, 69). Documentary sources on this and other famines of this early period (1904, 1907, and 1908) are sketchy; see *South African Pioneer* 17 (January 1904): 242; 20 (March 1907): 36; 21 (August 1908): 130. The evidence does not allow a full assessment of the effect of these annual crises on labor supply. See also Manning to Foreign Office, February 11, 1901, FO 2/469, PRO, for a report of a famine in the Highlands in 1901. The author does not, however, list the Valley as one of the areas suffering from food shortage in that year.

41 M. Page, "The Great War and Chewa Society in Malawi" (paper presented at a meeting of the African Studies Association, Baltimore, November 1978), 10. Between November 1918 and August 1919 there were 277 reported deaths in Chikwawa, where the epidemics were apparently not as virulent as in the southern districts. In the Lower Shire District especially they struck the victims of the Duladula floods who were crowded in msasa tents on the mphala bordering the marshes. By March 1920 there were 101 people reported to have died from smallpox in the Lower Shire District, a figure that the medical officer admitted to have been on the conservative side. Inoculation measures were rendered ineffective by the poor quality of the lymph administered (Lower Shire District Annual Report, 1919–20, S1/1077/19; 1920–21, S1/486/20, MNA. For Chikwawa District

see West Shire District Annual Report, 1918–19, S1/781/19; 1919–20, S1/1052/19; 1920–21, S1/474/20; for Ruo see Ruo District Annual Report, 1919–20, S1/1041/19; 1920–21, S1/487/20, MNA. See also *South African Pioneer* 33 [1920]: 17, 45; TVES5/6, 9).

42 Lower Shire District Book 1, 1907; Lower Shire District Annual Report, 1919–20, S1/1077/19, MNA. *South African Pioneer* 31 (August/September 1918): 71; 32 (March 1919): 20.

43 There are fewer documentary details on this famine than one might expect, especially for Chikwawa District, which was affected worse than its southern counterpart. The only detailed account I have come across is a description of food distribution organized by the agricultural officer, N. D. Clegg (Kherekhe), after whom the famine was called, in the central and northern parts of the Valley (the origin of the African name Mwamthota is unknown to me) (see A3/2/111, MNA). Another indication of the seriousness of the famine comes from population figures. Even if one grants the unreliability of most colonial figures, it is significant to note that the population of the Chikwawa section of the West Shire District in 1921 was 11,441. Two years later, in 1923, the figure was 10,640 (Chikwawa District Annual Report, 1922–23, NSC2/1/1, MNA). The decline is significant in view of the fact that Chikwawa District was much larger in 1923 as a result of the addition of the Makhwira chiefdom—the district's population center—after the dissolution of Ruo in 1922.

44 For events preceding the famine of 1922–23 see Chikwawa District Annual and Monthly Reports, 1918–19, S1/781/19; 1919–20, S1/1052/19; 1920–21, S1/474/20; 1922–23, NSC2/1/1; Lower Shire District Annual and Monthly Reports, 1918–19, S1/430/19; 1919–20, S1/1077/19; 1920–21, S1/486/20; 1921 (monthly reports), S1/299/21; 1922–26, NSP2/1/1; Ruo District Annual and Monthly Reports, 1919–20, S1/1041/19; 1920–21, S1/487/20; 1921 (monthly reports), S1/300/21; Ruo District Book 2, 1918–23, MNA. For events during the Depression see chaps. 5 and 7.

45 Lonsdale and Berman, "Coping with the Contradictions," 502.

46 Isaacman and Mandala, "From Porters to Labor Extractors."

47 Ibid.

48 For a discussion of Nyasaland's fiscal problems see L. Nthenda, "H.M. Treasury and the Problems of Nyasaland Public Finances, 1919 to 1940" (Ph.D. diss., Oxford University, 1972).

49 Johnston to Secretary of State for Foreign Affairs, January 22, 1894; Johnston, Report on the First Three Years, March 31, 1894, FO 2/66, PRO; Pachai, *Malawi,* 110–114. The Lower Shire District was among the first to be taxed, on the pretext that the people there were already used to paying taxes to the Portuguese. In 1893 the area contributed £400 in taxes.

50 Pachai, *Malawi,* 114; Sharpe, Report on the Trade and General Condition of British Central Africa, April 1, 1900, to March 31, 1901, FO 2/470, PRO.

51 Ruo District Book 2, 1918–23, July 1921 entry, MNA.
52 See, for example, TVES5/5; TVES6/4; Lower Shire District Annual Report, 1920–21, S1/486/20; 1923–24, NSP2/1/1; Ruo District Monthly Reports, 1920, S1/487/20, MNA. I haven't been able to find out when this apparently illegal practice started.
53 For the role of headmen in tax collection see, for example, Chikwawa District Annual Report, 1926–27, NSC2/1/2; Ruo District Book 2, 1918–23, MNA; Murray, *Handbook of Nyasaland,* 62–63. I have left out a discussion of public works partly because they were not so different from private works in terms of the dynamics of labor supply.
54 TVES4/9; TVES5/5, 7; TVES6/3, 4; Port Herald District Annual Report, 1931, S1/60F/32, MNA.
55 Port Herald District Annual Report, 1927, NSP2/1/2, MNA.
56 The workers received between one and two fathoms of cloth a trip (Buchanan, *The Shire Highlands,* 36; Drummond, *Tropical Africa,* 23; Cotterill, ed., *Travels and Researches,* 269).
57 *South African Pioneer* 19 (September 1906): 161. According to Ruo District Book 1, 1907, MNA, a porter received 3*d.* a day plus food.
58 TVES5/1; TVES6/3, 5. See also Pachai, *Malawi,* 115–119.
59 TVES5/1; TVES6/3, 5; Chikwawa District Annual Report, 1922–23, NSC2/1/1; Port Herald District Annual Report, 1922–23, NSP2/1/1, MNA.
60 Isaacman and Mandala, "From Porters to Labor Extractors," 230.
61 Morrison diaries 1 (July 27, 1882).
62 Buchanan, *The Shire Highlands,* 35–36; Macmillan, "Origins and Development," 187.
63 TVES4/9; TVES5/5, 7; TVES6/3, 4.
64 The following discussion is based on J. M. Schoffeleers, "From Socialization to Personal Enterprise: A History of the *Nomi* Labor Societies in Nsanje District of Malawi, c. 1891–1972," *Rural Africana* 20 (Spring 1973): 11–25.
65 F. J. T. Storrs, who administered the Lower Shire District from 1908 to 1910, was among the first Europeans to discover the trick (Lower Shire District 1, 1907, MNA). Chief Kapusi Chimombo was among the men raided in the nomi. Together with the others he was handed over to the African Lakes Company, which needed workers to cut firewood for its sternwheelers. The men spent four months in this occupation until, seeing no prospect of release, they ran away from the project (see also TVES5/8).
66 *South African Pioneer* 26 (July 1913): 105.
67 Chikwawa District Annual Report, 1927, NSC2/1/2, MNA.
68 *South African Pioneer* 18 (June 1905): 92; H. C. McDonald (Collector), Ruo District Annual Report, 1899–1900, FO 2/307, PRO.
69 Chikwawa District Annual Report, 1931, NSC2/1/3, MNA.
70 Ibid.

71 Lower Shire District Annual Report, 1920–21, S1/486/20, MNA; TVES5/5; TVES6/4.

72 Van Onselen, "Worker Consciousness."

73 E. D. Genovese, quoted in ibid., 249. See also Genovese, *Roll, Jordan, Roll,* 285–324.

74 Buchanan, *The Shire Highlands,* 36.

75 Morrison diaries 2 (October 5, 1883); 3 (March 16, 1884). Europeans often held the Kololo responsible for the thefts, which further complicated their relations with the rulers (see Isaacman and Mandala, "From Porters to Labor Extractors").

76 Mang'anja "thieves" were joined by the Lomwe from Mozambique, which greatly complicated the issue (Sharpe to the Governor of Zambezia, February 14, 1900, FO 2/306, PRO).

77 See, for example, Ruo District Book 1, 1907; Chikwawa District Annual Report, 1931, NSC2/1/3; 1932, S1/43B/33; 1934, S1/88B/35, MNA. The Chikunda (or Sena) were sometimes made an exception because they were good boatmen (see memorandums from Johnston and Sharpe, May–July 1897, FO 2/128, PRO).

78 Chikwawa District Annual Report, 1934, NSC1/88B/35, MNA.

79 Buchanan, *The Shire Highlands,* 36. The comparable weight of such loads at the beginning of this century was between fifty-six and seventy pounds (Ruo District Book 1, 1907, MNA).

80 Chief Secretary to Lower Shire District Commissioner, November 18, 1920, S1/487/20, MNA.

81 Port Herald District Annual Report, 1925–26, NSP2/1/1; 1927, NSP2/1/2, MNA.

82 Port Herald District Annual Report, 1927, NSP2/1/2, MNA.

83 Ibid. See also Port Herald District Annual Report, 1931, S1/60F/32, MNA. Elsewhere, administrators forced a railway company to pay its employees, who had apparently left employment before completing a three-month verbal "contract" (Chikwawa District Annual Report, 1932, NSC2/1/4, MNA).

84 Port Herald District Annual Report, 1931, S1/60F/32, MNA.

85 Chikwawa District Annual Report, 1922–23, NSC2/1/1, MNA. See also Port Herald District Annual Report, 1922–23, NSP2/1/1, MNA.

86 Port Herald District Annual Report, 1927, NSP2/1/2, MNA.

87 Port Herald District Annual Report, 1925–26, NSP2/1/1; 1931, S1/60F/32, MNA.

88 Port Herald District Annual Report, 1927, NSP2/1/2, MNA.

89 Port Herald District Annual Report, 1931, S1/60F/32, MNA. This practice apparently contributed to the abundance of labor in the area during the Depression.

90 Chikwawa District Annual Report, 1934, S1/88B/35, MNA.

91 J. S. J. McCall to British Cotton Growing Association (BCGA), December 3, 1910, A2/2/1, MNA; Pachai, *Malawi,* 110–127.

92 I will use the terms *settler, estate,* and *plantation* as if they were perfect synonyms.
93 Pachai, *Malawi,* 110–127.
94 Ibid., 100.
95 Refer to chap. 1, sec. 1.3.
96 S. Simpson to Colonial Office, July 11, 1906, CO 525/13, PRO; Simpson to District Resident (Blantyre), June 17, 1908, NSB1/1/1, MNA.
97 J. E. Chakanza, "The Rise and Decline of a Plantation Economy in Nsanje District, 1895–1945" (unpublished paper, Chancellor College, University of Malawi, 1976–77). After the coffee debacle, European settlers experimented with other crops such as tobacco and sisal. Tobacco farming was concentrated in Chikwawa District, whereas sisal estates were for the most part situated in the Lower Shire and Ruo districts. Best known among the latter was the Chipolopolo estate near Chiromo, which was closed only in the late 1930s.
98 Ibid.; J. B. Davey, "The Rise of the African Cotton Industry in Nyasaland," *Nyasaland Journal* 15 (July 1962): 14–15.
99 West Shire District Book 1, 1907; Ruo District Book 1, 1907; Lower Shire District Book 1, 1907; J. S. J. McCall, Cotton Growing by Natives, 1909, A2/1/3; Report on the Agricultural and Forestry Department for the Quarter Ending September 30, 1910, A2/3/1, MNA.
100 Director of Agriculture (DA) to Acting Deputy Governor, August 23, 1910, A2/3/1, MNA.
101 For a somewhat apologetic account of the association's activities see W. A. Wardle, "A History of the British Cotton Growing Association, 1902–39, with Special Reference to Its Operations in Northern Nigeria" (Ph.D. diss., University of Birmingham, 1980). See also J. A. Hutton (of the BCGA), review in the *Manchester Guardian* of July 29, 1916, A3/1/5; McCall, Memorandum on the Agricultural Development of Nyasaland as a Contribution to Empire Supplies, March 9, 1917, A3/2/67; Hutton to Undersecretary of State for the Colonies, May 14, 1917, A1/2/1; Acting DA, Report on the Operations of the BCGA in Nyasaland During the Year 1911, A2/1/6; BCGA to DA, March 31, 1913, A1/1/4; BCGA to DA, February 16, 1915, A3/2/57, MNA.
102 These obviously did not lead to actual increases in production during this phase; Empire Cotton Growing Corporation Circular Dispatch, August 31, 1917, A3/1/6, MNA.
103 See nn. 41–44 above.
104 Report for the Year 1916, A3/1/5; Empire Cotton Growing Corporation Circular Dispatch, August 31, 1917, A3/1/6, MNA.
105 Ruo District Annual and Monthly Reports, 1920–21, September 1920, S1/487/20, MNA.
106 DA to Acting Chief Secretary, December 17, 1917, A3/1/6. Only one of the plots was actually leased, and even this was probably never put to cultivation; the Duladula floods of 1918–19 swept everything away (see Lower

Shire District Annual Report, 1919–20, S1/430/19, MNA).

107 Governor Smith to Secretary of State for the Colonies, August 16, 1920, S1/557/20, MNA.

108 List of Estates in Nyasaland, 1921, A3/2/2, MNA. But see Ruo District Book 1, 1907, which lists only twenty-seven estates in the district in 1921. The area under cultivation in the district was the third largest of any district or subdistrict in the country (Ruo District Annual and Monthly Reports, 1920–21, S1/487/20, MNA). An agricultural report for 1925 (A3/2/233, MNA) gives 14,015 as the total number of acres under European cultivation that year, which represented, according to the figures of the same report, only 0.84 percent of the area's arable land. According to a 1926 report (List of Estate Owners, 1926, A3/2/96, MNA), Europeans owned about 102,000 acres. A major source of the discrepancies among these figures results, needless to say, from the fact that not all privately owned land was put into production at any time. In this respect, the figures for 1925 are closer to reality. European production was on the verge of collapse.

109 J. A. K. Kandawire, *Thangata: Forced Labor or Reciprocal Assistance?* (Zomba: University of Malawi Research and Publications Committee, 1979); Pachai, *Malawi,* 99–104.

110 Kandawire, *Thangata;* Pachai, *Malawi,* 99–104. For the Lower Tchiri see, for example, TVES1/10; TVES3/2, 7–9; TVES5/1–3; Ruo District Resident to DA, February 10, 1913, A1/1/4; Ruo District Book 1, 1907 (Headman Chenyera forced to pay rent labor by J. Dickie), MNA. A notable exception was planter Jennings who, according to oral testimonies, always demanded rent in cash (TVES5/2–3). Much of the work on his farm at Nyathando (Ndamera) was done by the nomi while the Ngoni from the north looked after his cattle.

111 Pachai, *Malawi,* 99–104; TVES3/9.

112 Ruo District Resident to DA, February 10, 1913, A1/1/4; McCall to Acting Government Secretary, March 25, 1913; McCall to Acting Government Secretary, March 7, 1913, A2/1/8, MNA.

113 McCall to Acting Government Secretary, March 25, 1913, MNA; TVES1/10; TVES3/2, 7–9; TVES5/1–3.

114 Chikwawa District Annual Report, 1925–26, NSC2/1/1, MNA.

115 Ruo District Book 1, 1907, MNA.

116 Chikwawa District Annual Report, 1931, NSC2/1/3, MNA.

117 TVES6/7.

118 Lower Shire District Book 1, 1907, MNA.

119 TVES3/9.

120 Chikwawa District Annual Report, 1925–26, NSC2/1/1; 1934, S1/88B/35, MNA.

121 These aggravating factors are cited by Chakanza, "Rise and Decline," but by none of the archival sources consulted by the present writer.

122 See chap. 4, sec. 4.2.

123 Vaughan, "Social and Economic Change."

124 See nn. 41–44 above. Shortage of labor had, for example, forced planters to curtail production in 1911–12, despite the money made available to them by the British Cotton Growing Association; Acting DA, Report on the Operations of the BCGA in Nyasaland During the Year 1911, A2/1/6, MNA.

125 Empire Cotton Growing Corporation Circular Dispatch, August 31, 1917, A3/1/6, MNA.

126 DA, Report on a Visit to the Lower Shire District, June 1923, A3/2/68, MNA.

127 Port Herald District Annual Report, 1922–23, NSP2/1/1, MNA.

128 DA, Report on a Visit to the Lower Shire District, June 1923, A3/2/68, MNA.

129 Chikwawa District Annual Report, 1922–23, NSC2/1/1, MNA.

130 Chikwawa District Annual Report, 1923–24, NSC2/1/1; Lower Shire District Book 1, 1907 (tax returns for 1918–19), MNA.

131 Chikwawa District Monthly Report, August 1926, NSC2/3/2, MNA. See also Chikwawa District Monthly Report, September 1926, NSC2/3/2; Port Herald District Annual Report, 1925–26, NSP2/1/1; Chikwawa District Annual Report, 1920–21, S1/474/20; 1934, S1/88B/35, MNA. The administration later reversed the policy and closed all doors to Lomwe immigration after the demise of the zunde system (see text below) (Port Herald District Annual Report, 1932, S1/43A/33; Lower Shire District Book 4, 1928–32 [March 22, 1929]; 5, 1933–37 [May 1935], MNA).

132 Port Herald District Annual Report, 1923–24, 1924–25, NSP2/1/1, MNA.

133 DA, Report on a Visit to the Lower Shire District, June 1923, A3/2/68, MNA.

134 Simpson to Colonial Office, July 11, 1906, CO 525, PRO; Simpson to District Resident (Blantyre), June 17, 1908, NSB1/1/1; McCall to Chief Secretary, January 1, 1916, A3/1/4, MNA.

135 McCall died in either 1921 or 1922, immediately after leaving Nyasaland for Tanganyika on a promotion. E. J. Wortley succeeded him as Nyasaland's second director of agriculture (BCGA Acting Manager to DA, July 1, 1922, A3/2/75; Annual Agricultural Report, 1924, A3/2/180, MNA).

136 Governor G. Smith to Secretary of State for the Colonies, August 16, 1920, S1/557/20, MNA.

137 McCall, Cotton Growing by Natives, 1909, A2/1/3, MNA. This was not a rebate in the sense that the sale of the required amount of cotton reduced the tax rate, as I have suggested in my earlier writings. The rebate was withdrawn at a very early stage (1911–12) in the Lower Shire District because peasants in the area did not need this form of encouragement (Government Secretary's Office to DA, June 6, 1911, A1/3/1, MNA).

138 McCall, Cotton Growing by Natives, 1909, A2/1/3, MNA.

139 McCall to BCGA, December 3, 1910, A2/2/1, MNA.

140 McCall, Report on Nyasaland Cotton, April 24, 1909, A2/1/3, MNA.

141 McCall to Acting Government Secretary, March 7, 1913, A2/1/8, MNA.

142 See, for example, A. Milner to G. Smith, March 29, 1920, S1/557/20, MNA.

143 As they apparently did in the interwar period.

144 See, for example, Agricultural Report, 1916, A3/1/5; McCall to Chief Secretary, January 1, 1916, A3/1/4; Extracts from a Special Meeting of the Executive Committee of the BCGA, London, September 9, 1919, A3/2/67, MNA.

145 BCGA to DA, January 16, 1916, A3/2/57; BCGA to DA, March 10, 1922, A3/2/59, MNA.

146 I have refrained from reproducing the figures on cotton raised on European estates as found in the Blue Books (1904–1907/8, 1920–22) and the published annual reports of the Department of Agriculture (1908–1919, 1923–40) for two main reasons. First, the units used have varied from tons to centals to hundredweights to pounds and from seed to lint cotton. Some of the shifts are made without any clear indication of the measures adopted. Second, my attempts to standardize the units have proved frustrating when I compared the figures given in the above-mentioned sources with those available for some years in the unpublished archival sources (see, for example, BCGA to DA, January 11, 1916, A3/2/57; DA to Killby, February 22, 1936; February 8, 1937, A3/2/70; Annual Agricultural Report, 1928, A3/2/182; 1930, A3/2/183; Production Per Head of Export Crops, 1925, A3/2/233, MNA). It was impossible to reconcile the figures found in the two sets of data. Part of the problem lies in the fact that buyers of European-grown cotton did not, unlike those merchants who purchased peasant-grown cotton, have to report their operations to the government (see DA to BCGA, July 4, 1935, A3/2/53, MNA). The only point on which all the data agree is that, with the possible exception of the period 1914–17, European planters never exported a thousand tons of seed cotton a year. The figures hover below five hundred tons, which is a pathetic record when compared with peasant output, especially after 1923.

147 Lonsdale and Berman, "Coping with the Contradictions," 505.

148 Chikwawa District Annual Report, 1930, NSC2/1/3, MNA.

149 See, for example, Chikwawa District Quarterly Reports, 1928–29, NSC2/1/1, NSC2/2/2, MNA.

150 Port Herald District Annual Report, 1933, NSP2/1/4, MNA.

151 Chikwawa District Annual Report, 1931, NSC2/1/3, MNA.

152 Ibid.

153 TVES3/9.

154 Ibid.

155 Chikwawa District Annual Report, 1931, NSC2/1/3, MNA.

156 Ibid.

157 Chikwawa District Annual Report, 1935, S1/79A/36, MNA.

158 The marketplace was not, however, all that free. Freedom to sell outside the estate meant in many years monopoly for the British Cotton Growing Association. See chaps. 4, sec. 4.2, and 5, sec. 5.3.

159 Chikwawa District Annual Report, 1931, NSC2/1/3; 1938, NSC2/1/5, MNA.
160 Ranger, "Growing from the Roots."
161 Lonsdale and Berman, "Coping with the Contradictions," 490.
162 Ranger, "Growing from the Roots."
163 Lonsdale and Berman, "Coping with the Contradictions," 502.
164 See, for example, Genovese, *Roll, Jordan, Roll,* 588–660.

4. The Ultimate Compromise: Peasant Cotton Agriculture, 1907–1939

1 Port Herald District Annual Report, 1932, S1/43A/33, MNA.
2 J. S. J. McCall, Some Problems Connected with the Introduction and Cultivation of Exotic Cottons in Nyasaland, 1910, A2/1/4, MNA.
3 Not all the cotton exported from the Valley did of course go to Britain. A good amount of it was also exported to India and other nodes of the capitalist world economy.
4 Port Herald District Annual Report, 1932, S1/43A/33, MNA.
5 McCall, Cotton Growing by Natives, 1909; Comparative Statement of Native Grown Seed Cotton Purchased by the African Lakes Company, 1907–1909, A2/1/3, MNA.
6 I have not found any evidence to support the idea of some colonial experts involved in the time of planting debate during the late 1930s (see, for example, F. Barker to Director of Agriculture [DA], November 8, 1934, A3/2/65, MNA; see also chap. 6) to the effect that some cultivators in the sparsely populated Chikwawa District or Tengani chiefdom in Port Herald District had planted cotton at the beginning of the rainy season (see E. C. Mandala, "Commodity Production, Subsistence and the State in Colonial Africa: Peasant Cotton Agriculture in the Lower Tchiri [Shire] Valley of Malawi, 1907–51," E. D. Genovese and L. Hochberg, eds., *Geographic Perspectives in History* [Oxford: Blackwell, 1989], 281–314). On the contrary, several reports indicate that even in Chikwawa, peasants were used to the "old style of planting cotton later than but in the same garden with maize" (Chikwawa District Annual Report, 1924–25, NSC2/1/1, MNA).
7 The data on the subject are overwhelming, especially for the 1930s. For the earlier period see, for example, DA to British Cotton Growing Association (BCGA) (Manchester), December 23, 1915, A3/1/3; Port Herald District Annual Report, 1925–26, NSP2/1/1, MNA; TVES4/4, 6. For Chikwawa District see Chikwawa District Annual Report, 1924–25, NSC2/1/1; 1937, NSC2/1/7, MNA. The government gave up the ruling by 1917, although it is not clear if this applied also to estate agriculture (Empire Cotton Growing Corporation Circular Dispatch, August 31, 1917, A3/1/6, MNA).

8 One possible explanation for this deviation may be found in demographic change.

9 There were probably several minor deviations from this standard schedule.

10 TVES1/12; TVES3/9; TVES4/4, 7; TVES5/2, 4, 5, 9; TVES6/6, 7. The system is described in detail after the arrival of a resident agricultural officer in the Valley in 1930 (see, for example, E. Lawrence to DA[?], January 8, 1931, A3/2/109; Annual Agricultural Report, 1930, A3/2/183; 1933, A3/2/58; Monthly Agricultural Reports, 1930–32, A3/2/200; 1933–35, A3/2/201; 1936–38, A3/2/202, MNA). The view (Agricultural Officer, Port Herald, to DA, August 16, 1915, A3/1/3, MNA) that it was the government which directed African growers to the dambo cannot be substantiated.

11 Monthly Agricultural Report, June 1909, A2/1/3, MNA.

12 McCall, Cotton Growing by Natives, 1909, A2/1/3, MNA.

13 Ibid.; Government Secretary's Office to DA, January 6, 1911, A1/3/1, MNA.

14 *South African Pioneer* 26 (April, July 1913): 61, 105.

15 Ibid.

16 Report for 1916, A3/1/5, MNA.

17 Governor to Secretary of State for the Colonies, August 16, 1920, S1/557/20; Empire Cotton Growing Corporation Circular Dispatch, August 31, 1917, A3/1/6, MNA.

18 Production Per Head of Export Crops, 1925, A3/2/233, MNA.

19 BCGA Local Manager to DA, January 19, 1926, A3/2/58, MNA.

20 The following gives a sampling of prices for selected years between 1909 and 1940 for one pound of first-grade cotton in the Valley, where prices were always higher than in any other part of the country because of proximity to the ocean and railway lines. (See also chap. 5, which also discusses the reasons why peasants in the Valley stepped up production during the Depression.)

Year	Price (in pence)
1909	1.00
1914	1.00
1917	1.125
1922	3.00
1923–25	2.50
1930	1.00
1931	0.62
1932	0.67
1933	0.70
1936	1.56
1937	1.46
1938	0.90
1939	1.00
1940	0.86

21 Port Herald District Annual Report, 1936, S1/66A/37; Monthly Agricultural Report, June 1909, A2/1/3, MNA; TVES5/4.
22 DA to Governor, December 17, 1917, A3/2/67, MNA.
23 Monthly Agricultural Report, July 1932, A3/2/200, MNA. There were 822 gardens classified as large out of a total of 13,102. The number of workers employed on the large gardens was 514. (There had been 22,531 gardens in 1931; ibid.) A year later large gardens represented only 1 percent of the total (Monthly Agricultural Report, June 1933, A3/2/201, MNA). For the difficulties facing the labor-employing peasant at this time see chaps. 5 and 7.
24 TVES1/11, 12, 13; TVES2/1; TVES5/1. Fatchi lived in the Dinde (Nyachikadza) until 1948, when he moved to Tengani (Duly, "The Lower Shire District," 27).
25 Port Herald District Annual Report, 1935, S1/79A/36, MNA. See also TVES5/2, 4; TVES6/2, 6; Port Herald District Annual Report, 1929, NSP2/1/3; 1936, S1/66A/37; Chikwawa District Annual Report, 1931, NSC2/1/3; 1934, S1/88B/35, MNA. The competition for these laborers was as stiff among the African farmers as it had been between them and their European rivals: "A large number of Portuguese natives do enter the district for temporary employment—but not enough to satisfy the demand. Vague complaints of 'enticing from employment' have been made though no definite charge has yet been proffered" (Port Herald District Annual Report, 1935, S1/79A/36, MNA).
26 Port Herald District Annual Report, 1929, NSP2/1/3, MNA; TVES5/2; TVES6/2, 6. Some government employees were said to have made between £20 and £300 from the sale of their cotton in 1917 (DA to Governor, December 27, 1917, A3/2/67, MNA). One Thomas from Chiromo, who was expected to produce thirty tons of cotton, was short of money for his laborers in 1922 (BCGA to DA, May 29, 1922, A3/2/75, MNA).
27 Memorandum on the Work and Experiments at Nyachiperi Farm (Port Herald) During 1915, A3/1/3, MNA.
28 Monthly Agricultural Report, December 1932, A3/2/200, MNA. These averages are not exactly the same as those given in other reports, but the departures are not very significant for the purpose of illustration.
29 TVES3/12.
30 H. C. Ducker to DA, December 15, 1936, A3/2/54, MNA.
31 Cotton Ordinance of 1910 (published 1912), A2/1/6, 7, MNA.
32 Ibid.
33 Ducker to DA, December 15, 1936, A3/2/54, MNA.
34 TVES3/12. See also DA to Chief Secretary, December 7, 1934, A3/2/3, MNA.
35 Chikwawa District Annual Report, 1936, S1/66B/37; 1937, NSC2/1/5, MNA.
36 Deputy Governor to Secretary of State for the Colonies, January 12, 1912, A1/1/3; DA to (?), November 17, 1911, A1/2/1, MNA. The British Cotton

Growing Association opened its first ginnery at Port Herald in January 1911 (Report for the Quarter Ending December 31, 1911, A2/1/6, MNA) and charged its customers very high rates.

37 J. M. Purves (Assistant DA) to Deputy Governor, March 28, 1912, A2/1/6, MNA.

38 Agreement with the BCGA, 1922, A3/2/55; Development of the Native Cotton Industry, May 9, 1923, A3/2/68, MNA. The initial contract was for five years and was to be renewed every three years afterward.

39 Agreement with the BCGA, 1922, A3/2/55; Development of the Native Cotton Industry, May 9, 1923, A3/2/68, MNA.

40 DA to British Central Africa Company, June 6, 1922, A3/2/67; Report on the African Cotton Industry, 1923, S1/481/24, MNA. For the governor's opposition see Acting Governor to Secretary of State for the Colonies, February 2, 1924, S1/481/24, MNA.

41 Churchill to Governor, October 21, 1922, A3/2/55, MNA. Passfield was for a price stabilization fund (Secretary of State for the Colonies to Governor, April 10, 1931, S1/552/40, MNA). On relations between the Nyasaland economy and the Imperial Treasury see Nthenda, "H.M. Treasury."

42 Annual Agricultural Report, 1924, A3/2/180; Report on the African Cotton Industry, 1923, S1/481/24; Port Herald District Annual Report, 1930, NSP2/1/3, MNA. In 1937 the state secured some funds for African cotton from the Colonial Development Fund (Acting DA to Acting Chief Secretary, June 16, 1937, S1/159/37, MNA).

43 See n. 20 above.

44 Port Herald District Annual Report, 1936, NSP2/1/5; 1937, NSP2/1/6; 1938, NSP2/1/7; 1939, NSP2/1/8; Lower Shire District Book 5, 1933–37, MNA. The African Lakes Company closed its shop in Chikwawa District because of poor trade (Chikwawa District Annual Report, 1938, NSC2/1/5, MNA).

45 Port Herald District Annual Report, 1939, NSP2/1/8, MNA.

46 Memorandum from DA, April 10, 1920, S1/225/20; BCGA Acting Manager to DA, July 1, 1922, A3/2/75, MNA.

47 Memorandum from DA, April 10, 1920, S1/225/20; BCGA Acting Manager to DA, July 1, 1922, A3/2/75, MNA. For the stiffness of the competition see, for example, Ruo District Annual Report, 1919, S1/1041/19, MNA, where it is reported that one market, Lalanje, had as many as thirty-seven buyers.

48 The system worked well for Indians during good cotton years but broke down during the Depression, when traders took their clients to court for failing to pay their debts. There were fifty-two such cases in Chikwawa District in 1930 alone (Chikwawa District Annual Report, 1930, NSC2/1/3, MNA). In Port Herald District the situation was so bad that one administrator recommended passing a law that would ban all credit by Indians

to peasants (Port Herald District Annual Report, 1931, S1/60F/32; 1932, NSP2/1/4; Lower Shire District Book 4, 1928–32, MNA).

49 Memorandum from DA, April 10, 1920, S1/225/20, MNA. This was one reason cited by the administration for discouraging Africans from owning large cotton fields, the cultivation of which would require paid labor. See n. 81 below.

50 Monthly Agricultural Report, December 1931, A3/2/200; April 1934, A3/2/201; Port Herald District Annual Report, 1933, NSP2/1/4; Chikwawa District Annual Report, 1934, S1/88B/35, MNA.

51 See the sources cited in the preceding note.

52 Empire Cotton Growing Corporation Circular Dispatch, August 31, 1917, A3/1/6, MNA.

53 Chikwawa District Annual Report, 1934, S1/88B/35, MNA.

54 Chikwawa District Annual Report, 1930, NSC2/1/3, MNA. The corresponding figure for 1930 was £2 5*s.* 0*d.*

55 See, for example, M. Muntemba, "Women and Agricultural Change in the Railway Region of Zambia, 1930–1970: Dispossession and Counterstrategies," E. Bay, ed., *Women and Work in Africa* (Boulder, Colo.: Westview, 1982): 83–103.

56 For variations on this theme refer to Etienne, "Women and Men, Cloth and Colonization."

57 S. Romalis, "Sexual Politics and Technological Change in Colonial Africa," *Occasional Papers in Anthropology,* vol. 1 (Buffalo: State University of New York, 1979), 177–185. For an inspiring argument against direct links between technological and social change see M. Wright, "Technology, Marriage and Women's Work in the History of Maize-Growers in Mazabuka, Zambia: A Reconnaissance," *Journal of Southern African Studies* 10 (October 1983): 71–85.

58 TVES3/9, 12.

59 TVES4/4, 7; TVES5/2, 4, 5; TVES6/6, 7; Port Herald District Annual Report, 1938, NSP2/1/7, MNA.

60 TVES5/2, 3, 9.

61 TVES4/3. See also TVES4/11–12. Misekete weighed about seventy pounds (McCall, Some Problems with the Cultivation of Exotic Cottons, 1910, A2/1/4, MNA).

62 The system was abolished at the beginning of the 1940s (see chap. 7).

63 Monthly Agricultural Report, June 1933, A3/2/201, MNA.

64 Elders recommended that such women be encouraged to marry so long as men paid only one tax regardless of the number of wives they had (District Council Meeting, September 2, 1932, Lower Shire District Book 4, 1928–32, MNA).

65 TVES5/2, 4, 6, 8; TVES6/2, 6; Duly, "The Lower Shire District," 36–40.

66 Chikwawa District Annual Report, 1930, NSC2/1/3; Port Herald District Annual Report, 1934, S1/88A/35, MNA.

67 Chikwawa District Annual Report, 1931, NSC2/1/3; 1934, S1/88B/35; 1935, S1/79B/36; Port Herald District Annual Report, 1935, S1/79A/36, MNA.
68 Port Herald District Annual Report, 1938, NSP2/1/7, MNA.
69 Chikwawa District Annual Report, 1930, NSC2/1/3, MNA.
70 TVES5/2.
71 District Commissioner (Port Herald) to Provincial Commissioner (Southern Province), March 3, 1931, S1/431/31, MNA.
72 TVES5/2, 4, 6, 8; TVES6/2, 6.
73 TVES1/5; Duly, "The Lower Shire District," 39.
74 The following summary is from J. M. Schoffeleers, *Evil Spirits and the Rites of Exorcism in the Lower Shire Valley of Malawi* (Limbe, Malawi: Montfort, 1967); idem, "Social Functional Aspects of Spirit Possession in the Lower Shire Valley of Malawi," Universities of East Africa Social Sciences Conference, *Religious Studies Papers* (1969): 51–63; idem, "Economic Change and Religious Polarization in an African Rural District," K. J. McCracken, ed., *Malawi: An Alternative Pattern of Development* (Edinburgh: Centre of African Studies, University of Edinburgh, 1984), 187–242.
75 According to Schoffeleers (personal communication, July 24, 1987), this was usually a foreign male spirit.
76 *South African Pioneer* 13 (December 1900): 213.
77 The movement does not appear to have won many converts among Mang'anja women.
78 See TVES3/12.
79 For the music see W. Van Zanten, "Traditional Malawi in Music, 1970–71," tape 8, track 4, item 7; for the challenges see works by Schoffeleers, esp. "Economic Change and Religious Polarization."
80 Schoffeleers, *Evil Spirits;* idem, "Social Functional Aspects."
81 Other factors included (a) colonial policies which were thoroughly inconsistent when it came to landownership by Africans; and (b) the tendency among zunde holders to use their money as bride-wealth for new wives. Section 5(1) of the Crown Lands Ordinance allowed Africans "a provisional leasehold tenure" at a reasonable rental in order to enhance the grower's interest in his holding. The government was expected to exercise "paternal" control by providing loans to such Africans so that they could employ labor (Extracts from a Meeting of the Executive Committee of the BCGA, September 9, 1919, A3/2/67; Chikwawa District Annual Report, 1930, NSC2/1/3, MNA). At the same time the state threatened to impose a 2*s*. rental on any African who had two acres of land or more. The aim was to discourage the rise of the large cotton grower who would pay his laborers with money borrowed from Indian traders, and who would, for all practical purposes, own the field without paying rent to the government (memorandum from DA, April 10, 1920, S1/225/20, MNA).
82 See, for example, A. Afonja, "Land Control: A Critical Factor in Yoruba

Gender Stratification," C. Robertson and I. Berger, eds., *Women and Class in Africa* (New York: Africana Publishing, 1986): 78–91. The conclusion that women constituted a distinct class among the peasantry (p. 90) is the least convincing aspect of this and several other studies in the collection.

83 Lower Shire District Book 4, 1928–32, MNA.

84 Meillassoux, " 'The Economy' "; Dupré and Rey, "Reflections"; Terray, *Marxism and "Primitive" Societies;* Terray, "Classes and Class Consciousness."

85 TVES1/9.

86 Chafulumira, *Mbiri ya Amang'anja,* 14; Chikwawa District Annual Report, 1930, NSC2/1/3, MNA.

87 Chikwawa District Annual Report, 1932, NSC2/1/4; 1936, S1/66B/37, MNA; I. and J. Linden, *Catholics, Peasants and Chewa Resistance in Nyasaland, 1889–1939* (London: Heinemann, 1974).

88 See the sources cited in the preceding note. The chiefs would join the missionaries in condemning the nyau only when Mang'anja headmen usurped the chiefs' right to stage the rituals (see chap. 3, sec. 3.1.2).

89 Chafulumira, *Mbiri ya Amang'anja,* 42; Van Zanten, "Traditional Malawi in Music," tape 8, track 11, item 18.

90 *South African Pioneer* 18 (June 1905): 95. See also D. R. Colman and G. K. Garbett, "The Labour Economy of a Peasant Community in Malawi," Second Report of the Socio-Economic Survey of the Lower Shire Valley (unpublished typescript, Shire Valley Agricultural Development Project, 1976).

91 See Meillassoux, " 'The Economy,' " 138.

92 *South African Pioneer* 27 (June 1914): 93; 28 (November 1915): 174.

93 An average family earned £2 3*s.* 6*d.* from the sale of its cotton in Chikwawa District in 1929 (Chikwawa District Annual Report, 1929, NSC2/1/3, MNA). The corresponding figure for Port Herald was slightly higher.

94 *South African Pioneer* 38 (September/October 1925): 105; 45 (August/September 1932): 108.

95 Lower Shire District Book 4, 1928–32 (September 2, 1932), MNA. See also TVES3/12; Port Herald District Annual Report, 1932, S1/43A/33, MNA.

96 Lower Shire District Book 4, 1928–32 (July 3, 1929), MNA.

97 The assertion by some administrators during the early 1930s that the nomi had declined (Port Herald District Annual Report, 1932, S1/43A/33; 1933, NSP2/1/4; 1935, S1/79A/36, MNA) could have reflected a real decline resulting from the exodus of boys for wage employment during the Depression. But in view of missionary reports (see, for example, *South African Pioneer* 45 [August/September 1932]: 108) it is more reasonable to think that the administrators were telling their superiors to ignore the accusations by missionaries; they did not want to be urged to go on anti-nomi campaigns and clash with the chiefs.

98 Colman and Garbett, "The Labour Economy."

99 Chikwawa District Annual Report, 1934, S1/88B/35, MNA. See also *South African Pioneer* 45 (October 1932): 127; 46 (August/September 1933): 103–104.

100 Chikwawa District Annual Report, 1934, S1/88B/35, MNA.

101 Port Herald District Annual Report, 1935, S1/79A/36, MNA.

102 Chikwawa District Annual Report, 1934, S1/88B/35, MNA.

103 Chikwawa District Annual Report, 1929, NSC2/1/3, MNA.

5. Structural and Conjunctural Strains in Food Production and Supply, 1907–1960

1 McCall, Some Problems with the Cultivation of Exotic Cottons, 1910, A2/1/4, MNA.

2 Governor's Message to Cotton Growers, August 6, 1930, S1/956/30, MNA.

3 Ibid.

4 One must consider this proposition as a hypothesis. I cannot demonstrate it for lack of evidence. The material I collected in the Malawi National Archives does not allow me to establish for most of the years covered by this study (a) the international prices for cotton; and (b) handling, insurance, transport, and other costs met by merchants. I hope to explore this problem in detail in a forthcoming study on famine in the Valley.

5 There were no fixed minimum prices for plantation cotton. Thus, when the highest price paid for peasants' seed cotton was 1.125*d.* a pound in 1916, the corresponding figure for European cotton was 9.50*d.* (Director of Agriculture [DA] to British Cotton Growing Association [BCGA], April 4, 1916, A3/1/5, MNA). See the *Nyasaland Times,* June 8, 1934, for settler opposition to the idea of fixed prices. It was only at the height of the Depression in 1930 that the government did not set guaranteed prices (Governor to Chief Secretary, August 6, 1930, S1/956/30, MNA).

6 McCall, History of a Movement to Establish Government Cotton Markets in Nyasaland, April 9, 1913, A2/1/8, MNA.

7 DA to Governor(?), June 24, 1912, A2/1/6; Acting Chief Secretary to BCGA, January 3, 1913, A1/1/4; DA to BCGA, September 12, 1921, A3/2/75, MNA. A notable exception to this happened in 1910, when McCall condemned outside buyers for driving up the price (McCall to BCGA, December 3, 1910, A2/2/1, MNA).

8 Extracts from a Meeting of the Executive Committee of the BCGA, September 9, 1919, A3/2/67, MNA. McCall, the director of agriculture, disputed this, saying that the association had never been forced to take the country's cotton during the previous ten years. However, see Report for 1916, A3/1/5, and DA (E. J. Wortley), Native Cotton Industry, 1922, A3/2/55, MNA, where the director admits that the association took all the cotton because there were no other buyers in 1915 and 1920.

9 Extracts from a Meeting of the Executive Committee of the BCGA, September 9, 1919, A3/2/67, MNA. See also BCGA to DA, July 1, 1922, A3/2/75; BCGA to McCall, March 4, 1913, A1/2/1, MNA, for the association's negative attitude toward competition and higher prices.

10 Memorandum from DA, April 10, 1920, S1/225/20; BCGA to DA, July 1, 1922, A3/2/75, MNA.

11 BCGA (Port Herald) to DA, July 1, 1922, A3/2/75, MNA.

12 McCall to Deputy Governor, December 21, 1909, A2/1/3; DA to BCGA (Port Herald), April 4, 1916, A3/1/5, MNA.

13 DA to BCGA, September 12, 1921, A3/2/75, MNA.

14 Agreement with the BCGA, 1922, A3/2/55; Development of the Native Cotton Industry, May 9, 1923, A3/2/68, MNA.

15 McCall to Deputy Governor, December 21, 1909, A2/1/3; McCall to Acting Deputy Governor, July 8, 1910, A2/3/1; BCGA to DA, March 4, 1913, A1/2/1; Government Secretary to DA, January 17, 1913, A1/1/4; Extracts from a Meeting of the Executive Committee of the BCGA, September 9, 1919, A3/2/67, MNA.

16 DA to BCGA (Port Herald), April 4, 1916, A3/1/5, MNA.

17 R. Rankine (Acting Governor) to Secretary of State for the Colonies, February 20, 1924, S1/481/24, MNA. But see Cotton Prices and Railway Rates, 1930, S1/956/30; Churchill to Governor, October 21, 1922, A3/2/55; and Governor to Chief Secretary, May 7, 1931, A3/2/56, MNA, for the opposition to the idea of subsidizing producer prices mounted by Governor Thomas and Churchill.

18 See, for example, BCGA to DA, April 19, 1911, A1/1/2; BCGA to (?), December 3, 1912, A1/1/3; Acting Chief Secretary to BCGA, January 3, 1913, A1/1/4; BCGA to DA, April 26, 1934, A3/2/53; Director, Liverpool-Uganda Cotton Company, to Chief Secretary, June 7, 1934, S1/269/34, MNA.

19 Report on Nyasaland Cotton, April 24, 1909, A2/1/3; see also African Lakes Company Report, March 1, 1911; McCall to Deputy Governor, March 3, 1911, A2/1/4; BCGA to (?), December 3, 1912, A1/1/3, MNA.

20 McCall, Some Problems with the Cultivation of Exotic Cottons, 1910, A2/1/4, MNA.

21 For a good beginning on the subject see Vail, "Railway Development and Colonial Underdevelopment."

22 Nyasaland Chamber of Agriculture and Commerce to Governor, November 20, 1915, A3/1/3, MNA.

23 BCGA Manager, Native Cotton Industry, Nyasaland, 1931, A3/2/56, MNA.

24 Pachai, *Malawi,* 152.

25 Cotton Prices and Railway Rates, 1930, S1/956/30, MNA.

26 BCGA to DA, August 5, 1931, A3/2/56; Report by the Committee Appointed to Make Recommendations for the Marketing of the 1931 Native Crop, June 12, 1931, A3/2/77, MNA.

27 DA(?) to Empire Cotton Growing Corporation, August 21, 1931, A3/2/70, MNA.
28 Shire Highlands Railway General Manager to Chief Secretary, May 31, 1931, S1/956/30; BCGA to DA, August 5, 1931, A3/2/56, MNA.
29 Chief Secretary to Provincial Commissioners, August 24, 1931, A3/2/77, MNA. The government and the British Cotton Growing Association contributed £2,000 and £15,000, respectively. The letter also notes that the railways contributed £700, although it is not clear in what form this contribution was made. On the basis of production figures for 1930 the reduction cost the railways only £386 6*s.* 5*d.* and not £1,180, as they claimed (BCGA to DA, August 5, 1931, A3/2/56, MNA).
30 DA to Chief Secretary, April 7, 1931, A3/2/56, MNA. The state preferred the renewal of the contract over two other options: (a) subsidizing the British Cotton Growing Association in order for it to purchase cotton from the northern belt; and (b) the government itself buying the cotton.
31 Chief Secretary to Shire Highlands Railway General Manager, May 4, 1931, S1/956/30, MNA.
32 See, for example, BCGA Manager, Native Cotton Industry, 1931, A3/2/56, MNA.
33 Report by the Committee Appointed to Make Recommendations for the Marketing of the 1931 Native Cotton Crop, A3/2/77, MNA.
34 K. L. Hall (Chief Secretary) to Provincial and District Commissioners, August 24, 1931, A3/2/77, MNA.
35 District Commissioner (Dedza) to Provincial Commissioner (Central Province), July 26, 1930, S1/956/30, MNA.
36 District Commissioner (Dedza) to Provincial Commissioner (Central Province), July 22, 1930, S1/956/30, MNA.
37 Chief Kachindamoto to District Commissioner (Dedza), July 27, 1930; Bishop M. Guillemé to Governor, July 26, 1930, S1/956/30, MNA.
38 District Commissioner (Dedza) to Provincial Commissioner (Central Province), July 22, 1930, S1/956/30, MNA.
39 District Commissioner (Dedza) to DA, July 26, 1930, A3/2/56, MNA.
40 Monthly Agricultural Report, November 1931, A3/2/200; May 1934, A3/2/201; June 1938, A3/2/202, MNA.
41 Monthly Agricultural Report, December 1933, A3/2/201, MNA. The details of this perception will be discussed in the next section.
42 According to some estimates, an acre in the southern part of Port Herald yielded 784 pounds of shelled nuts (Monthly Agricultural Report, April 1934, A3/2/201, MNA). Others placed the yield per acre at between five and six hundred pounds of unshelled nuts (Monthly Agricultural Report, April 1933, A3/2/201, MNA), whereas still other observers estimated that an acre could yield up to a thousand pounds of shelled nuts if there was a reliable market (Monthly Agricultural Report, August 1932, A3/2/200, MNA).

43 See, for example, Monthly Agricultural Report, April 1930; May, June 1932, A3/2/200; April, July 1933, A3/2/201, MNA.
44 Port Herald District Agriculturalist (H. Munro) to DA, July 22, 1915, A3/1/2; December 18, 1915, A3/1/3; April 1, 1916, A3/1/5, MNA.
45 Monthly Agricultural Report, December 1933, A3/2/201, MNA.
46 Ibid.; see also Monthly Agricultural Report, November 1931, A3/2/200, MNA.
47 Monthly Agricultural Report, May 1932, A3/2/200, MNA.
48 Monthly Agricultural Report, April 1932, A3/2/200, MNA.
49 Monthly Agricultural Report, May 1933, A3/2/201; Port Herald District Annual Report, 1933, NSP2/1/4, MNA.
50 Monthly Agricultural Report, May 1933, A3/2/201, MNA.
51 Monthly Agricultural Report, May 1934, A3/2/201, MNA.
52 Monthly Agricultural Report, April 1932 (see also June and December 1932), A3/2/200, MNA.
53 Monthly Agricultural Report, April 1932, A3/2/200, MNA.
54 Port Herald District Annual Report, 1933, NSP2/1/4, MNA.
55 Monthly Agricultural Report, June 1934, A3/2/201, MNA.
56 Monthly Agricultural Report, June 1936, A3/2/202, MNA.
57 DA to Chief Secretary, April 7, 23, 1931, A3/2/56, MNA.
58 DA(?) to Empire Cotton Growing Corporation, August 21, 1931, A3/2/70, MNA. According to the letter, a government subsidy of 0.25*d.* raised the minimum price in the northern areas to 0.50*d.*
59 E. Lawrence to DA(?), October 12, 1931, A3/2/200, MNA.
60 There were 8,409 fewer cotton growers and 9,429 fewer cotton gardens in 1932 than in the previous season, when there had been 21,214 growers and 22,531 gardens (Monthly Agricultural Report, July 1932, A3/2/200, MNA).
61 Monthly Agricultural Report, July 1933, A3/2/201, MNA.
62 Monthly Agricultural Report, March 1933, A3/2/201, MNA. For slightly different figures see Lower Shire District Book 5, 1933–37 (April 1933), MNA.
63 Monthly Agricultural Report, April, October 1933, A3/2/201, MNA.
64 Lower Shire District Book 4, 1928–32 (December 23, 1931), MNA.
65 Lower Shire District Book 5, 1933–37 (April 14, 1933), MNA.
66 Port Herald District Annual Report, 1931, S1/60F/32, MNA.
67 Port Herald District Annual Report, 1932, S1/43A/33, MNA.
68 Port Herald District Annual Report, 1933, NSP2/1/4, MNA.
69 Lower Shire District Book 4, 1928–32 (District Council Meeting, September 2, 1932), MNA.
70 Port Herald District Annual Report, 1930, NSP2/1/3, MNA.
71 Port Herald District Annual Report, 1931, S1/60F/32; 1932, S1/43A/33; Lower Shire District Book 4, 1928–32, MNA; *South African Pioneer* 46 (August/September 1933): 105.

72 Port Herald District Annual Report, 1931, S1/60F/32, MNA. According to one estimate, Indian traders at the tiny Chiromo township were owed £1,000 in small amounts by peasants of the neighborhood.
73 Chikwawa District Annual Report, 1930, NSC2/1/3, MNA.
74 Port Herald District Annual Report, 1931, S1/60F/32, MNA.
75 Ibid.
76 Port Herald District Annual Report, 1933, NSP2/1/4, MNA.
77 BCGA to Undersecretary of State for the Colonies, May 14, 1917, A1/2/1, MNA.
78 Monthly Agricultural Report, May 1934, A3/2/201, MNA.
79 Universities Mission to Central Africa, *Central Africa: A Record of the Work of the Universities Mission* 13 (1895): 66–67; Monthly Agricultural Report, September 1932, A3/2/200; Chikwawa District Annual Report, 1932, NSC2/1/4, MNA. People stopped eating locusts when they found that the insects were infested with worms (*mfunye*) (TVES4/5, 6; Monthly Agricultural Report, March 1934, A3/2/201, MNA).
80 Monthly Agricultural Report, January 1934, A3/2/201, MNA. By March the swarms left about fifty thousand people in the northern part of Port Herald District without food (Monthly Agricultural Report, March 1934, A3/2/201; see also Lower Shire District Book 5, 1933–37 [April 1933], MNA).
81 Monthly Agricultural Report, September 1933, A3/2/201; July 1937, A3/2/202; Soil Conservation Officer (Chikwawa) to DA, On a Visit to Eroded Areas in Lower Shire District, August 4, 1943, Ag. 2.17.7F/880, MNA; Schoffeleers, ed., *Guardians of the Land,* 1–8.
82 Monthly Agricultural Report, January 1934, February 1935, A3/2/201, MNA.
83 Monthly Agricultural Report, September 1933, A3/2/201, MNA. The swarms traveled seven miles a day on average (Monthly Agricultural Report, May 1933, A3/2/201, MNA).
84 Monthly Agricultural Report, March 1933, A3/2/201, MNA. See also Lower Shire District Book 5, 1933–37 (April 1933), MNA.
85 The original invaders apparently did little harm to early-planted crops that had become fully established by February (Monthly Agricultural Report, February 1933, February 1934, A3/2/201, MNA). The ravages were then confined to the late-planted crops, including cotton, that were still young by March.
86 Monthly Agricultural Report, February 1935, A3/2/201, MNA.
87 Monthly Agricultural Report, May, July 1933, A3/2/201, MNA.
88 Port Herald District Annual Report, 1935, S1/79A/36, MNA. See also Monthly Agricultural Report, February, April 1935, A3/2/201, MNA.
89 See chap. 6, sec. 6.1.
90 Port Herald District Annual Report, 1936, S1/66A/37; Chikwawa District Annual Report, 1937, S1/17B/38, MNA.

91 Monthly Agricultural Report, January, February, March 1936, A3/2/202; TVES4/5–6, 10–12. The battle against the locusts had started earlier but had not had much success. People suppressed information about the movements of the locusts for fear of being forced to take the measures listed in the text (Monthly Agricultural Report, March, November 1933, A3/2/201, MNA). Hunger may have to do with the earlier resistance.

92 Monthly Agricultural Report, January, February, July 1937; January, October, November 1938, A3/2/202, MNA.

93 Monthly Agricultural Report, April 1930, A3/2/200, MNA.

94 It appears from oral evidence that the drought of 1901–1902 did lead to a famine, known as Makanandula (T73/8; TVES1/9, 15; Malawi Congress Party, "Nsanje District Calendar of Events, [1859–1965]" [unpublished typescript, 1966]). There are, however, no detailed documentary reports on this famine.

95 *South African Pioneer* 20 (November 1907): 178.

96 *South African Pioneer* 21 (August 1908): 130.

97 Many people from the area migrated to Mozambique as a result of the shortage (Lower Shire District Book 1, 1907, MNA).

98 The shortage was preceded by excessive rains (*South African Pioneer* 25 [March 1912]: 37).

99 District Agricultural Officer (DAO) (Port Herald) to DA, March 19, April 1, 1912, A1/1/3, MNA.

100 *South African Pioneer* 25 (October 1912): 162. In areas such as Lulwe that did not have dambo land for the cultivation of sweet potatoes, the shortage was so severe that schools were closed.

101 *South African Pioneer* 26 (April 1913): 61. See also Lower Shire District Book 1, 1907, MNA.

102 See Table 4.1, p. 137, for the drop in cotton production. Peasants used the little grain they had in brewing beer in order to pay their taxes (see *South African Pioneer* 26 [July 1913]: 105).

103 *South African Pioneer* 48 (February 1935): 13.

104 A separate study is in progress on the famine.

105 It also affected the Mwanza-Neno area and parts of the Blantyre and Chiradzulu districts in the Highlands.

106 *South African Pioneer* 31 (August/September 1918): 71; 32 (March 1919): 20; Lower Shire District Book 1, 1907, MNA.

107 Between November 1918 and August 1919, 277 people were reported to have died from influenza in Chikwawa District, where the epidemic was considered mildest. Smallpox exacted a heavy toll in Port Herald District, especially among the fugitives from the flooded Dinde who were crowded in msasa tents on the mphala. By March 1920 there were 101 reported deaths in the district, a figure that the medical officer considered to have been on the conservative side. Inoculation measures were ineffective because of the poor quality of the lymph administered (Lower Shire District Annual

Report, 1919–20, S1/1077/19; 1920–21, S1/486/20). For the situation in Chikwawa District see Chikwawa District Annual Report, 1918–19, S1/781/19; 1919–20, S1/1052/19; 1920–21, S1/474/20; for the Ruo District see Ruo District Annual Report, 1919–20, S1/1041/19; 1920–21, S1/487/20, MNA. See also Ruo District Book 2, 1918–23 (November 11, 1918), MNA; *South African Pioneer* 33 (1920): 17, 45.

108 Ibid.

109 Lower Shire District Annual and Monthly Reports, 1920–21, December 1920, S1/468/20, MNA.

110 The government sent 385.5 tons of maize in all between September 1922 and March 1923. Of these only 95.67 tons were given free; the rest were sold at the exorbitant price of two pounds a penny (see N. D. Clegg to DA, September 22, 1922, through March 1923, A3/2/111, MNA).

111 Chafulumira, *Mbiri ya Amang'anja,* 3–5; TVES3/7, 14; TVES5/9; Chikwawa District Annual Report, 1922–23, NSC2/1/1; Port Herald District Annual Report, 1922–23, NSP2/1/1; Lower Shire District Monthly Report, April, May 1921, S1/299/21, MNA; TVES1/10–12, 14–15; TVES2/2–4; TVES3/1, 3, 7, 11–13, 15; TVES4/1.

112 *South African Pioneer* 35 (September/October 1922): 104; Port Herald District Annual Report, 1933, NSP2/1/4, MNA. See also J. M. Schoffeleers, *River of Blood* (forthcoming), chap. 4.

113 Some of the wild fruits and plants on which peasants lived during the famine were *mpama* (yam of genus *Dioscorea*); *bwemba* (*Tamarindus indica*); *mvumo* (*Borassus aethiopum*); *matondo* (fruit of the mtondo tree, *Cordyla africana*); *gugu* or *khundi* (*Sorghum verticilliflorum*) (Clegg to DA, February 7, 1923, A3/2/111, MNA; *South African Pioneer* 36 [April 1923]; and some of the oral testimonies cited in n. 111 above).

114 TVES1/1, 4, 11.

115 See chap. 4, sec. 4.1.

116 See, for example, Port Herald District Annual Report, 1938, NSP2/1/7, MNA.

117 BCGA to Undersecretary of State for the Colonies, May 14, 1917, A1/2/1, MNA.

118 See, for example, H. D. Aplin to DA, February 8, 1916, A3/1/4, MNA.

119 Monthly Agricultural Report, April 1930, A3/2/200, MNA.

120 Port Herald District Annual Report, 1930, NSP2/1/3, MNA.

121 Unlike during the 1930s, in the early 1910s peasants responded to the threat of hunger by cutting down cotton production (McCall to BCGA, January 4, 1913, A2/1/8, MNA).

122 Monthly Agricultural Report, January 1932; District Agricultural Officer (Port Herald) to DA, May 22, 1931, A3/2/200, MNA. The reason cited in the report was, of course, that peasants were lazy.

123 Monthly Agricultural Report, December 1935, A3/2/201, MNA.

124 Monthly Agricultural Report, February 1932; see also reports for November, December 1929; January, February 1930, A3/2/200, MNA.

125 Monthly Agricultural Report, April 1937, A3/2/202, MNA.
126 Monthly Agricultural Report, February, November 1934, A3/2/201, MNA.
127 Port Herald District Annual Report, 1925–26, NSP2/1/1, MNA.
128 Monthly Agricultural Report, April, May 1930, A3/2/200, MNA.
129 Monthly Agricultural Report, May 1931, A3/2/200, MNA.
130 DAO (E. Lawrence), Soil Erosion on the Lower Shire, April 3, 1931; Conservator of Forests, Memorandum on Soil Erosion, April 9, 1931; Lawrence, Memorandum on Soil Erosion, April 17, 1931; DA to Lawrence, Memorandum on Soil Erosion, May 2, 1931, A3/2/200, MNA.
131 Monthly Agricultural Report, April 1930; February 1931, A3/2/200, MNA. Hence the campaign at stalk destruction (see Monthly Agricultural Report, February, June 1931, A3/2/200, MNA).
132 For the view linking heavy seeding to the stem borer and other pests see Monthly Agricultural Report, April 1931; April 1932, A3/2/200, MNA. For an opposing view see Monthly Agricultural Report, December 1930, A3/2/200, MNA.
133 DAO (Lawrence) to DA, January 21, 1931, A3/2/109, MNA.
134 Lower Shire District Monthly Report, July 1919, S1/430/19; Monthly Agricultural Report, April 1938, A3/2/202, MNA.
135 Lawrence, Soil Erosion on the Lower Shire, April 3, 1931, A3/2/200, MNA.
136 H. C. Ducker, Notes on the Soil Erosion Problems of the Lower Shire in Reference to the Report by the DAO, April 23, 1931, A3/2/200, MNA. The point would become part of the argument against the ridging campaign during the late 1940s and 1950s. In 1931 Ducker raised the point only to underscore the need for further investigation into the problem.
137 Lawrence to DA, January 21, 1931, A3/2/109; Lawrence to DA, February 17, 1934, A3/2/53, MNA.
138 Lint Company of Zambia, *Cotton Pests in Africa* (Lusaka, Zambia: Lintco, n.d.), text facing plates 5 and 6.
139 See, for example, DAO to DA, March 23, 1917, A3/1/6; Report of the Chief Veterinary Officer, April 1, 1920, to December 31, 1922, A3/2/180, MNA. A notable exception occurred in 1930 when, according to Lawrence, the stainer did more damage than the red bollworm (Lawrence to the DA, January 17, 1930, A3/2/200, MNA). The two varieties of stainer found in the Valley were *Dysdercus nigrotasciatus* and *Dysdercus intermedius* (see, for example, Monthly Agricultural Report, September 1930, A3/2/200, MNA).
140 See Report for June 1909, A2/1/3, MNA, where it is referred to simply as a bollworm. The earliest references to the pest as the red bollworm are in the reports for the 1930s (e.g., Monthly Agricultural Report, August 1930, A3/2/200, MNA). Reports for the late 1930s also mention the presence of the American and the Sudanic bollworm (Monthly Agricultural Report, September 1936; April 1938, A3/2/202, MNA).
141 Record of a Meeting of the Special Committee Appointed to Consider the

Question of the Planting Date for Cotton in Nyasaland, November 26, 1937; Lawrence to DA, July 2, 1937, A3/2/54; Barker to DA, February 1, November 8, 1934; Ducker to DA, October 6, 1936; S. T. Hoyle, Memorandum on a Visit to the Lower River, September 1937, A3/2/65; Barker to DA, December 5, 1935, A3/2/71, MNA.

142 See, for example, J. A. Lee to DA, August 4, 1937, A3/2/54, MNA.

143 For the viewpoint of those supporting early planting see Barker to DA, February 1, November 8, 1934, A3/2/65; Barker to DA, December 5, 1935, A3/2/71, MNA. For arguments in favor of late planting see report of C. Smee, January 1937; Lawrence to DA, July 2, 1937; Ducker to DA, October 6, 1936, A3/2/65, MNA.

144 B. L. Mitchell, Survey of the Work in Progress in Nyasaland on the Red Bollworm, *Diparopsis castanea,* August 1939, S1/189/38; C. Smee et al., Pests and Diseases of Cotton in Nyasaland, 1939(?), S1/30/40, MNA; E. O. Pearson and B. L. Mitchell, *A Report on the Status and Control of Insect Pests of Cotton in the Lower River Districts of Nyasaland* (Zomba, Nyasaland: Government Press, 1945).

145 Smee et al., Pests and Diseases of Cotton, 1939(?), S1/30/40, MNA.

146 Ibid.

147 Lint Company of Zambia, *Cotton Pests in Africa,* text facing plates 5 and 6.

148 BCGA to DA, August 4, 1937, A3/2/54, MNA.

149 Smee et al., Pests and Diseases of Cotton, 1939(?), S1/30/40, MNA. In the northern belt moths emerged from the diapause from early December to the end of February. The corresponding period in the Valley was from February to early May. There were also variations in the Valley itself (see Mitchell, Survey of the Work in Progress, August 1939, S1/189/38, MNA).

150 Smee et al., Pests and Diseases of Cotton, 1939(?), S1/30/40, MNA.

151 Monthly Agricultural Report, February 1934, A3/2/201, MNA.

152 Monthly Agricultural Report, April 1936, A3/2/202, MNA.

153 Monthly Agricultural Report, May 1938, A3/2/202, MNA. The annual floods must have also reduced the reproductive capacity of the worm during the long pupal diapause.

154 Monthly Agricultural Report, July 1933, A3/2/201, MNA. See also Monthly Agricultural Report, May 1935, A3/2/201, MNA.

155 Monthly Agricultural Report, February, May, November 1934, A3/2/201, MNA.

156 Monthly Agricultural Report, February 1932, A3/2/200, MNA.

157 Monthly Agricultural Report, July 1933, A3/2/201, MNA.

158 Clegg to DA, August 20, 1927, A3/2/193, MNA.

159 J. Jennings to DA, May 2, 1917, A3/1/6, MNA.

160 Monthly Agricultural Report, March 1932, A3/2/200, MNA.

161 Monthly Agricultural Report, July 1933, A3/2/201, MNA.

162 Monthly Agricultural Report, September 1930, A3/2/200, MNA.

163 Monthly Agricultural Report, May 1932, A3/2/200, MNA.

164 Nyasaland Protectorate, *Nyasaland Government Gazette,* vols. 20–23 (1913–16), under "Rainfall, Crop Prospects, Conditions of Lake Nyasa, River Shire, &c."
165 Monthly Agricultural Report, June 1933; December 1934; January 1935, A3/2/201, MNA.
166 Monthly Agricultural Report, March 1934, A3/2/201, MNA.
167 Monthly Agricultural Report, January 1935, A3/2/201, MNA.
168 See, for example, A. E. Griffin, *A Report on the Flood Control and Reclamation on the Lower Shire River and Other Specified Areas in Nyasaland* (London: Crown Agents for the Colonies, 1949), 7–8.
169 Monthly Agricultural Report, March 1936, A3/2/202, MNA.
170 Monthly Agricultural Report, January 1938; see also the report for February 1938, A3/2/202, MNA.
171 Nyasaland Protectorate, *Annual Report of the Department of Agriculture,* 1939, pt. 1, p. 5.
172 Soil Conservation Officer (Chikwawa) to DA, August 4, 1943, Ag. 2.17.7F/880, MNA.
173 Southern Province Monthly Report, February 1945, Ag. 2.17.6F/873; Monthly Agricultural Report, January 1947; Acting Senior Agricultural Officer (Southern Province) to DA (Zomba), January 3, 1947, Ag. 5.6.4F/3499, MNA; Nyasaland Protectorate, *Annual Report of the Department of Agriculture,* 1952, pt. 1, p. 3.
174 Monthly Agricultural Report, March 1938, A3/2/202, MNA.
175 See Table 7.1, p. 238.
176 Department of Agriculture (Blantyre) to DA (Zomba), July 10, 1952, Ag. 2.13.8F/848, MNA; Nyasaland Protectorate, *Annual Report of the Department of Agriculture,* 1945, 1947, 1948.
177 See the sources cited in n. 173 above.
178 Department of Agriculture (Blantyre) to DA (Zomba), May 19, 1941, Ag. 2.17.7F/880, MNA.
179 Provincial Commissioner (Blantyre) to DA, September 24, 1941, Ag. 5.16.3R/2565, MNA.

6. Reactive Colonial Attempts to Restructure a Distorted Economy, 1930–1960

1 Port Herald District Annual Report, 1933, NSP2/1/4, MNA.
2 Soil Conservation Officer (Chikwawa) to DA, Visit to Eroded Areas in Lower Shire District, August 4, 1943, Ag. 2.17.7F/880, MNA.
3 H. C. Ducker, "Cotton in Nyasaland," *Nyasaland Agricultural Quarterly Journal* 10 (September 1951): 93.
4 H. C. Ducker to Director of Agriculture (DA), December 15, 1936, A3/2/54, MNA.

5 For an overview of the changes and continuity in legislation on peasant production in Malawi see C. Ng'ong'ola, "Malawi's Agricultural Economy and the Evolution of Legislation on the Production and Marketing of Peasant Economic Crops," *Journal of Southern African Studies* 12 (April 1986): 240–262.

6 Cotton Bill, ordinance no. 16 of 1934, A3/2/3, MNA.

7 British Cotton Growing Association (BCGA) (J. A. Lee) to DA, October 18, 1934; DA to Chief Secretary, November 19, 1934, A3/2/53, MNA. Nyasaland was divided into three main administrative units, called provinces. These were the Southern, Central, and Northern provinces.

8 BCGA (Lee) to DA, October 18, 1934; DA to Chief Secretary, November 19, 1934, A3/2/53, MNA.

9 DA to Chief Secretary, October 22, 1934; Governor's Deputy to Secretary of State for the Colonies, November 24, 1934, A3/2/53, MNA.

10 Governor's Deputy to Secretary of State for the Colonies, November 24, 1934, A3/2/53, MNA.

11 Governor to Chapelries (London), January 10, 1935, A3/2/53, MNA.

12 Ibid.

13 Cotton Purchases, 1938, Nyasaland Protectorate, *Nyasaland Government Gazette,* April 30, 1938; DA to Chief Secretary, March 11, 1938, S1/269/34, MNA.

14 DA, Native Cotton Industry, 1922, A3/2/55, MNA.

15 Ordinance no. 29 of 1951.

16 For two illuminating analyses of marketing boards in Malawi see Ng'ong'ola, "Malawi's Agricultural Economy"; and K. J. McCracken, "Planters, Peasants and the Colonial State: The Impact of the Native Tobacco Board in the Central Province of Malawi," *Journal of Southern African Studies* 9 (April 1983): 172–192.

17 District Agricultural Officer (DAO) (Port Herald) to DA, July 29, 1935; Crozier and Wright (Tobacco and Cotton Exporters) to DA, December 10, 1935, A3/2/53, MNA.

18 BCGA to DA, June 17, 1935, A3/2/53, MNA.

19 Ibid.

20 DA to Chief Secretary, March 11, June 1, 1938, S1/269/34; Agricultural Officer (E. Lawrence) to DA, February 11, 1938; A Few Notes on the Proposed Auctioning of Cotton Markets and Its Effects on Established Ginneries on the Lower River, 1938, A3/2/54, MNA.

21 See the sources cited in the previous note.

22 Cotton Bill of 1934, A3/2/3, MNA; Kareromwe, *Nyasaland Times,* July 8, 1934.

23 Kareromwe, *Nyasaland Times,* July 8, 1934.

24 DAO (Port Herald), Items for Discussion at the Cotton Conference to Be Held in Zomba, October 1935, A3/2/53, MNA.

25 DA to Chief Secretary, July 9, 1935, A3/2/53, MNA. The sources do not explain what was meant by "dumpy figures."

26 DAO (Port Herald), Items for Discussion, October 1935, A3/2/53, MNA.
27 DA to Chief Secretary, July 9, 1935, A3/2/53, MNA.
28 DA to Chief Secretary, December 7, 1935, A3/2/53, MNA.
29 DAO (Port Herald), Items for Discussion, October 1935, A3/2/53, MNA.
30 Ordinance no. 9 of 1936, Nyasaland Protectorate, *Nyasaland Government Gazette Supplement,* April 30, 1936.
31 Ibid., ordinance no. 24 of 1946, Nyasaland Protectorate, *Nyasaland Government Gazette Supplement,* December 28, 1946.
32 DA to Chief Secretary, May 25, 1935, A3/2/53, MNA. Tanganyika had a fixed formula for determining minimum rates. In Uganda minimum prices were based on the local lint market and the state did not fix minimum rates; it only made sure that growers were not given subminimum prices.
33 Cotton Purchases, 1938, Nyasaland Protectorate, *Nyasaland Government Gazette,* April 30, 1938.
34 DA to Chief Secretary, December 7, 1934, A3/2/3, MNA; ordinance no. 9 of 1936, Nyasaland Protectorate, *Nyasaland Government Gazette Supplement,* April 30, 1936.
35 Ordinance no. 9 of 1936, Nyasaland Protectorate, *Nyasaland Government Gazette Supplement,* April 30, 1936.
36 Ordinance no. 29 of 1951.
37 Ordinance no. 9 of 1936, Nyasaland Protectorate, *Nyasaland Government Gazette Supplement,* April 30, 1936; Cotton Purchases, 1938, idem, *Nyasaland Government Gazette,* April 30, 1938; ordinance no. 24 of 1946, idem, *Nyasaland Government Gazette Supplement,* December 28, 1946.
38 Ducker to DA, December 15, 1936, A3/2/54, MNA.
39 W. H. Evans, Notes on Cotton Buying Control, 1935, A3/2/54, MNA.
40 DAO (Port Herald) to DA, November 8, 1934, A3/2/65, MNA.
41 H. C. Ducker(?), Time of Planting Cotton in Nyasaland, 1934, A3/2/65, MNA.
42 DA to DAO (Port Herald), January 3, 1931, A3/2/109, MNA.
43 Empire Cotton Growing Corporation Circular Dispatch, August 31, 1917, A3/1/6; DAO (F. Barker) to DA, October 23, 1932, A3/2/70, MNA.
44 Ducker to DA, May 12, 1937, A3/2/65, MNA.
45 Empire Cotton Growing Corporation to DA, July 16, 1930, A3/2/71, MNA.
46 DA to DAO (Port Herald), January 3, 1931, A3/2/109, MNA.
47 Barker to DA, October 23, 1932, A3/2/70; Monthly Agricultural Report, November 1933, A3/2/201, MNA.
48 Annual Agricultural Report, 1930(?), A3/2/183; Monthly Agricultural Report, April, May, September 1931; March, June, September, December 1932, A3/2/200, MNA.
49 Monthly Agricultural Report, July, November 1933, A3/2/201, MNA.
50 N. D. Clegg to DA, February 1922, A3/2/193; Monthly Agricultural Report, May, June 1931; August 1933, A3/2/201; Monthly Agricultural Report, November 1936; May, November 1937, A3/2/202, MNA.

51 Monthly Agricultural Report, February, April, March 1931, A3/2/200; Monthly Agricultural Report, April 1938, A3/2/202, MNA. The system was imposed on an experimental basis in northeastern Chikwawa in 1938 (Chikwawa District Annual Report, 1938, 1939, NSC2/1/5, MNA).

52 There were nineteen such forested areas covering some 16,513 acres in Port Herald in 1934 (Port Herald District Annual Report, 1934, S1/88A/35, MNA).

53 Lawrence, Soil Erosion on the Lower Shire, April 3, 1931; Conservator of Forests, Memorandum on Soil Erosion, April 9, 1931; Lawrence, Memorandum on Soil Erosion, April 17, 1931; Ducker, Memorandum on Soil Erosion, April 23, 1931; DA to Lawrence, Memorandum on Soil Erosion, May 2, 1931, A3/2/200, MNA.

54 E. Lawrence to DA, December 30, 1929, A3/2/200; idem, A Description of the Land Lying to the South of the Lengwe Game Reserve in the Chikwawa District, October 24, 1933, A3/2/27, MNA.

55 See, for example, Ducker(?), Time of Planting Cotton, 1934, A3/2/65, MNA.

56 The actual dates vary from one memo to another, but the ones given in the text are the most representative (see Ducker to DA, October 6, 1936; May 12, 1937; Ducker[?], Time of Planting Cotton, 1934; Lawrence to DA, January 30, 1934, A3/2/65, MNA). For more literature on the time of planting debate see BCGA (Lee) to DA, February 7, 1934; S. T. Hoyle, Memorandum on a Visit to the Lower River, September 1937, A3/2/65; Cotton Propaganda Conference, April 10, 1936/37(?), A3/2/53, MNA.

57 Ducker to DA, May 12, 1937, A3/2/65; Lawrence to DA, July 2, 1937, A3/2/54, MNA.

58 Again, four different memorandums give slightly different dates from the ones I use in the text (Barker to DA, February 1, 21, November 8, 1934, A3/2/65; December 5, 1935, A3/2/71, MNA).

59 Barker to DA, December 5, 1935, A3/2/71, MNA.

60 Ibid.

61 Barker to DA, February 1, 1934, A3/2/65, MNA.

62 Ducker to DA, October 6, 1936; May 12, 1937, A3/2/65; see also Barker to DA, February 1, 1934, A3/2/65, MNA.

63 Ducker to DA, October 6, 1936, A3/2/65, MNA.

64 BCGA (Lee) to DA, August 4, 1937, A3/2/54, MNA.

65 See chap. 5, sec. 5.2.

66 Lawrence to DA, January 30, 1934, A3/2/65, MNA.

67 One of these explanations was that early-planted cotton was subject to heavy attack by insects, including the red bollworm. Late-planted cotton—so argued Ducker—escaped the period the red bollworm was most active, in March (H. C. Ducker, "A Talk on Cotton Growing in Lower Shire and Chikwawa Districts," *Nyasaland Agricultural Quarterly Journal* 1 [January 1941]: 14–15; Ducker[?], Time of Planting Cotton, 1934, A3/2/64, MNA).

Earlier, J. S. J. McCall had defended late planting as a method of checking bacterial blight on Egyptian cotton grown in the Valley (McCall to A. Rynevelt, January 31, 1913, A2/1/8, MNA).

68 Monthly Agricultural Report, December 1930, A3/2/200, MNA.

69 Monthly Agricultural Report, April 1932, A3/2/200, MNA.

70 DAO (Lawrence) to DA, January 8, 1931, A3/2/109, MNA.

71 Monthly Agricultural Report, November, December 1929; January, February 1930, A3/2/200, MNA.

72 Memorandum on Cotton Development and Propaganda, March 14, 1934, A3/2/53, MNA.

73 DAO (Lawrence) to DA, January 21, 1931, A3/2/109, MNA.

74 Nyasaland Protectorate, *Annual Report of the Department of Agriculture,* 1933, as cited in K. J. McCracken, "Experts and Expertise in Colonial Malawi," *African Affairs* 81 (January 1982): 104.

75 Nyasaland Protectorate, *Annual Report of the Department of Agriculture,* 1938, as cited in McCracken, "Experts and Expertise in Colonial Malawi," 104–105.

76 Ducker, "A Talk on Cotton Growing," 14–15.

77 R. W. Kettlewell, *An Outline of Agrarian Problems and Policy in Nyasaland* (Zomba, Nyasaland: Government Press, 1955), 2.

78 See chap. 5, sec. 5.3.

79 Nyasaland Protectorate, *Annual Report of the Department of Agriculture,* 1949, pt. 1, p. 3.

80 Lower Shire District Annual Report, 1943, NSP2/1/9, MNA.

81 Kettlewell, *An Outline of Agrarian Problems,* 5.

82 Soil Conservation Officer (Chikwawa) to DA, August 4, 1943; Department of Agriculture (Blantyre) to Agricultural Officer (Port Herald), July 18, 1944, Ag. 2.17.7F/880, MNA.

83 These were ordinance nos. 13 and 14 of 1933 (see Chikwawa District Annual Report, 1933, NSC2/1/4; 1934, S1/88B/35; Port Herald District Annual Report, 1933, NSP2/1/4; 1934, S1/88A/35, MNA). For the general application of the ordinances see Pachai, *Malawi,* 185–186.

84 See chap. 3, sec. 3.1.

85 Chikwawa District Annual Report, 1933, NSC2/1/4; 1934, S1/88B/35, MNA.

86 Port Herald District Annual Report, 1933, NSP2/1/4; 1934, S1/88A/35, MNA.

87 Chikwawa District Annual Report, 1935, S1/79B/36; Southern Province Annual Report, 1934, S1/88/35; Lower Shire Chiefs to District Commissioner (Port Herald), January 21, 1936; District Commissioner (Port Herald) to Provincial Commissioner (Southern Province), March 4, May 6, 1936, NSP1/15/1, MNA. Mang'anja chiefs from Mulanje also took part in the campaign, but the Kololo of Chikwawa and Ngabu opposed the scheme. Saizi Lundu was raised to paramountcy by the Malawi state in

1965. The position has meant almost nothing in reality.

88 Port Herald District Annual Report, 1933, NSP2/1/4; Monthly Agricultural Report, February 1934, A3/2/201, MNA. This was the first time since the famine of 1922–23 that a salima was found for Mbona. It should also be noted that 1933 was a year of crisis (see chap. 5, sec. 5.1).

89 Chikwawa District Annual Report, 1933, NSC2/1/4; 1934, S1/88B/35; Port Herald District Annual Report, 1933, NSP2/1/4; 1934, S1/88A/35, MNA.

90 Southern Province Annual Report, 1934, S1/88/35, MNA; Pachai, *Malawi,* 189. As a magistrate, a mfumu could impose fines of up to £5, £3, or £1 or imprisonment sentences of up to six months, three months, or one month, depending on whether he presided over a court of grade A, B, or C.

91 DA to Chief Secretary, April 20, 1944, Ag. 2.17.7F/880, MNA.

92 The actual reason cited was that the project would take away a considerable amount of land from cultivation (DA to DAO [Port Herald], May 2, 1931, A3/2/200, MNA). A similar argument was used later against the proposal that mechanical devices be used in contour bunding (District Commissioner [Port Herald] to Chief Soil Conservation Officer, November 7, 1949, Ag. 2.29.10R/2567, MNA).

93 Department of Agriculture (Blantyre) to Agricultural Officer (Masambanjati, Cholo), Soil Conservation Project: Lower Shire District, July 18, 1944, Ag. 2.17.7F/880; Department of Agriculture(?) to DA, Soil Conservation in Nyasaland, 1944; Department of Agriculture (Lilongwe) to DA, Answers to Soil Conservation Questionnaire, February 27, 1946; Reply to Questionnaire by Dr. Tempany, 1946, Ag. 3.17.7F/879; Department of Agriculture (Blantyre) to DA, Soil Conservation: Lower River, August 9, 1947, Ag. 2.17.7F/880, MNA. Other measures that were discussed but not applied in the Valley included grass stripping, strip cropping, terracing, and bunding.

94 Department of Agriculture (Blantyre) to District Commissioner (Port Herald), May 18, 1945, Ag. 2.17.7F/880, MNA.

95 Provincial Commissioner (Blantyre) to DA, September 24, 1941; Provincial Agricultural Officer to Provincial Commissioner (Southern Province), Food Situation: Lower River, May 11, 1941, Ag. 5.16.3R/2565, MNA. Work at the base of the foothills south of Port Herald was resumed and completed in 1944 (Port Herald District Annual Report, 1944, NSP2/1/9, MNA).

96 Department of Agriculture (Blantyre) to Agricultural Officer (Masambanjati, Cholo), Soil Conservation Project: Lower Shire District, July 18, 1944, Ag. 2.17.7F/880, MNA.

97 Agricultural Assistant (Port Herald) to Soil Conservation Officer (Blantyre), August 20, September 5, 1949, Ag. 2.29.10R/2565, MNA.

98 Department of Agriculture (Blantyre) to Agricultural Assistant (Chiromo), November 15, 1949, Ag. 2.29.10R/2565, MNA.

99 Reply to Questionnaire by Dr. Tempany, 1946, Ag. 3.17.7F/879, MNA.

100 Department of Agriculture (Lilongwe) to DA, Answers to Soil Conservation Questionnaire, February 27, 1946, Ag. 3.17.7F/879, MNA.

101 Reply to Questionnaire by Dr. Tempany, 1946, Ag. 3.17.7F/879, MNA.

102 Ibid.

103 Nyasaland Protectorate, *Annual Report of the Department of Agriculture,* 1952, pt. 1, p. 6; Chief Secretary (C. W. F. Footman), Crop Production Policy, 1952–53 Season, 1952, Ag. 2.13.8F/848, MNA.

104 Provincial Commissioner (Southern Province) to Chief Secretary, June 30, 1944, Ag. 5.16.6R/2596, MNA. The Native Authority of South Shire was formed in 1940 and disbanded in 1946.

105 Port Herald District Annual Report, 1946, NSP2/1/10, MNA. The shortage may have influenced one alarmist report on the colony's food situation issued by the director of agriculture (DA to Chief Secretary, Food Production in Nyasaland, March 21, 1946, Ag. 3.2.7R/1262, MNA). The year 1946 also saw the passage of a bill to control the sale of foodstuffs (DA to Senior Agricultural Officer [Lilongwe], Marketing of Native Produce, December 5, 1946; Department of Agriculture [Zomba] to Chief Secretary, Marketing of Native Produce, Amendment to Ordinance of 1946, January 2, 1947, Ag. 2.14.8F/855, MNA).

106 Lower River District (Chikwawa and Port Herald districts when they were administered as a single unit, 1947–195[?]) Annual Report, 1948, NS3/1/8, MNA. The subsequent countrywide famine of 1949 convinced many officials of the need for mitumbira. They were encouraged in this direction by the fact that the famine was less severe in the mountain areas where the system was widely adopted (Chief Soil Conservation Officer to [?], October 1949, Ag. 2.29.10R/2567, MNA).

107 District Commissioner (Port Herald) to Agricultural Officer (Cholo) and Agricultural Assistant (Chiromo), October 30, 1948, Ag. 2.17.7F/880, MNA.

108 Ibid.

109 Kettlewell, *An Outline of Agrarian Problems,* 3.

110 Soil Conservation Officer (Chikwawa) to DA, Visit to Eroded Areas in Lower Shire District, August 4, 1943, Ag. 2.17.7F/880, MNA.

111 Department of Agriculture (Cholo) to Senior Agricultural Officer (Blantyre), July 28, 1949, Ag. 2.17.7F/880, MNA.

112 Griffin, *A Report on Flood Control,* 9.

113 F. Debenham, *Nyasaland: The Land of the Lake* (London: Her Majesty's Stationery Office, 1955), 63–77.

114 Sir William Halcrow et al., *The Shire Valley Project: A Report on the Control and Development of Lake Nyasa and the Shire River,* vol. 1 (London: Crown Agents for Overseas Governments and Administrations, 1954). For a summary and criticism of the various consultants see Department of Agriculture (Zomba) to Chief Secretary, August 13, 1955, Ag. 2.17.5R/3335; Department of Agriculture (Zomba) to Chief Secretary, Shire Valley Project, October 9, 1956, Ag. 1.1.11R/3567, MNA.

115 Halcrow et al., *The Shire Valley Project.* This is but a crude layman's

summary of the complicated recommendations made by the engineers.

116 Lawrence, A Description of the Land Lying to the South of the Lengwe Game Reserve in the Chikwawa District, October 24, 1933, A3/2/27, MNA.

117 Lawrence to DA, December 30, 1929, A3/2/200; Provincial Commissioner (Southern Province) to Chief Secretary, Chikwawa and Port Herald Districts, November 29, 1952, Ag. 2.17.7F/880, MNA.

118 Agricultural Officer (Blantyre) to Senior Provincial Commissioner (Southern Province), Resettlement of Natives – Lower Shire District, December 2, 1941, Ag. 5.16.6R/2596, MNA.

119 Chief Soil Conservation Officer (Zomba) to Senior Agricultural Officer (Blantyre), Kakoma Farm, December 2, 1949; Agricultural Assistant (Blantyre) to Agricultural Assistant (Kakoma Farm), Handing Over Notes, January 14, 1950; Provincial Agricultural Officer (Southern Province) to Section Manager (Kakoma Farm), Kakoma, July 21, 1952, Ag. 2.29.10R/2595; DA to Provincial Agricultural Officer (Blantyre), Land Settlement – Kakoma, January 27, 1955, Ag. 15.7.3R/7921; Provincial Agricultural Officer (Southern Province) to DA, June 17, 1954, Ag. 5.16.6R/2596; DA to Provincial Agricultural Officer (Blantyre), June 25, 1954, Ag. 7.10.4R/3348; DA(?) to (?), Memorandum Regarding Appointment of F. E. Luscombe as Chief Agricultural Officer (Land Settlement), n.d., Ag. 15.7.3R/7921, MNA.

120 District Commissioner (Chikwawa) to Provincial Commissioner (Southern Province), Movement of Population from Port Herald to Chikwawa, February 24, 1956; Record of Meeting Held in the Provincial Commissioner's Office, February 11, 1956, Ag. 15.7.3R/7921; P. M. Lewis (Chairman, Chikwawa Land Use Committee) to DA(?), Land Settlement – Chikwawa, October 7, 1957; J. P. Mullins (Chairman, Chikwawa Land Use Committee), Memorandum on Land Settlement – Chikwawa, January 7, 1959, Ag. 2.2.5F/3667, MNA.

121 District Commissioner (Chikwawa) to Provincial Commissioner (Southern Province), Movement of Population from Port Herald to Chikwawa, February 24, 1956, Ag. 15.7.3R/7921, MNA.

122 Provincial Agricultural Officer (Blantyre) to Agricultural Supervisor (Chikwawa), Survey of Potential Resettlement Areas – Chikwawa, January 7, 1957, Ag. 2.2.5F/3667, MNA.

123 Lewis to DA(?), Land Settlement – Chikwawa, October 7, 1957, Ag. 2.2.5F/3667, MNA.

124 See, for example, W. Beinart, "Soil Erosion, Conservationism and Ideas about Development: A Southern African Exploration, 1900–1960," *Journal of Southern African Studies* 11 (October 1984): 52–83; idem, "Agricultural Planning and the Late Colonial Technical Imagination: The Lower Shire Valley in Malawi, 1940–1960," McCracken, ed., *Malawi,* 95–148.

125 Lawrence, A Description of the Land Lying to the South of the Lengwe Game Reserve in the Chikwawa District, October 24, 1933, A3/2/27,

MNA. Lawrence was not prepared to initiate projects that would interfere too much with local agricultural practices; he expected each peasant on the settlement schemes to "decide for himself" which crops to grow.

126 Governor G. F. T. Colby to Sir Godfrey Huggins, November 13, 1954, Ag. 2.17.5R/3335, MNA.

127 The soil conservation officer for Chikwawa had this to say when he saw the untouched sacred forest on Mount Malawi in 1943: "Adjoining this denuded belt, is a ridge of mountain, which, in local mythology, is considered to be the abode of the rain-god, and is untouched. The contrast is striking, and engenders the forlorn hope that this deity could be persuaded to extend his demesne to the southward" (Soil Conservation Officer [Chikwawa] to DA, Visit to Eroded Areas in Lower Shire District, August 4, 1943, Ag. 2.17.7F/880, MNA).

128 Soil Conservation Officer to DA, Preliminary Report on Proposed Area for Resettlement in the Mwanza Valley, October 25, 1943, Ag. 2.17.7F/880, MNA.

129 Chikwawa Settlement Scheme: 500 Families = 2175 Persons, 1943; Provincial Agricultural Officer (Blantyre) to Provincial Commissioner (Southern Province), December 16, 1952, Ag. 2.17.7F/880; Provincial Agricultural Officer (Southern Province) to DA, June 17, 1954, Ag. 5.16.6R/2596; DA to Provincial Agricultural Officer (Blantyre), Land Settlement—Kakoma, January 27, 1955, Ag. 15.7.3R/7921, MNA.

130 H. C. Ducker, "The Nyasaland Cotton Crop," *Nyasaland Agricultural Quarterly Journal* 10 (December 1951): 128.

131 DA to Provincial Agricultural Officer (Blantyre), June 25, 1954, Ag. 7.10.4R/3348, MNA.

132 Provincial Agricultural Officer (Blantyre) to Provincial Commissioner (Southern Province), December 16, 1952, Ag. 2.17.7F/880, MNA.

133 Lewis (Chikwawa Land Use Committee) to DA(?), Land Settlement—Chikwawa, October 7, 1957, Ag. 2.2.5F/3667, MNA. The idea of integrating cattle in the economy of Settlement Areas V and VI looked so attractive that planners were ready to examine ways of eradicating the tsetse fly in Area IV (Chikwawa Settlement Scheme: 500 Families = 2175 Persons, 1943, Ag. 2.17.7F/880, MNA).

134 Chikwawa Settlement Scheme: 500 Families = 2175 Persons, 1943, Ag. 2.17.7F/880, MNA.

135 Department of Agriculture (Cholo) to Senior Agricultural Officer (Blantyre), July 28, 1949, Ag. 2.17.7F/880, MNA; Pearson and Mitchell, *Report on the Status and Control of Insect Pests.*

136 Shire Valley Project, Federal Working Party Report by Members to Chairman on Activities of Working Party, May 25–29, 1955, Ag. 2.17.5R/3335, MNA.

137 Department of Agriculture (Zomba) to Chief Secretary, August 13, 1955, Ag. 2.17.5R/3335, MNA.

138 Sorghum and maize would be grown during the first and second year,

respectively. The land would lie fallow from the third through the fifth year, with the possible exception of low-lying areas, which would be put to rice cultivation.

139 Department of Agriculture (Cholo) to Senior Agricultural Officer (Blantyre), July 28, 1949, Ag. 2.17.7F/880, MNA.

140 DA to Chief Secretary, Control of Land—Shire Valley, May 20, 1955, Ag. 2.17.5R/3335, MNA.

141 Department of Agriculture (Cholo) to Senior Agricultural Officer (Blantyre), July 28, 1949, Ag. 2.17.7F/880, MNA.

142 The amounts were £2.5 million, £1 million, and £320,000 from cotton, rice, and food crops, respectively (Department of Agriculture [Zomba] to Chief Secretary, August 13, 1955, Ag. 2.17.5R/3335, MNA).

143 Department of Agriculture (Zomba) to Provincial Commissioners, Soil Conservation—Policy, September 21, 1948, Ag. 2.17.7F/879, MNA.

144 Provincial Agricultural Officer (Blantyre) to Provincial Commissioner (Southern Province), December 16, 1952, Ag. 2.17.7F/880. See also Provincial Agricultural Officer (Southern Province) to DA, June 17, 1954, Ag. 5.16.6R/2596; Record of Meeting Held in the Provincial Commissioner's Office, February 11, 1956, Ag. 15.7.3R/7921, MNA.

145 See, for example, Provincial Agricultural Officer (Southern Province) to DA, June 17, 1954, Ag. 5.16.6R/2596, MNA; and other sources cited in n. 144 above.

146 Department of Agriculture (Cholo) to Senior Agricultural Officer (Blantyre), July 28, 1949, Ag. 2.17.7F/880, MNA.

147 DA to Chief Secretary, Control of Land—Shire Valley, May 20, 1955, Ag. 2.17.5R/3335, MNA.

148 Governor Colby and sometimes the director of agriculture, R. W. Kettlewell, both of whom were trying to raise money for the project on the basis of its anticipated social and political benefits, opposed the scheme to reduce peasants to tenants. The governor stood firm on the idea that any organization that was willing to finance the project would do so on the understanding that the peasants would be its primary beneficiaries.

149 For a different position see Lonsdale and Berman, "Coping with the Contradictions," 505.

150 See, for example, Beinart, "Soil Erosion"; idem, "Agricultural Planning."

7. Constrained Peasant Initiatives and Agrarian Change, 1930–1960

1 Lower River District Annual Report, 1948, NS3/1/18, MNA.

2 Lower River District Annual Report, 1949, NS3/1/18, MNA.

3 K. Marx, "Preface to a Contribution to the Critique of Political Economy," *Karl Marx and Frederick Engels: Selected Works in One Volume* (New York: International Publishers, 1974), 183.

4 Director of Agriculture (DA), Report on a Visit to the Lower Shire District, June 1923, A3/2/68, MNA.

5 Governor Colby to Huggins, November 13, 1954, Ag. 2.17.5R/3335, MNA.

6 Lower Shire District Book 1, 1907, MNA.

7 Provincial Commissioner (Southern Province) to Chief Secretary, Scheme for the Resettlement in the Chikwawa District of Families from the Congested Areas in the Cholo District, September 4, 1944, Ag. 2.17.7F/880, MNA.

8 Ibid.

9 See, for example, Soil Conservation Officer to DA, Preliminary Report on Proposed Area for Resettlement in the Mwanza Valley, October 25, 1943, Ag. 2.17.7F/880; Record of a Meeting Held in the Provincial Commissioner's Office, February 11, 1956, Ag. 15.7.3R/7921, MNA.

10 J. P. Mullins (Chairman, Chikwawa Land Use Committee), Memorandum on Land Settlement—Chikwawa, January 7, 1959, Ag. 2.2.5F/3667, MNA.

11 Acting Geologist (D. G. G. Cooper) to DA, August 21, 1946, Ag. 2.17.7F/880, MNA.

12 See chap. 2, sec. 2.3.1.

13 Chikwawa District Quarterly Report, July–September 1929, NSC2/2/1, MNA.

14 Chikwawa District Annual Report, 1932, NSC2/1/4, MNA.

15 Chikwawa District Annual Report, 1936, S1/66B/37, MNA.

16 Lewis to DA(?), Land Settlement—Chikwawa, October 7, 1957, Ag. 2.2.5F/3667, MNA.

17 Memorandum to Chief Secretary, Nyamphota Agricultural Scheme, January 20, 1956, Ag. 16.5.4F/4938; W. H. J. Rangeley to Financial Secretary, Nyamphota Agricultural Scheme, May 9, 1956, Ag. 15.6.3F/7918, MNA.

18 See, for example, Soil Conservation Officer to DA, Preliminary Report on Proposed Area for Resettlement in the Mwanza Valley, October 25, 1943, Ag. 2.17.7F/880, MNA. The same rules were to be applied to the reclaimed dambo (Department of Agriculture [Cholo] to Senior Agricultural Officer [Blantyre], July 28, 1949, Ag. 2.17.7F/880; DA to Chief Secretary, Control of Land—Shire Valley, May 20, 1955, Ag. 2.17.5R/3335, MNA).

19 Memorandum to Chief Secretary, Nyamphota Agricultural Scheme, January 20, 1956, Ag. 16.5.4F/4938; Rangeley to Financial Secretary, Nyamphota Agricultural Scheme, May 9, 1956, Ag. 15.6.3F/7918; R. W. Kettlewell to Financial Secretary, May 11, 1956, Ag. 1.2.5F/3580; Précis for Executive Council, Nyamphota Agricultural Scheme, May 25, 1956, Ag. 15.6.3F/7918, MNA.

20 Memorandum to Chief Secretary, Nyamphota Agricultural Scheme, January 20, 1956, Ag. 16.5.4F/4938, MNA.

21 Rangeley to Financial Secretary, Nyamphota Agricultural Scheme, May 9, 1956, Ag. 15.6.3F/7918, MNA.

22 Kettlewell to Provincial Agricultural Officer (Blantyre), May 16, 1956, Ag. 5.17.4F/3580, MNA.

23 Record of a Meeting Held in the Provincial Commissioner's Office, February 11, 1956, Ag. 15.7.3R/7921, MNA.

24 District Commissioner (Chikwawa) to Provincial Commissioner (Southern Province), Movement of Population from Port Herald to Chikwawa, February 24, 1956, Ag. 15.7.3R/7921, MNA.

25 See, for example, Provincial Agricultural Officer (Southern Province) to DA, June 17, 1954, Ag. 5.16.6R/2596; Record of a Meeting Held in the Provincial Commissioner's Office, February 11, 1956, Ag. 15.7.3R/7921; Provincial Agricultural Officer (Blantyre) to Provincial Commissioner (Southern Province), December 16, 1952, Ag. 2.17.7F/880, MNA.

26 See chap. 4, sec. 4.3.

27 Lower Shire District Book 4, 1928–32 (March 22, 1929), MNA.

28 Lewis to DA(?), Land Settlement—Chikwawa, October 7, 1957, Ag. 2.2.5F/3667, MNA.

29 Mullins, Memorandum on Land Settlement—Chikwawa, January 7, 1959, Ag. 2.2.5F/3667, MNA.

30 E. Lawrence to DA, April 3, 1931, A3/2/200, MNA.

31 Soil Conservation Officer (Chikwawa) to DA, Visit to Eroded Areas in Lower Shire District, August 4, 1943, Ag. 2.17.7F/880, MNA.

32 District Commissioner (Port Herald) to Chief Soil Conservation Officer, November 7, 1949, Ag. 2.29.10R/2567, MNA.

33 Department of Agriculture (Blantyre) to District Commissioner (Port Herald), May 18, 1945, Ag. 2.17.7F/880, MNA.

34 Lewis to DA(?), Land Settlement—Chikwawa, October 7, 1957, Ag. 2.2.5F/3667, MNA.

35 DA to Provincial Agricultural Officer (Blantyre), June 25, 1954, Ag. 7.10.4R/3348, MNA.

36 Lewis to DA(?), Land Settlement—Chikwawa, October 7, 1957, Ag. 2.2.5F/3667, MNA.

37 Mullins, Memorandum on Land Settlement—Chikwawa, January 7, 1959, Ag. 2.2.5F/3667, MNA.

38 Lewis to DA(?), Land Settlement—Chikwawa, October 7, 1957, Ag. 2.2.5F/3667, MNA.

39 Record of a Meeting Held in the Provincial Commissioner's Office, February 11, 1956, Ag. 15.7.3R/7921, MNA.

40 District Commissioner (Chikwawa) to Provincial Commissioner (Southern Province), Movement of Population from Port Herald to Chikwawa, February 24, 1956, Ag. 15.7.3R/7921, MNA.

41 Provincial Agricultural Officer (Blantyre) to Agricultural Supervisor (Chikwawa), Survey of Potential Resettlement Areas—Chikwawa, January 7, 1957, Ag. 2.2.5F/3667, MNA.

42 Record of a Meeting Held in the Provincial Commissioner's Office, February 11, 1956, Ag. 15.7.3R/7921, MNA.

43 District Commissioner (Chikwawa) to Provincial Commissioner (Southern Province), Movement of Population from Port Herald to Chikwawa, February 24, 1956, Ag. 15.7.3R/7921, MNA.
44 DA(?) to (?), Memorandum Regarding F. E. Luscombe, n.d., Ag. 15.7.3R/7921, MNA.
45 See chap. 1, sec. 1.3.
46 Department of Agriculture (Blantyre) to DA, Soil Conservation: Lower River, August 9, 1947, Ag. 2.17.7F/880; Lower River District Annual Report, 1949, NS3/1/18, MNA.
47 Lower River District Annual Report, 1947, NS3/1/18, MNA.
48 Department of Agriculture (Blantyre) to DA, Soil Conservation: Lower River, August 9, 1947, Ag. 2.17.7F/880, MNA.
49 Ibid.
50 Ibid.
51 Reply to Questionnaire by Dr. Tempany, 1946, Ag. 3.17.7F/879, MNA.
52 Port Herald District Annual Report, 1943, NSP2/1/9, MNA. See also the report for 1944, NSP2/1/9, MNA.
53 Port Herald District Annual Report, 1943, NSP2/1/9, MNA.
54 Department of Agriculture (Blantyre) to DA, Soil Conservation: Lower River, August 9, 1947, Ag. 2.17.7F/880, MNA.
55 Mr. Bringer Antonio was one of the intellectuals who opposed mitumbira on this argument (see TVES6/6; T73/20; SM73/2). For a general description of the elite class in Port Herald see Port Herald District Commissioner to Provincial Commissioner (Southern Province), May 6, 1936, NSP1/15/1, MNA. The Devlin Commission Report, which investigated the uprisings of 1959 in Nyasaland, concluded that "all the rules are not universally considered to be beneficial, even by well informed opinion" (*Malawi News,* September 17, 1960, 8). Another observer reported that "the policy of our Southern neighbour [Mozambique] is to discourage ridging on the grounds that more damage is done when ridges break than by pure sheet erosion" (see Ecologist to the Department of Agriculture, Soil Conservation and Land Utilisation Policy, March 3, 1956, Ag. 5.6.3F/3330, MNA).
56 TVES6/6; T73/20; SM73/2.
57 Schoffeleers, ed., *Guardians of the Land,* 1–8.
58 Schoffeleers, *River of Blood,* chap. 4.
59 Lower River District Annual Report, 1947, NS3/1/18, MNA.
60 Mandala, "The Tengani Chieftaincy," 11.
61 Lower River District Annual Report, 1947, NS3/1/18, MNA.
62 Port Herald District Annual Report, 1943, NSP2/1/9, MNA.
63 Mandala, "The Tengani Chieftaincy," 9; Port Herald District Annual Report, 1946, NSP2/1/10, MNA.
64 Lower River District Annual Report, 1948, NS3/1/18, MNA.
65 Ibid.
66 Lower River District Annual Report, 1949, NS3/1/18, MNA.

67 Debenham, *Nyasaland,* 199.
68 Lower River District Annual Report, 1948, NS3/1/18, MNA.
69 Ibid.
70 Mandala, "The Tengani Chieftaincy," 10.
71 Tengani to District Commissioner (Port Herald), January 1938; District Commissioner (Port Herald) to Provincial Commissioner (Southern Province), March 28, 1938, NSP1/15/1(?), MNA.
72 Schoffeleers, *River of Blood,* chap. 4.
73 Monthly Agricultural Report, March 1938, A3/2/202, MNA.
74 Tengani's travels outside Nyasaland took him to such places as Uganda (Makerere College) in 1945, South Africa (Fort Hare College) in 1946, and Southern Rhodesia (Salisbury) in 1947. He was awarded the King's Medal twice, in 1943 and 1946, and attended a course in rural development at Jeans School in 1940 (Port Herald District Annual Report, 1940, NSP2/1/9; 1943, NSP2/1/9; 1945, NSP2/1/10; 1946, NSP2/1/10; Lower River District Annual Report, 1947, NSP3/1/18, MNA).
75 Mlolo once told the British to pack up and go home if they could not help the poor (Lower Shire District Book 5, 1933–37 [April 14, 1933], MNA). District Commissioner R. D. W. Martin explained Mlolo's abrasiveness with reference to his experience as a migrant laborer (Port Herald District Annual Report, 1940, NSP2/1/9, MNA). In his annual reports, Mlolo credited everything good to himself: "I did this and that."
76 See the chiefs' annual reports from 1943 onward in Port Herald District Annual Reports, 1943–44, NSP2/1/9; 1945–46, NSP2/1/10; Lower River District Annual Reports, 1947–49, NS3/1/18, MNA.
77 See Malawi Congress Party, "Nsanje District Calendar of Events, [1859–1965]," 1966. Like Chimombo, Ngabu and Chiphwembwe were fined in 1941 for neglecting cotton-uprooting rules (Port Herald District Annual Report, 1941, NSP2/1/9, MNA). The two chiefs were, according to one observer, "more interested in the Rain god (Mbona) than the problems of their people" (Port Herald District Annual Report, 1942, NSP2/1/9, MNA).
78 Mandala, "The Tengani Chieftaincy," 11.
79 Lower Shire District Book 1, 1907, MNA.
80 If one considers neocolonialism a form of Indirect Rule, the story of Mollen Tengani has a contemporary ring.
81 T73/2, 5, 20.
82 Lower River District Annual Report, 1949, NS3/1/18, MNA.
83 T73/2, 5, 20; see also Lower River District Annual Report, 1948, 1949, NS3/1/18, MNA.
84 T73/2, 5, 20.
85 Department of Agriculture (Blantyre) to DA, Soil Conservation: Lower River, August 9, 1947, Ag. 2.17.7F/880, MNA.
86 TVES4/6.

87 T73/2, 5, 20; TVES4/6.

88 Lower River District Annual Report, 1948, 1949, NS3/1/18; Port Herald District Annual Report, 1942, NSP2/1/9, MNA.

89 T73/2, 5, 20.

90 TVES5/1.

91 Lower River District Annual Report, 1948, NS3/1/18, MNA.

92 TVES5/4.

93 Nyachikadza did not have to construct mitumbira in his chiefdom because it was liable to annual flooding.

94 It is not clear why the father should be a Tonga except that the Tonga were reputed to be the most belligerent group among the Sena.

95 Quoted in *Malawi News,* September 17, 1960, 8.

96 Ibid., 2.

97 Ibid., 2–3.

98 Hyden, *Beyond Ujamaa in Tanzania.*

99 Soil Conservation Officer (Chikwawa) to DA, Visit to Eroded Areas in Lower Shire District, August 4, 1943, Ag. 2.17.7F/880, MNA.

100 A note of caution is necessary on the data listed in Table 7.1 for 1931 and 1945. It is difficult to reconcile the figures for 1931 with those given in the annual reports for Chikwawa and Port Herald districts for 1935 (S1/79A/36 and S1/79B/36, MNA), which indicate that the respective populations for the two districts were 30,616 and 86,830. Also, in 1945 the total population of Port Herald District was placed at 87,000 (Port Herald District Annual Report, 1945, NSP2/1/10, MNA). One day a revision may be necessary of J. G. Pike and G. J. Rimmington's *Malawi: A Geographical Study* (Oxford: Oxford University Press, 1965; see esp. p. 135), which is the source of Schoffeleers's *The Lower Shire Valley.*

101 Nyasaland Protectorate, *Report of the Census of 1945* (Zomba, Nyasaland: Government Press, 1946), 14.

102 Lower River District Annual Report, 1948, NS3/1/18, MNA.

103 Record of a Meeting Held in the Provincial Commissioner's Office, February 11, 1956, Ag. 15.7.3R/7921, MNA.

104 A. Isaacman et al., " 'Cotton is the Mother of Poverty': Peasant Resistance to Forced Cotton Production in Mozambique, 1936–1961," *International Journal of African Historical Studies* 13 (1980): 581–615.

105 Lower River District Annual Report, 1947, NS3/1/18, MNA.

106 TVES5/4; TVES6/2.

107 Lower River District Annual Report, 1948, NS3/1/18, MNA.

108 One important distortion had to do with the decline of the nonagricultural sector.

109 See, for example, A. Sharpe to Foreign Office, December 1, 1897, FO 2/129, PRO.

110 There were, for example, only 127 registered emigrants from Port Herald

in 1922–23 (Port Herald District Annual Report, 1922–23, NSP2/1/1, MNA). The corresponding figure for Chikwawa District in 1923–24 was 137 (Chikwawa District Annual Report, 1923–24, NSC2/1/1, MNA).

111 Port Herald District Annual Report, 1931, S1/60F/32, MNA. The commissioner for Port Herald ran out of passes to issue to the men who wanted to leave in 1931, when there were 2,060 registered emigrants.

112 Colman and Garbett, "The Labour Economy," 114, Table 8.1.

113 Chikwawa District Annual Report, 1940, NSC2/1/6, MNA.

114 Port Herald District Annual Report, 1940, NSP2/1/9, MNA.

115 Ibid.

116 Port Herald District Annual Reports, 1941–44, NSP2/1/9; 1945–46, NSP2/1/10, MNA.

117 Port Herald District Annual Report, 1940, NSP2/1/9, MNA.

118 *South African Pioneer* 52 (July 1938): 79.

119 Colman and Garbett, "The Labour Economy," 128.

120 Port Herald District Annual Report, 1946, NSP2/1/10; Lower River District Annual Report, 1949, NS3/1/18, MNA.

121 Record of a Meeting Held in the Provincial Commissioner's Office, February 11, 1956, Ag. 15.7.3R/7921, MNA.

122 Lower River District Annual Report, 1947, NS3/1/18, MNA.

123 Some observers in 1980 feared that much of the land in western Chikwawa, including makande soils, had lost its fertility.

124 Soil Conservation Officer (Chikwawa) to DA, Visit to Eroded Areas in Lower Shire District, August 4, 1943, Ag. 2.17.7F/880, MNA.

125 Précis for Executive Council, Native Development and Welfare Fund, Movement of People to Chikwawa Settlement Area, May 5, 1956, Ag. 9.3.1R/4938, MNA.

126 Port Herald District Annual Report, 1941, NSP2/1/9, MNA.

127 Thodi is the African version of the name Todd. A European employee of the Public Works Department, Todd was one of the Europeans who directed the famine relief program in the area (Lower River District Annual Report, 1949, NS3/1/18, MNA).

128 Port Herald and Lower River District Annual Report, 1943, NSP2/1/9; 1948, NSP3/1/18, MNA.

129 Lower River District Annual Report, 1949, NS3/1/18, MNA.

130 Ibid.

131 Agricultural Assistant (Port Herald) to Soil Conservation Officer (Blantyre), August 20, September 5, 1949, Ag. 2.29.10R/2565, MNA.

132 Lower River District Annual Report, 1949, NS3/1/18, MNA.

133 Bryceson, "Changes in Peasant Food Production."

134 Lower River District Annual Report, 1949, NS3/1/18, MNA.

135 Only cassava failed to take root in the Valley: the "truth is that cassava is not just a Chikunda crop . . . and the Lower Shire Mang'anja cannot be troubled to grow it at present" (Monthly Agricultural Report, November

1931, A3/2/200, MNA). The fact that other Mang'anja outside the Valley adopted the crop shows that there was nothing "tribal" about the resistance in the Valley.

136 *South African Pioneer* 20 (November 1907): 178.

137 *South African Pioneer* 21 (August 1908): 130.

138 Chap. 5, sec. 5.2.

139 See, for example, Monthly Agricultural Report, April, May, July, November, December 1930; January, March, April, October 1931, A3/2/200; January, May 1933, A3/2/201, MNA.

140 Monthly Agricultural Report, May 1931, A3/2/200, MNA.

141 Lower River District Annual Report, 1948, NS3/1/18, MNA.

142 TVES3/15; TVES5/9; TVES6/1–6, 9.

143 Lower River District Annual Report, 1948, NS3/1/18, MNA.

144 Port Herald District Annual Report, 1943, NSP2/1/9, MNA.

145 Monthly Agricultural Report, March 1933, A3/2/201, MNA.

146 Lower River District Annual Report, 1949, NS3/1/18, MNA.

147 Ibid.

148 Monthly Agricultural Report, July 1933, A3/2/201, MNA.

149 Ibid.

150 Port Herald District Annual Report, 1931, S1/60F/32, MNA.

151 Refer to chap. 1 for the sense in which I use the term *nonagricultural.*

152 TVES2/1; TVES3/5. Oral history attributes to the Sena the introduction of many more fishing techniques than the two discussed in the text. Identifying the ethnic origins of most techniques found in the Valley today is not an easy task. For a general survey of the techniques used in the early 1970s see Ratcliffe, "The Fishery of the Lower River Area." McCracken's "Fishing and the Colonial Economy" is the best historical account of the fishing industry in colonial Nyasaland.

153 See chap. 1, sec. 1.2.5.

154 McCracken, "Fishing and the Colonial Economy," 418–429.

155 Ibid., 420.

156 Ratcliffe, "The Fishery of the Lower River."

157 TVES2/1.

158 According to one informant an average kokota measured two hundred yards in length (see ibid.).

159 Ibid.; see also TVES3/5.

160 Ibid.

161 Duly, "The Lower Shire District," 43.

162 Ibid.; TVES2/1.

163 Port Herald District Annual Report, 1941, NSP2/1/9, MNA.

164 Duly, "The Lower Shire District," 42.

165 Lower River District Annual Report, 1949, NS3/1/18, MNA.

166 Port Herald District Annual Report, 1941, NSP2/1/9, MNA.

167 Lower River District Annual Report, 1949, NS3/1/18, MNA. See also

Lower River District Annual Report, 1947, 1948, NS3/1/18, MNA.

168 Monthly Agricultural Report, August 1934; September 1935, A3/2/201, MNA.

169 A penny could buy no more than two and a half pounds of maize in the early 1940s (Port Herald District Annual Report, 1940, NSP2/1/9, MNA). By 1948–49 a pound of maize cost 3*d.* (Lower River District Annual Report, 1948, 1949, NS3/1/18, MNA).

170 Lower River District Annual Report, 1949, NS3/1/18, MNA.

171 Wallis, ed., *Zambesi Expedition* 2:241; Bennett and Ylvisaker, eds., *Central African Journal,* 419.

172 Chikwawa District Annual Report, 1930, NSC2/1/3, MNA.

173 Chikwawa District Annual Report, 1931, NSC2/1/3, MNA.

174 Foskett, ed., *Zambesi Journal* 1:262.

175 Bennett and Ylvisaker, eds., *Central African Journal,* 420.

176 West Shire District Book 1, 1907, MNA.

177 Ibid.

178 Trypanosomiasis of Cattle, Lower Shire District, November–December 1923; Chief Veterinary Officer to Acting Chief Secretary, December 13, 1923, S1/3146/23, MNA. Colonial officials had suspected the presence of the tsetse fly at Kaombe estate in 1904 (F. B. Pearce, Tsetse Fly Near Chiromo, A1/3/1, MNA).

179 Minutes of the Standing Committee on Tsetse and Trypanosomiasis, July 8, October 8, 1952; April 14, 1953, Ag. 2.17.7F/880, MNA.

180 Chikwawa District Annual Report, 1931, NSC2/1/3, MNA.

181 Trypanosomiasis of Cattle, Lower Shire District, November–December 1923; Chief Veterinary Officer to Acting Chief Secretary, December 13, 1923, S1/3146/23, MNA.

182 Port Herald District Annual Report, 1942, 1943, NSP2/1/9; 1946, NSP2/1/10, MNA. An African veterinary assistant was posted to the area in 1942 (Port Herald District Annual Report, 1942, NSP2/1/9, MNA). The death of injected cattle in Mlolo's area, however, led to suspicion and resistance among cattle owners (Lower River District Annual Report, 1949, NS3/1/18, MNA). For a lively discussion of the problem in other areas of colonial Malawi see McCracken, "Experts and Expertise in Colonial Malawi," 101–116.

183 Colonial officials were not certain on this.

184 Port Herald District Annual Report, 1943, NSP2/1/9, MNA.

185 Nyasaland Protectorate, *Annual Report of the Department of Agriculture,* 1939, pt. 1, pp. 12–15. The corresponding figures for Chikwawa were 183 African-owned and 617 non-African-owned. The number of non-African-owned cattle had declined along with the collapse of the plantation system. There had been two thousand head of cattle owned by European and Asian planters in 1921 (Port Herald District Monthly Report, April 1921, S1/299/21, MNA). These figures are only rough estimates.

186 TVES2/1; TVES5/3.
187 Lower River District Annual Report, 1949, NS3/1/18, MNA; Shire Valley Agricultural Development Project, *Atlas,* under "Livestock."
188 Agricultural Officer (Nsanje District), personal communication, August 1980. Shire Valley Agricultural Development Project, *Atlas,* places the number of cattle in the region at fifty thousand in the early 1970s.
189 See, for example, TVES2/1; TVES5/3.
190 Ibid.
191 TVES5/3; see also TVES3/9; TVES5/8.
192 See, for example, Port Herald District Annual Report, 1927, NSP2/1/2, MNA, and the first section of this chapter.
193 TVES3/9; TVES5/3, 8.
194 Port Herald District Annual Report, 1945, NSP2/1/10, MNA.
195 It had not yet died, as suggested in my earlier writings (e.g., "Capitalism, Ecology and Society," chap. 5); Schoffeleers, personal communication, July 24, 1987.
196 Van Zanten, "Traditional Malawi in Music, 1970–71," tape 8, track 4, item 17.
197 This study has not explored the more difficult though critical issue of transformations in the household-based religious sphere.
198 Schoffeleers, "Economic Change and Religious Polarization."
199 SM73/5; T73/1.
200 Schoffeleers, "From Socialization to Personal Enterprise."
201 *South African Pioneer* 38 (September/October 1925): 105.
202 Duly, "The Lower Shire District," 41.
203 Ibid.
204 Schoffeleers, "From Socialization to Personal Enterprise."
205 Duly, "The Lower Shire District," 23. See also Port Herald District Annual Report, 1945, NSP2/1/10, MNA.
206 Schoffeleers, *The Lower Shire Valley of Malawi.*
207 See, for example, Port Herald District Annual Report, 1945, NSP2/1/10, MNA.
208 TVES4/3.
209 Port Herald District Annual Report, 1941, NSP2/1/9, MNA.
210 Port Herald District Annual Report, 1946, NSP2/1/10; Lower River District Annual Report, 1949, NS3/1/18, MNA.
211 Monthly Agricultural Report, June 1933, A3/2/201, MNA. The 25.5 percent figure was for the 1930–31 growing season. In 1931–32 the figure was 3.2 percent, whereas in 1932–33 the figure for Port Herald District was 19.3 percent. Colonial officials were surprised by the high percentages of women growers as well as by the annual variations.
212 The tensions must have contributed to the increase in the incidence of witchcraft accusations and of mwabvi poison ordeals.
213 Smee et al., Pests and Diseases of Cotton, 1939(?), S1/30/40, MNA.

214 Lower Shire District Book 4, 1928–32 (September 2, 1932), MNA.
215 Great Britain, Colonial Office, Nyasaland Protectorate, *A Report by Mr Eric Smith, Administrative Officer, on the Direct Taxation of Natives in the Nyasaland Protectorate and Other Cognate Matters* (London: Crown Agents for the Colonies, 1937), 10, CO 525/172–173, PRO.
216 Ibid.
217 Van Zanten, "Traditional Malawi in Music, 1970–71," tape 8, track 4, item 18.
218 This subject will be explored in another study.
219 Port Herald District Annual Report, 1941, NSP2/1/9, MNA.
220 Port Herald District Annual Report, 1942, NSP2/1/9, MNA.
221 Port Herald District Annual Report, 1944, NSP2/1/9, MNA.
222 Ibid. See also Port Herald District Annual Report, 1945, 1946, NSP2/1/10, MNA.
223 Duly, "The Lower Shire District," 36–37.
224 Ibid., 37.
225 Port Herald District Annual Report, 1944, NSP2/1/9, MNA. See also Port Herald District Annual Report, 1943, NSP2/1/9, MNA.

Conclusions: A Simple but Diverse Peasant World: The Lower Shire Valley Revisited

1 E. Durkheim, *The Elementary Forms of the Religious Life* (1915; London: Allen and Unwin, 1976), 6.
2 The Lower Tchiri Valley is in this sense a microcosm of Malawi itself; see S. Agnew, "Environment and History: The Malawian Setting," B. Pachai, ed., *The Early History of Malawi* (London: Longman, 1972), 28–48.
3 E. L. Hermitte, "An Economic History of Barotseland, 1800–1940" (Ph.D. diss., Northwestern University, 1974), 71–108.
4 See, for example, M. Miracle, *Agriculture in the Congo Basin* (Madison: University of Wisconsin Press, 1967).
5 Vaughan, "Social and Economic Change," 36–99.
6 Inikori, ed., *Forced Migration;* Lovejoy, *Transformations in Slavery.*
7 M. Mamdani, *Politics and Class Formation in Uganda* (New York: Monthly Review Press, 1976); C. Murray, *Families Divided: The Impact of Migrant Labour in Lesotho* (Cambridge: Cambridge University Press, 1981); S. S. Myambo, "The Shire Highlands Plantations: A Socio-economic History of the Plantation System of Production in Malawi, 1891–1938" (M.A. thesis, University of Malawi, 1973).
8 Durkheim, *Elementary Forms of the Religious Life,* 1–20.
9 I owe this reformulation of the problem to K. E. Fields's stimulating article, "Political Contingencies of Witchcraft in Colonial Central Africa: Culture and the State in Marxist Theory," *Canadian Journal of African Studies* 16 (1982): 567–598.

10 Sayer, "Epistemology and Conceptions," 28.
11 For a review of the literature on this problem see Berry, "The Food Crisis."
12 Tosh, "The Cash Crop Revolution," 80.
13 Bryceson, "Changes in Peasant Food Production"; Hyden, *Beyond Ujamaa,* 237–262. For a critique see Chipungu, *The State, Technology and Peasant Differentiation,* 1–17; Richards, "Ecological Change."
14 Isaacman, "Peasants and Rural Social Protest," 2.
15 Marwick, *Sorcery in Its Social Setting,* 111–167.
16 See, for example, P. Hill, *The Migrant Cocoa-Farmers of Southern Ghana* (Cambridge: Cambridge University Press, 1963).
17 For an illuminating analysis of the problem of rural accumulation see S. Berry, *Fathers Work for Their Sons: Accumulation, Mobility, and Class Formation in an Extended Yoruba Community* (Berkeley and Los Angeles: University of California Press, 1985).
18 S. Stern, "New Approaches to the Study of Peasant Rebellion and Consciousness: Implications of the Andean Experience," Stern, ed., *Resistance, Rebellion, and Consciousness in the Andean Peasant World, 18th to 20th Centuries* (Madison: University of Wisconsin Press, 1987), 9.
19 Isaacman, "Peasants and Rural Social Protest"; T. O. Ranger, "Connections Between 'Primary Resistance' Movements and Modern Mass Nationalism in East and Central Africa," *Journal of African History* 9 (1968): 437–453, 631–641; idem, "The People in African Resistance: A Review," *Journal of Southern African Studies* 4 (October 1977): 125–146; idem, *Peasant Consciousness and Guerrilla War in Zimbabwe* (Berkeley and Los Angeles: University of California Press, 1985). See also Beinart and Bundy, *Hidden Struggles in Rural South Africa;* J. C. Scott, *Weapons of the Weak: Everyday Forms of Peasant Resistance* (New Haven: Yale University Press, 1985); Stern, "New Approaches."
20 See the literature cited in the preceding note, esp. Ranger, "Connections."
21 The inclusiveness of the nkhondo-ya-mitumbira and its narrow focus on the colonial state may partly explain the conservative character of post-independence political developments in the Valley.
22 Genovese, *Roll, Jordan, Roll.*
23 S. Popkin, *The Rational Peasant: The Political Economy of Rural Society in Vietnam* (Berkeley and Los Angeles: University of California Press, 1979). Popkin's book is a response to J. C. Scott, *The Moral Economy of the Peasant: Rebellion and Subsistence in Southeast Asia* (New Haven: Yale University Press, 1976).
24 Isaacman, "Peasants and Rural Social Protest."
25 Hyden, *Beyond Ujamaa;* Lonsdale and Berman, "Coping with the Contradictions."
26 Palmer and Parsons, eds., *The Roots of Rural Poverty.* See Ranger, "Growing from the Roots," for a critique of this position.
27 Cohen, *Karl Marx's Theory of History;* Berry, "The Food Crisis."
28 Paraphrase of Marx, *Capital,* 284.

Bibliography

Oral Testimonies*

1. Tchiri Valley Economy and Society (TVES) (recorded in 1980)

TVES1/ 1 Aneala Baulo, 60 yrs., Mang'anja-Banda, salt maker; Austin Nazing'omba, 55 yrs., Mang'anja-Mbewe, headman. Malemia village (1), T.A.† Lundu, Chikwawa, Jan. 16.

TVES1/ 2 Willy Antonio, 70 yrs., Sena-Tembo; Elia Ganonga, 50 yrs., Mang'anja-Phiri; Evereji Tambala, 60 yrs., Mang'anja-Mbewe; Brown Tchalitchi, 65 yrs., Mang'anja-Banda, headman. Malemia Village (2), T.A. Lundu, Chikwawa, Jan. 17.

TVES1/ 3 Minezji Chiongano, 80 yrs., Sena-Mwenye. Bzyilomzyo Village, T.A. Lundu, Chikwawa, Jan. 17.

TVES1/ 4 Aneala Baulo and Austin Nazing'omba. *See* TVES1/1. Jan. 17.

TVES1/ 5 Dafleni Chimatiro, 70 yrs., Mang'anja-Banda, headman. Sekeni Village, T.A. Lundu, Chikwawa, Jan. 18.

TVES1/ 6 Rimpu Tizola, 55 yrs., Mang'anja-Banda, headman. Sekeni Village, T.A. Lundu, Chikwawa, Jan. 18.

TVES1/ 7 S. Mulira, 50 yrs., Mang'anja-Phiri, Nchalo Sugar Estate employee. Bzyilomzyo Village, T.A. Lundu, Chikwawa, Jan. 24.

TVES1/ 8 Redson Chipakuza, 45 yrs., Mang'anja-Phiri. Chipakuza Village, T.A. Lundu, Chikwawa, Jan. 25.

TVES1/ 9 Yakonja Mafale, 80 yrs., Mang'anja-Phiri, group village headman; Mrs. Mafale, 60 yrs., Lomwe. Mafale Village, T.A. Lundu, Chikwawa, Jan. 26.

TVES1/10 Hamilton Bankamu, 60 yrs., Mang'anja-Phiri; Dines Samu, 75 yrs., Mang'anja-Phiri; Sadriki Zimveka, 80 yrs., Mang'anja-Phiri. Chipakuza Village, T.A. Makhwira, Chikwawa, Jan. 30.

TVES1/11 Webster Ndafooka Nantusi, b. 1908, Mang'anja-Banda, headman. Nantusi Village, T.A. Makhwira, Chikwawa, Jan. 30.

TVES1/12 Martin Ndauza Leza, 75 yrs., Mang'anja-Banda, headman. Leza Village, T.A. Makhwira, Chikwawa, Jan. 30.

TVES1/13 Haneki Matimati Mpama, 75 yrs., Mang'anja-Phiri, headman; Janet Alufazema (Mrs. Mpama), 60 yrs., Mang'anja-Naphiri. Mpama Village, T.A. Makhwira, Chikwawa, Jan. 30.

TVES1/14 Nelson England, 80 yrs., Mang'anja-Phiri. Mtambo Village, T.A. Makhwira, Chikwawa, Jan. 31.

*Unless specified otherwise, ages of informants are only approximations.

†T.A. = Traditional Authority.

TVES1/15 Aradechi Kutsilikiza, b. 1911, Mang'anja-Phiri, headman. Dwanya Village, T.A. Makhwira, Chikwawa, Jan. 31.
TVES1/16 Elias Dzungumfunde, 70 yrs., Ngoni father and Mang'anja mother. Mfunde Village, T.A. Makhwira, Chikwawa, Jan. 31.

TVES2/ 1 Karim Khembo, 70 yrs., Sena-Mwenye. Chikwawa Township, Chikwawa, Feb. 25.
TVES2/ 2 Auzamele Bakaima, 80 yrs., Mang'anja-Phiri; David Musa, 65 yrs., Mang'anja-Banda. Ling'awa Village, T.A. Kasisi, Chikwawa, Feb. 26.
TVES2/ 3 Mathias Chimtanda Mlilima, b. 1907, Kololo-Banda, former chief. Mlilima Village, T.A. Kasisi, Chikwawa, Feb. 26.
TVES2/ 4 Joseph Maseya, 85 yrs., Kololo, chief; Clement Pemba, b. 1918, Yao-Banda. Frank Village, T.A. Maseya, Chikwawa, Feb. 27.

TVES3/ 1 Yohane Mzanji, 70 yrs., Mang'anja-Banda. Mtchenyera Village, S.T.A.* Mbenje, Nsanje, Apr. 1.
TVES3/ 2 Danson Kulima, b. 1905(?), Sena-Tonga, headman. Tambo Village, S.T.A. Mbenje, Nsanje, Apr. 1.
TVES3/ 3 Baker Minjale, b. 1917, Sena-Dzowa. Tambo Village, S.T.A. Mbenje, Nsanje, Apr. 1.
TVES3/ 4 Antonio Joachim Vaz, b. 1913, coloured father and Mang'anja mother. Tambo Village, S.T.A. Mbenje, Nsanje, Apr. 1.
TVES3/ 5 Anoki Martinyu, b. 1908(?), Sena-Bango; Stelia Nyang'a, b. 1922, Mang'anja-Phiri. Nyang'a Village, S.T.A. Mbenje, Nsanje, Apr. 2.
TVES3/ 6 Elias Ferrão, 65 yrs., Sena-Mwenye; Penda Kamtchichi, 65 yrs., Sena-Tonga. Chisamba Village, S.T.A. Mbenje, Nsanje, Apr. 2.
TVES3/ 7 Rhodesia Ngano, 80 yrs., Sena-Mrambala. Mtchenyera Village, S.T.A. Mbenje, Nsanje, Apr. 2.
TVES3/ 8 Alfred Phalula, b. 1928, Ngoni-Moyo. Mtchenyera Village, S.T.A. Mbenje, Nsanje, Apr. 3.
TVES3/ 9 Yohane Mzanji. *See* TVES3/1. Apr. 3.
TVES3/10 Joseni Nthonga, 75 yrs., Sena. Mtchenyera Village, S.T.A. Mbenje, Nsanje, Apr. 4.
TVES3/11 Maxwell Kalavina, b. 1908, Sena-Tonga. M'Bobo Village, S.T.A. Mbenje, Nsanje, Apr. 8.
TVES3/12 Lapukeni Amtamigu, 70 yrs., Sena-Tonga; Jailosi Chekani, 80 yrs., Mang'anja-Phiri; Adyanjao Dinyeiro, 80 yrs., Mang'anja-Kalonga; Moses Hedala, 60 yrs., Mang'anja-Kalonga; Fole Kalumphulalinga, 80 yrs., Mang'anja-Phiri; December Kaputanjuchi, 70 yrs., Mang'anja-Phiri; Sokosi Kaputanjuchi, 75 yrs., Mang'anja-Phiri; Mphetomwanyama Mgawira, 65 yrs., Mang'anja-Phiri; Moseyo

*S.T.A. = Sub-Traditional Authority.

Thimbwa, 70 yrs., Mang'anja-Phiri. Mbenje Village, S.T.A. Mbenje, Nsanje, Apr. 9.

TVES3/13 Million Kuyeli, b. 1901, Sena-Tonga; Jailosi Mlondanjira, 80 yrs., Mang'anja-Phiri; Marko Sorjin, 60 yrs., Sena-Tonga, headman. Sorjin Village, S.T.A. Mbenje, Nsanje, Apr. 9.

TVES3/14 Zaina Useni Mpsyangwa, 70 yrs., Sena-Mwenye, blacksmith. Nguluwe Village, S.T.A. Mbenje, Nsanje, Apr. 10.

TVES3/15 Juana Chamboko, 60 yrs., Sena-Tonga; Mailosi Njazi, 75 yrs., headman. Nguluwe Village, S.T.A. Mbenje, Nsanje, Apr. 10.

TVES4/ 1 Stonkeni Tengani, 75 yrs., Mang'anja-Phiri, chief. Tengani Village, T.A. Tengani, Nsanje, Sept. 1.

TVES4/ 2 Ezekia Mlongoti, 70 yrs., Mang'anja-Phiri. Nkhuku Village, T.A. Tengani, Nsanje, Sept. 1.

TVES4/ 3 Second Banzi, 65 yrs., Mang'anja-Phiri. Chikhau Village, T.A. Tengani, Nsanje, Sept. 2.

TVES4/ 4 Wizlam Machado Mwasalapa, 75 yrs., Mang'anja-Phiri, headman; Saikondi Kampira Godwa, 60 yrs., Mang'anja-Phiri. Mwasalapa Village, T.A. Tengani, Nsanje, Sept. 2.

TVES4/ 5 Ngona, Mang'anja-Phiri, headman. Ngona Village, T.A. Tengani, Nsanje, Sept. 3.

TVES4/ 6 Genti Tomasi, 70 yrs., Mang'anja-Phiri. Nyamula Village, T.A. Tengani, Nsanje, Sept. 4.

TVES4/ 7 Elias Dungummwamba, 60 yrs., Sena-Tonga. Kaeredzi Village, T.A. Tengani, Nsanje, Sept. 4.

TVES4/ 8 Harry Chimwenderere, 70 yrs., Sena-Tonga, headman. Chimwenderere Village, T.A. Tengani, Nsanje, Sept. 4.

TVES4/ 9 Jackson Kalumbi, 75 yrs., Mang'anja-Phiri, headman. Kalumbi Village, T.A. Tengani, Nsanje, Sept. 4.

TVES4/10 Donsa Chakanza, 60 yrs., Sena-Mrambara; Winiko Kuzendera, 60 yrs., Sena-Mwenye(?); Bitoni Soda, 60 yrs., Sena; Lapson Simbi Mkango, 50 yrs., Mang'anja-Phiri, headman. Mkango Village, T.A. Tengani, Nsanje, Sept. 4.

TVES5/ 1 Nthambire Chilema, 65 yrs., Sena-Tonga; Thuboyi Chilema, 70 yrs., Mang'anja-Phiri, headman. Chilema Village, T.A. Ndamera, Nsanje, Sept. 8.

TVES5/ 2 Harry Tchiku, b. 1910, Mang'anja-Phiri, chief. Ndamera Village, T.A. Ndamera, Nsanje, Sept. 8.

TVES5/ 3 Christino Chibanzi, 55 yrs., Mang'anja-Phiri; Nsayi Kanting'u, 60 yrs., Mang'anja-Phiri; Joakina Sekeni, 80 yrs., Sena-Mrambara. Nyathando Village, T.A. Ndamera, Nsanje, Sept. 8.

TVES5/ 4 Andreya Chisada, 70 yrs., Sena-Mrambara, confessor in Apostolic Church Movement; Mataya Chisada, 65 yrs., Mang'anja-Phiri.

Kungaecha Village, T.A. Ndamera, Nsanje, Sept. 9.

TVES5/ 5 Jimu Cholomali, 80 yrs., Sena-Tonga. Kungaecha Village, T.A. Ndamera, Nsanje, Sept. 9.

TVES5/ 6 Jackson Kwaibvamtowe, 75 yrs., Sena-Tonga. Tursida Village, S.T.A. Mbenje, Nsanje, Sept. 10.

TVES5/ 7 Andrea Mbanje, 70 yrs., Sena-Manyika. Mangani Village, T.A. Chimombo, Nsanje, Sept. 10.

TVES5/ 8 Kapusi Chimombo, 90 yrs., Mang'anja-Phiri, chief. Chimombo Village, T.A. Chimombo, Nsanje, Sept. 11.

TVES5/ 9 Rampi Masamba, 70 yrs., Sena-Barwe. Tizola Village, T.A. Chimombo, Nsanje, Sept. 11.

TVES6/ 1 Ngabu, 72 yrs., Mang'anja-Phiri, chief; Nyamdzikwi, 82 yrs., Mang'anja-Phiri; Mpachika, 90 yrs., Mang'anja-Phiri. Ngabu Village, T.A. Ngabu, Nsanje, Sept. 15.

TVES6/ 2 Simoni Nyantondola, b. 1914, Mang'anja-Phiri, Chief Nyachikadza (but his territory is permanently inundated). Njobvu Village, T.A. Ngabu, Nsanje, Sept. 15.

TVES6/ 3 Jairo Chibveu, 80 yrs., Mang'anja-Phiri. Mbeta Village, T.A. Tengani, Nsanje, Sept. 16.

TVES6/ 4 Weta Sumana, 60 yrs., Sena-Tonga. Lundu Village, T.A. Tengani, Nsanje, Sept. 16.

TVES6/ 5 Vasco Antonio Baptista, 70 yrs., Sena-Mwenye. Lundu Village, T.A. Tengani, Nsanje, Sept. 16.

TVES6/ 6 Bringer Antonio Phiri, b. 1902, Mang'anja-Phiri. Malemia Village, T.A. Malemia, Nsanje, Sept. 17.

TVES6/ 7 Menala Mutuwawira, 60 yrs., Sena-Tonga; Million Kandeya, b. 1926, Sena-Tonga. Mbangu Village, T.A. Malemia, Nsanje, Sept. 17.

TVES7/ 1 Mai Witness, 60 yrs., Sena-Tonga. Sekeni Village, T.A. Lundu, Chikwawa, Jan. 17–24. The informant recited the following folktales to music: "Atsikana a Maranche," "Bandera," "Kalindi," "Misase," "Nsayi Sinasembwa," "Sinja Malia," "Ndasala ndekha mdembe," "Sozinyu waimba ng'oma zautale," and "Wamuona, Misase."

TVES7/ 2 Mr. Bande, 60 yrs., Sena-Tonga. Kungaecha Village, T.A. Ndamera, Nsanje, Sept. 9–10. The informant recited the following folktales to music: "Analima mbanambwa," "Baba, ndiri kudza mndulimo," "Binzi," "Chingangulu, a ku nyika dododo kutapika matope," "Kapange mama, Chiposi," and "Katiki, anamala nyemba zanga mbani?"

TVES8/ 1 Mrs. Mifinu Kalosi Lichi, 50 yrs., Mang'anja-Phiri. Ngona Village,

T.A. Tengani, Nsanje, Sept. 2. The informant sang "Bobi, Thangata."

TVES8/ 2 Mrs. Fane Magaso, 55 yrs. Ngona Village, T.A. Tengani, Nsanje, Sept. 2. The informant sang "Iwe Lupata."

TVES8/ 3 Mrs. Esnati Nota, 50 yrs., Sena-Tonga. Ngona Village, T.A. Tengani, Nsanje, Sept. 3. The informant sang "Dzakuno, dzandiombole."

TVES8/ 4 Group of women at Ngona Village, T.A. Tengani, Nsanje, Sept. 4. The informants sang the following songs: "Achimwene, osapanga zaumbuli," "Antonyo, mama ndaledzera," "Ndipaseni shilini," "Nkhondo, Matekenya," "Oye, wachiona chikhalirewe," "Thete, famba mphole," and "Walira dziko."

2. The Kololo Interlude in Southern Malawi (M/CK) (recorded in 1976)

M/CK 1 Mathias Chimtanda Mlilima, b. 1907, Kololo-Banda, former chief. Mlilima Village, T.A. Kasisi, Chikwawa, Jan. 23.

M/CK 2 Lucias Kasisi, 60 yrs., Kololo, chief; Alindiana, 65 yrs., Mang'anja-Banda, headwoman; Lawrence Njereza, 70 yrs., Mang'anja-Phiri. Kasisi Village, T.A. Kasisi, Chikwawa, Jan. 25.

M/CK 3 Duckson Dzuweni, 70 yrs., Mang'anja-Banda; Thenson Katunga, 40 yrs., Kololo, chief; Silver Khonje, 60 yrs., Mang'anja-Phiri. Katunga Village, T.A. Katunga, Chikwawa, Jan. 30.

M/CK 4 Joseph Maseya, 80 yrs., Kololo, chief. Frank Village, T.A. Maseya, Chikwawa, Jan. 30.

M/CK 5 Chipakuza, 60 yrs., Yao, headman; Sadriki Zimveka, 70 yrs., Mang'anja-Phiri. Chipakuza Village, T.A. Makhwira, Chikwawa, Feb. 4.

M/CK 6 Lucias Chapananga, 64 yrs., Mang'anja-Phiri, chief. Mikolongo Village, T.A. Chapananga, Chikwawa, Jan. 26.

M/CK 7 Alano Chauluka, 57 yrs., Mang'anja-Phiri. T.A. Chapananga, Chikwawa, Jan. 24.

M/CK 8 George Katawala Kaphwiti, 60 yrs., Mang'anja-Phiri. Katawala Village, T.A. Chapananga, Chikwawa, Jan. 27.

M/CK 9 Evans Makosana Lundu, 60 yrs., Mang'anja-Phiri, lundu paramount. Mbewe-ya-Mitengo Village, T.A. Lundu, Chikwawa, Jan. 28.

M/CK10 Herbert Maluwa, 55 yrs., Mang'anja-Phiri. Makande, T.A. Ngabu, Chikwawa, Jan. 29.

M/CK11 Lawrence Nkunzi, 75 yrs., Mang'anja-Banda. Makande, T.A. Ngabu, Chikwawa, Jan. 29.

M/CK12 Moses Ganamba, 60 yrs., Mang'anja-Banda. Makande, T.A. Ngabu, Chikwawa, Jan. 29.

M/CK13 Liva Mlolo, 80 yrs., Mang'anja-Phiri, chief. Mlolo Village, T.A. Mlolo, Nsanje, Feb. 1.

M/CK14 Akashoni Bwatamba, 50 yrs., Mang'anja-Mbewe. Tsapa Village, T.A. Kasisi, Chikwawa, Jan. 23.

M/CK15 Jali Kanzimbi, 60 yrs., Mang'anja-Mbewe. Tsapa Village, T.A. Kasisi, Chikwawa, Jan. 21.

3. The Tengani Chieftaincy (T73) (recorded in 1973)

T73/ 1 Saimoni Alfase Nyantondola, b. 1914, Mang'anja-Phiri. Njobvu Village, T.A. Ngabu, Nsanje, Aug. 6.

T73/ 2 Moshtishu, 80 yrs., Mang'anja-Phiri. Chiphwembwe Village, T.A. Malemia, Nsanje, Aug. 9, 14.

T73/ 3 Stonkeni Falamenga, 68 yrs., Mang'anja-Phiri, headman. Nkuzaduka Village, T.A. Ngabu, Nsanje, Aug. 11.

T73/ 4 Rev. R. E. Barr, missionary in Nsanje from 1937 to 1963. Likhubula Bible Institute, Blantyre, Aug. 14.

T73/ 5 David Makoko, 80 yrs., Mang'anja-Phiri; Ostrich Makoko, 50 yrs., Mang'anja-Phiri, subchief. Makoko Village, T.A. Chimombo, Nsanje, Aug. 16.

T73/ 6 Ngabu, 65 yrs., Mang'anja-Phiri, chief; Mpachika, 80 yrs., Mang'anja-Phiri; Nyam'dzikwi, 75 yrs., Mang'anja-Phiri. Ngabu Village, T.A. Ngabu, Nsanje, Aug. 16.

T73/ 7 Kapusi Chimombo, 80 yrs., Mang'anja-Phiri, chief. Chimombo Village, T.A. Chimombo, Nsanje, Aug. 1972, Aug. 19.

T73/ 8 Mphamba, 50 yrs., Mang'anja-Phiri, headman. Mphamba Village, T.A. Malemia, Nsanje, Aug. 19.

T73/ 9 Vuntade Nyachikadza, 75 yrs., Mang'anja-Phiri, chief. Thuka Court, T.A. Nyachikadza, Nsanje, Aug. 20.

T73/10 Dalesi Ndamera, 60 yrs., Mang'anja-Phiri, chief. Ndamera Village, T.A. Ndamera, Nsanje, Aug. 21.

T73/11 Bobo Nyasaland, b. 1902, Mang'anja-Phiri. Ngabu Village, T.A. Ngabu, Nsanje, Aug. 22.

T73/12 Stonkeni Tengani, 70 yrs., Mang'anja-Phiri, chief. Tengani Village, T.A. Tengani, Nsanje, Aug. 23.

T73/13 Rev. J. Van Velden, missionary in Nsanje from 1942 to 1949, and in the early 1970s. Tengani Parish, T.A. Tengani, Nsanje, Aug. 23.

T73/14 Simoni Thole, 80 yrs., Sena-Tonga. Chataika Village, T.A. Malemia, Nsanje, Aug. 25.

T73/15 Mankhuso, 80 yrs., Mang'anja-Phiri. Chataika Village, T.A. Malemia, Nsanje, Sept. 24.

T73/16 Jonas Chiriwekha, 70 yrs., Sena-Tonga; Yohane Simenti, 59 yrs., Mang'anja-Phiri, headman. Nthole Village, T.A. Malemia, Nsanje, Aug. 25.

T73/17 Mtsangalambe, 75 yrs., Mang'anja-Phiri, headman. Mtsangalambe Village, T.A. Ngabu, Nsanje, Aug. 26.

T73/18 Jackson Falakeza, 72 yrs., Mang'anja-Banda; Yona Chiphwembwe, Mang'anja-Phiri; Joseph Chionadziwa, 70 yrs., Mang'anja-Phiri. Chiphwembwe Village, T.A. Malemia, Nsanje, Aug. 27.

T73/19 Harry Kampira, b. 1920, Mang'anja-Banda. Nthole Village, T.A. Malemia, Nsanje, Aug. 27.

T73/20 Bringer Antonio Phiri, b. 1902, Mang'anja-Phiri. Malemia Village, T.A. Malemia, Nsanje, Aug. 27.

T73/21 Luciano Thomu, 60 yrs., Mang'anja-Phiri, headman; Amosi Kalavina, 60 yrs., Mang'anja-Phiri. Nthukuso Village, T.A. Malemia, Nsanje, Aug. 28.

T73/22 Enos Mchinginji, 80 yrs., Mang'anja-Phiri, headman. Chapirira Village, T.A. Malemia, Nsanje, Aug. 30.

T73/23 Fraser Falamenga, 72 yrs., Mang'anja-Phiri. Nkuzaduka Village, T.A. Ngabu, Nsanje, Aug. 30.

T73/24 Rev. J. Dirkx, missionary in Nsanje from 1961 to 1973. Nsanje Parish, T.A. Malemia, Nsanje, Aug. 30.

4. Spirit Mediumship: J. M. Schoffeleers's Project (SM73) (recorded in 1973)

SM73/ 1 Chief Ngabu et al. *See* T73/6.

SM73/ 2 Bringer Antonio Phiri. *See* T73/20.

SM73/ 3 Rambiki, 63 yrs., Mang'anja-Phiri. Mphamba Village, T.A. Malemia, Nsanje, Aug. 31.

SM73/ 4 Joseph Chambote, 50 yrs., Mang'anja-Phiri, Mbona's medium. Nthole Village, T.A. Malemia, Nsanje, Sept. 17–18.

SM73/ 5 Nsayi Ndakuonetsani, 70 yrs., Mang'anja-Phiri, last female medium at Nyachikadza's court before giving up the profession in either 1962 or 1964. Chitsa Village, T.A. Tengani, Nsanje, Sept. 17.

SM73/ 6 James Charlie Nkhambala, 65 yrs., Mang'anja-Phiri. Nthole Village, T.A. Malemia, Nsanje, Sept. 18.

SM73/ 7 Semba Chingasala, 75 yrs., Sena-Tonga. Ndamera Village, T.A. Ndamera, Nsanje, Sept. 20.

SM73/ 8 Mpachika, 80 yrs., Mang'anja-Phiri. Ngabu Village, T.A. Ngabu, Nsanje, Sept. 20.

SM73/ 9 Mphamba. *See* T73/8. Sept. 20.

SM73/10 Sabe Mkhuche, 75 yrs., Mang'anja-Phiri, headman. Mkhuche Village, T.A. Malemia, Nsanje, Sept. 21.

SM73/11 Moshtishu. *See* T73/2. Sept. 21.

SM73/12 Daimoni Nyantusi, 70 yrs., Mang'anja-Phiri, headman; Thole Chitomeni, 85 yrs., Mang'anja-Phiri. Mchacha Village (1), T.A. Malemia, Nsanje, Sept. 22.

SM73/13 Mbangu, Mang'anja-Phiri, headman and official at Mbona shrine. Mbangu Village, T.A. Malemia, Nsanje, Sept. 22.

SM73/14 David Makoko et al. *See* T73/5. Sept. 22.
SM73/15 Mwanda, 75 yrs., Mang'anja-Phiri, headman. Mwanda Village, T.A. Malemia, Nsanje, Sept. 23.
SM73/16 Ngabu. *See* T73/6. Sept. 24.

Archival Materials

1. Malawi National Archives (MNA), Zomba

Chikwawa District (formerly part of West Shire District) monthly, quarterly, and annual reports. 1907–1946.
Department of Agriculture monthly, annual, and other reports. 1907–1960.
District books: Lower Shire (4 vols.); Ruo (2 vols.); West Shire (2 vols.). (Note that district commissioners for the Lower Shire continued to record their observations in vol. 1 until the 1950s).
Lower River District (Chikwawa and Port Herald when they were administered as a single unit, from 1947 to 195[?]) annual reports, 1947–1949.
Port Herald District (former Lower Shire and present Nsanje District) monthly, quarterly, and annual reports. 1907–1946.
Ruo (or Chiromo) District monthly, quarterly, and annual reports. 1907–1922.
Secretariat files, monthly and annual reports for Lower Shire, Ruo, and West Shire districts, 1907–1922.

2. Public Record Office (PRO), London

Great Britain. Colonial Office. Nyasaland. CO 525.
Great Britain. Foreign Office. Africa. FO 2.
Great Britain. Foreign Office. The Slave Trade. FO 84.

3. National Library of Scotland (NLS), Edinburgh

David Livingstone Papers.

4. University of Edinburgh Library

Frederick T. Morrison diaries (1882–1887).

5. Rhodes House, Oxford University

Horace Waller Papers, MSS. Afr s. 16, 10 vols.; Horace Waller diaries, 11 vols. (1860–1864).

Books, Articles, Periodicals, Dissertations, Theses

Afonja, A. "Land Control: A Critical Factor in Yoruba Gender Stratification." C. Robertson and I. Berger, eds., *Women and Class in Africa.* New York: Africana Publishing, 1986. 78-91.

Agnew, S. "Environment and History: The Malawian Setting." B. Pachai, ed., *The Early History of Malawi.* London: Longman, 1972. 28–48.

Alpers, E. A. *Ivory and Slaves in East Central Africa.* London: Heinemann, 1975.

Arrighi, G. "Labour Supplies in Historical Perspective: A Study of the Proletarianization of the African Peasantry in Rhodesia." G. Arrighi and J. Saul, eds., *Essays on the Political Economy of Africa.* New York: Monthly Review Press, 1973. 180–237.

Axelson, E. "Portugal's Attitude to Nyasaland During the Period of the Partition of Africa." B. Pachai, ed., *The Early History of Malawi.* London: Longman, 1972. 252-262.

Bazin, J. "War and Servitude in Segou." *Economy and Society* 3 (1974): 107–143.

Beinart, W. "Agricultural Planning and the Late Colonial Technical Imagination: The Lower Shire Valley in Malawi, 1940–1960." K. J. McCracken, ed., *Malawi: An Alternative Pattern of Development.* Edinburgh: Centre of African Studies, University of Edinburgh, 1984. 95–148.

Beinart, W. "Soil Erosion, Conservationism and Ideas About Development: A Southern African Exploration, 1900–1960." *Journal of Southern African Studies* 11 (October 1984): 52–83.

Beinart, W., and C. Bundy. *Hidden Struggles in Rural South Africa: Politics and Popular Movements in the Transkei and Eastern Cape, 1890–1930.* Berkeley and Los Angeles: University of California Press, 1987.

Bennett, N. R., and M. Ylvisaker, eds. *The Central African Journal of Lovell Procter, 1860–64.* Boston: Boston University Press, 1971.

Berry, S. *Fathers Work for Their Sons: Accumulation, Mobility, and Class Formation in an Extended Yoruba Community.* Berkeley and Los Angeles: University of California Press, 1985.

Berry, S. "The Food Crisis and Agrarian Change in Africa: A Review Essay." *African Studies Review* 27 (June 1984): 59–112.

Boserup, E. *Women's Role in Economic Development.* London: Allen and Unwin, 1970.

Bryceson, D. F. "Changes in Peasant Food Production and Food Supply in Relation to the Historical Development of Commodity Production in Pre-Colonial and Colonial Tanganyika." *Journal of Peasant Studies* 7 (April 1980): 281–311.

Buchanan, J. *The Shire Highlands (East Central Africa): As a Colony and Mission.* London: Blackwell and Sons, 1885.

Chadwick, O. *Mackenzie's Grave.* London: Hodder and Stoughton, 1959.

Chafulumira, E. W. *Mbiri ya Amang'anja* (A History of the Mang'anja). Zomba, Nyasaland: Government Press, 1948.

Chakanza, J. E. "The Rise and Decline of a Plantation Economy in Nsanje District, 1895–1945." Unpublished paper, Chancellor College, University of Malawi, 1976–77.

Chipungu, S. N. *The State, Technology and Peasant Differentiation in Zambia: A Case Study of the Southern Province, 1930–1986.* Lusaka: Historical Association of Zambia, 1988.

Clendennen, G. W., ed. "The Shire Journal of David Livingstone, 1861–1864." Unpublished typescript in author's possession.

Clendennen, G. W., and I. C. Cunningham, comps. *David Livingstone: A Catalogue of Documents.* Edinburgh: National Library of Scotland, 1979.

Cohen, G. A. *Karl Marx's Theory of History: A Defence.* Princeton: Princeton University Press, 1978.

Colman, D. R., and G. K. Garbett. "Economic and Social Issues in the Development of the Lower Shire Valley." First Report of the Socio-Economic Survey of the Lower Shire Valley. Unpublished typescript, Shire Valley Agricultural Development Project, 1973.

Colman, D. R., and G. K. Garbett. "The Labour Economy of a Peasant Community in Malawi." Second Report of the Socio-Economic Survey of the Lower Shire Valley. Unpublished typescript, Shire Valley Agricultural Development Project, 1976.

Colson, E. *Marriage and the Family Among the Plateau Tonga of Northern Rhodesia.* Manchester: Manchester University Press, 1958.

Cooper, F. "Peasants, Capitalists, and Historians: A Review Article." *Journal of Southern African Studies* 9 (April 1981): 285–314.

Cooper, F. "The Problem of Slavery in African Studies." *Journal of African History* 20 (1979): 103–125.

Copans, J., and D. Seddon. "Marxism and Anthropology: A Preliminary Survey." D. Seddon, ed., *Relations of Production: Marxist Approaches to Economic Anthropology.* London: Cass, 1978. 1–46.

Coquery-Vidrovitch, C., and P. Lovejoy, eds. *The Workers of African Trade.* Beverly Hills, Calif.: Sage, 1985.

Cordell, D., and J. W. Gregory, eds. *African Population and Capitalism: Historical Perspectives.* Boulder, Colo.: Westview, 1987.

Cotterill, H. B., ed. *Travels and Researches Among the Lakes and Mountains of Eastern and Central Africa: From the Journals of J. Frederick Elton.* London: Cass, 1968.

Coutinho, J. A. *Memorias de um Velho Marinheiro Soldado de Africa.* Lisbon: Bertrand, 1941.

Crossley, R. "High Levels of Lake Malawi." Unpublished paper, Chancellor College, University of Malawi, 1980.

Curtin, P., et al. *African History.* Boston: Little, Brown, 1978.
Davey, J. B. "The Rise of the African Cotton Industry in Nyasaland." *Nyasaland Journal* 15 (July 1962): 14–15.
Debenham, F. *Nyasaland: The Land of the Lake.* London: Her Majesty's Stationery Office, 1955.
Dos Santos, J. "Eastern Ethiopia." G. M. Theal, ed., *Records of South-East Africa.* 9 vols. 1899; Cape Town, South Africa: Struik, 1964. 7:258–304.
Drummond, H. *Tropical Africa.* London: Hodder and Stoughton, 1888.
Ducker, H. C. "Cotton in Nyasaland." *Nyasaland Agricultural Quarterly Journal* 10 (September 1951): 84–94.
Ducker, H. C. "The Nyasaland Cotton Crop." *Nyasaland Agricultural Quarterly Journal* 10 (December 1951): 127–134.
Ducker, H. C. "A Talk on Cotton Growing in Lower Shire and Chikwawa Districts." *Nyasaland Agricultural Quarterly Journal* 1 (January 1941): 14–25.
Duly, A. W. R. "The Lower Shire District: Notes on Land Tenure and Individual Rights." *Nyasaland Journal* 1 (July 1948): 1–44.
Dupré, G., and P. Rey. "Reflections on the Relevance of a Theory of the History of Exchange." D. Seddon, ed., *Relations of Production: Marxist Approaches to Economic Anthropology.* London: Cass, 1978. 171–208.
Durkheim, E. *The Elementary Forms of the Religious Life.* 1915. London: Allen and Unwin, 1976.
Edwards, E., M. Reich, and T. Weisskopf. *The Capitalist System.* 1972. Englewood Cliffs, N.J.: Prentice-Hall, 1978.
Etienne, M. "Women and Men, Cloth and Colonization: The Transformation of Production-Distribution Relations Among the Baule (Ivory Coast)." M. Etienne and E. Leacock, eds., *Women and Colonization: Anthropological Perspectives.* New York: Praeger, 1980. 214–238.
Fage, J. D. "Slaves and Society in Western Africa, c. 1445–c. 1700." *Journal of African History* 21 (1980): 289–310.
Fallers, L. A. *Bantu Bureaucracy: A Study of Integration and Conflict in the Political Institutions of an East African People.* Cambridge, England: Heffer and Sons, (1956).
Faulkner, H. *Elephant Haunts: Being a Sportsman's Narrative of the Search for Dr Livingstone, with Scenes of Elephant, Buffalo and Hippopotamus Hunting.* London: Hurst and Blackett, 1868.
Fields, K. E. "Political Contingencies of Witchcraft in Colonial Central Africa: Culture and the State in Marxist Theory." *Canadian Journal of African Studies* 16 (1982): 567–598.
Foskett, R., ed. *The Zambesi Journal of Dr. John Kirk, 1858–1863.* 2 vols. London: Oliver and Boyd, 1965.
Foster-Carter, A. "The Modes of Production Controversy." *New Left Review,* January/February 1978, 47–73.
Fox-Genovese, E., and E. D. Genovese. *Fruits of Merchant Capital: Slavery and Bourgeois Property in the Rise and Expansion of Capitalism.* Oxford: Oxford University Press, 1983.

Freeman, A. "A Preliminary Investigation into Dimba Cultivation in the Lower Shire Valley." Unpublished typescript, Shire Valley Agricultural Development Project, 1973.

Gamitto, A. C. P. *King Kazembe and the Marave, Cheva, Bisa, Bemba, Lunda, and Other Peoples of Southern Africa: Being the Diary of the Portuguese Expedition to That Potante in the Years 1831 and 1832.* 2 vols. Lisbon: Junta de Investigações do Ultramar, 1960.

Genovese, E. D. *Roll, Jordan, Roll: The World the Slaves Made.* 1972. New York: Vintage, 1976.

Godelier, M. *Perspectives in Marxist Anthropology.* 1973. Cambridge: Cambridge University Press, 1977.

Goody, J. *Technology, Tradition and the State in Africa.* Cambridge: Cambridge University Press, 1971.

Graham-Jolly, H. G. "Livingstone's Legacy: The Makololo Chiefs of Chikwawa District." *Nyasaland Journal* 19 (January 1966): 7–14.

Gregory, J. W., and E. C. Mandala. "Dimensions of Conflict: Emigrant Labor from Colonial Malawi and Zambia, 1900–1945." D. Cordell and J. W. Gregory, eds., *African Population and Capitalism: Historical Perspectives.* Boulder, Colo.: Westview, 1987. 221–240.

Griffin, A. E. *A Report on the Flood Control and Reclamation on the Lower Shire River and Other Specified Areas in Nyasaland.* London: Crown Agents for the Colonies, 1949.

Guyer, J. "Household and Community in African Studies." *African Studies Review* 24 (June/September 1981): 87–137.

Halcrow, Sir William, et al. *The Shire Valley Project: A Report on the Control and Development of Lake Nyasa and the Shire River.* Vol. 1. London: Crown Agents for Overseas Governments and Administrations, 1954.

Hermitte, E. L. "An Economic History of Barotseland, 1800–1940." Ph.D. diss., Northwestern University, 1974.

Hetherwick, A. *The Romance of Blantyre: How Livingstone's Dream Became True.* London: Clarke, n.d. (1931).

Hill, P. *The Migrant Cocoa-Farmers of Southern Ghana.* Cambridge: Cambridge University Press, 1963.

Hindess, B., and P. Hirst. *Pre-Capitalist Modes of Production.* London: Routledge and Kegan Paul, 1975.

Hyden, G. *Beyond Ujamaa in Tanzania: Underdevelopment and an Uncaptured Peasantry.* Berkeley and Los Angeles: University of California Press, 1980.

Inikori, J. E. "The Chaining of a Continent: Export Demand for Captives and the History of Africa South of the Sahara, 1450–1870." Unpublished typescript, UNESCO, 1986.

Inikori, J. E., ed. *Forced Migration: The Impact of the Export Slave Trade on African Societies.* New York: Africana Publishing, 1982.

Isaacman, A. *Mozambique: The Africanization of a European Institution, The Zambesi Prazos, 1750–1902.* Madison: University of Wisconsin Press, 1972.

Isaacman, A. "Peasants and Rural Social Protest in Africa." Paper commissioned by the joint American Council of Learned Societies–Social Science Research Council Africa Committee and presented at a meeting of the African Studies Association, Atlanta, November, 1989.

Isaacman, A., et al. " 'Cotton Is the Mother of Poverty': Peasant Resistance to Forced Cotton Production in Mozambique, 1936-1961." *International Journal of African Historical Studies* 13 (1980): 581–615.

Isaacman, A., and E. Mandala. "From Porters to Labor Extractors: The Chikunda and Kololo in the Lake Malawi and Tchiri River Area." C. Coquery-Vidrovitch and P. Lovejoy, eds., *The Workers of African Trade.* Beverly Hills, Calif.: Sage, 1985. 209–242.

Jackson, G., and P. O. Wiehe. *An Annotated Check List of Nyasaland Grasses.* Zomba, Nyasaland: Government Press, 1958.

Johnston, H. H. *British Central Africa: An Attempt to Give Some Account of a Portion of the Territories Under British Influence North of the Zambesi.* London: Methuen, 1897.

Kandawire, J. A. K. *Thangata: Forced Labor or Reciprocal Assistance?* Zomba: University of Malawi Research and Publications Committee, 1979.

Kerr, W. M. *The Far Interior: A Narrative of Travel and Adventure from the Cape of Good Hope Across the Zambesi to the Lake Regions of Central Africa.* 2 vols. London: Sampson Low, Marston, Searle and Rivington, 1887.

Kettlewell, R. W. *An Outline of Agrarian Problems and Policy in Nyasaland.* Zomba, Nyasaland: Government Press, 1955.

Kjekshus, H. *Ecology Control and Economic Development in East African History: The Case of Tanganyika, 1850–1950.* London: Heinemann, 1977.

Klein, M. "The Study of Slavery in Africa." *Journal of African History* 19 (1978): 599–609.

Klein, M., ed. *Peasants in Africa: Historical and Contemporary Perspectives.* Beverly Hills, Calif.: Sage, 1980. Introduction, 9–43.

Kopytoff, I., and S. Miers. "African 'Slavery' as an Institution of Marginality." S. Miers and I. Kopytoff, eds., *Slavery in Africa.* Madison: University of Wisconsin Press, 1977. 3–81.

Langworthy, H. "Understanding Malawi's Pre-Colonial History." *Society of Malawi Journal* 23 (January 1969): 36–45.

Linden, I. and J. *Catholics, Peasants and Chewa Resistance in Nyasaland, 1889–1939.* London: Heinemann, 1974.

Lint Company of Zambia. *Cotton Pests in Africa.* Lusaka, Zambia: Lintco, n.d.

Livingstone, D. *Missionary Travels and Researches in South Africa.* London: Murray, 1857.

Livingstone, D., and C. Livingstone. *The Narrative of an Expedition to the Zambesi and Its Tributaries and of the Discoveries of Lakes Shirwa and Nyassa.* London: Murray, 1865.

Livingstone, W. P. *Laws of Livingstonia: A Narrative of Missionary Adventure and Achievement.* London: Hodder and Stoughton, n.d.

Lonsdale, J., and B. Berman. "Coping with the Contradictions: The Development of the Colonial State in Kenya, 1895–1914." *Journal of African History* 20 (1979): 487–505.

Lovejoy, P. *Transformations in Slavery: A History of Slavery in Africa*. Cambridge: Cambridge University Press, 1983.

Macdonald, D. *Africana: The Heart of Heathen Africa*. London: Dawson of Pall Mall, 1969.

Macmillan, H. W. "The Origins and Development of the African Lakes Company, 1878–1908." Ph.D. diss., University of Edinburgh, 1970.

Mainga, M. *Bulozi Under the Luyana Kings: Political Formation in Pre-colonial Zambia*. London: Longman, 1973.

Malawi Congress Party. "Nsanje District Calendar of Events, [1859–1965]." Unpublished typescript, 1966.

Malawi Congress Party. *Malawi News*. 1959–60.

Malawi National Statistical Office. *Population Census, 1977: Preliminary Report*. Zomba, Malawi: Government Press, 1978.

Mamdani, M. *Politics and Class Formation in Uganda*. New York: Monthly Review Press, 1976.

Mandala, E. C. "Capitalism, Ecology and Society: The Lower Tchiri (Shire) Valley of Malawi, 1860–1960." Ph.D. diss., University of Minnesota, 1983.

Mandala, E. C. "Commodity Production, Subsistence and the State in Colonial Africa: Peasant Cotton Agriculture in the Lower Tchiri (Shire) Valley of Malawi, 1907–51." E. D. Genovese and L. Hochberg, eds., *Geographic Perspectives in History*. Oxford: Blackwell, 1989. 281–314.

Mandala, E. C. "The Kololo Interlude in Southern Malawi, 1861–95." M.A. thesis, University of Malawi, 1977.

Mandala, E. C. "The Nature and Substance of Mang'anja and Kololo Oral Traditions: A Preliminary Survey." *Society of Malawi Journal* 31 (January 1978): 1–14.

Mandala, E. C. "The Tengani Chieftaincy and Its Relations with Other Chieftaincies in Nsanje District, c. 1850–1951." Unpublished paper, Department of History, University of Malawi, 1973–74.

Marwick, M. G. *Sorcery in Its Social Setting: A Study of the Northern Rhodesia Chewa*. Manchester: Manchester University Press, 1965.

Marx, K. *Capital*. Vol. 1. Trans. B. Fowkes. New York: Vintage, 1977.

Marx, K. "Preface to a Contribution to the Critique of Political Economy." *Karl Marx and Frederick Engels: Selected Works in One Volume*. New York: International Publishers, 1974.

Marx, K., and F. Engels. *The German Ideology*. Ed. C. J. Arthur. New York: International Publishers, 1970.

Matecheta, H. K. *Blantyre Mission: Nkhani ya Ciyambi Cace* (Blantyre Mission: The Story of Its Origins). Blantyre, Nyasaland: Hetherwick, 1951.

McCracken, K. J. "Experts and Expertise in Colonial Malawi." *African Affairs* 81 (January 1982): 101–116.

McCracken, K. J. "Fishing and the Colonial Economy: The Case of Malawi." *Journal of African History* 27 (1987): 413–429.

McCracken, K. J. "Livingstonia Mission and the Evolution of Malawi, 1873–1939." Ph.D. diss., Cambridge University, 1967.

McCracken, K. J. "Planters, Peasants and the Colonial State: The Impact of the Native Tobacco Board in the Central Province of Malawi." *Journal of Southern African Studies* 9 (April 1983): 172–192.

McCracken, K. J., ed. *Malawi: An Alternative Pattern of Development.* Edinburgh: Centre of African Studies, University of Edinburgh, 1984.

Meillassoux, C. " 'The Economy' in Agricultural Self-Sustaining Societies: A Preliminary Analysis." D. Seddon, ed., *Relations of Production: Marxist Approaches to Economic Anthropology.* London: Cass, 1978. 127–157.

Meillassoux, C. "Female Slavery." C. Robertson and M. Klein, eds., *Women and Slavery in Africa.* Madison: University of Wisconsin Press, 1983. 49–66.

Meillassoux, C. *Maidens, Meal and Money: Capitalism and the Domestic Community.* 1975. Cambridge: Cambridge University Press, 1981.

Meillassoux, C. "The Role of Slavery in the Economic and Social History of Sahelo-Sudanic Africa." J. E. Inikori, ed., *Forced Migration: The Impact of the Export Slave Trade on African Societies.* New York: Africana Publishing, 1982. 74–99.

Miers, S., and I. Kopytoff, eds. *Slavery in Africa: Historical and Anthropological Perspectives.* Madison: University of Wisconsin Press, 1977.

Miracle, M. *Agriculture in the Congo Basin.* Madison: University of Wisconsin Press, 1967.

Mitchell, J. C. *The Yao Village.* Manchester: Manchester University Press, 1956.

Moir, F. L. M. *After Livingstone: An African Trade Romance.* London: Hodder and Stoughton, n.d.

Monclaro, F. "Account of the Journey Made by the Fathers of the Society of Jesus with Francisco Barreto in the Conquest of Monomotapa in the Year 1569." G. M. Theal, ed., *Records of South-East Africa.* 9 vols. 1899. Cape Town, South Africa: Struik, 1964. 3:229–235.

Morgan, W. B. "The Lower Shire Valley of Nyasaland: A Changing System of African Agriculture." *Geographical Journal* 119 (December 1953): 459–469.

Muntemba, M. "Women and Agricultural Change in the Railway Region of Zambia, 1930–1970: Dispossession and Counterstrategies." E. Bay, ed., *Women and Work in Africa.* Boulder, Colo.: Westview, 1982. 83–103.

Murray, C. *Families Divided: The Impact of Migrant Labour in Lesotho.* Cambridge: Cambridge University Press, 1981.

Murray, S. S. *Handbook of Nyasaland.* 1922. London: Crown Agents for the Colonies, 1932.

Myambo, S. S. "The Shire Highlands Plantations: A Socio-economic History of the Plantation System of Production in Malawi, 1891–1938." M.A. thesis, University of Malawi, 1973.

Newitt, M. D. D. *Portuguese Settlement on the Zambesi: Exploration, Land Tenure and Colonial Rule in East Africa.* London: Longman, 1973.

Ng'ong'ola, C. "Malawi's Agricultural Economy and the Evolution of Legislation on the Production and Marketing of Peasant Economic Crops." *Journal of Southern African Studies* 12 (April 1986): 240–262.

Northrup, N. R. "Southern Malawi, 1860–1891: A Case Study of Frontier Politics." Ph.D. diss., University of California, Los Angeles, 1978.

Nthenda, L. J. L. "H.M. Treasury and the Problems of Nyasaland Public Finances, 1919 to 1940." Ph.D. diss., Oxford University, 1972.

Nyasaland Protectorate. *Annual Report of the Department of Agriculture.* 1909–1960.

Nyasaland Protectorate. *Nyasaland Government Gazette.* 1896–1960.

Nyasaland Protectorate. *A Report by Mr Eric Smith, Administrative Officer, on the Direct Taxation of Natives in the Nyasaland Protectorate and Other Cognate Matters.* London: Crown Agents for the Colonies, 1937.

Nyasaland Protectorate. *Report of the Census of 1945.* Zomba, Nyasaland: Government Press, 1946.

Nyasaland Times (Blantyre). 1934.

Omer-Cooper, J. D. *The Zulu Aftermath: A Nineteenth Century Revolution in Bantu Africa.* London: Longman, 1966.

Pachai, B. *Malawi: The History of the Nation.* London: Longman, 1973.

Page, M. "The Great War and Chewa Society in Malawi." Paper presented at a meeting of the African Studies Association, Baltimore, November 1978.

Palmer, R., and N. Parsons, eds. *The Roots of Rural Poverty in Central and Southern Africa.* Berkeley and Los Angeles: University of California Press, 1977.

Pearson, E. O., and B. L. Mitchell. *A Report on the Status and Control of Insect Pests of Cotton in the Lower River Districts of Nyasaland.* Zomba, Nyasaland: Government Press, 1945.

Phiri, K. G. M. "Chewa History in Central Malawi and the Use of Oral Tradition, 1600–1920." Ph.D. diss., University of Wisconsin, 1975.

Phiri, K. G. M. "Some Changes in the Matrilineal Family System Among the Chewa of Malawi Since the Nineteenth Century." *Journal of African History* 24 (1983): 257–274.

Pike, J. G., and G. T. Rimmington. *Malawi: A Geographical Study.* Oxford: Oxford University Press, 1965.

Poewe, K. *Matrilineal Ideology: Male-Female Dynamics in Luapula, Zambia.* London: Academic Press, 1981.

Popkin, S. *The Rational Peasant: The Political Economy of Rural Society in Vietnam.* Berkeley and Los Angeles: University of California Press, 1979.

Ranger, T. O. "Connections Between 'Primary Resistance' Movements and Modern Mass Nationalism in East and Central Africa." *Journal of African History* 9 (1968): 437–453, 631–641.

Ranger, T. O. "Growing from the Roots: Reflections on Peasant Research in Central and Southern Africa." *Journal of Southern African Studies* 5 (October 1978): 99–133.

Ranger, T. O. *Peasant Consciousness and Guerrilla War in Zimbabwe.* Berkeley and Los Angeles: University of California Press, 1985.

Ranger, T. O. "The People in African Resistance: A Review." *Journal of Southern African Studies* 4 (October 1977): 125–146.
Rankin, D. J. *The Zambesi Basin and Nyasaland.* London: Blackwell and Sons, 1893.
Ratcliffe, C. "The Fishery of the Lower River Area, Malawi." Malawi Ministry of Agriculture, Fisheries Bulletin no. 3, 1972.
Richards, A. *Bemba Marriage and Present Economic Conditions.* Livingstone, Northern Rhodesia: Rhodes-Livingstone Institute, 1940.
Richards, P. "Ecological Change and the Politics of African Land Use." *African Studies Review* 26 (June 1983): 1–72.
Robertson, C., and M. Klein. "Women's Importance in African Slave Systems." C. Robertson and M. Klein, eds., *Women and Slavery in Africa.* Madison: University of Wisconsin Press, 1983. 3-25.
Rodney, W. "African Slavery and Other Forms of Social Oppression on the Upper Guinea in the Context of the Atlantic Slave Trade." *Journal of African History* 7 (1966): 431-443.
Romalis, S. "Sexual Politics and Technological Change in Colonial Africa." *Occasional Papers in Anthropology.* Vol. 1. Buffalo: State University of New York, 1979. 177–185.
Rowley, H. *The Story of the Universities Mission to Central Africa.* 1867. New York: Negro Universities Press, 1969.
Saul, J., and R. Woods. "African Peasantries." T. Shanin, ed., *Peasants and Peasant Societies.* New York: Penguin, 1971.
Sayer, A. "Epistemology and Conceptions of People and Nature in Geography." *Geoforum* 10 (1979): 19–43.
Schneider, D. M. "The Distinctive Features of Matrilineal Descent Groups." D. M. Schneider and K. Gough, eds., *Matrilineal Kinship.* Berkeley and Los Angeles: University of California Press, 1961. 1–29.
Schoffeleers, J. M. "The Chisumphi and Mbona Cults in Malawi: A Comparative History." J. M. Schoffeleers, ed., *Guardians of the Land: Essays in Central African Territorial Cults.* Gwelo, Zimbabwe: Mambo, 1978. 147–185.
Schoffeleers, J. M. "Crisis, Criticism, and Critique: An Interpretative Model of Territorial Mediumship Among the Chewa." *Journal of Social Science* 3 (1974): 74–80.
Schoffeleers, J. M. "Cult Idioms and the Dialectics of a Region." R. Werbner, ed., *Regional Cults.* London: Academic Press, 1977. 219–239.
Schoffeleers, J. M. "Economic Change and Religious Polarization in an African Rural District." K. J. McCracken, ed., *Malawi: An Alternative Pattern of Development.* Edinburgh: Centre of African Studies, University of Edinburgh, 1984. 187–242.
Schoffeleers, J. M. *Evil Spirits and the Rites of Exorcism in the Lower Shire Valley of Malawi.* Limbe, Malawi: Montfort Press, 1967.
Schoffeleers, J. M. "The History and Political Role of the Mbona Cult of the Mang'anja." T. O. Ranger and I. Kimambo, eds., *The Historical Study of*

African Religion. London: Heinemann, 1972. 73–94.

Schoffeleers, J. M. "Livingstone and the Mang'anja Chiefs." B. Pachai, ed., *Livingstone, Man of Africa: Memorial Essays, 1873–1973*. London: Longman, 1973. 111–130.

Schoffeleers, J. M. *The Lower Shire Valley of Malawi: Its Ecology, Population Distribution, Ethnic Divisions, and Systems of Marriage*. Limbe, Malawi: Montfort, 1968.

Schoffeleers, J. M. "Mbona, the Guardian Spirit of the Mang'anja." B.Litt. thesis, Oxford University, 1966.

Schoffeleers, J. M. "The Meaning and Use of the Name 'Malawi' in Oral Traditions and Pre-Colonial Documents." B. Pachai, ed., *The Early History of Malawi*. London: Longman, 1973. 91–103.

Schoffeleers, J. M. "The *Nyau* Societies: Our Present Understanding." *Society of Malawi Journal* 29 (January 1976): 59–68.

Schoffeleers, J. M. "Oral History and the Retrieval of the Distant Past: On the Use of Legendary Chronicles as Sources of Historical Information." J. M. Schoffeleers and W. Van Binsbergen, eds., *Theoretical Explorations in African Religion*. London: Routledge and Kegan Paul, 1985. 164–188.

Schoffeleers, J. M. *River of Blood*. Forthcoming.

Schoffeleers, J. M. "Social Functional Aspects of Spirit Possession in the Lower Shire Valley of Malawi." Universities of East Africa Social Sciences Conference, *Religious Studies Papers* (1969): 51–63.

Schoffeleers, J. M. "Symbolic and Social Aspects of Spirit Worship Among the Mang'anja." Ph.D. diss., Oxford University, 1968.

Schoffeleers, J. M. "Trade, Warfare and Social Inequality: The Case of the Lower Shire Valley of Malawi, 1590–1622." *Society of Malawi Journal* 33 (July 1980): 6–24.

Schoffeleers, J. M. "The Zimba and the Lundu State in the Late Sixteenth and Early Seventeenth Centuries." *Journal of African History* 28 (1987): 337–355.

Schoffeleers, J. M., ed. *Guardians of the Land: Essays on Central African Territorial Cults*. Gwelo, Zimbabwe: Mambo, 1978. Introduction, 1–46.

Schoffeleers, J. M., and A. A. Roscoe. *Land of Fire: Oral Literature from Malawi*. Limbe, Malawi: Popular Publications, 1985.

Scott, J. C. *The Moral Economy of the Peasant: Rebellion and Subsistence in Southeast Asia*. New Haven: Yale University Press, 1976.

Scott, J. C. *Weapons of the Weak: Everyday Forms of Peasant Resistance*. New Haven: Yale University Press, 1985.

Shire Valley Agricultural Development Project. *An Atlas of the Lower Shire Valley, Malawi*. Blantyre, Malawi: Department of Surveys, 1975.

South African Pioneer. Official newsletter of the South African General Mission, known today as the Africa Evangelical Fellowship. 1900–1938.

Stern, S. "New Approaches to the Study of Peasant Rebellion and Consciousness: Implications of the Andean Experience." S. Stern, ed., *Resistance, Rebellion, and Consciousness in the Andean Peasant World, 18th to 20th Centuries*. Madison: University of Wisconsin Press, 1987. 1–25.

Tabler, E. C., ed. *The Zambezi Papers of Richard Thornton: Geologist to Livingstone's Zambezi Expedition.* 2 vols. London: Chatto and Windus, 1963.

Terray, E. "Classes and Class Consciousness in the Abron Kingdom of Gyman." M. Bloch, ed., *Marxist Analyses and Social Anthropology.* London: Malaby, 1975. 85–135.

Terray, E. "Long-Distance Exchange and the Formation of the State." *Economy and Society* 3 (1974): 315–345.

Terray, E. *Marxism and 'Primitive' Societies.* New York: Monthly Review Press, 1972.

Theal, G. M., ed. *Records of South-East Africa.* 9 vols. 1899. Cape Town, South Africa: Struik, 1964.

Tosh, J. "The Cash Crop Revolution in Tropical Africa: An Agricultural Reappraisal." *African Affairs* 79 (1980): 79–94.

Universities Mission to Central Africa. *Central Africa: A Record of the Work of the Universities Mission.* Vol. 13. 1895.

Vail, L. "The Making of an Imperial Slum: Nyasaland and Her Railways, 1895–1935." *Journal of African History* 16 (1975): 89–112.

Vail, L. "Railway Development and Colonial Underdevelopment: The Nyasaland Case." R. Palmer and N. Parsons, eds., *The Roots of Rural Poverty in Central and Southern Africa.* Berkeley and Los Angeles: University of California Press, 1977. 365–395.

Vail, L., and L. White. *Capitalism and Colonialism in Mozambique: A Study of Quelimane District.* Minneapolis: University of Minnesota Press, 1980.

Van Onselen, C. "Worker Consciousness in Black Miners: Southern Rhodesia, 1900–1920." *Journal of African History* 14 (1973): 237–255.

Van Zanten, W. "Traditional Malawi in Music, 1970–71." Unpublished recordings.

Vaughan, M. "Social and Economic Change in Southern Malawi: A Study of Rural Communities in the Shire Highlands and Upper Shire Valley from the Mid-Nineteenth Century to 1915." Ph.D. diss., London University, 1981.

Vaughan, M. *The Story of an African Famine: Gender and Famine in Twentieth-Century Malawi.* Cambridge: Cambridge University Press, 1987.

Vaughan, M. "Which Family?: Problems in the Reconstruction of the History of the Family as an Economic and Cultural Unit." *Journal of African History* 24 (1983): 275–283.

Wallis, J. P. R., ed. *The Zambesi Expedition of David Livingstone, 1858–63.* 2 vols. London: Chatto and Windus, 1956.

Wallis, J. P. R., ed. *The Zambesi Journal of James Stewart, 1862–1863.* London: Chatto and Windus, 1952.

Wardle, W. A. "A History of the British Cotton Growing Association, 1902–39, with Special Reference to Its Operations in Northern Nigeria." Ph.D. diss., University of Birmingham, 1980.

Warhurst, P. R. "Portugal's Bid for Southern Malawi." G. W. Smith, B. Pachai, and R. K. Tangri, eds., *Malawi Past and Present.* Blantyre: Christian Literature Association in Malawi, 1971. 20–36.

Watts, M. "Good Try, Mr. Paul: Populism and the Politics of African Land-Use." *African Studies Review* 26 (June 1983): 78–83.

Williamson, J. *Useful Plants of Malawi.* 1956. Zomba, Malawi: Government Press, 1972.

Wrigley, C. C. "Historicism in Africa: Slavery and State Formation." *African Affairs* 70 (1971): 113–124.

Wright, M. "Technology, Marriage and Women's Work in the History of Maize-Growers in Mazabuka, Zambia: A Reconnaissance." *Journal of Southern African Studies* 10 (October 1983): 71–85.

Young, E. D. *The Search After Livingstone: A Diary Kept During the Investigation of His Reported Murder.* London: Letts, 1868.

Young, E. D. *Mission to Nyassa.* London: Murray, 1877.

Glossary

abambo: Fathers, village headman.
adzukulu: *See* **mdzukulu.**
afiti: *See* **mfiti.**
akamwini: *See* **mkamwini.**
akapolo: *See* **kapolo.**
amai: Mother.
amitala: *See* **wamitala.**
amtenga-tenga: *See* **wamtenga-tenga.**
ankhoswe: *See* **nkhoswe.**
anyakwawa: *See* **nyakwawa.**
anyamata-a-geni: Middleman traders, businessmen. The term combines the words *mnyamata* (boy, plural *anyamata*) and "gain."
anzache: A person's equals, friends.
aphajoni: Foreign troublemakers.
apongozi: *See* **mpongozi.**
apusi: Baboons.

bambaya: Sena word for sweet potatoes. Same as **mbatata** in Chimang'anja.
bande: A perennial grass which grows up to two meters tall along riverbanks and on the marshes. Uprooted by a strong current, an entire section of bande will float on the Tchiri River like an island during the flood season. The botanical name is *Echinochloa haploclada.*
bango: Chimang'anja word for reeds (*Phragmites mauritianus*). The Chisena equivalent is *mtete* (plural *mitete*).
banja: Family, household.
bayira: Anything that a seller gives to a buyer in addition to what the latter has actually paid for. The term came to be used to refer to the "presents" cotton producers received from Indian traders. Such presents constituted bayira because the merchants "bought" cotton by selling cloth and other merchandise. During the Depression traders gave nothing but bayira to cotton sellers.
Boma: Government.
Bomani: Floods of 1939. The word means to push, unsettle, or drive out.
bwalo: Open ground; meeting place for a group of families or a village; place (usually under a tree) where legal cases and other issues are discussed; courthouse.

bwazi: String-producing plant (*Securidaca longipendunculata*).
bwemba: Tamarind (*Tamarindus indica*).

chaina: Fast-ripening sweet potato that became popular in the Valley after the permanent inundation of the marshes in the late 1930s.
chambo: A fish of the genus *Tilapia;* one of the most numerous fish in Lake Malawi and the Tchiri River. Same as *mphende* in Chisena.
chaola: Famine.
chibutha: Harpoon. Same as *chidamba* in Chimang'anja.
chidamba: Harpoon for hippo hunting.
chigunda: A garden worked by and belonging to an unmarried girl or boy; same as *chilere.*
chikamwini: Bride-service among the matrilineal Mang'anja.
chikwati: Wedding or family.
chilere: *See* **chigunda.**
chimanga: Maize. Same as *mapiramanga* in Chisena.
Chimang'anja: The language of the Mang'anja.
chinamwali: Communal initiation ritual for girls.
chipala: Forge; place where (or action by which) a smith turns iron rods into implements.
chipata: Gate; a toll that merchants were required to give to a chief or headman in order to do business in a foreign territory.
chiperoni: Dry season rains that come in July and August.
Chisena: The language of the Sena.
chitedze: Buffalo plant.
chitowe: Sesame seeds; also known among the Sena as *ukaka* or *umphedza.*
chulu: Anthill.
chuma: Wealth; bride-wealth.

dambo: Floodland, marsh.
dawe: Nut grass.
demu: Small ax used by Zimba hunters.
dimba: River-fed agricultural system based on the cultivation of dambo floodland; garden on such land.
dindiro: Activities to protect crops, such as scaring birds or guarding against wild game.
dowe: Lung fish.
Duladula: The floods of 1918–19. *See also* **Mmbalu.**
dzombe: Red-winged locust (*Locusta migratoriodes*).

fodya: Tobacco.

gelo: Communal dormitory for boys or girls. The Chimang'anja equivalent is *gowelo*.
goli: Beam of wood used for chaining captives.
gondo: Cotton cloth. Also known in the nineteenth century as *maria,* and in the Portuguese records as *machila.* Also, the loom on which such cloth was produced.
gonkho: Millet (Guinea or kaffir corn, *Sorghum vulgare*). Same as *mapira* in Chimang'anja.
gowelo: Chimang'anja term for the Chisena *gelo* (q.v.).
gugu: Wild gonkho (*Sorghum verticilliflorum*) eaten in times of food shortage and famine; also known as *khundi* among the Sena.

kachasu: Locally brewed gin.
kaundula: Tax register kept by chiefs and headmen.
kanjere-mkwera: Small-grained but heat-resistant maize, originally grown on mathutu mounds.
kapitao: Overseer; instructor.
kapolo: "Slave" (plural *akapolo; ukapolo* = "slavery").
Kherekhe: One of the names given to the famine of 1922–23. The word is a corruption of the name of the agricultural officer who was responsible for famine relief measures, N. D. Clegg. The famine is also known as Mwamthota.
khoka: Flat trawl or seine net; the Chisena equivalent is *kokota.*
khola: Kraal made of tree poles.
khonga: Fish trap made of split bamboo or nchesi stalks. The Chimang'anja equivalent is *mono.*
khumbi: Temporary dwellings in the field. Same as *chisimba.*
khundi: *See* **gugu.**
kokota: Same as *khoka.*
kudza mchete: To be very poor.
kugwa thamanda: Communal fishing in a pool. The Chisena equivalent is *kugwa mlembwe.*
kulima: To work the land, cultivate.
kumasula: (Of crops.) To ripen, shoot flower, or tassel.
kuonja: To collect fish caught in a net or trap.
kusinja: To pound maize or any other grain in a wooden mortar.
kusompha: Fish spearing.
kuswa mphanje: To open a new field; the opening of a field.

kutcheza: To distill (salt).
kuwedza: To fish with a hook; angling.

lichelo: A flat winnowing basket made of split bamboo.
linga: Hedge.
lundu: Title of the highest-ranking ruler among the Mang'anja.

mabzyoka: Female spirit possession cult introduced in the Valley by the Sena.
mache: A fast-ripening sweet potato popular in the Valley after the permanent inundation of the marshes; the term also means "his or her mother."
machewere: *See* **mchewere.**
machila: Hammock used to carry European travelers; cotton cloth in pre-nineteenth-century Portuguese documents.
machona: The lost ones; nonreturning or nontraceable migrant workers.
mafumu: *See* **mfumu.**
magala: Royal fields.
magombo: Communal labor system.
makande: Basalt deposits from the Kirk Range found in the Ngabu chiefdom of Chikwawa District. Very fertile and good for cotton.
makumbi: Temporary dwellings erected in fields during the growing season.
malimidwe: Agricultural rules, policy.
malitchela: Gill net. Also known as *matchera* or *ukonde.*
malonda: Business.
mapira: Millet (*Sorghum vulgare*). Same as gonkho in Chisena.
maria: Nineteenth-century term for cotton cloth.
masamba: Leaves, vegetables.
masuku: Wood used to make charcoal.
matchera: Gill net. Same as *malitchela*
mathutu: Mounds on which the Mang'anja planted kanjere-mkwera maize.
matondo: African plum; fruit of the mtondo tree (*Codyla africana*).
maungu: Pumpkins; *matanga* in Chisena.
mbatata: Sweet potato; the Sena call it *bambaya.*
mbaza: Bag made from palm leaves; used in carrying salt.
Mbona: Guardian spirit of the Mang'anja.
mbudzi: Female leader in local rain-calling ceremonies known as *mgwetsa.*

mbumba: Matrilineage segment.
mbuna: Hunting trap.
mbvunguti: Sausage tree (*Kigelia aethiopica*).
mchere: Salt.
mchete: Color of skin exposed to cold.
mchewere: Bullrush or pearl millet (*Pennisetum typhoides*); the Chisena word is *machewere.*
mdzukulu: Grandchild, niece, or nephew.
mfiti: Witch (plural *afiti*).
mfumu: Chief (plural *mafumu*).
mfunye: Worms.
mgwetsa: Local rain-calling ceremonies.
midikhwa: Palm trees (*Borassus aethiopum*); same as *mvumo.*
minda: *See* **munda.**
misekete: Reed crates.
misikiri: Discarded hoes.
mitumbira: Ridges.
mkamwini: (Prospective) son-in-law (plural *akamwini*).
mkhombwe: Professional hippo hunter.
mlamba: Mudfish.
mlambe: Baobab tree (*Adansonia digitata*).
mlandu: Lawsuit.
mlomo: Mouth; idiomatically, fees paid to a chief or doctor before he would open his mouth.
Mmbalu: Cyclone winds that came with the floods of 1918–19. The floods are known as Madzi-a-Mmbalu or Madzi-a-Duladula.
mnjale: Tall tree indigenous to low-lying areas of Central Africa (*Sterculia appendiculata*).
momba: Spear used in killing fish.
mono: Fish trap; *khonga* in Chisena.
mpama: Yam of genus *Dioscorea.*
mphala: Dryland; agricultural production on this land depends on rainfall.
mphatso: Gift.
mphero: Grinding mill used for making flour.
mphingo: Ebony.
mphombo: Grasshopper.
mpongozi: Father- or mother-in-law.
mpunga: Rice.
msasa: Temporary tent.

Msasila: The floods of 1957.
mtenga-tenga: Porterage.
mtondo: Wooden mortar; also the name of a tree (*Codyla africana*) whose fruit is known as *matondo.*
mudzi: Village.
munda: Garden on mphala dryland; agricultural system based on cultivation of the mphala.
mvumo: Palm tree. Same as *midikhwa.*
mvuu: Hippopotamus.
mwabvi: Poison ordeal.
mwadiya: Dugout canoe; the Mang'anja call it *ngalawa.*
Mwamthota: The famine of 1922–23; also known as Kherekhe.
mwini-mbumba: "Owner" of the matrilineage group (mbumba); always a woman.
mzimbe: Sugarcane; *misale* in Chisena.
mzinda: Initiation school; town.
mzungu: European; white man.

nandolo: Pigeon pea.
nankungwi: Female instructor in puberty rites.
nansongole: A perennial grass found in the lowlands. It grows very high and has stiff, sharply pointed leaf blades. The botanical name is *Imperata cylindrica.*
nantusi: Clipper ant.
nchesi: Straw grass of hard hollow stalk used in making mono fish traps.
nchoche: Arrangement whereby people, especially those from the hills in the Lower Tchiri Valley and from the Tchiri Highlands, rented dimba gardens from valley dwellers. The users had to give a "present"—part of the harvest—to the owners of the garden.
ndiwo: Relish.
ngaiwa: Maize flour ground by machines without removing the bran; people usually do not eat such flour except in times of food shortage.
ngalawa: Dugout canoe; *mwadiya* in Chisena.
ng'anjo: Iron smelting which used to take place in the bush.
ng'ono: Younger, junior.
njala: Hunger; food shortage.
njobvu: Elephant; the Sena call it *nzou.*
nkhokwe: Granary.
nkhondo-ya-mitumbira: "War of the ridges."
nkhono: Medicine used to ward off thieves from a garden.

nkhoswe: A woman's elder brother (or her mother's brother) who acts as her guardian or marriage surety; always a man (plural *ankhoswe*).
nomi: Youth labor association, a Sena institution.
nsima: Hard porridge made of any flour; the main element in Mang'anja and Sena dishes.
nsomba: General term for fish among the Mang'anja; among the Sena the word refers to the mudfish (*mlamba* in Chimang'anja) only.
ntarato: Forced labor in Mozambique.
nthango: After-work meetings of nomi.
nthemba: Village segment.
nyahana: Female doctor, especially in mabzyoka rituals.
nyakwawa: Village headman—or, occasionally, woman (plural *anyakwawa*).
nyau: All-male secret society of masked dancers.
nyemba: Beans.
nyezi: A tuber of the coco yam family.
nyika: A water lily of the botanical family *Nymphaeaceae;* its roots were widely eaten in times of food scarcity (njala).
nyumba: House.
nzou: Elephant; the Mang'anja call it *njobvu.*

palasa: A compound used by nomi members.
prazo: A crown estate in Mozambique.
psyairo: Encircling fishing fences made of reed sheets woven together with palm strings; considered to be of Sena origin.

ropa: Slow-maturing sweet potato whose popularity has declined since the permanent inundation of the marshes in the late 1930s; the term also means black cloth.

salima: Mbona's "wife." The term literally means she (or he) who does not farm.
suludi: A plant from which the Mang'anja used to extract salt.

tchera: A trap consisting of a beam of up to six feet long with an iron spike that carries poison. The spike is suspended from the top of a pole overhanging a path used by animals. When an animal steps on the string the spike falls on it.
thamanda: Pool. *See also* **kugwa thamanda.**
thangata: Tenant labor.

Thodi: Local name of the countrywide famine of 1949. The term is derived from Todd, an employee of the Public Works Department, who was responsible for famine relief measures in the area.
thonje: Cotton.
thonje-kaja: Indigenous cotton found in the Valley in the nineteenth century; it was an annual.
thonje-manga: Cotton of foreign origin found in the Valley in the nineteenth century; it was a semi-perennial plant.
tsanja: Tower built in the fields from which boys scared birds.
tsanya: Mopane tree.
tsenjere: Elephant grass (*Pennisetum purpureum*).

uchifwamba: Kidnapping.
ufa: Flour.
ufiti: Witchcraft.
ukaka: Sesame seeds; also known as *chitowe* or *umphedza.*
ukapolo: Servitude.
ukonde: Gill net.
ulimi: Agriculture, farming; the verb is *kulima.*
umphedza: Sesame seeds. Same as *chitowe* or *ukaka.*
uzungu: Slavery under the white man; tenant labor.

wamitala: Polygynous husband.
wamtenga-tenga: Porter (plural *amtenga-tenga*).
wapambali: An outsider.

zunde: Large cotton field. The term originally referred to the garden of the chief.

Index